# THE AESTHETIC AND

# CRITICAL THEORIES OF

# JOHN RUSKIN

## BY GEORGE P. LANDOW

PRINCETON UNIVERSITY PRESS

PRINCETON, NEW JERSEY 1971

TO THE MEMORY OF

MY MOTHER

*Florence S. Landow*

(1914-1970)

# PREFACE

I would like to thank the Bodleian Library, Oxford and the Libraries of Princeton, Columbia, Cornell, and Yale Universities, the University of London, the British Museum, the Tate Gallery, the Fitzwilliam Museum, the Boston Museum of Fine Arts, the Fogg Art Museum of Harvard University, the Ruskin Museum, Coniston, and the National Galleries of London, Edinburgh, and Dublin. I am particularly indebted to the kindness of Marjorie G. Wynne of the Beinecke Rare Book and Manuscript Library of Yale University and Mr. William Rawdon-Smith of Coniston for their generous assistance in helping me obtain photocopies of Ruskin manuscripts. George Allen & Unwin Ltd. and the Ruskin Literary Trustees have kindly permitted me to publish sections from these manuscripts.

Portions of my first and second chapters previously appeared in slightly different form in *The British Journal of Aesthetics* and the *Journal of Aesthetics and Art Criticism*.

The Columbia University Council for Research in the Humanities provided me with a summer grant to study the sermon materials discussed in Chapters IV and V. I would especially like to thank the Society for the Humanities of Cornell University and its incomparable director Max Black for a fellowship during 1968-1969 which gave me the opportunity to complete the greater portion of this study.

Geoffrey Tillotson, A. Walton Litz, and Van Akin Burd gave me valuable advice and encouragement during the course of my research, and John D. Rosenberg, Harold Bloom, M. H. Abrams, and David Novarr kindly read portions of the manuscript. Barbara A. R. Burke,

PREFACE

Robert Fleder, Eugene Hill, and Billy T. Tracy kindly
helped me read proof. Most of all, I am indebted to
E. D. H. Johnson of Princeton University for his continual guidance while I was writing my dissertation on
Ruskin, for his encouragement, and for introducing me
to the study of Victorian literature.

# CONTENTS

# CONTENTS

# LIST OF ILLUSTRATIONS
## following page 436

xi

# THE AESTHETIC AND
# CRITICAL THEORIES OF
# JOHN RUSKIN

# INTRODUCTION

In *The Life of John Ruskin*, E. T. Cook praised the theories of beauty which Ruskin presented in the second volume of *Modern Painters* with an enthusiasm that these theories are unlikely to evoke in a reader today: "Ruskin's theory has been, and will be, assailed; but it is consistent with itself, it explains many of the phenomena, and it harmonises, better than any other philosophy of the beautiful, with a system of natural religion. . . . The volume has, moreover, a permanent value, independent of the theory which it expounds. No one, I think, can read the chapters on Infinity, Unity, Repose, Symmetry, Purity, and Moderation—or, again, those under the head of Vital Beauty—without having his ideas of the beautiful enlarged, or clarified."[1] In his recent anthology, *Ruskin Today*, Sir Kenneth Clark commented that "No other writer, perhaps, has suffered so great a fall in reputation as Ruskin,"[2] and one might well add that his philosophy of beauty has, more than any other part of his work, been neglected and has lost the prestige it once enjoyed. Readers no longer believe, with Cook, that Ruskin's theories are of much use in explaining the phenomena of beauty, and today most would be little moved by the fact that his conceptions harmonize with religious belief. Quentin Bell, author of a recent study of Ruskin's life and works, considers the volume that contains the burden of his aesthetic speculation to be a matter of "splendid inconsequence,"[3] and Clark warns that "we should be wasting our time to look for a coherent system of aesthetics

---

[1] Two vols. (London, 1911), I, 201.
[2] (London, 1964), p. xiii.
[3] *Ruskin* (Edinburgh and London, 1963), p. 21.

3

(two words he hated) in his works as a whole."[4] Joan Evans, who has contributed a biography, dismisses these theories of beauty almost without discussion.

Because noted students of Ruskin have thus dismissed his writings on the beautiful so lightly, a study of his aesthetics perhaps demands some apology or explanation. More than a century after he first became known to the British public, his reputation is again on the rise, though often, one must admit, for reasons that would have pained him. He hated to be considered a mere word painter, yet Miss Evans considers his great merit to lie in the fact that he was an "artist in words,"[5] and she has written that "Ruskin might consider himself a teacher and a moralist, but his true strength still lay in simple word painting."[6] Quentin Bell similarly believes that the reader "must learn to love the florid rhetorical prose of Ruskin's earlier manner, for it is in this—the ability to match great painting with language no less great—that Ruskin's achievement lies. He was the first art critic to create one masterpiece in praising another."[7] The recent appearance of five anthologies of his prose testifies in part to new interest in him as stylist.

Certainly, Ruskin wrote some of the finest, perhaps the finest, English prose of the nineteenth century, and his several styles well deserve the sensitive analysis John D. Rosenberg has recently accorded them.[8] Nonetheless, to dwell entirely on the values of his prose, neg-

4 *Ruskin Today*, p. 132.
5 *John Ruskin* (London, 1954), p. 87.
6 *Ibid.*, p. 221.          7 *Ruskin*, p. 117.
8 "Style and Sensibility in Ruskin's Prose," in *The Art of Victorian Prose*, eds. George Levine and William Madden (New York, London, and Toronto, 1968), pp. 177-200.

4

lecting as does Miss Evans the importance of Ruskin's ideas, unnecessarily deprives us of much we can ill afford to lose. To regard him *only* as an artist in words is to ignore Ruskin's value both to his own time and to ours; it is to suggest most erroneously that we have nothing to learn from his writings, and that his questions no longer interest us because we have answered them. Such complacency and such lack of curiosity hardly become an age whose arts, whose general surroundings, and whose conceptions of economics, education, and governmental responsibility Ruskin has so affected. The utensils we use, like the buildings we live in, show the influence of Ruskin. Fittingly, Nikolaus Pevsner's *Pioneers of Modern Design* opens with a quotation from his works; with equal justice a more recent history of English architecture closes with the reminder that the twentieth century and its buildings have ignored, rather than solved, the problems which Ruskin and his disciple Morris perceived. As a third architectural historian points out: "We still live in a continuation of the story."[9] Ruskin, in other words, is doubly useful, doubly relevant to us. First of all, his criticisms of society, his interpretations of art, his readings of literature remain valid, and while they may become dated when we have solved all our problems or when we no longer concern ourselves with art, literature, or the quality of human life, they continue to apply and will apply for some time to come. Secondly, Ruskin tells

[9] Rev. ed. (Penguin: n.p., 1960), p. 19. Peter Kidson, Peter Murray, and Paul Thompson, *A History of English Architecture*, rev. ed. (Penguin: n.p., 1965), p. 329: "The problem of work, so fundamental to the Victorians, to Ruskin and Morris, has been neglected rather than solved by the twentieth century" (Thompson). Robert Furneaux Jordan, *Victorian Architecture* (Penguin: n.p., 1966), p. 175.

us much about our past, and this ability to inform us about his age, our own, and the period between makes him of rare value.

*Modern Painters* and *The Stones of Venice* (my favorites, I admit) remain suggestive, rich, and necessary 100 years after their publication. Writing about Venice, Henry James once remarked that "it is Mr. Ruskin who beyond any one helps us to enjoy." James was right, and he was also right when he asserted that there "is no better reading at Venice . . . than Ruskin,"[10] for whether or not we agree, finally, with his evaluations of Renaissance and Gothic, Ruskin's words help us experience past arts better than those of anyone else. Several writers have considered Ruskin's ability to bring us to older painting and architecture with fresh eyes one of his greatest gifts. According to Lionello Venturi's *History of Art Criticism* (1936), his "justification of the value of mediaeval art" compels recognition that today "Ruskin as an art critic is more alive than ever, and that many of his positions are not superseded."[11] Like Venturi, Proust emphasized Ruskin's ability to bring medieval art to life:

L'unité de l'art chrétien au moyen âge, des bords de la Somme aux rives de l'Arno, nul ne l'a sentie comme lui, et il a réalisé dans nos coeurs le rêve des grands papes du moyen âge: l'"Europe chrétienne." Si, comme on l'a dit, son nom doit rester attaché au préraphaélisme, on devrait entendre parlà non celui d'après Turner, mais celui d'avant Raphaël. Nous pouvons oublier aujourd'hui les services qu'il a

[10] *The Art of Travel*, ed. Morton Dauwen Zabel (Garden City, N.Y., 1962), p. 335.
[11] Trans. Charles Marriott, rev. ed. (New York, 1964), p. 185.

rendus à Hunt, à Rossetti, à Millais; mais ce qu'il a fait pour Giotto, pour Carpaccio, pour Bellini, nous ne le pouvons pas. Son oeuvre divine ne fut pas de susciter des vivants, mais de ressusciter des morts.[12]

In addition to possessing rare value as one who can evoke our sympathetic interest in past art and guide our perceptions of it—I know of no one who can better aid our experience of St. Mark's—Ruskin has left valuable commentary on prenineteenth-century painting, poetry, and architecture. Even when subsequent work, like that of Emile Mâle, has superseded his views— often because it has elaborated upon them—his writings still point to significant problems of research and critical evaluation. And although recent scholarship no longer accepts all his conclusions, it treats him on occasion as an authority whose views are worthy of comment. For example, even though Paul Frankl's *Gothic Architecture*, the most authoritative study of its subject, does not finally accede to Ruskin's views of the role of rib-vaulting in Gothic style, it considers them important enough to discuss.

Furthermore, students of nineteenth-century arts have increasingly accepted the value of Ruskin's comments upon the painting of his own time. One only has to glance at recent studies of Turner to perceive how apposite his criticism remains: Ruskin's remarks on Turner's style, technique, and intentions prove valuable to the student of Turner, and even the critic's elaborate symbolical interpretations of the landscapist's work have recently gained favor.[13] Similarly, his com-

[12] *En mémoire des églises assassinées* in *Pastiches et Mélanges* (Paris, 1919), p. 161.
[13] For example, Eric Newton, *The Romantic Rebellion* (New York,

7

ments on the art of water color in the nineteenth century have retained their usefulness, so much so that Martin Hardie's authoritative *Water-Colour Painting in Britain* approvingly quotes his views not only of Turner but also of Girtin, Bonington, Cox, De Wint, Richardson, Fielding, and William Turner of Oxford.[14] Lately, those students of Pre-Raphaelitism who have perceived that both Ruskin and the Brotherhood wanted more from their art than a new realism have discovered that his influence and criticism provides a major aid to understanding these painters. His elaborate readings of Pre-Raphaelite art have proved, like his exegeses of Turner, to be very useful for those who wish to comprehend the intentions of this curious school of painting.[15] One should also point out that, as Sir Herbert Read has emphasized, Ruskin's theories find fulfillment, not in the art of the nineteenth century, but in the creations of twentieth-century Expressionism.[16] It is a sign of the far-reaching importance of Ruskin's writings on art that they help us to enjoy beauties which he never lived to see.

Like his writings on art, Ruskin's brilliant discussions and interpretations of literature continue to be of great value; and while his biographers have in general paid no attention whatsoever to his literary criticism, some of our finest critics have fortunately made up for this

---

1964), p. 115; and throughout Jack Lindsay's two studies of Turner's art and verse: *The Sunset Ship: The Poems of J.M.W. Turner* (London, 1966) and *J.M.W. Turner: His Life and Work* (New York, 1966).

[14] Eds. Dudley Snelgrove, Jonathan Mayne, and Basil Taylor, 3 vols. (London, 1967), II, 12, 22, 40-45, 183, 206, 220, 225, 231, 238.

[15] See below, pp. 420ff, for Ruskin's interpretations of Turner.

[16] "Human Art and Inhuman Nature," *The Philosophy of Modern Art* (New York, 1955), p. 81.

neglect. Harold Bloom, for example, indicates the nature of Ruskin's stature as a student of literature:

> Ruskin is very much an anticipatory critic in regard to some of the schools of literary criticism in our own time. Ruskin was one of the first, if not indeed the first, "myth" or "archetypal" critic, or more properly he is the linking and transitional figure between the allegorical critics of the elder, Renaissance kind, and those of the newer variety, like Northrop Frye. . . . Even if he did not have this unique historical position, Ruskin would stand as one of the handful of major literary critics in nineteenth-century England.[17]

Not unexpectedly, Northrop Frye himself has written about the value of Ruskin's conception of a "genuine criticism." In the "Polemical Introduction" to his *Anatomy of Criticism*, he first quotes one of Ruskin's etymological exegeses of names in Shakespeare, then gives Arnold's comment that such interpretation is provincial, and lastly remarks:

> Now whether Ruskin is right or wrong, he is attempting genuine criticism. He is trying to interpret Shakespeare in terms of a conceptual framework which belongs to the critic alone, and yet relates itself to the plays alone. Arnold is perfectly right in feeling that this is not the sort of material that the public critic can directly use. But he does not even seem to suspect the existence of a systematic criticism as distinct from the history of taste. Here it is Arnold who is the provincial. Ruskin has learned his trade

[17] "Introduction," *The Literary Criticism of John Ruskin* (Garden City, N.Y., 1965), p. xvi.

from the great iconological tradition which comes down through Classical and Biblical scholarship into Dante and Spenser, both of whom he had studied carefully, and which is incorporated in the medieval cathedrals he had pored over in such detail.[18]

This fascinating, central part of Ruskin's thought, which we shall later observe in detail, produces some of his most idiosyncratic, most unexpected, and yet most valuable insights into the arts of Giotto and Turner, Spenser and Milton. His literary criticism indicates again that our examination of his work serves a dual purpose: it enables us to deepen our understanding and enjoyment of art while simultaneously permitting us an invaluable historical perspective.

Arnold Hauser most helpfully reminds the modern reader both of his debt to Ruskin and the continuing value of Ruskin's ideas:

Artistic decay had never been regarded as the symptom of a disease involving the whole body of society and there has never been such a clear awareness of the organic relationship between art and life as since Ruskin. He was indubitably the first to interpret the decline of art and taste as the sign of a general cultural crisis, and to express the basic, and even today not sufficiently appreciated, principle that the conditions under which men live must first be changed, if their sense of beauty and their comprehension of art are to be awakened. . . . Ruskin was also the first person in England to emphasize the fact that art is a public concern and its cultivation one of the most important tasks of the state, in other words, that it represents a social necessity and that no nation can neglect it

[18] (Princeton, 1957), pp. 9-10.

without endangering its intellectual existence. He
was, finally, the first to proclaim the gospel that art
is not the privilege of artists, connoisseurs and the
educated classes, but is part of every man's inheritance and estate. . . . Ruskin attributed the decay of
art to the fact that the modern factory, with its mechanical mode of production and division of labour,
prevents a genuine relationship between the worker
and his work, that is to say, that it crushes out the
spiritual element and estranges the producer from
the product of his hands. . . . He . . . recalled his
contemporaries to the charms of solid, careful crafts-
manship as opposed to the spurious materials, senseless forms and crude, cheap execution of Victorian
products. His influence was extraordinary, almost beyond description. . . . The purposefulness and solid-
ity of modern architecture and industrial art are very
largely the result of Ruskin's endeavours and doctrines.[19]

Ruskin's words have already had important practical
effect, influencing our lives directly and indirectly for
the better; and by focusing our attention upon the dilemmas we still face, his thoughts prove themselves of
great value.

Our major enterprise in the following pages, however, will be not to examine Ruskin's present relevance
as critic of art or society but to use his writings to
understand our own past. An exploration of the 39 volumes which comprise the *Library Edition* of his works
reveals the many ways he provides an entrance into
the thoughts and feelings of a most complex age. In the
first place, Ruskin stands as an invaluable index of Vic-

19 *The Social History of Art*, 2 vols. (New York, 1952), II, 819-822.

torian taste. No writer on painting or architecture has ever possessed his influence in either England or America, and while we no longer believe, like many of his contemporaries, that he singlehandedly molded artistic preferences or initiated aesthetic movements, we cannot deny his major importance to the Victorian audience. Certainly, Ruskin did not discover Turner. Ever since A. J. Finberg showed that Turner, one of the most financially successful painters in the history of British art, enjoyed a wide reputation before Ruskin took up his cause in *Modern Painters,* no one has believed that he rescued the artist from obscurity;[20] and yet he did come to Turner's aid when he had lost much of his reputation and when the periodical critics were handling him savagely. In Ruskin, Turner found the greatest, most influential defender any great artist has had the good fortune to encounter while alive. In many ways Turner's situation was like that of Rembrandt: after great early success his art progressed beyond the capacities of his audience to understand and enjoy it, and although Turner, unlike the great Dutch artist, never suffered from poverty, he was equally hurt by the neglect and the attacks which his art received. Until very recently, the problem may have been that Ruskin did too much, for according to Sir Herbert Read, "we are still intimidated by the eloquence of Ruskin. Ruskin wrote so much and wrote so effectively about Turner, that Turner's reputation has actually been a little overshadowed, as in a cloud of golden dust."[21] Similarly, one no longer believes that Ruskin initiated either the Gothic Revival or the Pre-Raphaelite Movement, yet he con-

20 *The Life of J.M.W. Turner,* 2nd ed. rev. (Oxford, 1961) [1st ed. 1939], pp. 232-234.
21 *The Meaning of Art* (Baltimore, Md., 1949), p. 125.

tributed importantly to their progress, and without his advocacy neither would have achieved the popular success it did.[22] Again, Ruskin introduced neither the Italian Primitives nor Titian and Tintoretto to England, but he did do much to popularize and interpret them. The very fact that Ruskin was so long credited with having been the originator of aesthetic movements or having discovered major artists clearly demonstrates how important was his advocacy to the nineteenth-century public. About this subject we need to know more, and perhaps an examination of Ruskin's influence upon contemporary artists, critics, and audience will someday inform us more precisely about his major historical importance. Such a task, however, will not engage us here, for before we can profitably determine Ruskin's effect upon his contemporaries we need to know more about his writings themselves.

In particular, we need to perceive his relation to earlier authors, his major emphases, his habits of mind. To understand the Victorian age we must grasp what in his writings so appealed to his readers, what makes him a Victorian sage and a representative man. Despite growing interest in Ruskin, there has been little detailed examination of the kind we require to understand the writings of this most complex, often most perplexing man. After Ruskin's death Proust commented: "Aujourd'hui la mort a fait entrer l'humanité en possession de l'héritage immense que Ruskin lui avait légué."[23] We have not done enough to appreciate this immense inheritance. The past three decades have seen

---

[22] See Sir Kenneth Clark, *The Gothic Revival* (Penguin: n.p., 1964); Oswald Doughty, *A Victorian Romantic: Dante Gabriel Rossetti* (London, 1960).

[23] *En mémoire des églises assassinées*, p. 148.

a number of works which peer into Ruskin's madness, his unhappy marriage, and his penchant for young girls, but surely, however these aspects of his life may validly engage the biographer, they do not help us ascertain his value as much as would a close reading of his major works. Strangely enough, it almost seems necessary to point out that *Modern Painters* should concern us more than Rose La Touche, *The Stones of Venice* more than his later madness: we would reverence *Modern Painters* if Ruskin had never met Rose La Touche; we would not care much about the unfortunate Miss La Touche if he had not written *Modern Painters*.

The modern reader needs a convenient point at which to enter the formidable mass of Ruskin's works, and because his theories of the beautiful embody the concerns, methods, and dilemmas which characterize all his writings, they provide such an entrance. His aesthetic theories (by which I mean his theories of beauty and not his conceptions of art) provide what Ruskin would have called a type, an emblem, of all his thought. In the first place, both the origin and development of these aesthetic formulations are characteristic of his works whether on art or political economy; for he shaped his theories of beauty—like his theories of economics—polemically; which is to say, he formed them in conscious opposition to ideas he wished to confute and paid careful attention to the way his theories served such a purpose.

Secondly, they embody that characteristically Victorian eclecticism which appears throughout his thought. His conceptions of Typical and Vital Beauty draw upon Aristotle, Plato, Hooker, Bacon, Pope, Dr.

Johnson, Wordsworth, Reynolds, and many others; they combine notions derived from neoclassical poetry and criticism, Evangelical Anglican conceptions of scripture, and the late eighteenth-century Scottish moral philosophers. Such an assemblage of often contradictory sources well provides an emblem for the vigor, style, and dilemmas which mark the Victorian years. In particular, Ruskin's aesthetics, like much of his thought, informs us about the relation of Victorian ideas to those of the past. Like Tennyson and Arnold who return to ancient and medieval legend for materials with which to make a poetry relevant to contemporary life, Ruskin consciously attempts to enrich the present with the forms and inspiration of earlier times. Like the nineteenth-century architect who ransacks classical, medieval, and Renaissance buildings to find forms for present use, Ruskin collects and then pieces together elements from older thought and art to create a coherent shelter for pleasurable and profitable human existence; and, like the better Victorian architects, when he mines the past for present riches he moves beyond mere antiquarianism, mere use of dead forms, to produce a new consistency and order. This use of eclectically gathered materials to build a new order which characterizes all his writings is most evident in his theories of the beautiful, for in setting forth these theories Ruskin was concerned to demonstrate the orderly nature of beauty by relating it to a vision of universal order. A polemical defense of an artist led him to a theocentric aesthetics, and his theocentric aesthetics led him to propose a theory of the universe in which to enclose his conception of beauty. Like his theories of allegory, these descriptions of the beautiful appear as one of many nineteenth-century attempts to reconstruct by force of will, intellect, and imagination a meaningful world in which man can live.

The eclectic origin of Ruskin's theories also accounts for their frequently paradoxical quality. For example, while attempting to create a theoretical description of beauty adequate to the needs of his contemporaries, he transferred Evangelical typology to aesthetics, producing a view of life more congenial to the Middle Ages than to the reign of Queen Victoria. The very belief in typology, which so frequently plays an important role in his thought, was itself something of an anachronism in the nineteenth century, and only the extreme conservatism of the Evangelical party in the Church and related sects could long maintain such views in a hostile intellectual climate. Ruskin's allegorical vision, which evolves from Evangelical typology, produces some of the oddest and some of the most brilliant of his readings of art. Strangely enough, this use of figuralism, which permits Ruskin to incorporate ideas of the Church fathers and seventeenth-century Puritans into a Victorian theory of art, also leads to what Sir Herbert Read has called the most precise, most eloquent definition of twentieth-century Expressionism.[24] Again and again, his eclecticism produces such strange mixtures of anachronism and contemporaneity.

The same eclecticism appears less jarringly in his renovations of neoclassical theories of the sister arts, which importantly shape his descriptions of the beautiful. Joining eighteenth-century notions of painting to romantic theories of poetry, Ruskin formulated a Victorian theory of the arts which manages to pay careful

[24] See n. 16, above.

attention to the work of art, its creator, and its effects upon the audience. Characteristically, Ruskin could thus combine neoclassical and romantic views, because he shared with eighteenth-century authors conceptions of the imagination already conservative by the time he began *Modern Painters.*

A recognition of this eclecticism demands that we contradict views apparently widely held that Ruskin did not know very much about previous critical and aesthetic treatises, and that he was not interested in learning much about them. Several writers, of whom Joan Evans is the most important, have cast considerable doubt on Ruskin's knowledge of his subject. In fact, he was well acquainted with standard writings on aesthetics, art, and literature. In the early years of writing *Modern Painters,* for example, he cites among many others Alison, Burke, Cellini, Cenini, Harding, Hazlitt, Hunt, Mrs. Jameson, Leonardo, Rio, Schiller, Adam Smith, Dugald Stewart, and Winckelmann. He had early read the lectures of the Academicians, Barry and Fuseli as well as Reynolds, and his reading of J. D. Harding's numerous books informed him of standard sources. In addition, he read available studies of Indian and Japanese art, many treatises on technique, and a very large number of works on architecture and architectural theory. No one who has read Ruskin extensively can doubt his broad acquaintance with English, Continental, and American literature. Ruskin, for example, who always remained particularly indebted to the English romantic writers, made important use of Wordsworth's prefaces when they were neither well known nor easily accessible. On the other hand, Ruskin, it is true, did not know Kant, and whatever he learned of German philosophy came largely from Carlyle, but this is the only major gap one can discern in his knowledge.

Of course, a survey of his reading cannot reveal the importance of theories, attitudes, and details of technique he learned in conversation with J.M.W. Turner, George Richmond, J. D. Harding, Copley Fielding, and other painters. Perhaps most important was the astonishingly broad knowledge of individual works of art which so awed Proust. Writing of "la richesse infinie de son amour, de son savoir," he justly comments:

> Habituellement, chez un écrivain, le retour à de certains exemples préférés, sinon même la répétition de certains développements, vous rappelle que vous avez affaire à un homme qui eut une certaine vie, telles connaissances qui lui tiennent lieu de telles autres, une expérience limitée dont il tire tout le profit qu'il peut. Rien qu'en consultant les index des différents ouvrages de Ruskin, la perpétuelle nouveauté des oeuvres citées, plus encore le dédain d'une connaissance dont il s'est servi une fois et, bien souvent, son abandon à tout jamais, donnent l'idée de quelque chose de plus qu'humain, ou plutôt l'impression que chaque livre est d'un homme nouveau qui a un savoir différent, pas la même expérience, une autre vie.[25]

In her biography, Miss Evans, who displays a curious dislike for her subject, compares his degree of mastery with his century's "new and terrifying standards of professional knowledge of art."[26] Now, with all respect to Miss Evans, this is nonsense, and nonsense of a most un-

[25] *En mémoire des églises assassinées*, pp. 160-161.
[26] *John Ruskin*, p. 97.

grateful sort. Since Ruskin's popularizations of art, attacks on poor restoration, and encouragement of better museum practice led to the conveniences which the modern student enjoys, it is most ungracious and ungrateful to accuse him of not having the benefits for which he was in part responsible—and this, in essence, is what such criticism implies. In the first place, Ruskin's competence was superior to that of most professionals, and if one compares Ruskin's appraisals with those of contemporary professionals, such as Waagen, the author of *Modern Painters* fares rather well. For example, if one goes to examine the pictures in the Dulwich Gallery he criticized harshly, one finds them in storage, and when, through the generosity of the gallery staff, they are brought to light, one sees how correct Ruskin could be, how much better than the professionals of his day. Often forgetting that Ruskin saw many paintings which were greatly darkened by age and tinted varnish, we fail to remember how his criticism contributed to the standards of museum care and restoration whose benefits we now enjoy. Furthermore, unlike the modern student, he had the aid neither of careful, expert attribution nor of contemporary techniques in dating and the detection of forgery. Since his day the canons of some of the artists he discussed have been drastically narrowed, and some of the works which he suspected, but which his opponents did not, have proven to be poor copies or forgeries. Furthermore, reliable museum catalogues and photographic reproductions which make the art historian's life so much easier were lacking, and few who comment upon Ruskin's insularity would make the journeys he did on the chance that a work might prove worthy of inspection.

Ruskin has also been charged with insularity because he remained unaware of the French Impressionists, but, as Quentin Bell so correctly reminds us, it was most difficult to become aware of this school:

> It comes . . . as a shock to hear Ruskin allude to the muddy darkness of the modern French school, a school in which he could see only one supreme master, Edouard Frère. But it is even more shocking that the young revolutionaries of the 'seventies and 'eighties were themselves under the impression that the chief lessons that we had to learn from France was a lesson in tonality, in *les valeurs*, in drawing.
>
> Once again we see how easy it is to be misled by the judgments of history: we imagine that the visitor to Paris could hardly have avoided seeing the works of Monet, Renoir, Sisley, Pissarro and Manet, whereas the unavoidable painters would in fact have been Meissonier, Bonvin, Bésnard, Cormon and Bonnât. The Impressionists were there, but they were not easy to find. Monet does gradually emerge in the 1890's as a recognizable influence on British painting; but the rest are not clearly perceived until very late in the century.[27]

Professor Bell, one may add, is speaking about the difficulties of encountering work of the great French painters during the seventies and eighties—at the very least a decade after Ruskin completed *Modern Painters* and most of his major writings on the visual arts. On the other hand, although one can hardly blame Ruskin for not popularizing the pictures of Manet, Monet, and Renoir, most of whose works do not even appear until after the period with which we are primarily con-

[27] *Victorian Artists* (Cambridge, Mass., 1967), p. 78.

cerned, one might have expected him to mention Géricault and Delacroix. Géricault's *Raft of the Medusa*,
it is true, dates from the year of Ruskin's birth, and he
probably would have found little notice of this artist,
but Delacroix's paintings were accessible, and one is
surprised not to find mention of him in Ruskin's works.
Such omission is particularly striking since Rossetti
would have mentioned Delacroix, one of his favorites,
to the critic in the mid-fifties. Delacroix, one may conclude, was Ruskin's one major omission, but even so we
can hardly charge him with insularity, for, as an examination of his diaries, notebooks, and published works
reveals, Ruskin frequently obtained French works on
art soon after publication. Certainly, continually expanding artistic and intellectual horizons, rather than
insularity, characterize the first four or five decades of
Ruskin's life.

In fact, Ruskin's continual growth as a critic created
some of the difficulties we experience today in reading
*Modern Painters*, for as John D. Rosenberg has remarked, the "book would be less perplexing if Ruskin
had known more about art when he began it, or
learned less in the course of its composition."[28] He began his study of landscape painting with a definite
plan, but as he became more interested in the art of the
Middle Ages and Renaissance he modified his original
intentions. Once again, we may take his aesthetic
theories and their role in *Modern Painters* as a type for
the entire work. In the first place, he began *Modern
Painters* as a defense of J.M.W. Turner against the violent attacks of the periodical reviewers. The opening
volume therefore appropriately employs his embryonic

[28] *The Darkening Glass: A Portrait of Ruskin's Genius* (New York
and London, 1961), p. 2.

aesthetics largely as one more argument to prove the painter's superiority. By the time Ruskin came to write the second volume, however, he had changed his conception of the book, deciding that it would be, not merely a polemical defense of Turner which used a theory of art and beauty, but a complete theory of art and aesthetics which included Turner as one of the greatest of artists.[29] Having changed his initial conception, Ruskin thereupon revised his first volume to make it prepare more suitably for the calmer, less argumentative sections which followed. This modification of a work in progress well characterizes the complex, changing nature of Ruskin's thought. Furthermore, not only the role of his aesthetic theories but these theories themselves were modified during the course of writing *Modern Painters*, for as Ruskin lost the beliefs and attitudes which had originally grounded his conceptions of beauty, he found it increasingly difficult to maintain an exclusively theocentric aesthetic.

The individual volumes of *Modern Painters* and the works he wrote during the period of its composition record the stages of Ruskin's intellectual and spiritual development. Thus, the first volume (1843) proposes an early version of his conception of beauty as theophany; the second (1846) presents his fully developed theory; *The Seven Lamps of Architecture* (1848) and *The Stones of Venice* (1851-1853) offer descriptions of the sublime and picturesque, aesthetic categories more subjective than the beautiful—he had first denied that sublimity was distinct from beauty; the fourth volume (1856), published the same year as the third, states his developed theory of the picturesque; and the closing

---

[29] See my "Ruskin's Revisions of the Third Edition of *Modern Painters*, Volume I," *Victorian Newsletter*, xxxiii (1968), 12-16.

volume (1860) reveals new attitudes toward man and God which the changes in his aesthetics had presaged. One perceives in these theories of beauty that same developing, ever-groping quality which colors much Victorian work, for the changes in Ruskin's aesthetics, which relate so intimately to changes in other areas of his thought, make *Modern Painters* seem a work in process.

Nonetheless, taken together its volumes possess important unity, a unity created by a consistent, if continually developing, vision. One axis along which Ruskin's views develop appears in the initial outline presented in the first volume. It explained that *Modern Painters* would inform the reader about the three major criteria of great art—truth, beauty, and relation—and although he frequently turns back to present revisions, additions, and qualifications of his points, he does adhere to his stated plan. The major order which informs his works, however, is that of a growing, adapting organism, for his writings well exemplify his frequent descriptions of the organic development of thought and imagination. Like a growing plant, *Modern Painters* develops in relation to certain easily discernible axes, and if we can perceive these axes we can more easily sense the consistency of Ruskin's thought. During the seventeen years which Ruskin required to write the five volumes of *Modern Painters* (and the works on architecture which appeared between the second and third volumes), his thought developed in three directions: he became increasingly aware and increasingly interested in architecture and medieval and Renaissance painting; he concerned himself with the role of art in human life; and his religious faith, at its strongest in the second volume, gradually weakened and disappeared.

23

The continual evolution of his thought while his works were in progress demands that the student of Ruskin pay particular care to the context in which individual statements occur. Even when his ideas remain unchanged, such attention to context is absolutely essential. In the past, failure to perceive the setting of his ideas has led critics to charge Ruskin with more than his share of inconsistency. Despite the fact that both Ruskin and his editors carefully explained the purpose of his remarks about accurate representation of natural forms, one still encounters statements that his program entailed a mimetic theory of painting or a photographic "realism."[30] Ruskin carefully informed his readers that fact must provide the basis for subsequent imaginative creation, and that while the neophyte and unimaginative artist must restrict themselves to minute delineation of form, great art should not and cannot. The periodical reviewers claimed that however imaginative Turner's pictures might be they could not be true to nature. To counter these charges the opening volume of *Modern Painters* demonstrates that the artist's early work contains an astonishing record of visible fact— the foundation upon which he raised the imaginative vision of the much-attacked *Snow Storm* and *Mercury*

[30] See, for example, Roger B. Stein, *Ruskin and Aesthetic Thought in America, 1840-1900* (Cambridge, 1967), pp. 87, 113, 194; and my review, *JEGP* (April 1969). Quentin Bell, *Victorian Artists*, p. 41, quite accurately asserts that Ruskin's "celebrated advice: 'go to nature in all singleness of heart, rejecting nothing, selecting nothing, scorning nothing' was intended for students and he was of course delighted to find young painters who took his injunctions so much to heart. Holman Hunt had indeed read and been influenced by *Modern Painters* and it may be said that, in this sense, he remained a student of Ruskin all his life. But such prolonged apprenticeship was not what Ruskin wanted. In the sentence from which this quotation is taken he observed that, while young painters should make the early works of Turner their example his *latest* works were to be their object of emulation."

*and Argus.* In both this volume and the *Academy Notes* Ruskin emphasizes that the beginning painter must follow Turner's path through fact to imagination, but he never holds that great art, the art of Turner, Tintoretto, or Giotto, concerns itself with minute depiction. In fact, the inability of the Pre-Raphaelites to progress beyond the first necessary stage much troubled him.

In order to make our investigations of Ruskin's aesthetic thought and its background easier, the following pages will present a brief summary of *Modern Painters,* the center of his writings on the arts. His frequent cross references between *Modern Painters, The Seven Lamps of Architecture, The Stones of Venice,* his *Academy Notes,* and the lectures and essays of this period reveal that he considered his major writings to form a coherent whole, in essence one book of many volumes.

In the preface to the first edition of Volume 1 (1843), Ruskin informed the reader that "The work now laid before the public originated in indignation at the shallow and false criticisms of the periodicals of the day on the works of the great living artist [J.M.W. Turner] to whom it principally refers."[31] When the fifth and last volume appeared in 1860, Turner was no longer alive, and many other painters, among them Titian and Tintoretto, had rivaled Turner in Ruskin's estimation; and yet despite these changes of the historical context and of Ruskin's own interests, he generally followed his original intention to discuss the ideas of truth, beauty, and relation, which were at the center of his defense of Turner. Ruskin elaborated his projected outline of

[31] *Works, Library Edition,* eds. E. T. Cook and Alexander Wedderburn (London, 1903-1912), III, 3; hereafter cited in text, with Arabic rather than Roman numerals for volume numbers.

*Modern Painters* in a preface added to the second edition, which appeared in 1844:

> My task will naturally divide itself into three portions. In the first, I shall endeavour to investigate and arrange the facts of nature with scientific accuracy; showing as I proceed, by what total neglect of the very first base and groundwork of their art the idealities of some among the old masters are produced. This foundation once securely laid, I shall proceed, in the second portion of the work, to analyse and demonstrate the nature of the emotions of the Beautiful and Sublime; to examine the particular characters of every kind of scenery; and to bring to light, as far as may be in my power, that faultless, ceaseless, inconceivable, inexhaustible loveliness, which God has stamped upon all things, if man will only receive them as He gives them. Finally, I shall endeavour to trace the operation of all this on the hearts and minds of men; to exhibit the moral function and end of art; to prove the share which it ought to have in the thoughts, and influence on the lives, of all of us; to attach to the artist the responsibility of a preacher, and to kindle in the general mind that regard which such an office must demand. (3.48)

Ruskin opens Volume 1 with a brief exposition of five kinds of ideas important in the discussion of art:

> I think that all the sources of pleasure, or of any other good, to be derived from works of art, may be referred to five distinct heads.
>
> I. Ideas of Power.—The perception or conception of the mental or bodily powers by which the work has been produced.

II. Ideas of Imitation.—The perception that the thing produced resembles something else.

III. Ideas of Truth.—The perception of faithfulness in a statement of facts by the thing produced.

IV. Ideas of Beauty.—The perception of beauty, either in the thing produced, or in what it suggests or resembles.

V. Ideas of Relation.—The perception of intellectual relations in the thing produced, or in what it suggests or resembles. (3.93)

After he has provided the reader with this outline and with a brief exposition of the ideas that will be the subject of his yet unwritten volumes, Ruskin devotes the remainder of this first book to the project described in the 1844 preface:

For many a year we have heard nothing with respect to the works of Turner but accusations of their want of *truth*. To every observation on their power, sublimity, or beauty, there has been but one reply: They are not like nature. I therefore took my opponents on their own ground, and demonstrated, by thorough investigation of actual facts, that Turner *is* like nature, and paints more of nature than any man who ever lived. (3.51-52)

Ruskin begins this defense with an investigation of general truths, by which he means accurate representation of tone, color, chiaroscuro, and perspective. He then proceeds to demonstrate that Turner accurately presented the more specific truths of sky, earth, water, and vegetation—each chapter resounding with the refrain: "And let not arguments respecting the sublimity

27

or fidelity of *impression* be brought forward here. I have nothing whatever to do with this at present. I am not talking about what is sublime, but about what is true" (3.283). Work after work of the old masters are summoned so that Ruskin can show that Turner had a wider, as well as more exact, knowledge than any previous painter.

The second volume of *Modern Painters* (1846) contains Ruskin's theocentric system of aesthetics by which he explained the nature of beauty and demonstrated its importance. Beauty "is either the record of conscience, written in things external, or it is a symbolizing of Divine attributes in matter, or it is the felicity of living things, or the perfect fulfilment of their duties and functions. In all cases it is something Divine; either the approving voice of God, the glorious symbol of Him, the evidence of His kind presence, or the obedience to His will by Him induced and supported" (4.210). All beauty, if properly regarded, is theophany. Therefore, since art records, interprets, and conveys this beauty to man, art necessarily has moral and religious value. Ruskin has followed his outline by elucidating this theory of beauty and by describing the faculties of theoria and imagination, which perceive and create it in art. But he departs from the procedure of the first volume by drawing his examples, not from Turner, but from Italian religious and historical painters. Ruskin had read A. F. Rio's *De la Poésie Chrétienne* in 1844, and in the following year he set out, armed with new knowledge and new enthusiasms, to examine the art of Italy more closely than he had ever done before. Ruskin's notebooks from this trip reveal how carefully he studied Italian art, and this new interest dominated the second volume of *Modern*

*Painters,* which was written upon his return to England. In contrast to the treatment of Turner in Volume I, where Ruskin had cited many drawings and more than 40 oil paintings, the artist now appears all but neglected, and only one painting, *The Slave Ship,* is mentioned. Although there was nothing in Ruskin's original plan that would not permit such a change of method, the discussion of Italian religious and historical art led to problems which shaped the succeeding parts of *Modern Painters.*

When after the pause of a decade Ruskin resumed publication of *Modern Painters* in 1856 with Volumes III and IV, he felt it necessary to treat certain topics related to his studies in Italian art before he could proceed to the proposed closing section on truths of relation. But if the third volume, appropriately entitled "Of Many Things," leads the reader far from Ruskin's outline, the unexpected voyage is one to Serendip, and during the course of it one encounters some of Ruskin's most perceptive criticism of the art and the attitudes of his own time. This central volume again sets forth a romantic theory of painting, and all the concerns of romanticism are here—the nature of the artist, the importance of external nature, and the role of imagination, emotion, and detail in art. The book falls into two parts, both of which are related to Ruskin's interests in the history of European art. In the first section he defines the nature of great art in order to remove apparent contradictions between the first and second volumes which he had created by praising Giotto and Fra Angelico in Volume II. The praise of the Italian Primitives seemed inconsistent with his earlier demands that paintings should display a detailed knowledge of external nature. Ruskin solves the difficulty by explaining that "we might divide the art of Christian times into two great masses—Symbolic and Imitative"(5.262), and he points out that his demands for accurate representation had referred only to imitative art.

Ruskin begins his examination of greatness in art by discounting the neoclassical theory that a grand style is based on the imitation of *la belle nature*. After discussing Reynolds's assertion that "the grand style of Painting requires . . . minute attention [to nature's details] to be carefully avoided, and must be kept as separate from it as the style of Poetry from that of History"(5.21), Ruskin concludes: "Instead of finding, as we expected, the poetry distinguished from the history by the omission of details, we find it consist [*sic*] entirely in the *addition* of details; and instead of being characterised by regard only of the invariable, we find its whole power to consist in the clear expression of what is singular and particular. . . . Generally speaking, poetry runs into finer and more delicate details than prose; but the details are not poetical because they are more delicate, but because they are employed so as to bring out an affecting result"(5.26-27,30). After he has concluded that Reynolds's definition of the grand style will not do, Ruskin formulates his own, which is based upon four elements: noble subject, love of beauty, sincerity, and imaginative treatment. This last quality, imaginative treatment, is at the center of Ruskin's conception of ideal art which he had already explained in Volume II:

> Any work of art which represents, not a material object, but the mental conception of a material object, is, in the primary sense of the word, ideal. That is to say, it represents an idea and not a thing. Any

30

work of art which represents or realizes a material object is, in the primary sense of the term, unideal.

Ideal works of art . . . represent the result of an act of imagination, and are good or bad in proportion to the healthy condition and general power of the imagination whose acts they represent.

Unideal works of art (the studious production of which is termed Realism) represent actual existing things, and are good or bad in proportion to the perfection of the representation. (4.164-165)

When Ruskin describes the three healthy and powerful forms of ideal art, the purist, grotesque, and naturalist, he continues to use his notion that great art is "the expression of the spirits of great men"(5.69), and he relates these three branches of art to the nature of the minds which produce them. Thus purist art, such as that of Fra Angelico, "results from the unwillingness of men whose dispositions are more than ordinarily tender and holy, to contemplate the various forms of definite evil which necessarily occur in the daily aspects of the world around them. They shrink from them as from pollution, and endeavour to create for themselves an imaginary state, in which pain and imperfection either do not exist, or exist in some edgeless and enfeebled condition"(5.103-104). Purist art, which Ruskin finds noble only when instinctive and sincere, presents an incomplete picture of the world and is thus of a second order of greatness.

If the gaze of the purist idealist is averted from evil, that of the grotesque idealist is directed, often playfully or mockingly, into darkness. Ruskin had discussed the grotesque, which "is, in almost all cases, composed of two elements, one ludicrous, the other fearful"

(11.151), in *The Stones of Venice,* and following his usual procedure he refers the reader to that other work. *The Stones of Venice* and *Modern Painters* present a grotesque which can range from playfulness and satire to horror, but in all cases the grotesque is an incomplete, if necessary, view of reality.

In contrast to purist and grotesque art, the naturalist ideal—"naturalist, because studied from nature, and ideal, because it is mentally arranged in a certain manner"(5.113)—presents "things as they ARE, and accepts, in all of them, alike the evil and the good"(5.111). The steady, unshaken vision which creates the naturalist ideal is one quality of the great artist, whose portrait Ruskin draws in this third volume. Although he emphasizes that the ideal painter and poet must feel deeply, Ruskin is disturbed by the subjectivity that emotion produces: "All violent feelings have the same effect. They produce in us a falseness in all our impressions of external things, which I would generally characterize as the 'pathetic fallacy' "(5.205). As we shall see when we examine Ruskin's theories of beauty, he was always concerned to find ways to protect art and the perception of beauty based on emotion from the subjectivity which emotion causes. He tries to solve the problem of distorting emotion in art by the creation of an ideal artist, who, by definition, works with and yet controls and rises above strong feeling. Ruskin describes in detail the mind of Dante, who was such a perfect artist-poet:

> The high creative poet might even be thought, to a great extent, impassive (as shallow people think Dante stern), receiving indeed all feelings to the full, but having a great centre of reflection and knowl-

edge in which he stands serene, and watches the feeling, as it were, from afar off.

Dante, in his most intense moods, has entire command of himself, and can look around calmly, at all moments, for the image or the word that will best tell what he sees to the upper or lower world. But Keats and Tennyson, and the poets of the second order, are generally themselves subdued by the feelings under which they write, or, at least, write as choosing to be so. (5.210)

The calm veracity of the great artist creates the grand style. By relating his standard of greatness to the nature of the man who creates the picture or the poem, Ruskin has a means of embracing many kinds and many periods of art.

The rise of landscape painting, Ruskin's second concern in this volume, was an interest also occasioned by his study of Italian art. After he had begun a defense of Turner, a master of landscape, Ruskin had been diverted to other aspects of painting; in order to make his way back to Turner, Ruskin felt obliged to inform his reader why landscape, a comparatively new development in painting, had arisen. Classical, medieval, and modern attitudes toward external nature are considered in order to explain the growth of landscape feeling. In Homer, the prime example of classical attitudes, Ruskin points to "the utter absence of any trace of the feeling for what we call the picturesque, and the constant dwelling of the writer's mind on what was available, pleasant, or useful"(5.243). Like the classical mind, the medieval dislikes mountains and all other features of an awesome, unsubdued nature; and while the external world is no longer looked upon only in relation to its use, there is still nothing of the modern attitude which Ruskin describes as a "romantic love of beauty, forced to seek in history, and in external nature, the satisfaction it cannot find in ordinary life" (5.326). Drawing in part on what he believes were the effects of his own early love of nature, Ruskin concludes that landscape feeling, which is always dependent upon associations, many of which are literary, "will be found to bring with it such a sense of the presence and power of a Great Spirit as no mere reasoning can either induce or controvert"(5.378). After Ruskin has discussed the implications and importance of a love of external nature, he closes the third volume by examining the influence upon Turner of the French and Dutch landscape painters.

The fourth volume, published the same year as the third, often wanders far from its stated intention to discuss mountain beauty. After he has been led through long disquisitions on slaty crystallines, compact coherents, and the angles of aiguilles, the bored or bewildered reader may glance at the title page to reassure himself that he is still pursuing a work about Turner. The book opens with a discussion of the Turnerian picturesque, and the picturesque in general, which are the aesthetic categories specifically related to growth of landscape art. The volume closes with an examination of the influence of a mountain environment on the lives of men. In between, Ruskin places a very long geology lesson, which is largely a repetition, though in greater detail, of the section on truth of earth in the first volume.

The fifth volume, which was published in 1860, begins with sections on the beauty of leaves and clouds that are again second journeys through ground covered in the first volume. Next follows a discussion of formal relation, or composition, and then a demonstration of Turner's excellence in this aspect of the art. "Composition may best be defined as the help of everything in the picture by everything else"(7.205). This notion of help is central to Ruskin's theory of art, as it was to be in his theories of political economy, and he dwells on it at length, telling the reader that "The highest and first law of the universe—and the other name of life is, therefore, 'help' "(7.207). Composition, then, is the creation of an organic interrelationship between the formal elements of a work of art:

> A poet, or creator, is therefore a person who puts things together, not as a watchmaker steel, or a shoemaker leather, but who puts life into them.
>
> His work is essentially this: it is the gathering and arranging of material by imagination, so as to have in it at last the harmony or helpfulness of life, and the passion or emotion of life. (7.215)

Ruskin then demonstrates, by brilliant analyses of Turner's pictorial compositions, that this artist was a master of this aspect of visual art.

The relation of art to life, one of Ruskin's most important interests throughout his five volumes, is at the heart of the lengthy section on "Invention Spiritual" that concludes *Modern Painters*. In the course of stating what he believes to be the truths about human existence to which art must be related, Ruskin lays the foundations for his later work, and at the same time he suggests that he has begun to shift his attentions from the problems of art to the problems of society:

> In these books of mine, their distinctive character, as essays on art, is their bringing everything to a root

in human passion or human hope. Arising first not in any desire to explain the principles of art, but in the endeavour to defend an individual painter from injustice, they have been coloured throughout,—nay, continually altered in shape, and even warped and broken, by digressions respecting social questions, which had for me an interest tenfold greater than the work I had been forced into undertaking. Every principle of painting which I have stated is traced to some vital or spiritual fact; and in my works on architecture the preference accorded finally to one school over another, is founded on a comparison of their influences on the life of the workman—a question by all other writers on the subject of architecture wholly forgotten or despised. (7.257)

The following chapters relate art not to human hope, but to the lack of it which Ruskin believes to be a consequence of the Reformation. According to him, after the Reformation when men lost their firm belief in an afterlife, it was no longer possible to attain peace of mind, or to die hopefully. "Thenceforward human life became a school of debate, troubled and fearful. Fifteen hundred years of spiritual teaching were called into fearful question, whether indeed it had been teaching by angels or devils? Whatever it had been, there was no longer any way of trusting it peacefully" (7.301). After Ruskin has examined the remnants of faith which Salvator and Dürer possessed, he discusses the great landscapists Claude and Poussin, who, for him, are representative of painters without faith.

[They] founded a school of art properly called "classical," of which the following are the chief characteristics.

36

INTRODUCTION

The belief in a supreme benevolent Being having
ceased, and the sense of spiritual destitution fasten-
ing on the mind, together with the hopeless perception of ruin and decay in the existing world, the
imagination sought to quit itself from the oppression
of these ideas by realizing a perfect worldly felicity,
in which the inevitable ruin should at least be lovely,
and the necessarily short life entirely happy and refined. Labour must be banished, since it was to be
unrewarded. Humiliation and degradation of body
must be prevented, since there could be no compen-
sation for them by preparation of the soul for another world. Let us eat and drink (refinedly), for to-
morrow we die, and attain the highest possible dignity
as men in this world, since we shall have none as
spirits in the next. (7.315)

Rubens and Cuyp, the next artists whom Ruskin compares, do not even attempt, like the classical painters,
to compensate for their lost faith, and their works reveal that a decline in belief in an afterlife leads directly
to a loss of nobility and human dignity in art. Finally,
the effects of faithlessness appear even more distinctly
in the paintings of Wouwerman, an artist whose complete lack of spirituality Ruskin contrasts to the firm
religious belief of Fra Angelico. These contrasts prepare for a comparison of the boyhoods of Giorgione
and Turner. After Ruskin has shown the setting in
which Turner's mind developed, he devotes two chapters to elaborate exegeses of paintings which he
believes represent the faith of the artist and his England. The first picture to be examined, the *Garden of
the Hesperides*, "being the most important picture of
the first period"(7.392), is analyzed with care. Turner's

title for this painting, which is No. 477 in the National Gallery, was *The Goddess of Discord choosing the Apple of Contention in the Garden of the Hesperides* (see Plate 6). The editors of the *Library Edition* of Ruskin have included the explanatory note from the official catalogue at the British Institution, where the painting was exhibited in 1806:

> The three daughters of Hesperus, Aegle, Hespere, and Erytheïs, dwelt in this western garden, and had charge of the tree of the golden apples, the gift of Earth to Juno on her wedding day; the Hesperides and the garden were protected by the dragon Ladon. The Goddess of Discord, not having been invited to the marriage feast of Peleus and Thetis, threw one of these apples into the midst of the assembled gods, to be taken by the most beautiful. It was claimed by Juno, Minerva, and by Venus, and Jupiter ordered the contest to be decided by Paris, the son of Priam, who awarded the apple to Venus. This judgment of Paris was not only the cause of the destruction of Troy, but of countless misfortunes also to the Greeks. The Goddess of Discord is on the right in the act of receiving the golden apple (or orange) from one of the Hesperides. The dragon is seen lying along the summit of a lofty rock, in the middle distance.( 7.391n)

After Ruskin examines the darkness and haze of the picture, mentioning "the breaking of the bough of the tree by the weight of its apples—not healthily, but as a diseased tree would break"(7.407), he concludes: "Such then is our English painter's first great religious picture; and exponent of our English faith. A sad-coloured work, not executed in Angelico's white and gold; nor in Perugino's crimson and azure; but in a sulphurous hue, as relating to a paradise of smoke. That power, it appears, on the hill-top [the dragon] is our British Madonna"(7.407-408). The second painting Ruskin examines, *Apollo and Python* (1811; see Plate 7), also has a dragon, but a dragon defeated. Ruskin sees the contest of Apollo with the monster as "the strife of purity with pollution; of life with forgetfulness; of love, with the grave. I believe this great battle stood, in the Greek mind, for the type of the struggle of youth and manhood with deadly sin—venomous, infectious, irre-coverable sin. . . . Well did Turner know the meaning of that battle"(7.420). Even as Python is wounded "he bursts asunder in the midst, and melts to pieces, rather than dies, vomiting smoke—a smaller serpent-worm ris-ing out of his blood. Alas, for Turner! . . . In the midst of all the power and beauty of nature, he still saw this death-worm writhing among the weeds. . . . He was without hope"(7.420-421). Ruskin concludes that Turner is "the painter of the loveliness of nature, with the worm at its root: Rose and cankerworm,—both with his utmost strength; the one *never* separate from the other"(7.422). And the reason for Turner's fascina-tion with the destruction of beauty, and of his conse-quent lack of hope, lies, says Ruskin, in the nature of the age, an age which believes neither in man nor God, and which lets its great men die in isolation and despair. And in his next work, *Unto This Last*, which he completed the same year as this final volume of *Modern Painters*, Ruskin turned to attack the economic system which he believed to be the cause of the de-spairing, inhuman relations of men in society.

# CHAPTER ONE

# Ruskin's Theory of
# the Sister Arts

## I. Ruskin and the tradition of
## ut pictura poesis

THE WEARY tradition of *ut pictura poesis*, so popular
throughout the eighteenth century, had all but died by
1856 when John Ruskin published the third volume of
*Modern Painters*, and it is thus striking to encounter a
statement that "Painting is properly to be opposed to
*speaking* or *writing*, but not to *poetry*. Both painting
and speaking are methods of expression. Poetry is the
employment of either for the noblest purposes"(5.31).
In this same volume Ruskin again describes art as expression: "Great art is produced by men who feel
acutely and nobly; and it is in some sort an expression
of this personal feeling"(5.32). It is characteristic of
Ruskin's relation to previous criticism that he has
added a romantic emphasis on the expression of emotion to an older and rather unfashionable view that
verse and painting are analogous arts. If we can perceive the manner in which Ruskin drew upon both
these ways of considering art, we shall gain entrance
at an important point to his ideas about painting and
poetry. We shall, therefore, begin by examining the notion of *ut pictura poesis*, next consider the idea of art
based on expression of emotion, and then investigate
the ways in which these views, in the form Ruskin encountered them, occasionally conflicted.

Ruskin began *Modern Painters* as a defense of
J.M.W. Turner against charges that his works were not
true to life; and though this defense became entwined
with other interests and Ruskin was led far afield before he reached the final volume seventeen years after

43

he had begun the first, *Modern Painters* in part remained a vindication, a defense, just as Ruskin himself, to the end of his career, remained a missionary whose proselytizing devices ranged from golden descriptions to the harshest polemic. It is thus particularly appropriate that a work which had been undertaken to defend the value of painting should have referred to the principle of *ut pictura poesis*, for throughout the Renaissance and eighteenth century, poetry and painting had been juxtaposed as a means of defending the prestige of the visual art. In Renaissance Italy, in eighteenth-century England, and in the England of 1843, when Ruskin published the first volume of *Modern Painters*, painting was the younger sister of poetry, trying to edge into social acceptability on the arm of an elder relation. Since the Renaissance, artists had vehemently protested that their enterprise, like the poet's, was not merely a craft or trade but a liberal art requiring mental skills capable of providing great gifts for mankind. Modern notions of the fine arts had not existed in the Middle Ages and grew slowly. Painters of saddles and painters of fresco were often placed in the same guilds.[1] Poetry, on the other hand, had no connections with trade; and although, as in the English Renaissance, literary arts occasionally had to be guarded against charges of triviality or immorality, it was generally accepted that poetry was a liberal art possessing a long history of service for intellect and soul. As Rensselaer W. Lee has shown, the obvious defense of the painter's work and status was in a close alliance of the two arts which relied heavily upon support from the

[1] Thomas Munro, *The Arts and Their Interrelations* (New York, 1949), pp. 24-48.

classics.[2] Zeuxis and Simonides, Aristotle and Horace
were summoned to the defense, and their illustrative
comparisons became the basis of a widely held theory
of the arts. This hardening of analogies produced the
humanistic theory of painting which emphasized that
painting had to depend upon poetry, both as model
and source, for subject, content, and purpose. As
poetry drew painting upward, it impressed its own nature on the sister art.

Ruskin, who had encountered the principle of *ut
pictura poesis* in his favorite critics and in the practice
of his favorite artist, was well versed in this manner of
viewing the arts long before he began to write *Modern
Painters*. In addition to references to *ut pictura poesis*
which Ruskin would have found in eighteenth-century
literary criticism, he read the usual formulations in
Reynolds's *Discourses* and in the published versions of
similar lectures which Henri Fuseli and James Barry
delivered before the Royal Academy. It was probably
after finishing his first volume that Ruskin read another
famous work on the subject, Leonardo da Vinci's
*Treatise on Painting*. With the *Discourses* this remained in later years one of Ruskin's favorite works of
critical theory.

Turner, the painter whose works Ruskin knew best
when he began *Modern Painters*, believed in the principle of *ut pictura poesis*, and the titles and epigraphs
which he gave his paintings emphasize his own alliance
of poetry and painting.[3] Of the approximately 200 oil
paintings which Turner exhibited in his lifetime, 53

[2] Rensselaer W. Lee, "*Ut Pictura Poesis*: The Humanistic Theory of
Painting," *Art Bulletin*, XXII (1940), 197-269.

[3] See the list of Turner's works in A. J. Finberg, *The Life of J.M.W.
Turner, RA*, 2nd ed. (Oxford, 1961), pp. 456-516.

have poetic epigraphs, and 26 of these the artist composed himself. In addition Turner used five passages from the Bible. Of the poetic epigraphs which Turner appended to his paintings, six are from Thomson and three from Milton, both poets whom he discussed in his own lectures at the Academy. Byron, with whom Ruskin compared Turner in the last volume of *Modern Painters*, was the source of three epigraphs, and the painter also used selections from Rogers, Mallet, Gray, Langhorne, Ovid, Pope's *Iliad*, and Du Fresnoy's *Art of Painting*. The titles of sixty canvases, often those without epigraphs, make reference to Shakespeare, Byron, Ossian, and other poets, and in addition, many of the water colors similarly employ poetry for title or epigraph. For more than a century, Ruskin was the only critic to pay any close attention to Turner's use of poetry. In contrast, the painter's biographer, A. J. Finberg, a man most unsuited to his task, makes no use whatsoever of Turner's own "Fallacies of Hope" and pays little attention to the all important epigraphs. Indeed, not until the recent valuable work of Jack Lindsay, who has edited Turner's hitherto unpublished poems and contributed a critical biography, has there been an appreciation of the value of the painter's poetry comparable to Ruskin's.[4] The author of *Modern Painters* early perceived how the poems which the artist appended to his works provide major clues to his intentions. He points out that the "course of his mind may be traced"(13.125) through the poetry he attached to his works:

His first [epigraph] was given in 1798 (with the view

[4] *The Sunset Ship: The Poems of J.M.W. Turner* (London, 1966), and *J.M.W. Turner: His Life and Work* (New York, 1966).

of Coniston Fell, now numbered 461) from *Paradise Lost*, and there is a strange ominousness—as there is about much that great men do—in the choice of it. Consider how these four lines, the first he ever chose, express Turner's peculiar mission as distinguished from other landscapists:—

> "Ye mists and exhalations, that now rise
> From hill, or steaming lake, dusky or grey,
> Till the sun paint your fleecy skirts with gold,
> In honour to the world's great Author rise."

In this and the next year . . . came various quotations, descriptive of atmospheric effects, from Thomson, interspersed with two or three from Milton, and one from Mallet.

In 1800, some not very promising "anon" lines were attached to views of Dolbadern and Caernarvon Castles. Akenside and Ossian were next laid under contribution. Then Ovid, Callimachus, and Homer. At last, in 1812, the "Fallacies of Hope" begin, *apropos* of Hannibal's crossing the Alps: and this poem continues to be the principal text-book, with occasional recurrences to Thomson, one passage from Scott, and several from Byron. . . . The "Childe Harold" . . . is an important proof of his respect for the genius of Byron. (13.125-126)

Ruskin, then, was well aware of the continued importance of poetry to his favorite painter, and when we examine his interpretations of Turner in a later chapter, we shall perceive how sensitive was Ruskin to the implications of "The Fallacies of Hope." The author

47

of *Modern Painters*, who uses "the words painter and poet quite indifferently"(5.221), knew that he was following the precedent of Turner: the full title of one of the paintings exhibited in 1842 in whose behalf Ruskin began his book is *Snowstorm: Steamboat off a Harbour's Mouth making Signals in Shallow Water, and going by the Lead. The Author was in this Storm on the night the Ariel left Harwich* (see Plate 1). In his description of the Turner Bequest, Ruskin places an asterisk after *author* and instructs the reader to note "Turner's significant use of this word, instead of 'artist' "(13.161n).

Moreover, as Professor of Perspective at the Royal Academy, Turner delivered lectures between 1811 and 1823 which often considered the relation of the two arts. Jerrold Ziff's recent article, "J.M.W. Turner on Poetry and Painting," discusses the preparation and content of these hitherto unpublished and almost unknown writings.[5] Between the time Turner received his appointment in 1807 and four years later when he delivered his first lecture, he studied standard treatises on perspective and also read the usual works on art theory, including Charles Du Fresnoy, John Opie, Roger de Piles, Sir Joshua Reynolds, Jonathan Richardson, and Sir Martin Archer Shee. The lectures themselves contain discussions of verse by Milton and Thomson, these being the only known instances of the painter's written analyses of verse which he appended to his own paintings. Ziff quotes this paraphrase of Akenside's *Pleasures of the Imagination*, which Turner included in one of his lectures:

Painting and poetry, flowing from the same fount

[5] Ziff, in *Studies in Romanticism*, III (1964), 193-215.

48

mutually by vision, constantly comparing Poetic allusions by natural forms in one and applying forms found in nature to the other, meandering into streams by application, which reciprocally improve, reflect, and heighten each other's beauties like . . . mirrors.[6]

Ruskin probably encountered Turner's strangely written lectures when, during the years from 1856 to 1858, he arranged the Turner Bequest for the British Museum. They would have demonstrated even further that Turner believed poetry and painting were interdependent.

Well aware of the usual aims and methods of the critics who made use of the principle of *ut pictura poesis*, Ruskin referred to the older tradition with some cause, for the need for a polemical defensive alliance of the two arts continued in Ruskin's time. Art was gaining respectability (there was a Royal Academy), but painting had not achieved anything like the popularity or prestige of literature. Education of increasing numbers of people and new publishing practices had produced a sizeable reading public in England, and part of Ruskin's purpose in *Modern Painters* was to create and attract a similar audience among those, largely the middle classes, who were unaware of the art of painting.

Like most writers who allied arts in order to defend painting, Ruskin stressed its ability to convey information in the service of religion and morality. Unlike most who had preceded him, he did not defend painting on the ground that, like poetry, it educates and entertains by imitating nature. In the theory of poetry which Ruskin allied with pictorial art, the expression of noble emotion had replaced the earlier concerns with imita-

6 *Ibid.*, p. 203.

tion as a center of critical attention—a changed attitude toward imitation that was related to new views of
the nature of art.

From the Renaissance to the nineteenth century the
defense of the artist and poet against charges of frivol-
ity and immorality had been closely associated with the
theory of a particular kind of imitation. Although in the
eighteenth century imitation was occasionally used in
the sense of duplication or mechanical copying, it was
generally taken as a technical, philosophical term,
which conveniently removed it from comparison with
other more practical forms of human endeavor such as
the counterfeiting of money. One thing upon which
many writers on painting and poetry, including Dryden and Reynolds, agree is that imitation is a selective,
idealizing process which communicates the potential
best of nature. According to Dryden, *"both* these *Arts*
. . . are not only true imitations of Nature, but of the
best Nature, of that which is wrought up to a nobler
pitch. They present us with Images more perfect than
the Life in any individual: and we have the pleasure
to see all the scatter'd Beauties of Nature united by a
happy *Chymistry*, without its deformities or faults."[7]
Similarly, in his *Discourses* Reynolds quotes the statement of Proclus that the artist "who takes for his model
such forms as nature produces, and confines himself to
an exact imitation of them, will never attain to what is
perfectly beautiful. For the works of nature are full of
disproportion, and fall very short of the true standard
of beauty."[8] Dryden and Reynolds, with many others,

[7] "Preface of the Translator, with a Parallel of *Poetry* and *Painting*,"
in Charles Alphonse Du Fresnoy, *The Art of Painting* (London, 1695),
p. xxxiii.

[8] *Discourses on Art*, ed. Robert R. Wark (San Marino, Calif., 1959),
p. 42.

believed that the artist and poet working side by side repaired the accidents and errors of particular nature. As Reynolds put it: "Upon the whole . . . the object and intention of all the Arts is to supply the natural imperfection of things."[9]

Reynolds, whose criticism and painting Ruskin knew thoroughly, is the critic who may most fittingly be compared with the author of *Modern Painters* on the subject of imitation. Each was not only the major theorist of painting in his age but was also an important proponent of the alliance of painting with poetry. Both agree that the artist is a poet of lines and colors, but Reynolds's poet is of the eighteenth century, and Ruskin's of the nineteenth. The *Discourses* describe the ideal artist as a liberally educated man permeated with a knowledge of the rules and their decorums. While neither theorist believes that a man without innate genius can create great art, Reynolds, far more than Ruskin, held that abilities are developed through practice of the rules and through imitation of the ancients. But if Ruskin's painter and poet know the rules, they create despite rather than by means of them. "The knowing of rules and the exertion of judgment have a tendency to check and confuse the fancy in its flow; so that it will follow, that, in exact proportion as a master knows anything about rules of right and wrong, he is likely to be uninventive . . . [and thus he will work] not despising them, but simply feeling that between him and them there is nothing in common"(5.119). Reynolds's defense of the artist and his theory of imitating *la belle nature* are based on the belief, stated in the *Discourses,* that "the value and rank of every art is in proportion to the mental labour employed in it, or the

<hr />

[9] *Ibid.,* p. 244.

mental pleasure produced by it. As this principle is observed or neglected, our profession becomes either a
liberal art, or a mechanical trade."[10] Reynolds relates
this view of art to imitation in his *Idler* 79:

> Amongst the painters and the writers on painting
> there is one maxim universally admitted and continu-
> ally inculcated. "Imitate nature" is the invariable
> rule, but I know none who have explained in what
> manner this rule is to be understood; the conse-
> quence of which is that everyone takes it in the most
> obvious sense—that objects are represented naturally
> when they have such relief that they seem real. . . .
> It must be considered that if the excellency of a
> painter consisted only in this kind of imitation, paint-
> ing must lose its rank and be no longer considered
> as a liberal art and sister to poetry, this imitation be-
> ing merely mechanical, in which the slowest intellect
> is always sure to succeed best.[11]

Reynolds bases his defense of art on the old opposition
of physical and mental labor; since the art of painting,
like the art of poetry, demands the use of the intellect,
it should therefore be accorded the greater respect due
an intellectual art. Reynolds's opposition of the mechanical and the fine arts is based on a psychology that
could not conceive the unconscious creative processes
or theories of aesthetic-moral emotion that were important in nineteenth-century conceptions of poetry. Ruskin, in contrast, allies painting to a romantic view of
poetry, and his theory of arts is characteristically centered not on intellect but emotion:

[10] *Ibid.*, p. 57.
[11] *Eighteenth-Century Critical Essays*, ed. Scott Elledge, 2 vols. (Ithaca, N.Y., 1961), II, 831-832.

MANUFACTURE is, according to the etymology and right use of the word, "the making of anything by hands,"—directly or indirectly, with or without the help of instruments or machines. . . . ART is the operation of the hand and the intelligence of man together. . . . Then FINE ART is that in which the hand, the head, and the *heart* of man go together. (16.294)

Since his romantic defense of the allied arts could not gain prestige for painting by employing Reynolds's major argument—that they require intellect—Ruskin had to find other means to demonstrate the value of Turner's glorious representations of color and form.

## II. *The use and moral value of art*

FOR more than forty years Ruskin emphasized man's essential need for the arts and considered such vindication a major part of his critical enterprise. With Wordsworth, probably the most important source of his critical theory, he felt intense dislike for men who, as the poet complained, "talk of Poetry as of a matter of amusement and idle pleasure; who will converse with us as gravely about a *taste* for Poetry, as they express it, as if it were a thing as indifferent as a taste for ropedancing, or Frontiniac or Sherry."[12] Although Ruskin, as we shall see, redefines the term "taste" to suit his purposes, he, too, on occasion felt uncomfortable with the employment of such a word in relation to the arts. Possibly echoing Wordsworth, he explained in the third volume of *Modern Painters* that "the name which is given to the feeling [of pleasure and preference in

12 *The Poetical Works*, eds. E. de Selincourt and Helen Darbishire, 5 vols. (Oxford, 1940-1952), II, 394.

art],—Taste, Goût, Gusto,—in all languages indicates the baseness of it, for it implies that art gives only a kind of pleasure analogous to that derived from eating by the palate"(5.96). Such an implication Ruskin will not admit, for as he had earlier insisted, "Art, properly so called, is no recreation; it cannot be learned at spare moments, nor pursued when we have nothing better to do. It is no handiwork for drawing-room tables, no relief of the ennui of boudoirs; it must be understood and undertaken seriously, or not at all. To advance it men's lives must be given, and to receive it, their hearts" (4.26).

Nonetheless, one must admit that, despite his continuing emphasis on the importance of the visual arts, rarely has a passionate advocate of painting so candidly admitted his doubts about its moral effectiveness. Twice in *Modern Painters*, for example, he publicly expressed such doubt. In concluding the last volume of *Modern Painters*, he confided in the reader: "What the final use may be to men, of landscape painting, or of any painting, or of natural beauty, I do not yet know. . . . Full of far deeper reverence for Turner's art than I felt when this task of his defence was undertaken. . . , I am more in doubt respecting the real use to mankind of . . . art; incomprehensible as it must always be to the mass of men"(7.423,441). During a time when he turned increasingly to the problems of society and the common man, he briefly questioned the value of something which most men could not understand or enjoy; but, as later works demonstrate, he never lost hope for long, continuing throughout his career to search for, discover, and explicate the uses of art to man. In the 1844 preface to the first volume of *Modern Painters*, written near the beginning of his career, he had commented that it is "a question which, in spite of the claims of Painting to be called the sister of Poetry, appears . . . to admit of considerable doubt, whether art has ever, except in its earliest and rudest stages, possessed anything like efficient moral influence on mankind"(3.20-21). In particular, landscape painting, the specific kind of art he had set out to explain and defend, had conspicuously failed to achieve anything of moral worth, and he remarks on "the utter inutility of all that has been hitherto accomplished by the painters of landscape. No moral end has been answered, no permanent good effected, by any of their works"(3.21). According to him, "all hitherto done in landscape, by those commonly conceived its masters, has never prompted one holy thought in the minds of nations" (3.24), but the cause of such failure, he insists, was an accidental, not an essential, condition of art: Claude, Salvator Rosa, and the Dutch—the painters idolized by the periodical critics and other detractors of Turner— had turned away from God and nature, using their great talents merely for the sake of proud displays of virtuosity. Turner and all great artists paint differently, says Ruskin, and therefore he will dedicate *Modern Painters* "to exhibit the moral function and end of art; to prove the share which it ought to have in the thoughts, and the influence on the lives, of all of us; to attach to the artist the responsibility of a preacher, and to kindle in the general mind that regard which such an office must demand"(3.48).

In the first place, art possesses major value because it embodies the essence of past ages of greatness: "Whole æras of mighty history are summed, and the passions of dead myriads are concentrated, in the existence of a noble art"(18.170). From such great painting, from such great poetry, we can learn more deeply than

in any other manner the wisdom, beliefs, and feelings
of men and societies now vanished into the darkness
of time. Art, which has the power to release us from
the limitations of our own time, can thus reveal truths
which we have neglected or of which we are ignorant;
and by so doing it furnishes us with a necessary perspective from which to view our own assumptions and
complacencies. Painting, poetry, and architecture contributed importantly to Ruskin's own growth as a man,
and he frequently uses the evidence of the arts to stimulate the intellectual and moral sympathies of his audience. Ruskin, whose experience of Catholic art had
gradually dissolved his Evangelical Anglican bigotry,
tried to bring a similar experience to the readers of
*The Stones of Venice.* Addressing his work to a Protestant, and presumably anti-Catholic, audience, he insists
that medieval legends, for example, deserve attention
"on this ground, if on no other, that they have once
been sincerely believed by good men, and have had no
ineffective agency in the formation of the existent European mind" (10.42). The art of Venice, the painting of
Giotto, and the myths of Greece provide modern man
with examples of sincere belief and virtuous life which
he may use to examine his own strengths and weak-
nesses.

Moreover, since Ruskin firmly believes "the art of
any country *is the exponent of its social and political
virtues"*(20.39), he searches the artistic creations of the
past for lessons he can apply to the present. In particular, much troubled by "the apparent connection of
great success in art with subsequent national degradation"(16.263), he examines the arts of India and Italy to
see if it is possible to discover causes of national decline in their painting and architecture. *The Stones of*

*Venice,* his major endeavor to derive lessons of contemporary value from an earlier art, opens with the
famous and beautiful lines that compare England to
her predecessors: "Since first the dominion of men was
asserted over the ocean, three thrones, of mark beyond
all others, have been set upon its sands: the thrones of
Tyre, Venice, and England. Of the First of these great
powers only the memory remains; of the Second, the
ruin; the Third, which inherits their greatness, if it forget their example, may be led through prouder eminence to less pitied destruction"(9.17). Desiring to record for his contemporaries "the warning . . . uttered
by every one of the fast-gaining waves, that beat like
passing bells, against the STONES OF VENICE"(9.17), Ruskin undertakes to examine "the relation of the art of
Venice to her moral temper"(9.14). Since he believes
the Renaissance was the age when Venice declined
from its previous greatness, he juxtaposes Gothic and
Renaissance work to determine how the spirit of the
city, once truly religious, changed. Comparing the
tomb sculptures of the Doges Tomaso Mocenigo and
Andrea Vendramin, the latter "unanimously declared
the *chef d'oeuvre* of Renaissance sepulchral work"
(9.50), he discovers that whereas the earlier artist dedi-
cated his skill to create a "noble image of a king's mor-
tality"(9.49), the Renaissance sculptor—a man, it turns
out, later banished for forgery—saved time, money,
and energy to lavish on putti by carving only the side
of the dead man's effigy nearest the spectator. That
such deception, coarseness, and "utter coldness of feeling"(9.52), which turned memorial into mockery, found
favor in Venice indicates much about both artist and
audience. Ruskin returns to these and other examples
of tomb sculpture in the last volume of *The Stones of*

57

*Venice* when he traces the evolution of Renaissance sepulchral work from its origins in primitive simplicity and sure belief. Summoning example after example, he demonstrates in detail how sculptors increasingly eager to display their skill created monuments to Venetian vanity and worldly success. From this evidence Ruskin concludes:

Exactly in proportion to the degree of the pride of life expressed in any monument, would be also the fear of death; and therefore, as these tombs increase in splendour, in size, and beauty of workmanship, we perceive a gradual desire to *take away from the definite character of the sarcophagus.* In the earliest times, as we have seen, it was a gloomy mass of stone; gradually it became charged with religious sculpture; but never with the slightest desire to disguise its form, until towards the middle of the fifteenth century. It then becomes enriched with flower-work and hidden by the Virtues: and, finally, losing its four-square form, it is modelled on graceful types of ancient vases, made as little like a coffin as possible, and refined away in various elegances, till it becomes, at last, a mere pedestal or stage for the portrait statue. This statue, in the meantime, has been gradually coming back to life, through a curious series of transitions. The Vendramin monument is one of the last which shows, or pretends to show, the recumbent figure laid in death. A few years later, this idea became disagreeable to polite minds; and lo! the figures, which before had been laid at rest upon the tomb pillow, raised themselves on their elbows, and began to look round them. The soul of the sixteenth century dared not contemplate its body in death. . . . The statue rose up, and presented itself in front of the tomb, like an actor upon a stage, surrounded now not merely, or not at all, by the Virtues, but by allegorical figures of Fame and Victory, by genii and muses, by personifications of humbled kingdoms and adoring nations, and by every circumstance of pomp, and symbol of adulation, that flattery could suggest, or insolence could claim. (11.109-110,111)

However much these gaudy monuments fail to memorialize those hidden inside, they blazon forth, because they embody, an age afraid of death, an age which has lost true faith in either God or man. In this third volume Ruskin confirms other evidence of Venetian decline he had presented in his opening chapter. After comparing the tombs of Mocenigo and Vendramin, he had compared a Gothic capital bearing a figure of Hope from the Ducal Palace with its Renaissance imitation from the same building. He observed the later work to be not only more crudely chiseled but missing its essential iconographical attribute, the hand of God coming forth from the sun—"a curious and striking type of the spirit which had then become dominant in the world"(9.55). Ruskin, we must notice, does not hold that this art or that of the tomb sculptures is a *cause* of Venetian decline, but merely a very "readable," and hence most valuable, *sign* of it.

Such investigations of Renaissance art disclose the general, and not the specific, causes of what Ruskin believes to be the cause of Venetian disaster. One specific cause, upon which Ruskin places great emphasis, appears in his justly famous chapter "The Nature of Gothic." Contrasting Gothic and Renaissance architecture, he finds that the later style, which demands that

59

everything follow a rigid, predetermined plan, necessitates turning the worker into a slave, a "machine," a mere "animated tool"(10.192). Such an art, says Ruskin, bespeaks the ideals and spiritual condition of the society which chooses it. When he discusses the failures of Renaissance tombs and Renaissance capitals, he chiefly dwells on the spirit of the past; but when he turns to Renaissance architecture, still popular with many of his contemporaries, he indicts his own time as well—and not merely because many in Victorian England prefer Renaissance to Gothic buildings. No, he sees this architecture as a fitting emblem of modern manufacture, modern tyranny, and incipient modern disaster. Ruskin warns that for men "to feel their souls withering within them, unthanked, to find their whole being sunk into an unrecognized abyss, to be counted off into a heap of mechanism numbered with its wheels, and weighed with its hammer strokes—this, nature bade not,—this, God blesses not,—this, humanity for no long time is able to endure"(10.195). If England forgets the example of Venice, it may be led, he warns, through prouder eminence to less pitied destruction.

Ruskin not only thus draws upon the arts of the past but, as one might expect, applies the same methods to contemporary works of art. In "Traffic," for example, he examines the implications, not of medieval, but of Victorian Gothic building and points out that mid-nineteenth-century use of Gothic for churches and Italianate modes for "mills and mansions" indicates a serious divorce of religion from daily life. He therefore instructs his audience that although they may consider "Gothic a pre-eminently sacred and beautiful mode of building, which you think, like fine frankincense, should be mixed for the tabernacle only, and reserved for your religious services," such a conviction, so foreign to the period of genuine Gothic, only means "you have separated your religion from your life"(18.440). Modern faith in Mammon—the true faith of the nineteenth century and the belief by which the age lives—embodies itself, he says, in warehouses and railroads, in factories and stock exchanges, and it is to them one must go to perceive the conditions of life and worship.

Art, thus considered as the creation and embodiment of a culture, provides invaluable evidence about the political, social, and spiritual state of its creators. Great art, the product of a healthy, vital era, furnishes later times with an ideal to emulate, while less successful art teaches them what to avoid. And when one considers the art of the present, discovering symptoms of an unhealthy society, one has received a warning, especially compelling because unintended if inevitable.

Nonetheless, however important Ruskin may find painting, poetry, and architecture as an exponent of a nation's ethical life, such an indirect and archaeological use of the arts provides no essential argument for their continued creation. His chief defense of the arts comes rather from what he conceives to be their distinguishing capacity to communicate and record matters particularly important to men, matters with which neither science nor philosophy can adequately deal. Ruskin, we have already seen, believes painting a form of language, and the greatest painting a form of poetry. At its simplest level, then, the pictorial arts function as a medium for conveying and making permanent truths which would otherwise be lost. In *Sesame and Lilies* (1865) he pointed out that "a book is written, not to multiply the voice merely, not to carry it merely, but to perpetuate it"(18.61), and we may take this assertion as applying to the sister art as well. Thus, in its most basic form, the art of painting and drawing serves chiefly as a means of fixing images—of making permanent record of visible fact. Ruskin discusses this idea of visual art as notation in his lecture "Education in Art"(1858), which he appended to *A Joy For Ever*: "Drawing, so far as it is possible to the multitude, is mainly to be considered as a means of obtaining and communicating knowledge. He who can accurately represent the form of an object, and match its colour, has unquestionably a power of notation and description greater in most instances than that of words"(16.143). A decade earlier *The Seven Lamps of Architecture* had similarly explained that "the whole art of painting" functions to state

> certain facts, in the clearest possible way. For instance: I desire to give an account of a mountain or of a rock; I begin by telling its shape. But words will not do this distinctly, and I draw its shape and say "This was its shape." Next: I would fain represent its colour: but words will not do this either, and I dye the paper, and say, "This was its colour." (8.58-59)

Ruskin, we see, takes quite literally the idea that painting and drawing serve as a means of stating visible fact. As I have explained elsewhere, Ruskin's conception of painting as language permits him to replace an older theory of imitation, traditionally central to views of art, with the theory that painting utilizes systems of visual relationships which figure forth the essentially inimitable tones, tints, and forms of nature.[13]

Even this most basic function of art bears great gifts

[13] See my "J. D. Harding and John Ruskin on Nature's Infinite Variety," *JAAC*, XXVII (1970), 369-380.

to man, if he will only accept them; for by recording the truths of sky, mountain, and sea, painting can bring an awareness of nature into the dark confines of an industrial age. Ruskin, who believes that much human strength and health of spirit comes from nature, tells his Victorian readers: "You have cut yourselves off voluntarily, presumptuously, insolently, from the whole teaching of your Maker in His universe"(16.289). But art can remind man what he has lost and, to a degree, restore it.

Although this elemental form of art can thus perform an important service for man, it remains, says Ruskin, the kind of painting and drawing to which beginners and those without imagination must devote themselves. The great artist, however, does not merely record the facts of appearance. Rather, he treats his subject differently, "giving not the actual facts of it, but the impression it made on his mind. . . . The aim of the great inventive landscape painter must be to give the far higher and deeper truth of mental vision, rather than that of the physical facts, and to reach a representation which . . . shall yet be capable of producing on the far-away beholder's mind precisely the impression which the reality would have produced, and putting his heart into the same state in which it would have been" (6.32,35-36) had he been at the scene. According to Ruskin, then, the greatest painting, like the greatest verse—both of which deserve the title "poetry" —reproduce the artist's impression of fact rather than the fact itself. In other words, art concerns itself with man and his human, phenomenological relations to his world:

Science deals exclusively with things as they are in

themselves; and art exclusively with things as they affect the human sense and human soul. Her work is to portray the appearances of things, and to deepen the natural impressions which they produce upon living creatures. The work of science is to substitute facts for appearances, and demonstrations for impressions. Both, observe, are equally concerned with truth; the one with truth of aspect, the other with truth of essence. Art does not represent things falsely, but truly as they appear to mankind. Science studies the relations of things to each other: but art studies only their relations to man: and it requires of everything . . . only this,—what that thing is to the human eyes and human heart, what it has to say to men, and what it can become to them. (11.47-48)

This passage from the concluding volume of *The Stones of Venice* echoes Wordsworth's statement that "The appropriate business of poetry, (which, nevertheless, if genuine, is as permanent as pure science,) her appropriate employment, her privilege and her *duty*, is to treat of things not as they *are*, but as they *appear*; not as they exist in themselves, but as they *seem* to exist to the *senses*, and to the *passions*."[14] Here we have but one example of the way Ruskin transfers to the visual arts romantic descriptions of the nature and function of poetry.

He similarly adopts much of the Wordsworthian description of the poet. Ruskin's artist, like Wordsworth's poet, "thinks and feels in the spirit of human passions," and "is chiefly distinguished from other men by a greater promptness to think and feel without immediate external excitement, and a greater power in

14 *Works*, II, 410.

expressing such thoughts and feelings as are produced in him in that manner."[15] The painter's greater sympathies, sensibility, and imagination, according to Ruskin, make art particularly valuable to us; for the great artist, the man who sees farther and more deeply, makes the spectator "a sharer in his own strong feelings and quick thoughts . . . and leaves him more than delighted,—ennobled and instructed, under the sense . . . of having held communion with a new mind, and having been endowed for a time with the keen perception and the impetuous emotions of a nobler and more penetrating intelligence"(3.134). Art, which deals in the truths of *experience*, adds to the wealth of human knowledge by permitting us to see and feel with the faculties of another greater than ourselves. For this reason, truly imaginative paintings have an "infinite advantage"(5.186) over our actual presence at the scene they depict since they provide a "penetrative sight" and "kindly guidance"(5.187) that, like an imaginative lens, increases our powers of beholding nature and man. In other words, the great artist allows us to stand on the shoulders of a giant.

Imaginative art, as Ruskin explains in the second volume of *Modern Painters*, serves the cause of religion and morality in an even more direct way. According to him, the imagination's "first and noblest use is, to enable us to bring sensibly to our sight the things which are recorded as belonging to our future state, or as invisibly surrounding us in this"(5.72). Therefore, the imagination and the art which embodies it enable the worshipper to envisage the truths of religion and morality, thereby stimulating him to follow the precepts of the Bible. At the time Ruskin wrote the second

[15] *Ibid.*, pp. 398, 397.

volume of *Modern Painters* he would have been most concerned with the imagination's ability not only to vivify scriptural history but also to figure forth the joys of salvation and the torments of damnation.

In addition, the imagination—that faculty which is "an eminent beholder of things *when* and *where* they are NOT"(5.181)—also aids man when it creates art that records secular history and legend. Turner's *Apollo and Python* (see Plate 7), his *Bay of Baiae,* and his series of paintings on Carthage permit us to see and feel the past just as his steamship in a snowstorm (see Plate 1) gives us the experience of a raging sea. In contrast to that imaginative art and poetry which convey a heightened experience of the world, there is another form, the symbolical, which embodies abstract truths in type, allegory, and symbol. Both forms of imaginative art, according to Ruskin, are equally great, and the "abstract and symbolical suggestion will always appeal to one order of minds, the dramatic completeness to another"(24.101). Whereas the imaginative painting of experience enables the spectator to see the exterior world in new ways, the imaginative art which employs allegory and symbolism communicates abstract truth more effectively than any other manner.

The wonderful capacity of the visual arts to communicate fact, feeling, and belief enables them to have a profound influence on the lives of men. Ruskin, who continually insists that art must appeal to the whole man, believes that taste, in its largest sense, is a moral quality; as he tells us in "Traffic," "What we *like* determines what we *are,* and is the sign of what we are; and to teach taste is inevitably to form character" (18.436). Ruskin, in other words, says of art what Plato says of philosophy: that it leads us toward the Good.

66

"And all delight in fine art, and all love of it, resolve themselves into simple love of that which deserves love. That deserving is the quality which we call 'loveliness' . . . and it is not an indifferent nor optional thing whether we love this or that; but it is just the vital function of all our being"(18.436). The fact that art and morality act and react upon one another is the reason Ruskin feels it a matter of urgency whether one delights in a Teniers tavern brawl or a Turner landscape.

Despite his fervent belief that art can aid morality, Ruskin rejects usual notions of didactic painting and poetry. Thus, when writing in *The Queen of the Air* about the "ethical conception of the Homeric poems," he pauses, correcting himself, and mentions instead "their ethical nature; for they are not conceived didactically, but are didactic in their essence, as all good art is"(19.307). Hence although he attached "to the artist the responsibility of a preacher"(3.48), he forbids him to preach. Denying that the artist achieves moral ends by direct instruction, he writes of the *Iliad* that "all pieces of such art are didactic in the purest way, indirectly and occultly, so that, first, you shall only be bettered by them if you are already hard at work in bettering yourself; and when you *are* bettered by them it shall be partly with a general acceptance of their influence, so constant and subtle that you shall be no more conscious of it than of the healthy digestion of food; and partly by a gift of unexpected truth, which you shall only find by slow mining for it"(19.308). According to this view of "didacticism," art must work indirectly, gradually adding to the knowledge of its audience. In addition, art can improve man "indirectly and occultly" by developing his moral sense: Ruskin's moral theories rely on the notion of an imaginative sympathy which projects us into the emotional position of another human being, thus enabling us to experience how it feels to be acted upon; this experience then produces moral action. Anything which contributes to such experience, or to the sympathetic imagination that produces it, also contributes to the betterment of our moral nature. Since painting, like poetry, exercises this essential faculty, sharpening and perfecting our moral perceptions, it is of great potential moral value. In *The Queen of the Air* Ruskin explains another way that art functions didactically: "As all lovely art is rooted in virtue, so it bears fruit of virtue, and is didactic in its own nature. It is often didactic also in actually expressed thought, as Giotto's, Michael Angelo's, Dürer's, and hundreds more; but that is not its special function, —*it is didactic chiefly by being beautiful*; but beautiful with haunting thought, no less than with form"(19.394; italics mine). Art can be didactic by being beautiful in two ways. First, perception of certain modes of beauty exercises moral sympathy; and, second, since according to Ruskin, the beautiful is a symbol of God, its perception becomes an essentially religious act which "indirectly and occultly" informs the beholder of the nature of God. Ruskin's deep faith in the value of art appears nowhere more strikingly than in his affirmation that painting and poetry are most useful and teach most by conveying images of beauty. In the second volume of *Modern Painters*, which sets forth his aesthetic theories, he argues that "men in the present century understand the word Useful in a strange way . . . as if houses and lands, and food and raiment were alone useful, and as if Sight, Thought, and Admiration were all profitless, so that men insolently call themselves Utilitarians, who would turn, if they had their way, themselves and their race into vegetables"(4.28,29). Ruskin, in contrast, finds that useful which makes man more alive, and for this reason he believes that art is truly useful and truly necessary.

## III. Ruskin's conception of painting and poetry as expressive arts

BEFORE we examine the effects of this alliance of painting and poetry upon Ruskin's philosophy of beauty and theories of meaning in art, it will be necessary to analyze further the nature of the romantic, or expressive, poetry which he wished to league with painting. In characterizing romantic critical theory by its emphasis upon expression, I am following M. H. Abrams, whose useful descriptions of romantic criticism will illuminate important aspects of Ruskin's ideas on art. In *The Mirror and the Lamp* he writes:

> Almost all the major critics of the English romantic generation phrased definitions or key statements showing a parallel alignment from work to poet. Poetry is the overflow, utterance, or projection of the thought and feelings of the poet; or else (in the chief variant formulation) poetry is defined in terms of the imaginative process which modifies and synthesizes the images, thoughts, and feelings of the poet. . . . A work of art is essentially the internal made external, resulting from a creative process operating under the impulse of feeling, and embodying the combined product of the poet's perceptions, thoughts, and feelings.[16]

[16] M. H. Abrams, *The Mirror and the Lamp: Romantic Theory and the Critical Tradition* (New York, 1953), pp. 21-22.

Studies of seventeenth- and eighteenth-century English aesthetic theory have done much to explain the development of the critical attitudes described by Abrams.[17] In particular, the genetic relation of theories of the sublime to romantic criticism is important to a study of Ruskin, not only because he discusses the sublime himself but because ideas derived from the sublime otherwise influence his views of art. For example, the origin of certain aspects of romantic critical theory in notions of the sublime accounts for the criteria which romantic criticism, including that of Ruskin, applies to art. The notion of reaction is at the center of theories of the sublime: the spectator, upon encountering sublimity in art or nature, reacts emotionally in much the same unconscious, natural manner as does a seed with its environment. This idea of reaction is also important to expressive theories of art, for, as we shall demonstrate from

[17] Ernest Lee Tuveson's recent *The Imagination as a Means of Grace: Locke and the Aesthetics of Romanticism* (Berkeley and Los Angeles, 1960), p. 2, proposes that Locke's new model of the mind transferred "the 'locus of reality' [from the exterior world] to the perceiving mind," bringing with it this acceptance of subjectivity new theories of knowledge and new attitudes toward relations of the mind to the exterior world. By focusing attention on formation of ideas within the mind, Locke's *Essay Concerning Human Understanding* promoted interest in psychological processes and occasioned the development of theories of the imagination and the moral sense. Whereas Tuveson is primarily concerned with the role of psychologies and theories of imagination which lead to romanticism, Marjorie Hope Nicolson treats the change in preromantic attitudes toward external nature. Her *Mountain Gloom and Mountain Glory: The Development of the Aesthetics of the Infinite* (New York, 1963) demonstrates how the theological controversy surrounding Thomas Burnet's *Sacred Theory of the Earth* (1684) created modern awareness of external nature and led to a taste for the great and overpowering. We may observe the development of this taste for the massive and overpowering into theories of the sublime in Samuel Holt Monk's pioneering study on the subject, *The Sublime: A Study of Critical Theories in XVIII-Century England* (Ann Arbor, Mich., 1960), in which he describes how seventeenth- and eighteenth-century aestheticians used Longinus's *Peri Hupsous* as a framework within which to consider the role of emotion in art.

Ruskin's statements, the criteria of poetry and painting in expressive theory are those which insure that the aesthetic reaction takes place and that it is portrayed accurately.

First and before all, the work of art and the man who creates it must be sincere: without sincerity we can neither trust the artist's reaction nor his presentation of it. In a late work, *The Laws of Fésole* (1878-1879), Ruskin wrote that "The greatest art represents everything with absolute sincerity, as far as it is able"(15.359) and in the final volume of *Modern Painters* we are informed that the lesson to be learned from the life of Turner, England's greatest artist, "is broadly this, that all the power of it came of its mercy and sincerity" (7.442).

A second criterion which owes much to the eighteenth-century roots of romanticism is intensity. Theories of sublimity, which were frequently concerned with violent emotional reactions, made the intensity of an aesthetic experience a matter of concern; and intensity became even more important with the growth, in the eighteenth century, of epistemologies that conceived that emotion and imagination—not conscious intellect—grasp all that is important to man and art. As Ruskin explains, since we perceive by means of the imagination's emotional processes, the more intense our emotion, the deeper will be the imagination's glance, the surer its grasp of truth: "Wholly in proportion to the intensity of feeling which you bring to the subject you have chosen, will be the depth and justice of your perception of its character"(16.370). Elsewhere, Ruskin explains this relationship between intensity of feeling and perception in more detail: "There is reciprocal action between the intensity of moral feeling and the power of imagination; for, on the one hand, those who have keenest sympathy are those who look closest and pierce deepest, and hold securest; and on the other, those who have so pierced and seen the melancholy deeps of things are filled with the most intense passion and gentleness of sympathy"(4.257). In other words, the imagination's distinguishing quality and strength is that it *sees with intensity*: "The virtue of the Imagination is its reaching, by intuition and intensity of gaze (not by reasoning, but by its authoritative opening and revealing power), a more essential truth than is seen at the surface of things"(4.284). Therefore, since intensity is so closely related to the means of perceiving what is true, intensity becomes a criterion of both artistic perception and aesthetic experience.

Thirdly, the work of art should in some way be original. Originality is an appropriate criterion for a theory of art which centers on individual reactions; for if the artist and poet differ from other men because they have the ability to react with greater sensitivity to nature, then art which expresses these valued reactions will be praised because it appears unique, or even strange to the audience. Ruskin believed that true originality came not from mere novelty but from better apprehension of truth: "That virtue of originality that men so strain after is not *newness*, as they vainly think (there is nothing new), it is only *genuineness*" (4.253). But as Ruskin tells us in *"A Joy For Ever"* (1857), the very freshness of the artist's vision creates difficulties; for "Precisely in the degree in which any painter possesses original genius, is at present the increase of moral certainty that during his early years he will have a hard battle to fight"(16.31). Since the poet and painter present truth in new and strikingly original ways, great art will rarely meet or adapt itself very much to the expectations of an audience; for, indeed, art's very purpose is to increase the audience's range of knowledge and expectations. The audience must thus be sympathetic to originality:

> The highest art, being based on sensations of peculiar minds, sensations occurring to *them* only at particular times, and to a plurality of mankind perhaps never, and being expressive of thoughts which could only rise out of a mass of the most extended knowledge, and of dispositions modified . . . by peculiarity of intellect, can only be met and understood by persons having some sort of sympathy with the high and solitary minds which produced it. (3.135-136)

But audiences do not tend to be sympathetic, and therefore isolation and alienation are the natural conditions in which the great artist must create. So it was, we are told, with Turner:

> Now the condition of mind in which Turner did all his great work was simply this: "What I do must be done rightly; but I know also that no man now living in Europe cares to understand it; and the better I do it, the less he will see the meaning of it." There never was yet, so far as I can hear or read, isolation of a great spirit so utterly desolate. . . . So far as in it lay, this century has caused every one of its great men, whose hearts were kindest, and whose spirits most perceptive of the work of God, to die without hope: —Scott, Keats, Byron, Shelley, Turner. (7.452,455)

Since the artist is thus isolated by the very quality which makes his work valuable to his audience, it will be necessary for the artist's work to be interpreted to, and often defended from, the mass of men for whom he creates. Such was the case with Turner, and such was the reason that *Modern Painters* was begun in 1843.

### IV. Conditions of the alliance

ALTHOUGH there was adequate occasion for Ruskin to defend painting by allying it with poetry, the alliance was not easy to effect because changes in critical theory had destroyed some of the old points of comparison. As long as critics considered poetry a mimetic art, its natural analogue was painting; but once it became an art whose central operation and purpose were expressive, poetry's natural analogue became music.[18] Changes in theories of the imagination also tended to dissolve the alliance of the arts: eighteenth-century theories of the imagination which considered it an image-making faculty had supported the parallel of painting and poetry, but the growth of notions of the sympathetic imagination in the late eighteenth century did not serve the same function. The gradual shift from the imagination as maker of images to the imagination as creator of emotional states or sympathies tended to divide the two allied arts.

[18] Ruskin, who states that "Music rightly so called is the expression of the joy or grief of noble minds for noble causes"(19.175), also makes it one of the sister arts. His discussions, however, rarely concern themselves chiefly with music, and his frequent mentions of the art serve in most cases to draw simple analogies between music and her sisters or to emphasize the irrational, hidden nature of imaginative creation. Ruskin, who believes color the embodiment of feeling, writes of "playing on a colour-violin . . . and inventing your tune as you play it" (15.416). He also mentions that "the painter's faculty, or masterhood over colour" is "as subtle as the musician's over sound"(20.203), and that "no musical philosophy will ever teach a girl to sing, or a master to compose; and no colour-philosophy will ever teach a man of science to enjoy a picture, or a dull painter to invent one"(15.433).

Thomas Hobbes and John Locke were the chief
sources of the belief, so widely encountered in eighteenth-century critics, that the mind deals with visual
images. There was in reality nothing new about Locke's
idea that "sight [is] the most comprehensive of all our
senses, conveying to our minds the ideas of light and
colours, which are peculiar only to that sense; and also
the far different ideas of space, figure, and motion."[19]
That the eye was the most important link between the
mind and the external world had been a commonplace
long before Palamon cried to Arcite, "I was hurt right
now thurghout myn ye into myn herte" by sight of
Emelye. The novelty is in Locke's theory that there are
no ideas innate to the mind; for if the mind is at origin
a *tabula rasa*, all knowledge must enter from without.
Since the sight provides most of the impressions that
enter the mind, it thereby becomes the most important
of all faculties. In addition to the emphasis on sight created by this predominantly visual epistemology, a further emphasis was made by the Hobbes-Lockean
psychology which regarded ideas as visual images, or,
in the words of Hobbes, as *"decaying sense."*[20] Ernest
Lee Tuveson has suggested that one major influence of
Locke on English poetry was a new emphasis on visual
qualities.[21] Addison, an important popularizer of
Locke, stressed the importance of the visual faculties
in his first *Spectator* on "The Pleasures of the
Imagination"(1712):

> Our sight is the most perfect and most delightful of
> all our senses. It fills the mind with the largest va-

19 *An Essay Concerning Human Understanding*, ed. Alexander Campbell Fraser (New York, 1959), I, 188.
20 "Of Imagination," *Leviathan* (New York and London, 1950), p. 10.
21 Tuveson, *The Imagination as a Means of Grace*, pp. 72-73.

riety of ideas, converses with its objects at the greatest distance, and continues the longest in action without being tired or satiated with its proper enjoyments. . . . It is this sense which furnishes the imagination with its ideas; so that by the pleasures of the imagination or fancy (which I shall use promiscuously) I here mean such as arise from visible objects, either when we have them actually in our view or when we call up their ideas into our minds by paintings, statues, descriptions, or any the like occasion. We cannot indeed have a single image in the fancy that did not make its first entrance through the sight; but we have the power of retaining, altering, and compounding those images.[22]

John Baillies's *Essay on the Sublime* (1747) specifically uses this theory of the imagination for describing poetry: "What, indeed, is *Poetry* but the Art of throwing a Number of agreeable *Images* together, whence each of them yields a greater *Delight* than they could *separately*."[23] By the time that Dr. Johnson writes his "Life of Cowley" (1778), the idea that the poet should write in visual images has become such a critical commonplace that he censures Cowley and the metaphysicals for failing to write thus: "One of the great sources of poetical delight is description, or the power of presenting pictures to the mind. Cowley gives inferences instead of images, and shows not what may be supposed to have been seen, but what thoughts the sight might have suggested."[24] Both Dr. Johnson's conception of the imagination and his ideal of description depend

---

[22] *Eighteenth-Century Critical Essays*, I, 42.

[23] *An Essay on the Sublime* (London, 1747), Augustan Reprint Society (Los Angeles, 1953), p. 37.

[24] *Lives of the English Poets* (London and New York, 1925), I, 34.

upon theories that language conveys or summons up images within the mind.

In his work on the critical history of Thomson's *Seasons*, Ralph Cohen has detailed the shift from a picture-theory of language to a language and description concerned with effects on the mind.[25] The earlier picture-theory of language had begun to die out with the growth of theories of the sympathetic imagination. In 1751 James Harris's universal grammar, *Hermes*, had attacked the picture-theory of language, and the far more influential Edmund Burke's *On the Sublime* (1757) attempted to confute what the writer held to be the usual view of language:

> It is not only of those ideas which are commonly called abstract, and of which no image at all *can* be formed, but even of particular real beings, that we converse without having any idea of them excited in the imagination. . . . Indeed so little does poetry depend for its effect on the power of raising sensible images, that I am convinced it would lose a very considerable part of its energy, if this were the necessary result of all description.[26]

A few pages later Burke's notion of language is the basis of an opposition of painting and poetry:

> Poetry and rhetoric do not succeed in exact description so well as painting does; their business is to affect rather by sympathy than imitation; to display rather the effect of things on the mind of the speaker,

[25] *The Art of Discrimination: Thomson's "The Seasons" and the Language of Criticism* (London, 1964), pp. 131-187.

[26] *A Philosophical Enquiry into the Origin of our Ideas of the Sublime and Beautiful*, ed. J. T. Boulton (London, 1958), p. 170.

or of others, than to present a clear idea of the things themselves.[27]

Burke's attitude generally held sway in the next century. William Hazlitt, for example, who wrote extensively on both painting and poetry, felt that the two arts should be strongly contradistinguished: "When artists or connoisseurs talk on stilts about the poetry of painting, they show that they know little about poetry, and have little love for the art. Painting gives the object itself; poetry what it implies."[28] Hazlitt's other writings confirm what this passage suggests—that while Hazlitt accepted a conservative imitative theory of painting, he believed that poetry was, as he put it, "only the highest eloquence of passion."[29]

Ruskin, on the other hand, holds that both painting and poetry are expressive arts, but he supports his romantic version of *ut pictura poesis* with some conservative ideas. Most important of these is that like Locke, Addison, and Johnson, whose writings he knew very well, Ruskin believes in a visual imagination. Although Ruskin's ideas of the imagination were heavily influenced by the writings of British moral philosophers, such as Dugald Stewart and Sydney Smith, who described the imagination as working with sympathies and emotional states, Ruskin believes that the imagination works with images. In *The Two Paths* (1859) Ruskin describes the visual nature of the imagination: "We all have a general and sufficient idea of imagination, and of its work with our hands and in our hearts: we understand it, I suppose, as the imaging or

[27] *Ibid.*, p. 172.
[28] "On Poetry in General," *The Complete Works*, ed. P. P. Howe (London and Toronto, 1934), v, 7.
[29] *Ibid.*, p. 10.

picturing of new things in our thoughts"(16.347). In an 1883 note to the second volume of *Modern Painters,* which contains his longer discussions of the various aspects of imagination, he stated: "I meant, and always do mean by it, primarily, the power of seeing anything we describe as if it were real"(4.226n). While his knowledge of Locke and eighteenth-century writers supported his belief in a visual imagination, this belief was largely derived, one feels, from what Ruskin himself described in *Praeterita* as a "sensual faculty of pleasure in sight, as far as I know unparalleled"(35.619). This autobiographical remark is the proper note to strike in a discussion of Ruskin's relation to earlier and to contemporary critical writings. It is a highly personal factor that enables and encourages him simultaneously to draw both from neoclassical theories of painting and from romantic theories of poetry in order to formulate his own view of the allied arts.

### V. Implications of the alliance

RUSKIN'S renovations of older theories of *ut pictura poesis* are important not only because they indicate both his characteristically eclectic formulation of ideas and his major debt to the eighteenth century, but also because they reveal that romantic poetic theory served as his model for the other arts. We have thus far observed that he applied to painting ideas of poetry derived from Wordsworth and others. These same ideas he also applies to architecture and sculpture. Ruskin, who at the age of sixteen had published a series of articles in *The Architectural Magazine* entitled "The Poetry of Architecture"(1837-1838), believed that the art of building is in part a language like speaking and

writing. In *The Stones of Venice* he explained that this
art has two functions "acting and talking:—acting, as
to defend us from weather or violence; talking, as the
duty of monuments or tombs, to record facts and express feelings; or of churches, temples, public edifices,
treated as books of history, to tell such history clearly
and forcibly"(9.60). Significantly, Ruskin's most em-
phatic assertion that expression is the central principle
of the arts occurs in this same work on architecture.
*The Stones of Venice* continually emphasizes "the great
principle . . . that art is valuable or otherwise, only as
it expresses the personality, activity, and living perception of a good and great human soul. . . . It is the expression of one soul talking to another, and is precious
according to the greatness of the soul that utters it. And
consider what mighty consequences follow from our acceptance of this truth! what a key we have herein given
us for the interpretation of the art of all time!"(11.201,
220) The consequences which follow from Ruskin's acceptance of this idea are many and include some of his
most characteristic views on the art of building.

First of all, architecture, the art which shelters man,
expresses his needs and his entire nature. As Ruskin
explains when he compares architecture to painting,
poetry, and sculpture, "A picture or poem is often little
more than a feeble utterance of man's admiration of
something out of himself; but architecture approaches
more to a creation of his own, born of his necessities,
and expressive of his nature. It is also, in some sort, the
work of the whole race, while the picture or statue is
the work of one only"(10.213). Architecture, then, is in
some sense a group enterprise, and while it expresses
the nature of the architect, it also expresses both the
nature of the men for whom he builds and that of the

80

workers whose skill carries out his intentions. St. Mark's, for example, expresses the piety of architects and patrons and the free vitality of the men who carved its capitals and erected its walls.

Ruskin, who came to criticism of society through the study of architecture, increasingly concerned himself with the role of the individual worker. As early as *The Seven Lamps of Architecture* (1848) he wrote that "the right question to ask, respecting all [architectural] ornament, is simply this: Was it done with enjoyment— was the carver happy while he was about it?"(8.218) Great architecture, then, embodies the happiness, the fulfillment, the human activity of the workman. According to *The Stones of Venice*, "All art is great, and good, and true, only so far as it is distinctively the work of *manhood* in its entire and highest sense; that is to say, not the work of limbs and fingers, but of the soul, aided, according to her necessities, by the inferior powers"(11.201). Ruskin, in other words, wishes to solve the problems of Victorian England and Victorian architecture by making the workman an artist. In fact, one might argue that he became increasingly aware of the dilemmas of the modern age once he realized that the average worker, unlike the painter, had no means to express himself, develop his capacities as a man, or engage in truly useful labor. By the time he wrote *Fors Clavigera* he had closely associated the role of artist and worker, and according to the eleventh letter to the workingmen of England, "a true artist is only a beautiful development of tailor or carpenter. As the peasant provides the dinner, so the artist provides the clothes and house"(27.186). A romantic theory of art, as we have seen, concentrates on the nature and function of the artist. Ruskin begins with such a romantic theory of the arts, applies its criteria to architecture, and recognizing the plight of the worker whom he considers potentially an artist, moves away from the problems of art to the problems of society.

Thus holding a romantic conception of architecture, he judges this art by the same criteria he applies to romantic poetry and painting. A building, for example, should be sincere. As he comments in *The Seven Lamps of Architecture*, "We may not be able to command good, or beautiful, or inventive, architecture; but we *can* command an honest architecture: the meagreness of poverty may be pardoned, the sternness of utility respected; but what is there but scorn for the meanness of deception?"(8.60) According to Ruskin, therefore, a building must in general express its structure, materials, and degree of handwork. Speaking of structural deceits, he notes that although the architect is not bound to reveal structure, "nevertheless, that building will generally be the noblest, which to an intelligent eye discovers the great secrets of its structure, as an animal form does, although from a careless observer they may be concealed"(8.61). One should note Ruskin's emphasis here on the "intelligent eye," for he explains that convention may transform something potentially insincere, such as gilding, to a commonplace which all understand. Similarly, "in the vaulting of a Gothic roof it is no deceit to throw the strength into the ribs of it, and make the intermediate vault a mere shell. Such a structure would be presumed by an intelligent observer, the first time he saw such a roof; and the beauty of its traceries would be enhanced to him if they confessed and followed the lines of its main strength. If, however, the intermediate shell were made of wood instead of stone, and whitewashed to look like the rest,—this

would, of course, be direct deceit, and altogether unpardonable"(8.61). The need for honesty in building
similarly forbids the "use of cast or machine-made
ornaments of any kind"(8.60), since decoration, the
proper task of the worker, cannot be tacked on at so
much a yard. Sincerity in relation to structure expresses the nature of architect and patron, whereas sincerity in relation to handmade ornament expresses the
worker as well: if a man chooses things he truly loves
and carves them on capitals and moldings, the building
thus decorated will bear an impress of the carver's
vitality, interest, and sincerity. If, however, the worker
—whether through choice or command—carves subjects which bore him, such as rows upon rows of gar-
lands, hunting horns, or cherubim, then the work will
be as insincere as it is lifeless. At this point one should
observe that Ruskin closely joins architecture and
sculpture, considering sculpture chiefly as an adjunct
to building and architecture chiefly the art of decorat-
ing structure with carving. Much of his criticism of the
art of building, therefore, usually concerns the nature
of ornament, and it is to this subject that his romantic
criteria most fittingly apply. For example, although he
made influential pronouncements about sincerity in
structure, the chief use of this criterion occurs in his
discussion of capitals, moldings, and other embellishments. Similarly, when Ruskin desires originality in
building, he wants not the originality of new, fanciful
styles but merely the originality that comes from individual work in carving: "Exactly so far as architecture works on known rules, and from given models, it
is not an art, but a manufacture; and it is, of the two
procedures, rather less rational . . . to copy capitals or
mouldings from Phidias, and call ourselves architects,

than to copy heads and hands from Titian, and call ourselves painters"(10.207). Imaginativeness, another romantic criterion, enters both the design of the entire
structure and the creation of ornament, whereas sympathy, which Ruskin closely associates with imagination, primarily concerns decoration. He explains in
"The Nature of Gothic" that the great variety of Gothic
carving, the profuseness with which the builders lavished natural forms on St. Mark's and the Ducal
Palace, expresses a sympathy, an imaginative grasp, of
man's "Desire of Change"(10.214). Whereas, according
to Ruskin, Renaissance style demands an all too educated eye, the Gothic modes of building frankly confess man's instability and consequent love of variety,
and hence provide something which all men can enjoy.
For him, a building, like a painting, poem, or statue,
must give delight: delight in its many forms is architecture's highest utility. This final criterion, which sums
all the others, arises, once again, in Ruskin's conception
of poetry.

Ruskin's habit of impressing the nature of verbal
upon visual art occurs again in his theories of interpretation. He not only believes that the arts function as
language to communicate fact, but also that painting
and architecture should be read, like poetry, for complex symbolical meanings. This belief naturally serves
to join the arts even more firmly in one happy family
among whose members poetry acts as an acknowledged
elder sister. *The Stones of Venice*, which mentions
"reading a building as we would read Milton or Dante"
(10.206), explains that St. Mark's "is to be regarded less
as a temple wherein to pray, than as itself a Book of
Common Prayer, a vast illuminated missal, bound with
alabaster instead of parchment, studded with porphyry

pillars instead of jewels, and written within and without in letters of enamel and gold"(10.112).[30] For a building to serve such a verbal function its users must have prior knowledge of the literature which defines its images. "A building which recorded the Bible history by means of a series of sculptural pictures, would be perfectly useless to a person unacquainted with the Bible beforehand"(9.61). From this recognition follows the principle, central to Ruskin's brilliant readings of art, that one can neither interpret nor criticize the intended symbolism of a work "until we can fully place ourselves in the position of those to whom . . . [it] was originally addressed, and until we are certain that we understand every symbol, and are capable of being touched by every association which its builders employed as letters of their language"(9.61). Throughout his works Ruskin therefore endeavors to set visual art within its proper linguistic context, and this belief in the essential union of word and image produced, as we shall see, not only his fine readings of Turner and Giotto, but also his concern with allegory, iconography, and mythology.

Lastly, his theory of the sister arts is important because it led him to devise a philosophy of beauty appropriate to both painting and poetry. His alliance of the arts produced, paradoxically enough, a bifurcated

---

[30] Ruskin later adds: "I have above spoken of the whole church as a great Book of Common Prayer; the mosaics were its illuminations, and the common people of the time were taught their Scripture history by means of them, more impressively perhaps, though far less fully, than ours are now by Scripture reading. They had no other Bible, and—Protestants do not often enough consider this—*could* have no other. We find it somewhat difficult to furnish our poor with printed Bibles; consider what the difficulty must have been when they could be given only in manuscript. The walls of the church necessarily became the poor man's Bible, and a picture was more easily read upon the walls than a chapter" (10.129-130).

aesthetic, of which one half—which he called "Typical Beauty"—was concerned primarily with visual beauty, while the other—which he called "Vital Beauty"—was concerned with emotional states and their expression. It has often been commented that aestheticians tend to found their conceptions of the beautiful upon the arts with which they are most familiar. Ruskin's concern with painting (and his belief in a visual imagination) led him to formulate his theory of Typical Beauty, which draws its details, if not its ultimate explanations, from conceptions of the beautiful that emphasize qualities most suitable for painting, that is, the visual, the external, the element of form. Vital Beauty, on the other hand, draws heavily on romantic theories of poetry, and on notions of moral emotion and sympathy which are associated with romantic philosophies of art. Vital Beauty, which is the beauty of living things, depends on the internal made external, on expression.

# CHAPTER TWO

# Ruskin's Theories
# of Beauty

That Beauty is not, as fond men misdeem,
An outward show of things, that only seem;
But that fair lamp, from whose celestial ray
That light proceeds which kindleth lover's fire,
Shall never be extinguished nor decay;
But, when the vital spirits do expire,
Unto her native planet shall retire,
For it is heavenly born and cannot die,
Being a parcel of the purest sky.

—Edmund Spenser, quoted by Ruskin (4.207)

## I. Ruskin's refutation of "False Opinions held concerning Beauty"

JOHN RUSKIN'S aesthetic theories are a type of his entire thought and writings, and they deserve careful attention not only because they play an essential role in *Modern Painters*, but also because their relation to sources, their formulation, and their evolution are characteristic of much that is important in his works. The same concerns, attitudes, and procedures which mark his aesthetics also characterize aspects of his work as different as his pronouncements on poetry and politics. The presentation of these theories of beauty is, for example, characteristically polemical. In aesthetics, as in politics, Ruskin rarely advances a point without casting down a gauntlet—though it occasionally be to a straw knight on a straw horse. The theories of Typical and Vital Beauty are proposed with the same urgency, the same contentiousness, and the same sense of speaking the only truth with which Ruskin usually presents his own ideas. This polemical tone is appropriate, for, as we have noted earlier, Ruskin originally formulated these theories of beauty in order to defend Turner. The first volume of *Modern Painters* attempts to prove that Turner was the most truthful painter of landscapes, and the role of the second is in part to present an aesthetic theory in relation to which Turner's paintings could appear as not only the most truthful but the most beautiful creations of English art. But Ruskin's aesthetics are polemical for other reasons than the aggressive tone with which they are presented, for his theories of beauty are advanced and even formed in conscious opposition to ideas which Ruskin wanted to confute. He developed his conception of theoria, for example, almost entirely to oppose another view of beauty—in this case the notion that the study of beauty is the study of perception alone and is hence divorced from the study of morality and religion. A pure aestheticism, or a theory of beauty divorced from morality, would not do for Ruskin since he was trying to demonstrate that the perception of beauty (especially the beauties of Turner) has an important relationship to man's moral and religious nature. It is thus fitting that in setting forth his aesthetic doctrine, Ruskin frequently sounds as though he were preaching from the pulpit or seeking converts among the heathen. His earnest, urgent, sermonizing tone is appropriate to his theories of beauty which had grown from the body of his religious beliefs. Ruskin's early Evangelicalism affected his aesthetics as his later humanism influenced his political-economics; and as his political and economic theories were formed by his loss of religious belief, so his conceptions of beauty were informed by an early piety which is evident throughout the second volume of *Modern Painters.*

Furthermore, a study of Ruskin's aesthetics is necessary to an understanding of his non-aesthetic writings, because these propositions about the beautiful attempt, but finally fail, to solve problems that recur throughout his works. If, for example, one can perceive the reasons for his ultimate inability to demonstrate that beauty is the embodiment and representation of immutable order, one can explain more clearly such major changes in *Modern Painters* as the movement from the problems of art to the problems of society. An examination of Ruskin's aesthetic writings reveals that when he first proposed his theories of beauty he wished most of all to emphasize the importance of the beautiful; and he was able to make this emphasis because he believed that beauty was a reflection of God's nature in visible things. Since the beautiful was a *speculum dei* it could not, therefore, vary; nor could it depend upon subjective factors such as personal associations. Once Ruskin began to question his religious faith, his attention shifted from the relation of man to God to the relations of man to man. At about the same time that he became interested in the problems of society, Ruskin began to allow that there were human, not divine, sources of beauty. But when he thus granted that personal and historical associations could create beauty, his attempt at an aesthetic system failed. At a first glance it might seem that since his aesthetic theories were one of his early, and rare, endeavors to be systematic they therefore cannot be taken as characteristic of his work; but in fact his failure to create a coherent system, and his subsequent inconsistencies, were caused by developments in his theories of beauty which paralleled his later loss of religion and his then growing interest in social reform.

The best introduction to what we may call the dilemma of Ruskin's aesthetic theories is that section in the second volume of *Modern Painters* where, before advancing his own views, he pauses in imitation of Edmund Burke to attack ideas concerning the nature of beauty which he thought mistaken. "Those erring or inconsistent positions" which he dismisses are: "the first, that the Beautiful is the True; the second, that the Beautiful is the Useful; the third, that it is dependent on Custom; and the fourth, that it is dependent on the Association of Ideas"(4.66). When Ruskin mentions the

first "erring" position, he may have had Keats in mind.[1]
He quickly refutes this proposition by pointing out that
to make such an equation between truth and beauty is
to confuse a quality of statements with a quality of matter. Unlike the three other views he opposes, and
despite his remarks to the contrary, this notion, that
truth is beauty and beauty truth, was not an important
position.

In contrast with this, the other positions which he
wanted to refute were widely held throughout the last
half of the eighteenth and the first half of the nineteenth centuries; and Ruskin's attack on them reveals
important points about his own notions of beauty. Most
important, his opposition indicates how conservative
were his aesthetics. Any study of Ruskin's theories of
beauty as they relate to his theories of art must begin
with the realization that although he proposed a romantic, emotionalist theory of painting and poetry,
many of his most characteristic ideas and attitudes were
reactions against what he recognized as the limitations
of a subjectivist aesthetic. In fact Ruskin used his theories of beauty as one way of solving the problem of subjectivity in romantic art. A classical theory of beauty,
such as that which he elects, considers beauty as a quality which, residing in the object, embodies a principle
of order. The statement that beauty is order and takes
the form of proportion, symmetry, and a mixture of

[1] While Ruskin provides no evidence that he was familiar with the
writings of Anthony Cooper, Lord Shaftesbury, it is possible that he
may have been referring to Shaftesbury's statement: "The most natural
beauty in the world is honesty and moral truth. For all beauty is truth.
True features make the beauty of a face; and true proportions the
beauty of architecture" (*Characteristics of Men, Manners, Opinions,*
ed. John M. Robertson, 2 vols. [1963], I, 94). By "true" Shaftesbury
evidently meant "correct" and were his statement the object of Ruskin's
criticism, that criticism would be valid and to the point.

unity and variety is frequently encountered in eighteenth-century writings on art, and it is from these notions of the beauty of order that Ruskin created his own theory of Typical Beauty. On the other hand, a romantic, or at least an internalized, aesthetic considers beauty as an emotion and discusses it not in terms of external qualities of the object but in terms of the psychological experiences of the beholder. The three eighteenth-century positions which Ruskin here opposes historically occupy a medial position in the development of British aesthetics. Thus although these theories are still concerned with qualities of the beautiful object, they do not consider beauty as the embodiment of some metaphysical order. The movement of speculative interest from metaphysics to psychology that is so characteristic of the eighteenth century affected aesthetics in much the same way that it changed views of language: in both cases the influence of Hobbes and Locke, particularly the influence of their new models for the mind, caused men to discuss the nature of both beauty and language in terms of psychological inquiry. In the case of writings about beauty the result was that, although writers still discussed the qualities of beauty, they were primarily concerned to investigate why these qualities were received as pleasing by the mind. Ruskin, who was well aware of the difficulties inherent in his theories, spoke of beauty as both quality and feeling; but in an attempt to demonstrate the objective, unvarying existence of the beautiful he suggested that everyone receives identical emotions from certain visual qualities much as everyone receives identical sensations of sweetness from sugar. Men react so, he said, because it is God's will and because all men have a divine element in their nature. In order to propose his theory of uniform emotional reactions, Ruskin must first deny the psychological explanations of earlier aestheticians, particularly since derivations of beauty from custom and association allow great variations in the beautiful. His attempt and failure to exclude all these subjectivist, variable elements of beauty indicate how conservative—and how tenuous—was his attempt to solve the problems of romanticism in art by appealing to a metaphysical order.

We see one threat to Ruskin's theory in the second position he attacked, namely that the beautiful is the useful or is largely dependent upon utility. David Hume, who emphasized the importance of utility in morals, stated the usual case for the relationship between beauty and utility in his early *Treatise on Human Nature* (1739). According to him, most works of art are adjudged beautiful "in proportion to their fitness for the use of man,"[2] and many of the beauties of nature are considered to be so because of a similar utility. Hume believed that beauty was a relative not an absolute quality, and that it "pleases us by nothing but its tendency to produce an end that is agreeable."[3] Walter J. Hipple, Jr., a recent commentator on his aesthetic theories, points out that by utility Hume means, not usefulness toward any end, but usefulness in the creation of human happiness. Thus, according to Hipple, an efficient device such as an engine of torture, though in one sense useful, would not be beautiful.[4] Despite Hipple's clarification of this aspect of the idea of utility, other confusions remain because Hume used

[2] Eds. T. H. Green and T. H. Grose (London, 1832), II, 36. Quoted by Walter J. Hipple, Jr., *The Beautiful, the Sublime, and the Picturesque in Eighteenth-Century British Aesthetic Theory* (Carbondale, Ill., 1957), p. 40.
[3] *Ibid.*, p. 40.      [4] *Ibid.*, p. 41.

the notion of happiness in several different ways. This
confusion appears most noticeably when he discusses
the beauty of animals. In the *Inquiry Concerning the
Principles of Morals* (1752), for example, he states that
"one considerable source of *beauty* in all animals is the
advantage which they reap from the particular structure of their limbs and members, suitably to the particular manner of life to which they are by nature
destined."[5] By this statement Hume apparently means
that the beauty of animals is derived from a fitness,
such as strength, which contributes to their own well-
being. In the next sentence, however, he states that certain "just proportions" are accepted as beautiful for a
horse since these are related to qualities of the animal
useful to man. Thus there seem to be two notions of
happiness and usefulness, one considered in relation to
the animal and one in relation to the owner of the animal. In other words, the attempt to derive beauty from
psychology here leads to a confusion of the psychology
of man and horse. Perhaps the most important point to
be drawn from his works about the notion of the beauty
of utility is that despite apparently simple, clear statements that the beautiful is the useful, this theory is never
presented without some modification such as that offered by Hume.

Adam Smith's *Theory of the Moral Sentiments*
(1759), which Ruskin read before he began *Modern
Painters*, presents another modification of the theory
of fitness. Smith states the basic notion that beauty is
derived from the useful but then adds that utility is
often more valued as a quality "than the very end for
which it was intended," and that therefore the appearance of utility is frequently more valued as an aesthetic

5 Ed. Charles W. Hendel (New York, 1957), p. 69.

95

quality than the "conveniency or pleasure" which it was supposed to provide.[6] Both streamlined steam-irons and Bauhaus furniture prove the justice of Smith's proposition that usefulness or its appearance (for, as with the steam-iron, utility may not in fact be present) can become an aesthetic quality.

Henri Fuseli, an early favorite with Ruskin, provides an example of a third, somewhat confused, form of the idea that utility is beauty. Fuseli, a Swiss-born member of the Royal Academy who painted nightmares and other wildly dramatic scenes, delivered a series of lectures at the Academy (1801-1825), which in the light of his own art are surprisingly neoclassical both in taste and in tenet. He several times suggests that beauty is closely related to utility; but since utility is always joined with other qualities in his statements, the exact relations are rather confusing. At one point Fuseli states that: "Beauty, whether individual or idea, consists in the concurrence of parts to one end, or the union of the simple or the various."[7] At another point he claims: "The beauty which we acknowledge is that harmonious whole of the human frame, that unison of parts to one end, which enchants us."[8] It is unclear whether the "one end" to which Fuseli refers is a function, a use to self, or whether it is the "end" of being a beautiful whole, a unity. Fuseli's combination of utility theory with the notion that beauty is harmony makes his formulation even more confusing. If he meant that each thing that lends itself to a harmonious whole is beautiful, then Ruskin would have agreed. If, however, Fuseli meant that parts of a whole are beautiful be-

[6] (Edinburgh, 1813), I, 406-408.
[7] *The Life and Writings*, ed. John Knowles, 3 vols. (London, 1811), III, 76.
[8] *Ibid.*, II, 22.

cause they perform a function, then Ruskin would have disagreed with him.

Ruskin dismisses the notion that the beautiful is the useful without discussion, and he is able to treat it so curtly because this idea had in his opinion already been convincingly refuted by Edmund Burke's *Philosophical Enquiry into the Origin of our Ideas of the Sublime and the Beautiful* (1757). From the frequency with which he refers to *On the Sublime,* and from the allusion to it in a footnote,[9] it seems clear that Ruskin expects the reader to be acquainted with this most influential English treatise on aesthetics. In the section "FITNESS not the cause of BEAUTY," Burke answers the proposition "that the idea of utility, or of a part's being well adapted to answer its end, is the cause of beauty" with an appeal to experience. He suggests that if utility were indeed the cause of beauty, then "on that principle, the wedge-like snout of a swine, with its tough cartilage at the end, the little sunk eyes, and the whole make of the head, so well adapted to its offices of digging, and rooting, would be extremely beautiful."[10] Burke has followed the procedure, usually more useful in satire than in philosophy, of accepting another's terms at their most literal and then applying them in this literal sense. Burke's wedge-snouted swine is, however, the perfect counterexample for Hume's well-proportioned horse; for the swine's physical makeup is as well suited to its own happiness as it is to the ultimate happiness of men, who will profit from its successful rooting in the mud. Whatever way Hume and others

[9] "He was the first English writer on art who used his common sense and reason on this subject [proportion]. The essay on the Sublime and the Beautiful is, like all his writing, extremely rational and forcible; and deserves most careful and reverent reading" (4.109n).

[10] Burke, *On the Sublime,* pp. 104-105.

intended the notion of utility to be taken, in these terms the swine would have been beautiful. And swine are not beautiful.

Ruskin may have been able to dismiss the theory that the beautiful is the useful so summarily because Burke had already refuted it, but he does so with such vehemence because this notion repelled him and was so opposed to his own basic conceptions of beauty and its role in man's life. According to Ruskin, to hold that beauty is derived from usefulness "is to confound admiration with hunger, love with lust, and life with sensation; it is to assert that the human creature has no ideas and no feelings except those ultimately referable to its brutal appetites"(4.67). First of all he rejects this theory because he believes that it neglects the needs of the spirit and mistakenly derives beauty from an inadequate, selfish (and hence necessarily subjective) psychology. Moreover, at this point in his career Ruskin was not only concerned to emphasize the needs of the human spirit, of which beauty is a most important one, but he was also opposed to Utilitarianism, with which he apparently connects this aesthetic theory. He desires to impress upon his reader that beauty is contemplated for its own sake, and that the pleasure derived from the contemplation of beauty is disinterested. The conception of disinterestedness, which is lacking in most eighteenth-century British aesthetic theories, is at the center of Ruskin's idea of beauty; and although many aspects of his aesthetics, and the attitudes upon which they were based, changed, his emphasis on the disinterestedness of aesthetic perception did not. In the preface which he added to the second volume of *Modern Painters* in 1883, he wrote of this volume that "its first great assertion is, that beautiful things are

useful to men because they are beautiful, and for the
sake of their beauty only"(4.4). Ruskin thus continued
to believe that his early assertion, that beauty was independent of utility, was one of the most important
ideas in *Modern Painters*.

Ruskin devotes little more space to refuting the third
view, that custom is the source of the beautiful or that
"the sense of the Beautiful arises from Familiarity with
the object"(4.67). That beauty depends upon custom
was a theory popular in the eighteenth century, as
might be expected in an age whose literature and moral
philosophy were so directed toward society. Ruskin,
who was widely read in standard works of the time,
had encountered this theory in many places, including
the works of Oliver Goldsmith and Sir Joshua Reynolds.[11] He several times refers to Goldsmith's Citizen
of the World, a Chinese gentleman who had at first
been shocked by the long feet and white teeth of English women but who, after becoming accustomed to
these features, found them attractive and sadly concluded that "there is no universal standard for beauty."[12]
In one of his essays in *The Idler* (1759) Reynolds similarly attaches great importance to the influence of
custom upon the beautiful. According to him, since we
are "more accustomed to beauty than deformity, we
may conclude that to be the reason why we approve
and admire it. . . . Though habit and custom cannot be
said to be the cause of beauty, it [*sic*] is certainly the
cause of our liking it."[13] Although he tries to avoid

11 "But the theory that beauty was merely a result of custom was
very common in Johnson's time. Goldsmith has, I think, expressed
it with more force and wit than any other writer, in various passages of
the *Citizen of the World*" (5.45). There is also an 1883 note, 4.67n.
12 *The Citizen of the World, The Works of Oliver Goldsmith*, ed.
J.W.M. Gibbs (London, 1885), III, 154.
13 *Eighteenth-Century Critical Essays*, II, 835.

some of the difficulties inherent in this position by proposing that custom does not create beauty but only makes us prefer beauty, his argument causes additional difficulties. For if custom creates our preference for what we believe to be beautiful, we can have no way of distinguishing between that which is truly beautiful and that which is merely thought to be beautiful because it is familiar. Reynolds also seems willing to admit that if men were more accustomed to ugliness than beauty, then ugliness would seem beautiful. This last conclusion probably did not trouble him, however, since in his opinion men are accustomed to beauty and not ugliness and therefore the theoretical confusion of the beautiful and the ugly is not in actuality possible. Adam Smith, who recognizes the implications of such a position, cannot grant that "custom is the sole principle of beauty"; yet he does believe that no form could or can please "if quite contrary to custom, and unlike what we have been used to in that species of things."[14] British moral philosophers of the eighteenth and nineteenth centuries, like Smith, derived the sense of beauty from the moral sense. But although they maintained that the moral sense was basically unchanging, as was necessary to the objective reality of morals, they allowed that beauty was changeable and that custom plays an important role in determining ideas of beauty.

Ruskin, however, who propounds that beauty has an objective, unchanging existence, cannot grant that something as ever-changing as custom can have much effect on beauty. Although he admits that custom has some small effect on the perception of the beautiful, he does not in any way allow that it makes us prefer beauty to ugliness; for he believes that such preference

[14] Smith, *Theory of the Moral Sentiments*, II, 15.

must be instinctive. Ruskin proposes that custom both deadens the "frequency and force of repeated impressions" and endears "the familiar object to the affections"(4.68). One possible difficulty or inconsistency in Ruskin's rejection of this position is that, while he says that custom can endear the familiar object, he holds that it cannot make that object seem beautiful. In other places he speaks of joy, admiration, and love as the emotions produced by the perception of beauty, and it is difficult to see where in his own terms there is a difference between the love created by familiarity and the love created by true beauty. The problem arises because he tries to connect the perception of the beautiful with the moral emotions, and he hence finds it difficult to distinguish between the two forms or varieties of love.

The notion that the perception of beauty is dependent upon custom is closely related to the theory that beauty is dependent upon association, the last of the four theories that Ruskin attacks. The Associationist theory of beauty is the most important of the positions which he opposes both because it was popular and because it presented the greatest threat to Ruskin's idea that beauty has an objective, unchanging existence. More than any other position he rejects, Associationism removes beauty from the heavens and places it within the changeable and limited territories of the human mind. Among the various British writers on aesthetics who made association important in their theories of beauty, Archibald Alison, against whom Ruskin directed his argument, held the most extreme position, for he proposed that association creates all natural and artificial beauty. Although it was common for eighteenth-century writers to explain the beauties of music and color by association,[15] Alison was the first to extend this notion to all areas of the beautiful. According to his *Essays on the Nature and Principles of Taste* (1790), "the Sublimity or Beauty of Forms arises altogether from the Associations we connect with them, or the Qualities of which they are expressive."[16] When Alison uses the term "expressive" he does not mean that forms express something, but that, by association, they come to represent beauty or grandeur.[17] Alison subsumes all the traditionally contributory aspects of beauty—utility, form, and harmony—under the theory of association. He derives the beauty of form, for example, from an association of pleasantness with qualities which are in turn associated with form. According to him, then, "The greater part of those bodies in Nature, which possess Hardness, Strength, or Durability, are distinguished by angular Forms," while those which possess "Weakness, Fragility or Delicacy" have winding or curvilinear shapes. Angularity thus comes to represent strength and curves delicacy.[18] These qualities, strength and delicacy, are in turn associated by their effects with the sublime and the beautiful. Alison even proposes that since proportion is generally traditional and related to custom, its effect is also achieved by as-

[15] James Boswell comments, for example, in *The Life of Samuel Johnson*, "Much of the effect of musick, I am satisfied, is owing to the association of ideas. That air, which instantly and irresistibly excites in the Swiss, when in a foreign land, the *maladie du pais* [*sic*], has, I am told, no intrinsick power of sound. And I know from my own experience, that Scotch reels, though brisk, make me melancholy, because I used to hear them in my early years. . . . Whereas the airs in *The Beggar's Opera*, many of which are very soft, never fail to render me gay, because they are associated with the warm sensations and high spirits of London" (Everyman Library: New York, 1906), II, 144.

[16] 2 vols. (Edinburgh, 1817), I, 317-318.

[17] *Ibid*., p. 325.        [18] *Ibid*., pp. 330-331.

sociation of ideas and not by any inherent beauty in proportions themselves.

The *Essays on the Nature and Principles of Taste* were very popular in the early nineteenth century and editions appeared in 1812, 1815, 1817, 1825, and 1842.[19] Alison's ideas provided the basis for Jeffrey's article on beauty in the fifth edition of the *Encyclopaedia Britannica* (1795), which did much to disseminate the Association theory. The popularity of this aesthetic theory and the effect which the *Britannica* article had upon its diffusion are attested in part by Sir George Steuart Mackenzie's *Essay on Taste* (1817), written to refute Alison's Associationism. Mackenzie states that Alison is commonly accepted as the "author of the Theory of Association,"[20] and he quotes Jeffrey's version of the theory as evidence of the prevalence of this position. According to Jeffrey, the beauty of

> outward objects, is nothing more than the reflection of our inward sensations, and is made up entirely of certain little portions of love, pity, and affection, which have been connected with these objects, and still adhere, as it were, to them, and move us anew whenever they are presented to our observation.[21]

Mackenzie wants to deny the validity of this aesthetic theory because, like Ruskin, he believes that it necessarily reduces beauty to a transient gleam and puts it on the level of "those grovelling pleasures, indulgence in which induces satiety, disgust, and nausea."[22]

Ruskin disapproves of Alison's position not only because it discounts the objective, permanent nature of

---

[19] Hipple, *The Beautiful . . . in British Aesthetic Theory*, p. 158.
[20] (Edinburgh, 1817), p. 42.      [21] *Ibid.*, pp. 43-44.
[22] *Ibid.*, p. 189.

beauty, in which Ruskin himself believed, but also because Associationism is a purely aesthetic theory; which is to say that Associationism is a self-contained explanation of the beautiful which cannot readily be derived from moral or metaphysical order. Alison, then, derives beauty from principles of the human mind which are most affected not by eternal law but local situation, not by essence but accident, not by order but disorder. To complicate the issue for Ruskin is the fact that he believes that association does have some influence on our judgment of beauty. He attacks an inconsistent passage in Alison's *Essay* which suggests that beauty is, simultaneously, something less powerful than association and the same thing as association, and then dismisses Alison in a few sentences without having disproved his points. Ruskin himself next proceeds to observe the effects which he believes association does have on the sense of beauty. He proposes that there are two kinds of association, rational and accidental; and he is most concerned with the second form of association which is "the accidental connection of ideas and memories with material things, owing to which those material things are regarded as agreeable or otherwise"(4.71-72). At the same time he emphasizes that these associations do not create beauty, Ruskin insists that all powerful emotions and "all circumstances of exciting interest, leave their light and shadow on the senseless things and instruments among which, or through whose agency, they have been felt or learned"(4.72), and that we always project "a spirit and a life"(4.72) upon all material things in moments of extreme happiness or extreme depression. These effects are important because "in many who have no definite rules of judgment, preference is decided by little else, and thus, unfortunately, its operations are mistaken for, or rather substituted for, those of inherent beauty"(4.73). Thus although Ruskin admits the importance of association, he continues to maintain that beauty and association are basically independent.

Since Ruskin considers personal association to be so important, it is somewhat surprising to observe him dismiss Rational Association so quickly. Rational Association is "the interest which any object may bear historically, as having been in some way connected with the affairs or affections of men; an interest shared in the minds of all who are aware of such connection" (4.71). The attitude and tone with which he rejects this form of association are interesting because of the glimpse they provide into his belief about the importance and nature of human life. For Ruskin, to call the pleasures of association beauty

> is mere and gross confusion of terms; it is no theory to be confuted, but a misuse of language to be set aside, a misuse involving the positions that in uninhabited countries the vegetation has no grace, the rock no dignity, the cloud no colour, and that the snowy summits of the Alps receive no loveliness from the sunset light, because they have not been polluted by the wrath, ravage, and misery of men. (4.71)

But the position which Ruskin here dismisses so contemptuously is approximately that which he chose a few years after writing this passage. When *The Seven Lamps of Architecture* appeared in 1848, two years after the second volume of *Modern Painters*, it contained a description of a beautiful scene in the Jura which reveals a changed attitude toward the importance of man and the importance of Rational Association in the beautiful. After Ruskin has described his "mountain symphonies" in spring, he continues:

> It would be difficult to conceive a scene less dependent upon any other interest than that of its own secluded and serious beauty; but the writer well remembers the sudden blankness and chill which were cast upon it when he endeavoured, in order more strictly to arrive at the sources of its impressiveness, to imagine it, for a moment, a scene in some aboriginal forest of the New Continent. The flowers in an instant lost their light, the river its music; the hills became oppressively desolate; a heaviness in the boughs of the darkened forest showed how much of their former power had been dependent upon a life which was not theirs, how much of the glory of the imperishable, or continually renewed, creation is reflected from things more precious in their memories than it, in its renewing. Those ever springing flowers and ever flowing streams had been dyed by the deep colours of human endurance, valour, and virtue; and the crests of the sable hills that rose against the evening sky received a deeper worship, because their far shadows fell eastward over the iron walls of Joux and the four-square keep of Granson. (8.223-224)

The contempt for man which appears in the second volume of *Modern Painters* is replaced in *The Seven Lamps of Architecture* by praise which, if it does not put man at the center of all things, does at least make the beauty of all things dependent upon his presence. Moreover, Ruskin now appears to believe that historical associations can create beauty, something which he had earlier denied. The difference of subject and purpose in these two works explains their different attitudes toward man and toward historical association. In *Modern Painters*, Volume II, Ruskin wants to demonstrate that beauty is essential to the health of the human spirit. This purpose is related to the fact that if he can demonstrate this, he will have shown that the painting and poetry which create, portray, and interpret this beauty are also important. In order to prove that beauty is essential to man, he relates the beautiful to religion and morality, to principles which are permanent, unchanging, and greater than man. Hence he cannot allow historical associations, the associations of man, to determine the nature of beauty. On the other hand, *The Seven Lamps of Architecture*, which is concerned with an art that shelters human life, relates beauty not to principles above man but to man himself. This new emphasis allows Ruskin to accept Associationism; but although the new theme may permit him to derive beauty from historical associations, his reason for doing so is that it aids his criticism of contemporary architecture. Ruskin finds the homes and public buildings of his England constructed without style, without regard to permanence and without meaning for the men who inhabit them. Since he wishes to correct these deficiencies, he places great emphasis upon historical associations, whose presence, he says, will insure both that an edifice influence the life of the inhabitant and that it be solidly constructed—this latter because if a building is to endure long enough for historical associations to accrue, then it must be well made.

Although it is clear that Ruskin places new importance on historical associations in *The Seven Lamps of Architecture*, it is not certain that he believed that these associations create beauty. The chapter "The

Lamp of Beauty" reaffirms his belief in the aesthetic theories of *Modern Painters*; but while he clearly maintains the major tenets of his earlier books, it is difficult to determine whether he has truly modified the details of his position, as he appears to have done. In most cases there is not much evidence as to Ruskin's exact aesthetic beliefs after *Modern Painters*, Volume II. Although the notes added to the 1883 edition of *Modern Painters* qualify his theories of beauty long after the fact, he never presented a new aesthetic system, and thus, in order to follow the development of Ruskin's aesthetics, it is necessary to consult evidence external to *Modern Painters*, much of which is inconclusive. But in this particular case we are fortunate that entries in Ruskin's diaries confirm the apparent acceptance of Associationism that appears in his work on architecture. The first sign of Ruskin's changed attitude appears in his entry for 19 April 1846: "I felt it more than usual, but it struck me suddenly how utterly different the impression of such a scene would be, if it were in a strange land and in one without history. How dear to the feeling is the pine of Switzerland compared to that of Canada! I have allowed too little weight to these deep sympathies."[23] A year after the publication of *The Seven Lamps of Architecture* Ruskin returned once again to his beloved Switzerland and noted his reactions: "I repeated 'I am in *Switzerland*' over and over again, till the name brought back the true group of associations—and I felt I had a soul, like my boy's soul, once again. I have not insisted enough on this source of all great contemplative art."[24] Although Ruskin is

[23] *The Diaries of John Ruskin*, eds. Joan Evans and John Howard Whitehouse, 3 vols. (Oxford, 1958), I, 325.
[24] *Ibid.*, II, 381.

here writing of personal, possibly accidental associations, his new emphasis would seem to demonstrate a general acceptance of association, and this later acceptance of Associationism in turn shows that Ruskin was not consistently able to oppose Alison's aesthetic theories. Despite his desire for a tidy, coherent, and convincing aesthetic system, Ruskin apparently modified his earlier statements about the relationship of association and beauty.

But his opposition to Alison's theory, however inconsistent, and his opposition to other aesthetic theories reveal aspects of his own conceptions of the beautiful. First of all, Ruskin believed that beauty is disinterested, and thus cannot be affected by considerations of utility; secondly, that it has an objective and unchanging reality, and thus cannot be importantly affected either by local custom or by association. Furthermore, Ruskin's opposition to the idea that beauty is dependent upon use, custom, and association reveals the extent to which he not only was acquainted with eighteenth-century writings but also considered them to have a major relevance to himself and his contemporaries.

The final and perhaps most important thing that Ruskin's attempt to confute these aesthetic positions can tell us is that despite his early assurance he could create a conception of the beautiful which was independent of subjective elements, this was to be impossible. After denying the validity of the four "erring" positions, he proceeded to propose his own bifurcated aesthetics, of which one part—Typical Beauty—is symbolic of the order that is the nature of God, and the second—Vital Beauty—is created by moral order, the ordinance of God. But when Ruskin lost his religious faith in 1858 he also lost the basis of these theories of beauty; and convinced that he had to turn his energies toward improving life on this earth (he no longer believed in a future life), he increasingly centered his writing on the needs of man. This focus on man, which begins to emerge in the section "On the Nature of Gothic" in *The Stones of Venice* (1853) and which evolves into the humanism of the last volume of *Modern Painters* (1860) and the political economy of *Unto This Last* (1860), first appears in Ruskin's difficulties with a theory of beauty that does not depend on the human element of association.

## II. Ruskin's theory of Typical Beauty

IN THE second volume of *Modern Painters* Ruskin advanced his idiosyncratic, eclectic, and often puzzling theocentric system of aesthetics by which he hoped to explain the nature and demonstrate the importance of beauty. Beauty, he wrote, "is either the record of conscience, written in things external, or it is the symbolizing of Divine attributes in matter, or it is the felicity of living things, or the perfect fulfilment of their duties and functions. In all cases it is something Divine; either the approving voice of God, the glorious symbol of Him, the evidence of His kind presence, or the obedience to His will by Him induced and supported" (4.210). All beauty, then, relates to the nature of God, and, if properly understood, is theophany; but Typical Beauty—"the symbolizing of divine attributes in matter"—most directly partakes of the Holy.

A manuscript originally intended for the second volume of *Modern Painters* reveals that this conception of the beautiful came to Ruskin as he gazed wonderingly upon a storm in the Alps. One dark, still July evening he lay beside the fountain of Brevent in the valley of Chamonix.

Suddenly, there came in the direction of Dome du Goûter a crash—of prolonged thunder; and when I looked up, I saw the cloud cloven, as it were by the avalanche itself, whose white stream came bounding down the eastern slope of the mountain, like slow lightning. The vapour parted before its fall, pierced by the whirlwind of its motion; the gap widened, the dark shade melted away on either side; and, like a risen spirit casting off its garment of corruption, and flushed with eternity of life, the Aiguilles of the south broke through the black foam of the storm clouds. One by one, pyramid above pyramid, the mighty range of its companions shot off their shrouds, and took to themselves their glory—all fire—no shade— no dimness. Spire of ice—dome of snow—wedge of rock—*all* fire in the light of the sunset, sank into the hollows of the crags—and pierced through the prisms of the glaciers, and dwelt within them—as it does in clouds. The ponderous storm writhed and moaned beneath them, the forests wailed and waved in the evening wind, the steep river flashed and leaped along the valley; but the mighty pyramids stood calmly—in the very heart of the high heaven— a celestial city with walls of amethyst and gates of gold—filled with the light and clothed with the Peace of God. And then I learned—what till then I had not known—the real meaning of the word Beautiful. With all that I had ever seen before—there had come mingled the associations of humanity—the exertion of human power—the action of human mind. The

image of self had not been effaced in that of God.
. . . It was then that I understood that all which is the
type of God's attributes . . . can turn the human soul
from gazing upon itself . . . and fix the spirit . . . on
the types of that which is to be its food for eternity;
—this and this only is in the pure and right sense of
the word BEAUTIFUL. (4.364-365)

John D. Rosenberg points out that this passage is "a
Christian rendering of the Romantics' vision of nature,"[25] and one might add that Ruskin's apocalyptic
vision presses even further toward complete effacement
of self in nature than Wordsworth's ever did. As Ruskin
looked upon the serene peaks rising amid the tumult,
he experienced "the absorption of soul and spirit—the
prostration of all power—and the cessation of all will
—before, and in the Presence of, the manifested Deity.
It was then only that I understood that to become nothing might be to become more than Man"(4.364). His
confrontation with the Holy, his sense of the glories of
becoming nothing before God, led him directly to
formulate a theory of the beautiful, which, denying the
importance of human elements, derived all from the
eternal, the unchanging, the infinite.

One may say of Ruskin's aesthetic theories what he
said of the arts—that they are in some sort an expression of deeply felt emotion, the recasting of intensely
felt experience. One such experience impelled him to
create his theory of Typical Beauty, while another almost as powerful led him, a few years later, to change
direction and admit the importance of association—a
human element—in the beautiful. Although his most in-

---

[25] *The Darkening Glass: A Portrait of Ruskin's Genius* (New York
and London, 1961), p. 19.

tensely felt emotional events, and not purely theoretical investigation, engendered his aesthetics, these views about beauty nonetheless bear the characteristic impress of Ruskin's thought; for, like his conception of the sister arts, they are derived in large part from neoclassical writings and serve a polemical purpose. In particular, his statements about the nature of beauty permit him to answer certain problems which an emotionally centered theory of art presents.

The difficulties Ruskin must solve appear first in the brief mentions of the beautiful which he makes in the opening volume of *Modern Painters*. In the chapter "Of Ideas of Beauty," he states that "any material object which can give us pleasure . . . without any direct and definite exertion of the intellect, I call in some way, or in some degree, beautiful"(3.109). The perception of beauty is thus an act of some non-intellectual part of the mind—non-intellectual, because he later states that ideas of beauty "are the subjects of moral, but not of intellectual perception"(3.111). Ruskin believes beauty, then, to be a disinterested pleasure which has an objective reality and which is perceived by the non-intellectual part of the mind. Although Ruskin, in contrast to many English aestheticians of the eighteenth and nineteenth centuries, believes that beauty is an objectively existing thing or quality, he yet speaks of "the emotions of the Beautiful and Sublime"(3.48). Emotion is subjective, and it is difficult to see how it could be thought to be objectively verifiable, since emotions, which are the product of the non-intellectual, the "moral" part of the mind,[26] cannot, as can conceptual thought, be reasoned over or even compared with each other. If emotion is thus subjective, and if beauty is an emotion, it is difficult to see how

[26] See below, pp. 156-58.

Ruskin believes that beauty can be objective. He attempts to solve the problem of feeling in beauty by reasoning that all men perceive, or should perceive, certain qualities with the same emotion much in the same manner that all men find sugar sweet and wormwood bitter. Men react so, says Ruskin, because it is God's will and because all men have a divine element in their nature, but men do not receive pleasure from certain forms and colors "*because* they are illustrative of it [God's nature], nor from any perception that they are illustrative of it, but instinctively and necessarily, as we derive sensual pleasure from the scent of a rose" (3.109). By appealing to an order that is ultimately divine, Ruskin thus proves to his satisfaction, if not, alas, to ours, that aesthetic emotions are both uniform and essential. In other words, he has found a theological reason for claiming that "Ideas of beauty are among the noblest which can be presented to the human mind, invariably exalting and purifying it" (3.111). He has also found the perfect defense of art, for if it is allowed that beauty is the image of God, then it is also easily allowed that the painting and poetry which create, portray, and interpret this beauty are important as well.

According to the second volume of *Modern Painters*, Typical Beauty, "the symbolizing of Divine attributes in matter"(4.210), has six aspects or modes: 1) infinity, or the type of divine incomprehensibility; 2) unity, or the type of divine comprehensiveness; 3) repose, or the type of divine permanence; 4) symmetry, or the type of divine justice; 5) purity, or the type of divine energy; and 6) moderation, or the type of government by law. The traditional notions of beauty which Ruskin incorporates into his own aesthetics appear under these six headings, and their inclusion is appropriate, for Typical Beauty is an aspect of universal order and those traditional aesthetic theories which emphasize the orderliness of beauty, or its dependence upon order, here find a ready place.

The emphasis upon an order in nature and in the beautiful was current in the eighteenth century, and it was from eighteenth-century writings that Ruskin received the details of his theory. Many of the meanings of the central term of neoclassical criticism, "nature," refer to some kind of order. Nature, for example, often meant pattern or law which functioned as pattern, as was the case when nature was spoken of as Platonic essence imperfectly realized, or as generic type or mode. The sense of nature as an empirical reality to be observed in humankind, the universe, and the connections between the two is also frequently encountered in neoclassical criticism. Although it is thus possible to distinguish between the various usages of the term "nature" in the eighteenth century, it does not appear that many writers carefully separated the various meanings, or, indeed, that they were always aware of them. But whatever the critics intended by the term, they were generally in agreement that this nature was informed by an order which was to be imitated. All would have agreed with Pope that

> The gen'ral ORDER, since the whole began,
> Is kept in NATURE, and is kept in Man.[27]

This general emphasis upon order in nature and its recreation or representation in art is related to the idea that the perception of order is itself pleasing and that

[27] "An Essay on Man," *The Twickenham Edition of the Poems of Alexander Pope*, ed. Maynard Mack (London, 1950), III, 36; ll. 171-172.

order produces all or part of the phenomenon of beauty. De Piles, the French translator of Du Fresnoy's widely read Latin work on the sister arts, *De Arte Graphica*, supported his demand for order by citing the ancients: *"Nothing pleases a Man so much as Order* (says *Xenophon*); and *Horace*, in his *Art of Poetry*, lays it down as a rule."[28] Francis Hutcheson, an aesthetician of the early eighteenth century, believed that order was such an important source of beauty that Locke and Newton, who had perceived new sources of order in man and nature, were rightfully to be considered as unveilers of the beautiful.[29] Even John Dennis, who was primarily concerned with the emotions of the violent sublime, emphasized the importance of order:

> The work of every reasonable creature must derive its beauty from regularity, for reason is rule and order, and nothing can be irregular either in our conceptions or our actions any further than it swerves from rule, that is, from reason. As man is the more perfect the more he resembles his Creator, the works of men must needs be more perfect the more they resemble his Maker's. Now the works of God, though infinitely various, are extremely regular.
>
> The universe is regular in all its parts, and it is to that exact regularity that it owes its admirable beauty. The microcosm owes the beauty and health both of its body and soul to order.[30]

[28] In Charles Alphonse Du Fresnoy, *De Arte Graphica: The Art of Painting . . . with Remarks [by Roger de Piles]. Translated into English together with an Original Preface [by] Mr. Dryden* (London, 1750), p. 116.

[29] *An Inquiry into our Ideas of Beauty and Virtue . . .* (London, 1726), p. 34.

[30] "The Grounds of Criticism in Poetry" (1704), *Eighteenth-Century Critical Essays*, I, 102.

Ruskin, like Dennis, believes that order is a primary cause of the beautiful, or better, that order is itself beautiful. This belief lies at the center of Ruskin's theory of Typical Beauty. In outlining his theory, Ruskin shows that all forms of Typical Beauty please because these forms symbolize divine order in material things. Similarly, when he explains the individual forms of this kind of beauty, he shows that they relate to a vision of universal, pleasing order.

In his chapter on the beauty of unity Ruskin includes two of the most common traditional formulations of the idea that beauty is order. He first subscribes to the theory, popular throughout the eighteenth century, that the beautiful is a properly composed mixture of unity and variety, an idea which appears in various contexts and with varying emphases throughout the writings of his predecessors. Francis Hutcheson, for example, who speaks not of unity but uniformity, states that beauty can be defined with much the same precision as that Newton attained with physical and mathematical science. According to Hutcheson, "What we call Beautiful in Objects, to speak in the Mathematical Style, seems to be in a compound *Ratio* of *Uniformity* and *Variety*; so that where the *Uniformity* of Bodys [*sic*] is equal, the Beauty is as the *Variety*; and where the *Variety* is equal, the Beauty is as the *Uniformity*."[31] Pretensions, such as Hutcheson's, to mathematical rigor are rare, and most writers do not present similarly careful definitions. Henry Fuseli merely states as part of his definition of the beautiful that it consists of the "union of the simple and the various."[32] Many authors whom Ruskin knew, however, do stress either

[31] Hutcheson, *An Inquiry into our Ideas of Beauty and Virtue*, p. 17.
[32] Fuseli, *The Life and Writings*, III, 76.

term of this aesthetic equation, depending on whether they wish to emphasize the pleasures of variety or those created by the unifying principle of order. In the *Essay on Criticism*, Pope, for instance, stresses the importance of order, and he thus emphasizes unity:

> In Wit, as Nature, what affects our Hearts
> Is not th'Exactness of peculiar Parts;
> 'Tis not a *Lip*, or *Eye*, we Beauty call,
> But the joint force and full *Result* of *all*.
> Thus when we view some well-proportion'd Dome,
> (The *World*'s just Wonder, and ev'n *thine* O *Rome!*)
> No single Parts unequally surprize;
> All comes *united* to th' admiring Eyes.[33]

Pope's concern with an ordering, embracing unity is present in other authors with whom Ruskin was familiar. Abbe Winckelmann, whose *Reflections on the Painting and Sculpture of the Greeks* Ruskin read either soon before or soon after writing *Modern Painters*, Volume II, held that unity is one of the ideas that "ennoble the more scattered and weaker beauties of our Nature."[34] The degree to which Winckelmann's conception of beauty relies on harmony and unity is clear from his remark that "the bodies of the Greeks, as well as the works of their artists, were framed with more unity of system, a nobler harmony of parts, and a completeness of the whole"[35] greater than that found in any later art or people. Although Winckelmann's book is justly known for creating interest in Greek art, he presented this art to his contemporaries in terms of their own belief in the beauty of order and unity.

[33] *Twickenham Edition*, eds. E. Audra and Aubrey Williams (London and New Haven, 1961), I, 267-268; ll. 243-250.
[34] Trans. Henry Fuseli (London, 1765), p. 19.
[35] *Ibid.*, p. 16.

In setting forth the theory of unity amid variety, Ruskin emphasizes the first term, "unity," and this stress on the element of order is perhaps an intentioned contrast to the writings of his older friend and teacher, the artist J. D. Harding, whose *Principles and Practice of Art* (1845) had stated:

> Variety is essential to beauty, and is so inseparable from it, that there can be no beauty where there is no variety. . . . As variety is indispensable to beauty, so perfect beauty requires that variety to be infinite. It is this infinite variety which constitutes the perfection of Nature, and the want of it which occasions every work of Art to be imperfect.[36]

According to Harding, who cites Hogarth's "line of beauty," the visible manifestation of this principle of variety is the curved line which thus must be the basis of all beautiful art.[37] Although Ruskin adds a final qualification to his teacher's praise of variety, he follows Harding's main points in his section on the Typical Beauty of infinity. Ruskin, for example, assumes "that all forms of acknowledged beauty are composed exclusively of curves will, I believe, be at once allowed. . . . What curvature is to lines, gradation is to shades and colours. It is their infinity, and divides them into an infinite number of degrees"(4.88,89). Throughout his own writings he emphasizes, in agreement with Harding, that the inexhaustible, infinite variety of nature is one of its most beautiful and important characteristics.

Ruskin's theory of beautiful variety relates directly to his practice as an art critic, for he judges the beauty, as well as the truth, of a painting by its ability to con-

[36] (London, 1845), p. 39.
[37] *Ibid.*, pp. 44-46.

vey impressions of nature's infinite change. Ruskin, who believes that nature never repeats herself(3.542), insists that "there is not one of her shadows, tints, or lines that is not in a state of perpetual variation: I do not mean in time, but in space. There is not a leaf in the world which has the *same colour* visible over its whole surface"(3.294). Therefore, unvaried color or tone in a painting that purports to convey an image of nature is both ugly and false, and he criticizes Salvator's *Mercury and the Woodman* and Claude's *Sinon before Priam* [National Gallery, London, Nos. 84 and 6] for portraying rocks and mountains with monotonous, unvarying browns. Turner, in contrast, had an "inimitable power" of varying color, "so as never to give a quarter of an inch of canvas without a change in it, a melody as well as a harmony of one kind or another" (3.293-294). In the first volume of *Modern Painters* he thus praises not only the intensity but also the infinite variation of Turner's palette. Drawing his examples of excellence from paintings the periodical critics had attacked, he lauds *The Slave Ship* (see Plate 5), *Snow Storm: Steamboat off a Harbour's Mouth* (see Plate 1), *War* (see Plate 8), and *Mercury and Argus*. Of this last painting he writes:

> In the Mercury and Argus, the pale and vaporous blue of the heated sky is broken with grey and pearly white, the gold colour of the light warming it more or less as it approaches or retires from the sun; but, throughout, there is not a grain of pure blue; all is subdued and warmed at the same time by the mingling grey and gold, up to the very zenith, where, breaking through the flaky mist, the transparent and deep azure of the sky is expressed with a single

crumbling touch; the keynote of the whole is given, and every part of it passes at once far into glowing and aërial space. (3.292-293)

After he has described the truth and beauties of Turner's art, he reminds the reader of those paintings "with great names attached to them"(3.293) in which the sky is a monotonous panel of unvarying grey.[38] Ruskin's practice as an art critic suggests that however abstract the details of his theological aesthetic may at first appear, they were grounded in personal experience of nature and art. Like his drawing teacher, he believes that nature's infinite variety provides a treasure hoard from which every great artist borrows.

But in contrast to Harding, Ruskin believes that variety is not itself beautiful, and that "it is a mistake which has led to many unfortunate results, in matters respecting art, to insist on any inherent agreeableness of variety, without reference to a farther end"(4.96). After his praise of variety in the chapter on infinity, Ruskin adds as a qualification in the chapter on unity that it is only a unified, ordered variety which is beautiful: "It is therefore only harmonious and chordal variety, that variety which is necessary to secure and extend unity . . . which is rightly agreeable; and so I

[38] A page later Ruskin continues: "A mass of mountain seen against the light, may at first appear all of one blue; and so it is, blue as a whole, by comparison with other parts of the landscape. But look how that blue is made up. There are black shadows in it under the crags, there are green shadows along the turf, there are grey half-lights upon the rocks, there are faint touches of stealthy warmth and cautious light along their edges; every bush, every stone, every tuft of moss has its voice in the matter, and joins with individual character in the universal will. Who is there who can do this as Turner will? The old masters would have settled the matter at once with a transparent, agreeable, but monotonous grey. . . . Turner only would give the uncertainty; the palpitating, perpetual change . . . the unity of action with infinity of agent" (3.294).

name not Variety as essential to beauty, because it is only so in a secondary and casual sense"(4.96-97). The final emphasis, for Ruskin, must be upon the divine element of unity, one of the most important laws of the universe. A beautiful object, a work of art, a healthy man, a functioning society, physical nature, and, ultimately, God are all perfected by the necessary presence of unity.

> Now of that which is thus necessary to the perfection of all things, all appearance, sign, type, or suggestion must be beautiful, in whatever matter it may appear; and the appearance of some species of unity is, in the most determined sense of the word, essential to the perfection of beauty in lines, colours, or forms. (4.94)

In fact, it is from the need for this perfecting unity that Ruskin deduces the need for variety; for, according to him, if different things are to create a unity, "there must be difference of variety. . . . Hence, out of the necessity of Unity, arises that of Variety"(4.95-96). Thus unity, the order which is a symbol and manifestation of eternal order, is the major term in Ruskin's aesthetic formula.[39]

---

[39] Significantly, the one work in which Ruskin emphasizes the element of variety by itself is *The Stones of Venice*. Defining "The Nature of Gothic," he explains that one major characteristic of the style is "CHANGEFULNESS, or Variety" (10.204), and he finds "the perpetual variety of every feature"(10.204) of a Gothic structure admirable, since "change or variety is as much a necessity to the human heart and brain in buildings as in books" (10.207). Thus, although his theories of beauty derive from a love of order and repose, he here states that "It is that strange *disquietude* of the Gothic spirit that is its greatness" (10.214). Yet, even while stressing the delights of variety, he admits both that too much change soon palls and that "order, in its highest sense, is one of the necessities of art" (10.205). Order in its highest sense is unity, and the Gothic has many unifying factors, such

All great art necessarily embodies this "Essential Unity," which binds "things separately imperfect into a perfect whole"(4.95). In a fine painting every aspect of technique, expression, and subject contributes its strength to create a unified whole, a complete work of art. For example, the infinitely various hues of Turner's *Mercury and Argus* become beautiful not because the painter employs blues as well as "grey and pearly white," but because he makes every tint harmoniously build upon every other. Similarly, all lines, like all colours, must contribute to this essential "unity of Membership"(4.95). Ruskin's most extended discussion of this aspect of painting occurs in the fifth volume of *Modern Painters*, in which he explains the theory and practice of composition. His definition reveals that for him this highest of the artist's gifts creates beautiful unity: "Composition," he states, "may be best defined as the help of everything in the picture by everything else"(7.205), or, again, it "signifies an arrangement, in which everything in the work is thus consistent with all things else, and helpful to all else"(7.208-209). He next points out that "a great composition always has a leading emotional purpose, technically called its motive, to which all its lines and forms have some relation"(7.217),

---

as proportion, repetition, and harmony, which blend all this delightful variety into a beautiful whole. Nonetheless, although *The Stones of Venice* (which cites the theories of beauty presented in *Modern Painters*, Volume II) does not repudiate his earlier conceptions of the beautiful, it does shift his earlier emphases, praising the human element of variety at the expense of order. Ruskin's increasing concern for the individual worker apparently led him to grant more importance to human, as opposed to divine, elements in his aesthetic theories; for it was the need to stimulate the worker and delight the common man which evoked his praise of Gothic variety. If such an explanation for this new emphasis is correct, then both Ruskin's modified view of association and his praise of architectural variety anticipate the approaching change in his thought.

and he further explains that whereas undulating lines express action, horizontal or angular ones express rest and strength. After examining an example of repose, Ruskin sets out to elucidate the essential unity of "a composition in which the motive is one of tumult: that of the Fall of Shaffhausen"(7.221; illus. facing 222). It is worth our while to quote most of this compositional study, because it not only demonstrates Ruskin to be an astonishingly perceptive critic of Turner, but also shows how directly he derived his theories of beauty from the practice of art:

> The line of fall is straight and monotonous in reality. Turner wants to get the great concave sweep and rush of the river well felt, in spite of the unbroken form. The column of spray, rocks, mills, and bank, all radiate like a plume, sweeping round together in grand curves to the left, where the group of figures, hurried about the ferry boat, rises like a dash of spray; they also radiating: so as to form one perfectly connected cluster, with the two gens-d'armes and the millstones; the millstones at the bottom being the root of it; the two soldiers laid right and left to sustain the branch of figures beyond, balanced just as a tree bough would be.
>
> One of the gens-d'armes is flirting with a young lady in a round cap and full sleeves, under pretence of wanting her to show him what she has in her bandbox. The motive of which flirtation is, so far as Turner is concerned in it, primarily the bandbox: this and the millstones below, give him a series of concave lines, which, concentrated by the recumbent soldiers, intensify the hollow sweep of the fall, pre-

cisely as the ring on the stone does the Loire eddies. These curves are carried out on the right by the small plate of eggs, laid to be washed at the spring; and, all these concave lines being a little too quiet and recumbent, the staggering casks are set on the left, and the ill-balanced milk-pail on the right, to give a general feeling of things being rolled over and over. The things which are to give this sense of rolling are dark, in order to hint at the way in which the cataract rolls boulders of rock; while the forms which are to give the sense of its sweeping force are white. The little spring, splashing out of its pine-trough, is to give contrast with the power of the fall,—while it carries out the general sense of splashing water. (7.221-222)

Turner's images of people, water, and rocks build toward one complete emotional impression of the scene; for in this work, as in all great painting, the most minute details contribute to a whole that is far greater than the sum of its parts.

After he has explained the theory of unity amid variety, Ruskin proceeds to his second aesthetic formulation of order, the theory that proportion is beauty. He derives proportion, the ordered relation of quantities, from a form of unity different from that mentioned in relation to the beauty of unity and variety. The beauty of unity and variety arises when a "harmonious and chordal variety" creates the unity of membership, "that unity of things separately imperfect [formed] into a perfect whole"(4.95). Proportion, on the other hand, creates a unity of sequence, a unity which is the ordering principle in changing, developing things. Following

his usual procedure, Ruskin explains how this kind of
Typical Beauty symbolizes a principle of the physical
and moral world. Thus, the unity of sequence

> is that of things that form links in chains, and steps
> in ascents, and stages in journeys; and this, in matter,
> is the unity of communicable forces in their continu-
> ance from one thing to another; and it is the passing
> upwards and downwards of beneficient effects
> among all things, the melody of sounds, the continu-
> ity of lines, and the orderly succession of motions
> and times; and in spiritual creatures it is their own
> constant building up, by true knowledge and con-
> tinuous reasoning, to higher perfection, and the sin-
> gleness and straightforwardness of their tendencies
> to more complete communion with God. (4.94-95)

The unity which results from this melodious variety
appears throughout the world in which man lives, and
in each case its manifestation is the simultaneous effect
and symbol, or type, of universal and divinely created
law. In the unity of sequence the pleasing effects of this
kind of variety are "best exemplified by the melodies
of music, wherein, by the differences of the notes, they
are connected with each other in certain pleasant relations. This connection, taking place in quantities, is
Proportion"(4.102). The proportions which inform the
human body, works of art, and all beautiful things are,
in Ruskin's terms, the music, or melody, of quantities,
while melody in return is proportion in sound. When
Ruskin thus discusses proportion and music as though
they are manifestations of the same law of nature, he
follows a tradition that had originated with Pythagoras
and Plato, developed to its greatest complexity in the
Italian Renaissance, and then, as its metaphysical and

mathematical bases were forgotten in the eighteenth century, had gradually dissolved and died away. Although Ruskin did mention the *Timaeus*, the Platonic source of the older theories of proportion, in his section on the beauty of unity and variety, he apparently was unaware of its traditional importance to ideas of proportion, for he did not mention this dialogue in his own discussion of the subject. His knowledge of the theory of proportions at the time he wrote the second volume of *Modern Painters* was confined to statements of English and Continental writers who wished to emphasize the element of order in beauty. Many of the critics with whom Ruskin was familiar, including Addison, Johnson, and Winckelmann, made proportion an important part of the beautiful. In his series on "The Pleasures of the Imagination"(1712) Addison includes proportion as one of the sources of that secret delight caused by the beautiful,[40] and in the second half of the century Dr. Johnson offered, as his *Dictionary*'s first definition of the beautiful: "That assemblage of graces, or proportion of parts, which pleases the eye." Winckelmann, advocate of a calm, ordered, classical beauty, stated that "Beauty consists in harmony of the various parts of an individual,"[41] and from his insistence that "Nature keeps proportion,"[42] it seems clear that proportion is a major source of this harmony.

Addison, Johnson, and Winckelmann are the eighteenth-century heirs to an almost vanished heritage of Italian architects and aesthetic theoreticians. In his *Architectural Principles in the Age of Humanism* (1949) Rudolph Wittkower has shown that Alberti, Palladio,

[40] *The Spectator*, No. 412, in *Eighteenth-Century Critical Essays*, I, 47.
[41] Winckelmann, *Reflections*, p. 259.
[42] *Ibid.*, p. 157.

and other fifteenth- and sixteenth-century Italian architects based their elaborate systems of proportion on
Pythagorean conceptions of musical harmony known
to them through Plato's *Timaeus,* Ficino's commentary
on the *Timaeus,* and Boethius's medieval treatise *De
Musica.*[43] Pythagoras's discovery that arithmetical and
geometrical relationships were the organizing principle
of the musical octave convinced him that number was
the primary law of existence, the principle whose perception revealed the one in the many, the order amidst
apparent disorder. Certain that these Pythagorean discoveries held the key to the universe, Renaissance
architects believed that number, geometry, and music
were varying appearances of one principle, and they
therefore used these terms interchangeably, speaking
of their buildings as spatial music. Alberti and Palladio
assumed that the same musical and mathematical order
informs nature and man and in so doing reflects the
image of God in material things. Since the laws of
harmonic number pervade all things, these theorists
reasoned, these laws must also exist in the human soul.
And because the human soul is an analogue, a minor
image, of a major, all-pervading order, the soul instinctively responds to other manifestations of God's order
and finds these other harmonies beautiful. A natural
affinity of souls to each other permits man instinctively
to enjoy harmony; but the human reason may also consciously discover the laws of this greater order, thus
enabling man to recreate divine, natural harmony in
human art and architecture. These architects corre-
spondingly subscribe to mathematical definitions of
beauty. Palladio, here following Alberti, states that

[43] 3rd ed. (London, 1962), pp. 23, 111-112. My discussions of proportion are dependent upon Professor Wittkower's study.

"Beauty will result from the beautiful form and from the correspondence of the whole to the parts, of the parts amongst themselves, and of these again to the whole."[44] For Alberti, Palladio, and other Renaissance theoreticians, the sources of this beautiful order were three simple mathematical ratios, those which produce the arithmetic, geometric, and "harmonic" means between two extremes. In practice these means were used to furnish the proper dimensions for details and other architectural elements.[45] Sculptors and painters also tried, though with less success, to derive proportional systems from the human body that would reflect the same order of God in nature that the architects had discovered.

These theories were the source of eighteenth-century ideas that proportion was beauty. But although eighteenth-century painters, architects, and sculptors often worked from Renaissance copy-books of proportions, the artists were ignorant of the means by which the proportions were attained. As William Gilpin, who proclaimed the aesthetic of an irregular, "picturesque" beauty, pointed out in 1792: "The secret is lost. The ancients had it. . . . If we could only discover their principles of proportion."[46] As the theoretical sources of proportion were forgotten, aestheticians began to offer other explanations for the relation between proportion and beauty. Hume, for example, who derived beauty from utility, thought that proportions are beautiful only when they are related to a useful end,[47] while Alison, the Associationist, held that proportions are en-

45 *Ibid.*, pp. 107-113.
46 *Three Essays on Picturesque Beauty* (London, 1792), p. 32. Quoted in Wittkower, *Architectural Principles*, p. 145.
47 See *An Inquiry Concerning the Principles of Morals*, pp. 40-42.

tirely arbitrary and beautiful only because they are familiar through custom and hence association.[48] Edmund Burke, against whom Ruskin in part directed his discussion of the aesthetics of proportion, went even further and denied that proportions were beautiful. Burke's first argument against the identification of proportion and beauty is that "Proportion relates almost wholly to convenience, as every idea of order seems to do; and it must therefore be considered as a creature of the understanding, rather than a primary cause acting on the senses and imagination. It is not by the force of long attention and enquiry that we find any object to be beautiful."[49] This argument makes four points, none of which seems necessarily joined by logic to the others. First, Burke assumes that proportion relates to convenience, that is, that proportion is a matter of utility. This assumption that proportion must necessarily be connected to use reveals his ignorance of the older theories of proportion. Secondly, Burke makes the assumption, equally foreign to the old aesthetic, that order is similarly related to utility, and thirdly, he assumes that order is not enjoyed aesthetically without reference to use. Fourthly, he confuses the discovery of a proportion with its enjoyment when he states that proportions can only be perceived by the understanding, in contrast to beauty which is received and enjoyed instinctively. Burke's second major argument is that, since different species of animals have different proportions, and since each species has its own beauty, proportion therefore cannot contribute to beauty. In other words, Burke assumes, rather illogically, that since *one* proportion or set of proportions is not found

[48] Alison, *Essays on the Nature and Principles of Taste*, II, 137.
[49] Burke, *On the Sublime*, p. 92.

in all beautiful things, proportion cannot be the basis of beauty. As a final touch Burke attempts his usual method of reducing the ideas of his opponents to absurdity with an attack on the proposition that proportions found in the human body are used in architecture:

> It has been said long since, and echoed . . . that the proportions of building have been taken from those of the human body. To make this forced analogy complete, they represent a man with his arms raised and extended at full length, and then describe a sort of square, as it is formed by passing lines along the extremities of this strange figure. But it appears very clearly to me, that the human figure never supplied the architect with any of his ideas. For in the first place, men are very rarely seen in this strained posture.[50]

Burke's ingenuousness, whether assumed or actual, reveals the extent to which the older theories of proportion had been forgotten.

Ruskin does not answer this last objection of Burke, and he also ignores Burke's first argument, which he can do, because he has already shown that order is not related to utility and that it is instinctively perceived and enjoyed as beauty. In regard to his predecessor's second objection, however, Ruskin mentions the "curious error of Burke, in imagining that because he could not fix upon some one given proportion of lines as better than any other, therefore proportion had no value or influence at all. It would be as just to conclude that there is no such thing as melody in music, because no one melody can be fixed upon as best"(4.108). His use

[50] *Ibid.*, p. 100.

of a musical analogy demonstrates at once both how similar and unlike Ruskin's ideas of proportion are to those of the Renaissance. For Alberti and Palladio musical harmony is the incorporation of order, and so it is for Ruskin; but whereas the earlier theorists mention harmony in relation to proportion, Ruskin speaks of harmony in relation to his idea of unity amid variety. For Ruskin, proportion is represented not by harmony, but by melody; not by the ordering element that the reason perceives, but by the melodic connection created and perceived by the imagination. When Ruskin makes musical analogies, as he frequently does throughout *Modern Painters*, music represents not a rationally perceived and recreatable order, but the expression of the imagination that surpasses reason. There is an order, an emotional, imaginative order, in melody and proportion, but it is not the order of number.

In his discussion of Burke, Ruskin concentrates on his predecessor's relation of fitness to proportion, and he makes the admission that Burke was in part correct, that one kind of proportion, constructive proportion, is related to use. Constructive proportion, primarily of importance in architecture, is a ratio of the strength, quantity, and bearing purpose of materials. Though an appropriate ratio of these three factors will seem pleasant to the knowledgeable observer, the pleasure produced by this ratio arises from a conscious recognition of skill and is not an innate reaction such as that which characterizes the perception of beauty.

The second form of proportion, that with which Ruskin is primarily concerned, is apparent proportion, which "takes place between quantities for the sake of connection only, without any ultimate object or causal necessity"(4.102). This apparent proportion, a law of nature, "which is itself, seemingly, the end of operation to many of the forces of nature, is therefore at the root of all our delight in any beautiful form whatsoever"(4.107-108). Apparent proportion, then, which parallels in so many ways the proportional theories of the Renaissance, is that which creates the unity of sequence. Since Ruskin's theological and aesthetic explanations of proportion are so like those of Alberti and Palladio, it is particularly ironic that he should have so harshly condemned an architecture that incorporated his own beliefs about beauty. But the very irony of Ruskin's lack of recognition points out most clearly both how much traditional theories of aesthetic order had been forgotten by the nineteenth century, and how conservative was his emphasis upon the beauty of order.

This belief in the importance and beauty of order also informs Ruskin's brief chapter on the typical beauty of symmetry. Most Continental and English writers, such as Alberti, Congreve, and Johnson, who mention the relation of symmetry and beauty, consider symmetry as an aspect of proportion. In his "Discourse on the Pindaric Ode" (1706) William Congreve wrote that "Nothing can be called beautiful without proportion. When symmetry and harmony are wanting, neither the eye nor the ear can be pleased."[51] In his statement Congreve, like most writers, apparently uses the terms synonymously, and in the *Dictionary* Dr. Johnson presents symmetry and proportion as synonyms. But Ruskin, unlike those who preceded him, differentiates between these two forms of aesthetic order: "Symmetry is the *opposition* of *equal* quantities

[51] *Eighteenth-Century Critical Essays*, I, 146.

to each other; proportion, the *connection* of *unequal* quantities with each other. The property of a tree sending out equal boughs on opposite sides is symmetrical; its sending out shorter and smaller towards the top, proportional"(4.125-126). Proportion, a relationship of changing, developing things, creates the unity of sequence, while symmetry, which is static, creates opposition and balance. In other words, proportion is kinetic order, symmetry static order. Ruskin emphasizes that this necessary "reciprocal balance" is formed not by the opposition of identical things, but by things which balance each other: "Absolute equality is not required, still less absolute similarity. A mass of subdued colour may be balanced by a point of a powerful one"(4.125). Ruskin professes to find it strange that such aesthetic balance could ever have been thought to be synonymous with proportion; but the explanation is simple and lies in the fact that whereas he considers symmetry alone to be a form of balance, earlier writers considered both symmetry and proportion to be so. In fact, this earlier identification of both terms appears in Aristotle's *Nicomachean Ethics*, an important source of Ruskin's moral conception of symmetry.

Following his usual procedure, Ruskin derives this form of aesthetic order from moral laws which, in turn, are derived from the nature of God. Accordingly, symmetry is the type of divine justice. Ruskin's suggestion that symmetry may in part be pleasurable because of its relation to Aristotle's notion of abstract justice provides the reader with several clues as to both the source and nature of Ruskin's moral conception of symmetry. First, there is his citation of the Aristotelian idea of abstract justice. In the *Ethics* Aristotle states that justice is receiving that which one deserves according to one's merit. The philosopher explains his conception of justice by comparing that which is just for two different people. Thus, since person A and person B should each receive what is commensurate with his merit, the rewards A' and B' will be related A + A' = B + B'. Aristotle concludes that "This, then, is what the just is—the proportional; the unjust is what violates the proportion."[52] Aristotle here presents proportion as balance, and the proportionate balance of rewards and merits as justice. Except for the fact that Ruskin writes of symmetry and not proportion, though he apparently means much the same as Aristotle, he follows the philosopher's notion of justice, and from this notion of justice—which he derives from divine nature—he explains the moral nature of symmetry.

The *Ethics* also explain Ruskin's theory of the typical beauty of symmetry. Aristotle's entire theory of virtues is based on the recognition of what a recent scholar calls "the necessity of introducing system, or as Aristotle says, symmetry, into the manifold tendencies which exist within us."[53] The virtue of courage, for example, is a mean which balances the deficiency of cowardice against the excess of recklessness. While symmetry is itself thus not a virtue, it is a principle in all virtue. This conception of symmetry seems to enter Ruskin's notion of the typical beauty of symmetry. He states that symmetry "is rather a mode of arrangement of qualities than a quality itself"(4.126), and hence that it has little power over the mind unless connected with other beauties. Ruskin therefore relates symmetry to

[52] Trans. W. D. Ross, *The Basic Works*, ed. Richard McKeon (New York, 1941), p. 1007.

[53] W. D. Ross, *Aristotle: A Complete Exposition of his Works and Thought* (New York, 1959), pp. 191-192. In his own translation Ross uses "proportionate" (*The Basic Works*, p. 954).

beauty as Aristotle relates it to forms of virtue—as a principle of order which creates the desired quality. Just as the symmetry of the mean is necessary for the dignity of man, so, too, symmetry is necessary for "the dignity of every form"(4.126) in art. Order, representative of moral order and ultimately derived from it, is the source of this beauty of symmetry:

> Orderly balance and arrangement are essential to the perfect operation of the more earnest and solemn qualities of the Beautiful, as being heavenly in their nature, and contrary to the violence and disorganization of sin; so that the seeking of them, and submission to them, are characteristic of minds that have been subjected to high moral discipline. (4.126-127)

Ruskin thus adds an Evangelical Anglican flavor to his Aristotelian sources, relating the beauty of symmetry to the balance of divine justice and of right conduct among men.

From his theory of the typical beauty of symmetry Ruskin deduces the value of balance in art, praising in particular the symmetrical groupings that Giotto, Ghirlandajo, and Tintoretto employ. On the other hand, although he devotes much care to setting forth his theory of beautiful proportion, no such practical criteria follow from this mode of Typical Beauty. Because Ruskin believes that proportions "are as infinite . . . as possible airs in music"(8.163), he cannot advocate any one proportional system for the arts. The relation of this aspect of his aesthetic theory to his practice as a critic appears not in proscriptions for beauty but in his careful analyses of architecture. In *The Stones of Venice*, for instance, he details the measurements of San Donato in Murano, discovering that the distance between columns in the church's apse provides a modular which its builders employed throughout the building: the width of the aisle measures twice the interval between shafts, the transept three times, and the nave four(10.46). In addition, he determines other proportional gradations along the length of the shafts themselves. Thus, Ruskin's firm belief in the beauties of order encourages him to search for order in beautiful architecture, producing a method of critical, if not artistic, practice.

This same emphasis on order, appropriate and perhaps expectable in an aesthetic theory presented as part of a metaphysic, appears in the three remaining branches of Typical Beauty—repose, moderation, and purity. Whereas unity amid variety, proportion, and symmetry are themselves forms of order, repose and moderation are qualities produced by order or associated with it. Like the Solitary in Wordsworth's *Excursion*, that poem so beloved of Ruskin at this point in his career, he emphasizes

> The universal instinct of repose,
> The longing for confirmed tranquillity,
> Inward and outward.[54]

All art, says Ruskin, must have an element of repose, the symbol of divine permanence. This element of repose may be "a simple appearance of permanence and quietness"(4.114), or else it may be repose proper, "the rest of things in which there is vitality or capability of

---

[54] *Works*, v, 87. Ruskin quotes these lines in a note to the chapter on repose, adding: "But compare carefully (for this is put into the mouth of one diseased in thought and erring in seeking) the opening of the ninth book; and observe the difference between the mildew of inaction—the slumber of Death; and the patience of the Saints—the rest of the Sabbath Eternal. Rev. xiv. 13" (4.117n).

motion actual or imagined"(4.114). Repose would seem to answer yearnings for peace, stability, and order, both in life and in art. "In architecture, in music, in acting, in dancing, in whatsoever art, great or mean, there are yet degrees of greatness or meanness entirely dependent on this single quality of repose"(4.119). Ruskin believes that repose symbolizes divine permanence, that aspect of God's nature which is in greatest contrast to the change and effort of human existence:

> As opposed to passion, change, fulness, or laborious exertion, Repose is the especial and separating characteristic of the eternal mind and power. It is the "I am" of the Creator opposed to the "I become" of all creatures; it is the sign alike of the supreme knowledge which is incapable of surprise, the supreme power which is incapable of labour, the supreme volition which is incapable of change; it is the stillness of the beams of the eternal chambers laid upon the variable waters of ministering creatures. (4.113)

Here peacefulness and permanence are the aspects of order which please changing, changeable men, who always desire the calm of order.

In the experience which occasioned Ruskin's theory of typical beauty, it was the sight of the *aiguilles* standing "calmly" amid the writhing, moaning storm that brought him a vision of "the Peace of God"(4.364); and throughout his writings he delighted in impressions of repose. John D. Rosenberg has suggested that "in art as in life he was most moved by the kind of beauty which possesses the unchanging . . . remoteness of death."[55] Ruskin's praise of della Quercia's sepulchral

[55] *The Darkening Glass*, p. 205. "Peace, youth, and death were always associated with Ruskin's moments of profoundest feeling: with the

monument for Ilaria di Caretto [illus. facing 4.122], his careful attention to tomb sculpture in *The Stones of Venice*, and his strong approval of Wallis's *Death of Chatterton* (see Plate 13) and Millais's *Ophelia* (see Plate 14) all argue for Rosenberg's view. At the same time, Ruskin's love of the intense and infinitely various hues of nature (and of her prophet Turner) does not permit one to accept the idea that such beauty *most* moved him: one remembers that his vision of the Alps, like Turner's art, mixed tumult and calm, change and permanence, conflict and peace.

It is nonetheless true that his writings about art, society, and self frequently reveal an intense yearning for peace and permanence. He once wrote that "the Greek could stay in his triglyph furrow, and be at peace; but the work of the Gothic heart is fretwork still, and it can neither rest in, nor from, its labour, but must pass on, sleeplessly, until its love of change shall be pacified for ever in the change that must come alike on them that wake and them that sleep"(10.214). Ruskin had a Gothic heart but he continually desired to make himself at least partially a Greek. His writings on art, his entire works, indeed his life, appear in retrospect a peregrination without rest, a continuing voyage of exploration and discovery; for the goals of Ruskin's pilgrim's progress, like the ends of his holy war, frequently changed or vanished. In particular, *Modern Painters*, an emblem of changefulness, grew and recast itself, leading him through many areas of life and art of which he had at first been unaware. The publication

---

'marble-like' beauty of the girl at Turin, who lay motionless on the sand, 'Like a dead Niobid'; with the girls at Winnington, immobile and innocent, as they listened to music; with the perfect repose of Della Quercia's figure of the sleeping *Ilaria di Caretto*, which he loved above all other statues . . ." p. 205.

of the second volume in 1846, and his subsequent revisions of the first, reveal his defense of art to be an ongoing, ever-changing work-in-progress which continually incorporated new discoveries, embodied developing attitudes, and ended, seventeen years after it had begun, far longer and far different than its author had at first expected. Certainly, in *Modern Painters* there are many central themes which in part determined its form—a form sometimes unexpected but always relevant to the main purposes. Certainly, an order, a unity of the kind Ruskin demanded, does exist in his work, but it is the order of a changing, growing thing like the unity of a living organism, like the unity of Ruskin's own life: complex and ever in transition.

It is no surprise, then, that a man aware of his own changefulness, a man pained at the cruel effects of time on men and their creations, should long for signs of permanence and peace in art. His praise of Dante, the ideal artist, who, though intensely emotional, stands unmoved, is thus not only Ruskin's revision of romantic conceptions of the poet, but also a much desired, if unattainable, ideal for himself.[56]

This yearning for repose enters both his aesthetics and critical practice, coloring his preferences for sub-

[56] John D. Rosenberg, who has written brilliantly of the tempest raging within Ruskin in the 1860's (*ibid.*, pp. 147-152), also points out: "Physically as well as intellectually he spent these ten years [after 1860] in transit, shifting from subject to subject as rapidly as he hastened from place to place, seeking an anchorage he could not find and fleeing from a chaos he was powerless to avoid" (p. 148). Similarly, John Lewis Bradley's fine introduction to his edition of *The Letters of John Ruskin to Lord and Lady Mount-Temple* (Ohio State University Press: n.p., 1964), pp. 4-5, states: "Most apparent about the Ruskin of the '60's is a growing discursiveness, an almost maniacal tendency to dart from one lecture hall to another, from one town to the next, to talk, and to write as well, on strikingly varied subjects. . . . With the death of his father in 1864 and the intensification of his passion for Rose La Touche, he casts himself into one activity after another."

ject, lighting, composition, and emotional effect. Ruskin, who delighted in images of the eternal rest of men and mountains, intensely disliked most portrayals of violence or violent emotion in art. He realized, like Lessing, that the power of art to fixate images of transient emotion led more frequently to the ludicrous and horrible than to the beautiful.[57] Despising the *Laocoön*, he found the Elgin marbles, particularly the Theseus, ideal embodiments of the beauty of repose(4.119). Similarly, he criticized Raphael's attempt to portray acute anguish in *The Massacre of the Innocents*(4.204), and, among contemporaries, he criticized the morbidity of William Windus's *Too Late*(14.233-234). In Windus's rather unfortunate painting (see Plate 16), which he exhibited at the Royal Academy in 1859, we can observe the worst of Victorian pathos, the very thing

[57] Gotthold Ephraim Lessing, *Laocoön: An Essay on the Limits of Painting and Poetry*, trans. E. A. McCormick (Indianapolis, Ind., 1962), p. 17, wrote that the portrayal in the visual arts of pain, or any strong emotion, inevitably becomes grotesque: "Simply imagine Laocoön's mouth forced wide open, and then judge! Imagine him screaming, and then look! . . . The wide-open mouth, aside from the fact that the rest of the face is thereby twisted and distorted in an unnatural and loathsome manner, becomes in painting a mere spot and in sculpture a cavity, with most repulsive effect." According to Lessing, a "single moment, if it is to receive immutable permanence from art, must express nothing transitory. . . . The prolongation of such [transitory] phenomena in art, whether agreeable or otherwise, gives them such an unnatural appearance that they make a weaker impression the more often we look at them, until they finally fill us with disgust or horror" (p. 20). Citing the ancient painter Timomachus, he explains that the proper way to "display extreme passion" (p. 20) is to portray the moment before or after the transitory event or effect, so that the audience's imagination completes the situation. This notion of the decisive moment, which one encounters in many writers on the arts, informs both Ruskin's own attitudes toward the depiction of emotion (4.203-205) and his idea that landscape painting should capture the sense of growth and change in scenery. He writes, for example, that "the great quality about Turner's drawings which more especially proves their transcendent truth is, the capability they afford us of reasoning on past and future phenomena" (3.487).

Ruskin was trying to discourage: a young man has returned too late to his gaunt-cheeked beloved, who, dying of consumption, supports herself weakly by a cane, while the lover buries his head in his arms as a little girl looks at him with reproach.[58]

Ruskin's other modes of Typical Beauty create the specific technical criteria of repose. In his chapter on infinity, Ruskin, who had only contempt for dramatic

[58] Raymond Lister, *Victorian Narrative Paintings* (London, 1966), p. 80, writes: "The artist, who was a neurotic, was deeply hurt [by Ruskin's criticism] and this, with the death of his wife in 1862, caused him to abandon professional painting and to destroy nearly all he had so far painted." Graham Reynolds, *Victorian Painting* (London, 1966), p. 67, rather strangely writes that the artist unfortunately "encountered Ruskin in one of his more unbalanced moods." Neither Ruskin's comment on the painting nor his actions at this period suggests that he was in any way "unbalanced," and since Reynolds, who admits the "morbidity" of the painting, apparently agrees with Ruskin, one finds it difficult to understand the reason for such commentary.
Ever since Wilenski's cruel and rather inept attempt at a psychological biography, critics who feel unhappy with Ruskin's judgments attribute them to insanity. Wilenski's *John Ruskin, An Introduction to the Further Study of His Life and Work* (London, 1933), which throughout contains amateur psychological analyses of the most pernicious kind, frequently appears more an essay in character assassination than a prolegomena to the study of Ruskin's work. The author paints Ruskin's portrait in darkest colors, holding that he was insane throughout his life and only clearheaded at brief moments. For example, Wilenski states that Ruskin never worked very hard (!), though to do so he must ignore the enormous body of sketching and writing that he produced. He makes Ruskin's statements that he was recording buildings about to be torn down or defaced seem untrue, whereas E. T. Cook and others have demonstrated the importance of this work. Similarly, he informs the reader that Ruskin was mad enough to pay high prices for rocks and even collected shells on the beach—a sure sign of insanity—but fails to mention until much later that Ruskin was an amateur geologist with publications to his credit. Perhaps the most astonishing example of motive-mongering comes when Wilenski explains many reasons for Ruskin's donation of his beloved Turners to Oxford, including (1) desire to buy his way into the good graces of the university; (2) guilt at his own wealth; (3) loss of interest in art; (4) an attempt to forestall accusations that he was inflating the prices of Turner for his own profit. He does not feel it necessary, however, to mention Ruskin's stated intention of acquainting students with the artist's work.

Rembrandtesque lighting, praised diffused lighting and "the preciousness of the luminous sky"(4.86). He also finds closely associated with this lighting the portrayal of a luminous distance exemplified by the painters of the early Florentine Renaissance(4.84-85). Similarly, both symmetry and proportion, which create a visual order in painting, aid the effect of repose.

Purity, which less obviously partakes of Ruskin's emphasis upon order, is the type of divine energy, and its best example is light—"not *all* light, but light possessing the universal qualities of beauty, diffused or infinite rather than in points; tranquil, not startling and variable; pure, not sullied or oppressed"(4.128). Purity, referable to God, cannot mean sinlessness, because, according to Ruskin, one cannot define God in negatives. He therefore explains that purity must signify some sort of energy, and from his remarks about the tranquil, constant nature of beautiful light it would appear that purity refers specifically to restrained divine energy. If this interpretation of his idea of purity is correct, then purity, thus taken to mean restrained energy, readily has a place in his aesthetic of order beside the other branches of Typical Beauty.

His remarks about diffused or infinite light further suggest that this mode of the beautiful is associated closely with the typical beauty of infinity; but whereas this other mode of beauty most concerns light considered as illumination, purity concerns light as color. Throughout his career Ruskin closely associates purity and color, several times undertaking theological justification of this connection. In the last volume of *Modern Painters*, for example, he insists that color "is the purifying or sanctifying element of material beauty" (7.417n), and he attempts to support his claim by the use in Leviticus of the scarlet hyssop as a purifying element in the sacrifice. Similarly, in the fourth volume, in which he also asserts the "sacredness of colour" (6.68), he both argues that God appointed blue, purple, scarlet, white, and gold for the tabernacle, and that He has made color accompany "all that is purest, most innocent, and most precious"(6.68).

Ruskin's criticism of individual paintings demonstrates that for him the beauty of purity is embodied in bright, clear, intense hues—in the reds and golds of medieval painting, in the palette of the Pre-Raphaelites, and, above all, in the scarlets, blues, and yellows of Turner. In particular, his favorite artist's *Ulysses Deriding Polyphemus*, *The Slave Ship*, *San Benedetto*, and *Napoleon* exemplify his conception of this mode of the beautiful. His preferences lead one to conclude that Ruskin, who considers color the visible embodiment of feeling, "the type of love"(7.419), believes that intense colors more suitably convey the emotional impression of a scene than do violent action or the depiction of faces under the influence of strong passions.

Nevertheless, as he explains in his chapter on moderation, the sixth and last branch of Typical Beauty, the painter's colors, though intense, must avoid the glaring and discordant. Like all other aspects of painting, color demands moderation, which Ruskin believes to be "the girdle and safeguard of all the rest, and in this respect the most essential of all"(4.139) forms of beauty. The appearance in material things of "self-restrained liberty" is beautiful, says Ruskin, because it is "the image of that acting of God with regard to all His creation, wherein, though free to operate in whatever arbitrary, sudden, violent, or inconstant ways He will, He yet, if we may reverently so speak, restrains in Himself this

His omnipotent liberty, and works always in consistent modes, called by us laws"(4.138). In the course of his discussion Ruskin mentions Richard Hooker's *Laws of Ecclesiastical Polity*, a work on which he modeled the style of the second volume of *Modern Painters*,[59] but even more important as an influence, perhaps, is again Aristotle's *Ethics*; for the ideas of the mean, of symmetrical virtue, are in essence ideas of moderation. Ruskin insists on the moral and artistic superiority of moderate things to "the loose, the lawless, the exaggerated, the insolent, and the profane"(4.140) —to things, to men, to colors and forms which are disordered and hence unrelated to divine nature. According to him, one who would achieve this mode of the beautiful should emulate "the pure and severe curves of the draperies of the religious painters"(4.140). Similarly, in color "it is not red, but rose colour, which is most beautiful . . . and so of all colours; not that they may not sometimes be deep and full, but that there is a solemn moderation even in their very fulness, and a holy reference . . . to great harmonies by which they are governed"(4.140). Such a criterion for orderly, moderate color would seem to go against his praise of Turner's stridently red *Napoleon*, but since the hues of this work turned, losing all their harmony, within a decade after the artist laid them on his canvas(13.160), one cannot ascertain whether Ruskin argues inconsistently. The general principle remains: all elements of

---

[59] In the tenth number of *Fors Clavigera*, which appeared in October 1871, Ruskin mentions his "affectation to write like Hooker and George Herbert" (27.168), and in the 1871 preface to *Sesame and Lilies* he mentions the imitation of Hooker in the second volume of *Modern Painters* (18.32). See also Malcolm Mackenzie Ross, "Ruskin, Hooker, and 'the Christian Theoria,'" *Essays in English Literature from the Renaissance to the Victorian Age* (Toronto, 1963), pp. 283-301.

painting, even color which is the embodiment of feeling, require order and moderation.

Ruskin's theory of Typical Beauty is an Apollonian, classical aesthetic of order, and as such apparently incongruous with his romantic conceptions of painting and literature. His incorporation of the idea of infinity, long an important element in conceptions of a powerful, often violent sublime, shows the extent to which Ruskin avoids elements of disorder in his system of Typical Beauty. Rather than deriving some traditional form of overpowering beauty or sublimity from infinity, Ruskin tamely confines infinity to gradations in color and line, and in the following chapter on the beauty of unity these elements of variation are then made subservient to unity, a principle of order. The beauty of purity presents a similar example, for, again, rather than using the notion of divine energy and power to create a sublime aesthetic, Ruskin instead emphasizes a mild, calm beauty. This Apollonian beauty is all the more surprising, since Ruskin had stated in the previous volume that sublimity was not an aesthetic category separate from beauty but was contained in beauty. When we examine his conceptions of sublimity in the following chapter, we shall see that after Ruskin discovered he could find no place for the disordering elements of emotion in his theories of beauty, he made use of the sublime, in the manner of eighteenth-century writers, to accommodate the pleasures of the awesome, the terrific, and the vast.

## III. Ruskin's theory of Vital Beauty

AFTER he has presented his theory of Typical Beauty, Ruskin then turns to the more emotional part of his aesthetic, Vital Beauty, the beauty of living things. He begins with a word painting that contains contrasted examples of both forms of the beautiful, and this is followed by an explanation of the principles of Vital Beauty:

> I have already noticed the example of very pure and high typical beauty which is to be found in the lines and gradations of unsullied snow: if, passing to the edge of a sheet of it, upon the Lower Alps, early in May, we find, as we are nearly sure to find, two or three little round openings pierced in it, and through these emergent, a slender, pensive, fragile flower, whose small, dark purple, fringed bell hangs down and shudders over the icy cleft that it has cloven, as if partly wondering at its own recent grave, and partly dying of very fatigue after its hard-won victory; we shall be, or we ought to be, moved by a totally different impression of loveliness from that which we receive among the dead ice and the idle clouds. There is now uttered to us a call for sympathy, now offered to us an image of moral purpose and achievement, which, however unconscious or senseless the creature may indeed be that so seems to call, cannot be heard without affection, nor contemplated without worship, by any of us whose heart is rightly tuned, or whose mind is clearly and surely sighted.
>
> Throughout the whole of the organic creation every being in a perfect state exhibits certain appearances or evidences of happiness; and is in its nature, its desires, its modes of nourishment, habitation, and death, illustrative or expressive of certain moral dispositions or principles. Now, first, in the keenness of

the sympathy which we feel in the happiness, real or apparent, of all organic beings, and which, as we shall presently see, invariably prompts us, from the joy we have in it, *to look upon those as most lovely which are most happy*; and, secondly, in the justness of the moral sense which rightly reads the lesson they are all intended to teach . . . consists, I say, the ultimately perfect condition of that noble Theoretic faculty, whose place in the system of our nature I have already partly vindicated with respect to typical, but which can only fully be established with respect to vital beauty. (4.146-147)

To clarify the second, often puzzling, theory which Ruskin presents about the beautiful, it will be advisable to continue the contrast he has begun between Typical and Vital Beauty. If one relates both forms of beauty to Ruskin's metaphysics and religion, it will be seen that although both Typical and Vital Beauty are affected by Ruskin's religious beliefs at the time he was writing *Modern Painters*, Volume II, the connection between Vital Beauty and God is not as clear as Ruskin obviously believed it to be. Typical Beauty is the beauty of forms and of certain qualities of forms, which Ruskin now tentatively and now firmly asserts to be aesthetically pleasing because they represent and embody divine nature. Vital Beauty, on the other hand, is the beauty of living things, and it is concerned not with form but expression—with the expression of the happiness and energy of life, and, in a different manner, with the representation of moral truths by living things. Now, Typical Beauty, which figures forth God's being, is clearly a part of Ruskin's metaphysical system, and so also is that part of Vital Beauty produced by the presentation of moral truths. This second form of Vital Beauty is closely related to Ruskin's religious world-view, since these beautiful truths exist as part of a divinely ordained great chain of being in which each living creature plays a role as agent and as living emblem of divine intention. The first problem with this form of Vital Beauty is that such recognition of moral truth seems inconsistent with Ruskin's continual assertion of the non-rational nature of the aesthetic perception. A second problem is that the beauty of happiness, the first aspect of Vital Beauty Ruskin mentions, seems only partially at home with his other aesthetic ideas.

More problems and more clues are forthcoming if one realizes that, taken together, Typical and Vital Beauty comprise a kind of sister arts aesthetic. It has often been stated that aestheticians tend to base their ideas of beauty upon the arts with which they are most familiar. This assertion is obviously true about writers of the eighteenth century, who, believing in a visual imagination, emphasized the qualities of painting and the beauties which it presented as models for all the arts. As one might expect, this same emphasis on the visual is found in Ruskin, and, in particular, his theory of Typical Beauty draws its details, if not its ultimate explanations, from theories of beauty concerned largely with the visual, the external, the element of form. But as we have seen, Ruskin draws to a large extent on expressive ideas of poetry, and these also enter his aesthetic system. For Vital Beauty, which is based on romantic theories of poetry, is concerned with emotions, with internal reactions, and with notions of psychology and morality on which romantic poetic theory depends. The extent to which Vital Beauty has a different basis than Typical Beauty is seen in the different accounts which Ruskin provides to explain their reception in the mind. A concern with internal reactions and processes of thought is characteristic of expressive theories of art, and it is appropriate that such an interest should enter what is in essence an expressive theory of beauty. For whereas Ruskin merely states that the contemplative faculty, theoria, instinctively perceives Typical Beauty as pleasurable, he describes the mechanism by which the observer perceives both the happiness and moral significance of a living being to be beautiful. This process, act, or faculty—one cannot be sure which it is—is sympathy. To solve the problems, first, of how the mind enjoys the internal mental and emotional state of another, and, second, of how moral truth is perceived by a non-rational part of the mind, one must examine the history of the term "sympathy" and attempt to show what Ruskin believed sympathy to be.

In *Modern Painters* Ruskin usually defines his critical terminology with care both in order to make his argument clear to the reader and to create an impression of originality and precise reasoning. In the first volume Ruskin introduces the definitions he will use for imitation, beauty, sublimity, relation, and idea. The following volume, largely devoted to his aesthetic system, defines imagination, beauty, and theoria, and the final three volumes inform the reader of what Ruskin considers to be the correct meanings of picturesque and of landscape. Sympathy, on the other hand, is one of the few terms in *Modern Painters* Ruskin does not trouble to define at the outset of the discussion in which it plays a part. Many years later when he addressed *Fors Clavigera* to the workingmen of England, he explained that sympathy, "the imaginative understanding of the natures of others, and the power of putting ourselves in their place, is the faculty on which the virtue depends"(27.627). From the fact that Ruskin did not trouble to define the term in *Modern Painters* one can infer that he assumed that his readers would have been aware of the various common psychological and moral associations of this term. But because it is just these associations which are most likely to trouble anyone who now attempts to follow Ruskin's aesthetic speculations, it will be necessary to examine the history of the term and its development amid systems of moral philosophy.

During the second half of the eighteenth century and throughout most of the nineteenth, sympathy, which today signifies little more than compassion or pity, was a word of almost magical significance that described a particular mixture of emotional perception and emotional communication. According to Johnson's *Dictionary* (1755), sympathy is "Fellow-feeling; mutual sensibility; the quality of being affected by the affections of another." For Dr. Johnson, sympathy is, first, fellow-feeling, an emotion brought forth or called into being in some manner by another human being; secondly, it is a shared interaction of emotions by several people; and, thirdly, it is the "quality" of being emotionally stirred by another's emotions. Dr. Johnson's definition of sympathy is derived from a British school of moral philosophy which referred ethics to feeling.

For this sentimentalist or emotionalist school of ethics to have developed, it was necessary that there be changes in the traditional moral psychology that had been handed down, virtually unchanged, from ancient

Greece through Rome to Europe of the Middle Ages and Renaissance.[60] These changes were brought about by the English empiricists Thomas Hobbes and John Locke, and the sentimentalist theories of ethics attempted to answer problems which these philosophers had raised about the nature of moral action. Thomas Burnet and Anthony Cooper, Lord Shaftesbury, originators of the emotionalist school of moral philosophy, based their theories of moral behavior upon emotional reactions in attempts to replace innate ideas, whose existence Locke had denied, with another means of making man innately aware of good and evil. Since Locke had demonstrated to their satisfaction that the mind cannot possess inborn ideas of God and moral right, they attempted to find another manner in which man might make moral valuations. Extending Locke's own notion that the mind has an innate power or principle that perceives differences in color, Burnet suggested that it is by means of a similar innate power that the mind perceives differences of moral value. According to Shaftesbury, the more influential of the two writers, man's power of perceiving right and wrong resides in "his natural moral sense,"[61] an internal sense much like the senses of sight, hearing, and taste. By analogy to the "feelings" of sight and sound, the subject feelings of this moral sense were thought to be the affections or emotions. This notion of a moral sense became quite important in British ethical theory and influenced Ruskin, who accepts the existence of an innate "moral sense" that deals with emotions.[62]

60 Tuveson, *The Imagination as a Means of Grace*, pp. 42-55.

61 Shaftesbury, *Characteristics*, I, 262.

62 *"A Joy for Ever"* (1873) perhaps best states Ruskin's acceptance of the traditional emotionalist position: "To this fixed conception of a difference between Better and Worse, or, when carried to the extreme,

One of the changes wrought by this school of emotionalist ethics to which Ruskin was indebted was a new concentration on the emotions in ethical speculation. Since the affections, or emotions, were thought to produce moral behavior, moral philosophy naturally became the study of the affections. For this shift of emphasis from reason to emotion to occur, it was necessary for older conceptions of emotion to change. One of the premises of Shaftesbury's ethical writings, which was ultimately of great significance in theories of art and morality, is the principle that the emotions are not only equally valuable, but in certain cases superior to the conceptions of the rational, thinking mind. The emotionalist ethics based on this premise did not develop, and probably could not have developed, until Hobbes and Locke had replaced the classical and medieval hierarchical model of the mind with one in which all the faculties were in a sense equal. For centuries moral philosophy had been founded on a psychology in which reason, lord and rightful ruler of the soul, checked the often rebellious urgings of the lower faculties, sense and will. Hobbes and Locke replaced this moral psychology, in which reason dominated the hierarchy, with a psychology in which reason was dependent upon sense-data. Locke wrote his *Essay Concerning Human Understanding*, as he informed his reader, in order to limit to a proper sphere the endeavors of the too ambitious human mind; and the first limitation which Locke imposed, or rather, revealed, is that the understanding can only work with ideas that enter the mind through the senses. This limitation not

---

between good and evil in conduct, we all, it seems to me, instinctively, and, therefore rightly, attach the term of Moral sense" (16.164).

only denies the possibility of innate ideas, it also destroys the older descriptions of the mind as capable of the immediate apprehension of truth. Locke's restriction of the understanding and his insistence that it is dependent for its ideas on the senses shatters the older hierarchical model of the mind and consequently changes attitudes toward reason and emotion. When Shaftesbury, using Latitudinarian theories of the benevolent affections, places the burden of moral behavior on the emotions, then emotion, for the first time, becomes of greater value than reason in moral theory.

When Hobbes and Locke attacked previously conceptions of reason and the hierarchical psychology with which they were associated, these philosophers clearly did not foresee that their attempts to make men aware of the true nature and importance of reason would, paradoxically, become the basis of psychologies in which feeling was not only more important than reason but in which even the role of a Lockean conception of the understanding was disparaged. Even Shaftesbury, who derived morality from the feelings and not from reason, was very much a man of his age and would have denied the great claims which those he influenced made about the role of the emotions. The Scottish school of moral philosophers, with which Ruskin was well acquainted and from which he derived many of his ideas, was the philosophical heir of both Locke and Shaftesbury, and it is in the works of Adam Smith, Dugald Stewart, and Thomas Reid, the leaders of this school, that one can observe the development of Locke's and Shaftesbury's new attitudes toward mind and reason. In Adam Smith's *Theory of the Moral Sentiments*, for example, reason is presented as playing a very small role in moral action. Since Smith believes that all behavior comes within the scope of morality, he believes, in effect, that reason plays but a small role in the conduct of human life. After the great paeans to reason which one finds in the Cambridge Platonists of the seventeenth century, and after the attempts of Hobbes and Locke to clarify the all important function of reason, it is surprising to encounter the intensity with which Smith denies that reason is important in decisions about moral right:

> Though reason is undoubtedly the source of the general rules of morality, and of all the moral judgments we form by means of them; it is altogether absurd and unintelligible to suppose that the first perceptions of right and wrong can be derived from reason, even in those particular cases upon the experience of which the general rules are formed. These first perceptions, as well as all other experiments upon which any general rules are founded, cannot be the object of reason, but of immediate sense and feeling. . . . If virtue, therefore, in every particular instance, necessarily pleases for its own sake, and if vice as certainly displeases the mind, it cannot be reason, but immediate sense and feeling, which, in this manner, reconciles us to the one, and alienates us from the other.[63]

Smith's assertion that the first perceptions of moral right as well as everyday moral decisions are made by the emotions, and not by the reason, is accepted by Ruskin as one of his moral and artistic premises. According to Ruskin, the imagination is not only "dependent on acuteness of moral emotion; [but] in fact, all moral truth can only thus be apprehended"(4.287).

---

[63] Smith, *Theory of the Moral Sentiments*, I, 569.

Ruskin was familiar with Smith's moral treatise,[64] but since the emotionalistic ethics it propounded were so widely accepted and could have been encountered anywhere from Wordsworth to Dickens, it is improbable that he derived this conception of morality from any one source. Ruskin's acceptance of this kind of ethical theory explains how, when he believed that beauty was instinctive and non-conceptual, he could find beautiful something that today we believe requires the exercise of conceptual thought processes.

Another premise of emotionalist moral theory which ultimately had great effect on Ruskin's ideas was the notion that the study of the processes of the mind, chiefly of the emotions, was the proper sphere of moral philosophy. Shaftesbury himself wrote that since all moral value depends upon the affections, the study of these affections must be the subject and method of moral philosophy.[65] Because psychology had developed as a part of moral philosophy, these fields of inquiry used the same terminology, and this terminology, as much as any other factor, was responsible for the continuing close alignment of studies of psychology and morals well into the nineteenth century. The alignment can be observed in Ruskin's use of the word "moral." Much of the time it is difficult to tell whether by moral Ruskin means ethical or whether he means psychological, and one is forced to conclude that he did not

[64] In Ruskin's early "Essay on Literature," which he wrote in 1836, he mentions Adam Smith (1.370), and the editors reason (1.370n) that since Ruskin was at this time unacquainted with Smith's *Wealth of Nations*, he was almost certainly referring to *The Theory of the Moral Sentiments*.

[65] "Since it is therefore by affection merely that a creature is esteemed good or ill, natural or unnatural, our business will be to examine which are the good and natural, and which the ill and unnatural affections" (Shaftesbury, *Characteristics*, I, 247).

differentiate between a philosophy of mind and a philosophy of morality.[66] It is not that Ruskin aligns the two subjects, but rather that for him psychology and moral philosophy had never been separated. Since the emotionalist moral philosophers with whose works Ruskin was familiar, particularly Smith, did not distinguish the study of what we today would call unconscious mental processes from the study of moral decisions, it is easy to understand how Ruskin could use the term "moral" to mean simultaneously "ethical" and "referring to all mental processes." From this point of view, then, Ruskin's statement about beauty becomes somewhat clearer: "Ideas of beauty, then, be it remembered, are the subjects of moral, but not of intellectual perception"(3.111). By this statement, I take it that Ruskin refers both to the fact that he believes aesthetic perception to be unconscious and automatic, and also to his belief that aesthetic responses are made by the same faculty which makes moral valuations.

The fact that the term "moral" referred both to the study of ethics and to the study of psychology helps explain why Ruskin could consider aesthetics to be a part of the study of morality. A lack of specialized vocabularies for philosophies of morality, psychology, and beauty encouraged the continuing close relationship between these three areas of inquiry. The implications of this association appear as early as Shaftesbury. He believed both that the sublime arouses violent emotion and that emotion is the agent of moral behavior. Since Shaftesbury did not distinguish between aesthetic and moral emotion, he assumed that the perception of the sublime is, in some manner, a moral act, and that it is

66 I am indebted to Professor Geoffrey Tillotson, Birkbeck College, London, who pointed this out to me.

good for the perceiver because it exercises his moral emotions. This same connection is made with similar results throughout the eighteenth and nineteenth centuries. James Beattie, Wordsworth, Hazlitt, Shelley, and Ruskin are a few of the many who believe that the perception of the beautiful is a moral act. Ruskin's theoretic faculty, he writes, "is concerned with the moral perception and appreciation of ideas of beauty" (4.35). Ruskin here makes the same identifications as had Shaftesbury, and it appears that he also draws the same conclusion, that aesthetic emotion is morally valuable to the perceiver. Ruskin makes the point in the first volume of *Modern Painters* when he states that "Ideas of beauty are among the noblest which can be presented to the human mind, invariably exalting and purifying it"(3.111).

At the time, however, when Ruskin was writing *Modern Painters*, the idea was current that theories of beauty should be divorced from the study of morals and made the subject of aesthetics, a separate discipline. Alexander Baumgarten, a German philosopher, had introduced the term "aesthetic" in 1735 with the suggestion that the study of beauty should be concerned merely with the adequacy of the object to perception, that is, that aesthetics should be a separate, independent concern dealing only with pleasures of perception.[67] Baumgarten's ideas were already known in England, too well known for Ruskin's pleasure, and he insists several times that calling the perception of beauty aesthetic is "degrading it to a mere operation

[67] Alexander Gottlieb Baumgarten, *Meditationes Philosophicae de Nonnullis ad Poema Pertinentibus* (1735), ed. and trans. K. Aschenbrenner and W. B. Holther (Berkeley and Los Angeles, 1954). This work is cited and discussed by F. E. Sparshott, *The Structure of Aesthetics* (Toronto and London, 1963), pp. 4, 54.

of sense"(4.35), when it is in fact an operation of the moral faculty, theoria, and hence should be called "theoretic." Ruskin probably borrowed the name of his contemplative moral faculty, theoria, from Aristotle and formed its adjective, theoretic, so as to have a counterterm that he could oppose to Baumgarten's "aesthetic" which would permit him to relate beauty to a faculty concerned both with the beautiful and the good. He was impelled to defend the importance of beauty with such high moral seriousness because he had accepted the identification, made by the emotionalist school of ethics, of aesthetic and moral emotion, and because he had accepted the general views of emotion subscribed to by this school of moralists.

Now that we have looked at the conceptions of psychology which were associated with sympathy and which permitted its development as a term of moral philosophy, we can continue with the history of the term "sympathy." Shaftesbury, who conceives of sympathy as fellow-feeling, mentions it as one of several sources of the benevolent affections which are, in turn, the source of moral action. He believes that these natural moral affections are primarily social and must be developed within a social context. (Recently J. B. Broadbent succinctly described Shaftesbury's ethics as the aesthetic of an aristocracy, a morality to make men comfortable in the club of Augustan society.)[68] Edmund Burke, who wrote almost five decades after Shaftesbury, also considers sympathy primarily as one of the "social passions"[69] which harmoniously bind men together in civilized society, but for Burke sympathy is

[68] "Shaftesbury's Horses of Instruction," *The English Mind: Studies in the English Moralists presented to Basil Willey*, eds. Hugh Sykes Davies and George Watson (Cambridge, Eng., 1964), p. 80.
[69] Burke, *On the Sublime*, p. 43.

159

far more than fellow-feeling. It is rather an entire process of emotional identification and perception. In *On the Sublime* (1757) Burke explains that sympathy is the means by which we enter into the interests of other men and are forced to be moved by their actions and emotional reactions: "For sympathy must be considered as a sort of substitution, by which we are put into the place of another man, and affected in many respects as he is affected."[70] Whereas for Shaftesbury sympathy is the shared social affection of social equals, for Burke, whose conception is more typical of later authors, sympathy is an almost mystical communion by means of which the observer places himself in the emotional point of view of another person.

Shaftesbury's notion of sympathy is that it is one of the means by which the moral affections are aroused, and although he mentions a "natural moral sense,"[71] he does not connect the two, and neither does Francis Hutcheson, another moral philosopher who centered his moral theory upon this idea of an internal moral sense.[72] It was not until Adam Smith, following Douglas Hume, identified sympathy with the internal moral sense that it became the center of ethical theory.[73] In his *Theory of the Moral Sentiments*, Smith, much in the

[70] *Ibid.*, p. 44.    [71] Shaftesbury, *Characteristics*, I, 262.

[72] "We are not to imagine, that this *moral Sense*, more than other Senses, supposes any *innate Ideas, Knowledge*, or *practical Proposition*: We mean by it only *a Determination of our Minds to receive amiable or disagreeable Ideas of Actions, when they occur to our Observation, antecedent to any Opinions of Advantage or Loss to redound to our selves from them*; even as we are pleas'd with a *regular Form*, or an *harmonious Composition*, without having any Knowledge of *Mathematicks*, or seeing any *Advantage* in that Form, or Composition, different from the immediate Pleasure" (Hutcheson, *An Inquiry into our Ideas of Beauty and Virtue*, p. 135).

[73] Walter Jackson Bate, "The Sympathetic Imagination in Eighteenth-Century English Criticism," *ELH*, XII (1945), 146-147.

manner of Burke, describes sympathy as a means of entering another person's emotions, and he explains that the imagination carries man beyond the limitations of his senses, thus creating what Burke had called a "substitution." It is interesting to observe the manner in which Smith, a philosopher consciously working in the tradition of Locke, assumes that imagination can effect a mystical identification or communion with other human beings. The sympathy evoked by this process of imaginative identification is the means by which the morality of all acts is perceived. For we approve or disapprove the conduct of another person when, placing ourselves in his stead, we either can or cannot sympathize with his motives; and similarly we approve or disapprove our own actions, "according as we feel that, when we place ourselves in the situation of another man, and view, as it were with his own eyes and from his station, we either can or cannot enter into and sympathize with the sentiments and motives which influenced it."[74] Sympathy, then, is in a sense a psychological explanation of the golden rule: one acts as he would be acted upon, both because one can perceive how it feels to be acted upon, and because one can perceive the other person's judgment of one's own motives. Furthermore, since the one who is acting can, by means of sympathetic perception, be the other person for a few brief moments, he is, in a sense, acting upon himself.

This conception of moral sympathy allows us to see how vital beauty conforms to Ruskin's general statements concerning the beautiful. First of all, the notion of disinterested pleasure is at the center of Ruskin's aesthetic theory, and depending on whether he is writ-

[74] Smith, *Theory of the Moral Sentiments*, I, 188-189.

ing about beauty as emotion or beauty as quality which produces this emotion, Ruskin considers beauty to be either a feeling of disinterested pleasure or a quality which produces this feeling of disinterested pleasure. Now, since sympathy is a means of partaking of the feelings of another, and since happiness is a feeling of pleasure or some combination of pleasures, the necessarily disinterested pleasure that is produced by sympathizing must, according to Ruskin's system, therefore be beautiful. Thus, the vital beauty of happiness is simply the pleasure of another which the observer disinterestedly enjoys by means of sympathetic perception —that is, by entering for an instant into that person's feelings and making that person's pleasure his own to the extent that it can be enjoyed.

Although the history of moral sympathy clarifies to an extent what Ruskin means by the beauty of human happiness, his remarks on the Vital Beauty of plants and animals remain difficult to understand. For since happiness implies a form of consciousness rarely accorded to dogs and never to delphiniums, it seems confusing to apply the notion of happiness to animals, and even meaningless to mention it in relation to plants. Ruskin was well aware of the difficulties in his theory of Vital Beauty, and he began his discussion of it at this, its most difficult part, with an examination of happiness in organisms in which "it is doubtful, or only seeming"(4.150). He seems quite undecided as to the true nature of happiness in plants, for while he is attracted to the idea that all living things have some form of soul, a basic conservatism prevents him from definitely and finally stating that this is so. But this does not help his theory much, for if plants can't be happy, then their Vital Beauty would seem to be based, at

least in part, on illusory appearance. Ruskin suggests
that the truly perceptive observer may in fact perceive
happiness in the mountain gentian, his first example,
but then he also suggests that the percipient associates
this idea of happiness with the plant because it appears
to be healthy and strong. Ruskin's lack of decision is
evident in his statement, that after one has discounted
the effects of Typical Beauty, "the pleasure afforded by
every organic form is in proportion to its appearance
of healthy vital energy. . . . The amount of pleasure we
receive is in exact proportion to the appearance of
vigour and sensibility in the plant"(4.151). The central
term would here seem to be "appearance," for Ruskin
seems willing to settle for a mere appearance of sensibility. He had earlier tried to deny that association, a
subjective element, had a role in the beautiful, but
when he permits an illusory appearance to be a partial
basis of Vital Beauty, it seems that he has now allowed
association to play a most important part in his aesthetic theory. The one thing of which the reader can be
certain is that happiness for plants is chiefly to be seen
in the appearance (true not illusory) of life and health.
And since man, a higher being, has the added dimensions of mind and spirit, it would seem that human
Vital Beauty based on the appearance of life and health
must be derived, in part, from the appearance of mental and spiritual health and vitality.

Two passages in the second volume of *Modern
Painters* furnish an idea of what Ruskin meant by happiness, and hence by the Vital Beauty of happiness.
First, there is the preface to the 1883 edition in which
he explains that his own conception of happiness is derived from Aristotle's *Nicomachean Ethics*. After trans-
lating a passage which in the earlier editions had ap-

peared in the original Greek, Ruskin continues with his own remarks on happiness: " 'And perfect happiness is some sort of energy of Contemplation, for all the life of the gods is (therein) glad; and that of men, glad in the degree in which some likeness to the gods in this energy belongs to them. For none other of living creatures (but men only) can be happy, since in no way can they have any part in Contemplation.' This, as I have said [writes Ruskin], goes far beyond my own statement; for *I* call any creature 'happy' that can love, or that can exult in its sense of life: and I hold the kinds of happiness common to children and lambs . . . no less god-like than the most refined raptures of contemplation attained to by philosophers"(4.7). The passage makes it clear that although Ruskin does not restrict happiness to the Aristotelian idea of contemplative pleasure, he still envisages it as requiring some form of consciousness: the happy being (whom we find beautiful) is able, he tells us, to love and to exult in its own sense of life, and both loving and exultation are activities which would require consciousness in some form. Although it is possible and even probable that Ruskin believed that animals have such a consciousness, it seems unlikely that he believed that plants could be aware of and exult in their own vitality. So the problem is not solved.

A second piece of evidence, however, casts more light on the problem of what Ruskin meant by happiness. When, near the beginning of the second volume of *Modern Painters*, Ruskin introduces his theory of Vital Beauty, he states that it is "the appearance of felicitous fulfilment of function in living things, more especially of the joyful and right exertion of perfect life in man"(4.64). This connection of happiness and function is reminiscent of the *Nicomachean Ethics,* and the manner in which Ruskin introduces the idea of function makes it clear that he is following Aristotle's procedure. At the beginning of *Modern Painters,* Volume II, where Ruskin demonstrates the importance of the theoretic faculty, he proposes to determine, first, what is useful and hence important to man:

> [Anything is useful to another thing] which enables it rightly and fully to perform the functions appointed to it by its Creator. Therefore, that we may determine what is chiefly useful to man, it is necessary first to determine the use of Man himself.
>
> Man's use and function (and let him who will not grant me this follow me no farther . . .) are, to be the witness of the glory of God, and to advance that glory by his reasonable obedience and resultant happiness. (4.28-29)

According to Ruskin, then, it is the function of man to glorify God and by his obedience (obedience it is presumed to moral law) to achieve happiness. This passage apparently refracts Aristotle's definition of happiness through Ruskin's religious belief. In the *Ethics,* after Aristotle has informed the reader that happiness is something final and self-sufficient, he admits that to say that happiness is the greatest good seems merely to be a platitude, and that a more definite idea being necessary, "This might perhaps be given, if we could first ascertain the function of man."[75] Aristotle first excludes the life of nutrition and growth common to all living things, and he next excludes the life of perception, i.e., mere physical pleasure, common to men and animals. "There remains, then, an active life of the ele-

[75] Aristotle, *The Basic Works,* p. 942.

ment that has a rational principle. . . . Now if the function of man is an activity of soul which follows or implies a rational principle [which is what Aristotle concludes] . . . human good turns out to be activity of soul in accordance with virtue."[76] Man's function, according to Aristotle, is virtuous activity, and this virtuous activity produces happiness. Man's function, according to Ruskin, is man's obedience to God's law, which is consequently virtuous activity and hence productive of happiness; and, according to Ruskin, by being happy man is beautiful. In his attempt to extend the conception of happiness to all living things, Ruskin has simply followed Aristotle's chain of reasoning backward, so to speak, allowing those things to be happy (animals and plants) which the philosopher had excluded. Since lesser animals can only partake of lesser, non-spiritual kinds of activity, their "happiness" is merely in vitality and health. Although Ruskin's sources thus help to explain how he came to formulate his notion of happiness, they do not dispel the apparently intentional ambiguities in his theory of Vital Beauty. I can only propose that Ruskin, here formulating an emotionalistic aesthetic, was willing to admit a subjective element to his system—although he was earlier unable to admit that beauty itself was subjective. Hence Ruskin's indecision and his multiple explanations for the perception of Vital Beauty.

Because Ruskin bases his theory of Vital Beauty on an extended conception of human happiness, one might expect that his chapter "Of Vital Beauty in Man" would have concentrated on the forms and qualities of a beauty more complete than any found in the animals of the field or in the oak and mountain flower; but, in

[76] *Ibid.*, pp. 942-943.

fact, although he briefly mentions the effects of happiness on the human face and form, he devotes the larger part of his chapter to those things, evil passions of sensuality, pride, fear, and ferocity, which destroy the beautiful in man. When he formulated his aesthetic theories, Ruskin was still a devout, rather puritanical Evangelical Anglican; and, more troubled by man's fallen state than pleased by man's beauties, he begins his chapter on human beauty with a reminder of the loss of Eden, showing next how the "present operation of the Adamite curse"(4.184) shatters the image of the beautiful which should, and which in some small degree still does, dwell in the features of men. The entire chapter is marked by theological assertions which later embarrassed Ruskin, so much so that when in 1883 he added notes to *Modern Painters*, 37 years after the publication of the second volume, he felt obliged both to apologize for his earlier belief and to assure the reader that it was not necessary for him to "believe the literal story of the Fall, but only that, in some way, 'Sin entered into the world, and Death by Sin'" (4.184n). There is evil in man's nature; and man dies. These assertions, acceptable to the reader without reference to particular religious belief, are far different from Ruskin's earlier attempts to paint the darkened image of a sin-ridden creature whose potential beauty can never be even partially realized this side of paradise.

Ruskin's puritanical attitudes and his penchant for theological speculation shaped his aesthetic theory to such an extent that, without reference to his religion, it would be as difficult to understand his ideas of beauty as it would be to understand the reason for the sermonizing tone with which he presents them. The emotional tone, the intellectual attitudes, and the very articles of belief which form Ruskin's religion permeate this second volume of *Modern Painters*, entering all aspects of his aesthetic theory, sometimes as source and sometimes as support for his ideas of beauty. Typical Beauty, for example, has its obvious inspiration in Ruskin's theology—so much so that in a final analysis his theory of Typical Beauty is best seen, not as an aesthetic theory related to his religious belief, but rather as a natural extension of this religious belief into the realm of aesthetics. The theory of Vital Beauty, in contrast, does not have as its basis any single theological principle, such as the figuring of divine nature in earthly objects; but here also Ruskin's faith plays a very important part. Although a religious theory of happiness is one major principle of Vital Beauty, in most parts of this aesthetic theory his belief does not so much shape or originate as merely support nonreligious descriptions and explanations of the beautiful.

Ruskin's religion, for example, supports an aspect of his philosophy of beauty when he derives the characteristic romantic demand for particularity and detail in art from his own belief in man's fallen state. The fall of man, according to Ruskin, caused an "evil diversity" (4.176) in mankind, so that, unlike other living things, there is no ideal state or central form of human beauty. He concludes from this lack of a single ideal of human beauty, that ideal beauty, such as exists in men, is attainable only in portraiture, and that neoclassical theories of generalization, such as those of Reynolds, are inapplicable.

Another characteristic Ruskinian fusion of religion and romanticism leads to his proposition that facial expression is the chief source of human beauty. Because his puritanical attitudes toward the human body prevent his enjoying the nude in art, Ruskin has to replace classical and Renaissance conceptions of human beauty with one which does not emphasize the body. He dislikes the portrayal of the human form in art, because he believes, at this point in his career, that the body and its pleasures were necessarily suspect because necessarily corrupting. Ruskin therefore finds sensuality distasteful, and sexuality disgusting—with the result that the nude, particularly the female nude, is considered always a potentially dangerous subject for the artist to attempt, since it so easily strays into that "which is luscious and foul"(4.194). Ruskin says that few moderns, if any, have been able to avoid the dangers of this subject; and in northern painting where the nude figure looks "as if accidentally undressed"(4.198), the distrust of the nude, which Ruskin believes a modern characteristic, creates additional problems, for "from the very fear and doubt with which we approach the nude, it becomes expressive of evil"(4.198). Although Ruskin believes that moderns cannot successfully paint the nude figure, he admits that the great religious painters "with Michael Angelo and most of the Venetians, form a great group, pure in sight and aim, between which and all other schools by which the nude has been treated, there is a gulf fixed"(4.196). Prior to these men the Greeks achieved a depiction of the human form ideal in its bodily health and strength; but, for Ruskin, this perfection of the human body is but a minor part of man's true beauty.

Man's true beauty, according to Ruskin, is not found in equal degree throughout the entire body but is concentrated in the features, and this beauty appears in or upon these features when they express man's spiritual and intellectual nature. Ruskin thus uses a form of the romantic notion of expression to solve the aesthetic problem created by the opposition that he believes exists between the body and spirit, between the material and immaterial. He asserts that expression is the means by which spirit and intellect inform the face, thus making it beautiful. Human Vital Beauty is, in particular, the expression of three mental operations: that of the intellect, of the intellect joined with moral emotion, and of faith. The action of intellect engenders the appearance of "energy and intensity"(4.179)—qualities which Ruskin had earlier mentioned as characterizing non-human Vital Beauty. The appearance of the intellect working conjointly with the moral emotions creates, on the other hand, a peculiarly human form of the beautiful, the "sweetness which that higher serenity (of happiness), and the dignity which that higher authority (of divine law, and not human reason), can and must stamp on the features"(4.181). The operation of faith leaves both face and body "conquered and outworn, and with signs of hard struggle and bitter pain upon it"(4.186). Here it is the human form weakened by faith that is beautiful, the signs of submission and bodily weakness that are appealing.

These conceptions of the beautiful, like the first part of Ruskin's aesthetic, embody criteria by which he evaluates individual paintings. To create images of Vital Beauty in man, for example, the painter must necessarily avoid depicting violent or debasing emotions. Ruskin, who desires something very like a classical restraint in art, believes that the "use and value of passion is not as a subject of contemplation in itself, but as it breaks up the fountains of the great deep of the human mind"(4.204). Accepting emotionalist theories of art and moral perception, he emphasizes that the painter should only depict emotion to attain a further end, such as the rendering of character. Since he places such importance on the noble emotions, he despises a sensationalistic art which portrays violent passion only to titillate its audience, and, in fact, he holds that "all passion which attains overwhelming power . . . is unfit for high art"(4.204).

In addition to avoiding violent emotion, the artist who would create images of human beauty must beware presenting the appearance of pride, lust, fear, or cruelty which are destructive of the best in man. Ruskin's previously encountered remarks about the nude constitute his chief emphasis upon the avoidance of sensuality in art. In the course of warning against signs of pride, he singles out contemporary portraiture to which he opposes the "glorious severity of Holbein, and the mighty and simple modesty of Raffaelle, Titian, Giorgione, and Tintoret"(4.193). Lastly, "of all subjects that can be admitted to sight, the expressions of fear and ferocity are the most foul and detestable"(4.200), for these present not the healthy energy of man's body, mind, and spirit, but the disordered, debasing emotions which man received upon his fall from grace. Prohibiting all non-satirical presentation of fear, hatred, cruelty, and ferocity in art, he holds that the artist should particularly avoid scenes of war, hell, and death by violence. He thus attacks with especial fervor Nicolas Poussin's *Deluge* (Louvre), a "monstrous abortion . . . whose subject is pure, acute, mortal fear" (4.200), and he similarly criticizes Salvator's battle piece in the Pitti Palace "wherein the chief figure in the foreground is a man with his arm cut off at the shoulder, run through the other hand into the breast with a lance"(4.201). Furthermore, writing at a time when he still accepted Evangelical estimates of Roman Catholicism, he expresses strong distaste for both representations of hell and those "horrible images of the Passion, by which vulgar Romanism has always striven to excite the languid sympathies of its untaught flocks. . . . There has always been a morbid tendency in Romanism toward the contemplation of bodily pain, owing to the attribution of saving power to it; which, like every other moral error, has been of fatal effect in art" (4.201-202). According to Ruskin, far different subjects should appear in religious painting, for he would have it portray the highest form of Vital Beauty in man— the effects of spirit upon body.

The beauty of living things, therefore, not only provides criteria for what the painter should avoid but also instructs him what to seek. In landscape, for example, it demands signs of energy, strength, and growth in trees and vegetation. Ruskin's conception of Vital Beauty thus accounts for the care with which the first and fifth volumes of *Modern Painters* explain the principles of tree form: only by teaching his audience to recognize signs of life in growing things can Ruskin hope to create a correct taste in landscape, an appreciation of beauty. His belief in Vital Beauty also explains his emphasis in *The Seven Lamps of Architecture* that beauty must depend upon natural form, for, according to him, the architect can only learn to express energy in structure and decoration by observing the power and life of natural forms. Vital Beauty also provides criteria for animal painting, requiring that the artist convey appearances, not only of physical energy and health, but also of consciousness or such intelligence as the subject may possess. Ruskin's praise of Sir Edwin

Landseer's *Old Shepherd's Chief Mourner* in the first volume of *Modern Painters* reveals his attitude toward Vital Beauty in animals:

> Here the exquisite execution of the glossy and crisp hair of the dog, the bright sharp touching of the green bough beside it, the clear painting of the wood of the coffin and the folds of the blanket, are language—language clear and expressive in the highest degree. But the close pressure of the dog's breast against the wood, the convulsive clinging of the paws, which has dragged the blanket off the trestle, the total powerlessness of the head laid, close and motionless, upon its folds, the fixed and tearful fall of the eye in its utter hopelessness, the rigidity of repose which remarks that there has been no motion nor change in the trance of agony since the last blow was struck on the coffin-lid . . . these are all thoughts —thoughts by which the picture is separated at once from hundreds of equal merit, as far as mere painting goes. (3.88-89)

The glossy, crisp hair of the dog indicates its physical health and vitality, but Ruskin concerns himself far more with qualities in the picture that express the animal's sorrow and loneliness. The painting, which is not as mawkish as much of the artist's later work, conveys the simple fact that the dog remains alone, its head resting on the coffin, after all others have left; and anyone who has ever seen a dog whose master has left it behind can admit that the picture, though not to modern taste, is not excessively sentimental. Ruskin, however, would take the reading farther than I have, finding human qualities, human virtues, in the animal's bearing; and at this point, most people today, except dog fanciers, would part company with the great Victorian. But whether one likes the painting or not, one must notice that the primary characteristic Ruskin admires is its ability to convey an emotion with restraint: all the signs that he interprets indicate past movements; now all is still, all is in repose.

Of far greater importance to his art criticism are the criteria which Vital Beauty provides for the painting of human beings. Ruskin's words of praise in his *Academy Notes* for Arthur Hughes's *April Love* (R. A., 1856; see Plate 17) indicate that he believes this painter, an associate though not a member of the Pre-Raphaelite Brotherhood, has succeeded in portraying feminine beauty: "Exquisite in every way; lovely in colour, most subtle in the quivering expression of the lips, and sweetness of the tender face, shaken, like a leaf by winds upon its dew, and hesitating back into peace"(14.68). Upon examining this painting (which William Morris purchased from the artist) one perceives that Ruskin is praising, once again, a restrained, quiet representation of feeling. Similarly, Ruskin's praise in the *Academy Notes* for several of Millais's works reveals a preference for subtle depictions of quiet emotion. For example, his delight in this painter's *Autumn Leaves* (R. A., 1856), which he considered "the most poetical work the painter has yet conceived" (14.66), derives, one is led to believe, both from its "perfectly painted twilight"(14.67) and the lovely expressions of quiet reverie on the faces of the four girls. Again, his excessive praise of Millais's *The Rescue* (R. A., 1855), a painting of a fireman returning two young children to their joyful mother, was evoked both by the impassive figure of the rescuer and the noble emotion on the mother's face. Pensiveness, joy, nobility

—the expression of all these, believes Ruskin, creates human beauty.

Perhaps the finest example of the kind of serene emotion Ruskin desired in art occurs in Giotto's Arena Chapel frescos in Padua. Between 1853 and 1860 he composed a series of commentaries to accompany the Arundel Society's reproductions of Giotto's paintings of the lives of Mary and Christ—the editors of the *Library Edition* have included the illustrations with Ruskin's text. Although he occasionally points out the artist's shortcomings, he more frequently lauds the painter's superb images of spiritual beauty. He thus praises the "submissive grace"(24.96) of the two standing apostles in the panel devoted to *The Washing of the Feet*; and of *The Meeting at the Golden Gate* (of Joachim and Anna) he writes: "The face of St. Anna, half seen, is most touching in its depth of expression; and it is very interesting to observe how Giotto has enhanced its sweetness, by giving a harder and grosser character than is usual with him to the heads of the other two principal female figures (not but that this cast of feature is found frequently in the figures of somewhat earlier art), and by the rough and weatherbeaten countenance of the entering shepherd"(24.58). Ruskin finds that despite the painter's limited means, his restraint produces nobly powerful images of human beauty, and although he admits that Giotto cannot depict physical beauty very well(24.68), he believes his skill and restraint portray the more important beauties of the spirit—the admiration, hope, and love necessary to great art—better than could painters of the Renaissance. Emphasizing how much this great artist's handling of subject differs from that of later men, he comments about *The Salutation*:

Of majestic women bowing themselves to beautiful and meek girls, both wearing gorgeous robes in the midst of lovely scenery, or at the doors of Palladian palaces, we have enough; but I do not know any picture which seems to me to give so truthful an idea of the action with which Elizabeth and Mary must actually have met,—which gives so exactly the way in which Elizabeth would stretch her arms, and stoop and gaze into Mary's face, and the way in which Mary's hand would slip beneath Elizabeth's arms, and raise her up to kiss her. I know not any Elizabeth so full of intense love, and joy, and humbleness; hardly any Madonna in which tenderness and dignity are so quietly blended. (24.69-70)

This praise handily summarizes Ruskin's notions of the highest form of Vital Beauty in man, for it emphasizes the way quiet, imaginatively conceived gesture, gentle expression, and lofty theme produce the highest beauty. The emphasis upon the spiritual, which remains implicit in many of Ruskin's critiques of Giotto, appears most overtly in his praise for *The Raising of Lazarus*: "Later designers dwell on vulgar conditions of wonder or horror, such as they could conceive likely to attend the resuscitation of a corpse; but with Giotto the physical reanimation is the type of a spiritual one, and, though shown to be miraculous, is yet in all its deeper aspects unperturbed, and calm in awfulness" (24.88). Grasping the spiritual, and particularly the typological and symbolical, significance of Christ's miracle, this great artist presents the essential and most noble reactions to the event. In this particular panel, the painter sets his scene not in time and space but, more appropriately, in the realm of the spirit, and he

176

thus portrays his important subject from the vantage point of eternal order, eternal peace, and eternal life. Hence in this picture of the spirit animating flesh the principle of Vital Beauty appears most clearly, for the rebirth of Lazarus is the image of the way the spirit creates beauty in fallen flesh. We here perceive the principle at the heart of Ruskin's delight in the fact that Giotto rendered admiration, tenderness, joy, dignity, and love—the noble feelings which produce noble beauty—so excellently. Here as in his theoretical writing Ruskin places emphasis upon the ascendancy of face over body, spirit over flesh, and love over all. The spirit gives life, and hence the spirit creates beauty.

In the final volume of *Modern Painters* (1860), after Ruskin had abandoned his early religion and much of its corollary puritanism, he expounded a new humanism that provided no place for his earlier belief that body and spirit necessarily exist in a state of conflict, or that the human body weakened and submissive is beautiful. His changed attitudes led him to dispraise medieval Christian art for the same tendency to emphasize the spiritual and to show the body outworn that he himself had earlier advocated. Writing fourteen years after *Modern Painters*, Volume II, Ruskin would say that man's "nature is nobly animal, nobly spiritual—coherently and irrevocably so; neither part of it may, but at its peril, expel, despise, or defy the other"(7.264). But in the earlier volume he emphasizes that human beauty depends entirely on the spiritual dimensions of man. In each of the three cases Ruskin mentions, the spirit is expressed upon the features, and it is not the human face itself which is beautiful, but only the face as symbol, as tablet upon which the mind and spirit can inscribe their images. His theory that mind and spirit create human beauty permits him to perform a tour de force, the formulation of a theory of human visible, material beauty based on that which is invisible and immaterial.

Expression is also the principle of Typical Beauty. In both Typical and Vital Beauty the physical object expresses and represents the immaterial. In both forms of the beautiful, the material object, that which is directly perceived, whether it be a human face suffused by joy and nobility or a sweep of Alpine snow glorying in unity and moderation, is a symbol through which, or on which, appear the signs of spiritual law. Vital Beauty expresses spirit, mind, and the energy of life, all informed, ultimately, by God. Typical Beauty expresses the nature of God. The twin, and in this case interchangeable, ideas of symbolization and expression grant Ruskin the means of reconciling material and immaterial, for they grant him a way of showing that the beautiful object is beautiful, as far as it is beautiful, because it is spiritual. These ideas of symbolization and expression permit Ruskin to state that beauty is, in the full sense of the word, essential, and they also allow him to defend the pleasures of aesthetic perception as moral, even religious exercises.

But the religious beliefs in which these aesthetic theories were rooted changed, and when they changed it became difficult for Ruskin to retain his theories in their original form. His loss of belief most strongly affected the theory of Typical Beauty; for after Ruskin lost his early belief, his more theological aesthetic became both intellectually untenable and emotionally uncongenial. Ruskin added a note to his chapter on Typical Beauty in 1883, many years after he had to some extent regained his faith, and in this note he in-

formed the reader that typical now meant "any character in material things by which they convey an idea of immaterial ones"(4.76n). The central theological principle is gone, and once it had departed the theory of Typical Beauty lost all its force; for whereas one can hold that the symbolization in material things of moral qualities is beautiful, unless one can also hold that such symbolization is universal and intentional—a law of nature—beauty becomes a matter of subjective responses. It was thus that the explanation of beauty which most emphasized the objective, universal nature of aesthetic qualities became, once Ruskin lost his faith, an implicitly subjective, personal theory. Vital Beauty, on the other hand, fared somewhat better when Ruskin's beliefs changed, for based as it was on an Aristotelian notion of the happiness of function, it could easily be modified. To retain the theory of Vital Beauty Ruskin had only to return the central idea of function to its original Aristotelian acceptation and the theory could stand independently.

Ruskin's aesthetic theories are the product and the type of irreconcilable dilemmas in his thought. When he wrote the second volume of *Modern Painters*, he wished to take into account the subjective nature of beauty and yet make it a universal, objective phenomenon. Having begun with the premise that emotion is the basis of art, beauty, and morality, he wished to avoid the disordering, as well as the subjective, nature of emotion. And, arguing from the principle that the physical, the material, is only dross, he wished to show that the beauty of physically existing things is of greater value than the things themselves.

# CHAPTER THREE

# Ruskin's Theories of the Sublime and Picturesque

I was one day admiring one of the falls of the Clyde; and ruminating upon what descriptive term could be most fitly applied to it, I came to the conclusion that the epithet "majestic" was the most appropriate. While I was still contemplating the scene a gentleman and a lady came up, neither of whose faces bore much of the stamp of superior intelligence, and the first words the gentleman uttered were "It is very majestic." I was pleased to find such a confirmation of my opinion, and I complimented the spectator upon the choice of his epithet, saying that he had used the best word that could have been selected from our language: "Yes, sir," replied the gentleman, "I say it is very majestic: it is sublime, it is beautiful, it is grand, it is picturesque."—"Ay (added the lady), it is the prettiest thing I ever saw." I own that I was not a little disconcerted.

—Samuel Taylor Coleridge[1]

[1] *Coleridge's Shakespearean Criticism*, ed. T. M. Raysor, 2nd ed., 2 vols. (London and New York, 1960), II, 37.

## I. Ruskin's theory of the sublime

RUSKIN used his theory of the sublime, like the theory of beauty which it complements, to solve the problem of the role of emotion in beauty and art. Ruskin's theoretical formulations of the sublime changed during the writing of *Modern Painters*, and the course of this change is an index of his attempts to find place for the disordering, subjective elements of emotion in his aesthetic system. Since he at first believed that his notion of beauty could embrace what earlier authors had relegated to the sublime, he thought his aesthetic would not require a theory of sublimity. In the first volume of *Modern Painters*, when Ruskin is outlining his theory of art, he pauses to inform the reader why he has neither taken any notice of the sublime in art nor once used the term:

> The fact is, that sublimity is not a specific term,—not a term descriptive of the effect of a particular class of ideas. Anything which elevates the mind is sublime, and elevation of mind is produced by the contemplation of greatness of any kind. . . . Sublimity is, therefore, only another word for the effect of greatness upon the feelings;—greatness, whether of matter, space, power, virtue, or beauty. . . . The sublime is not distinct from what is beautiful, nor from other sources of pleasure in art, but is only a particular mode and manifestation of them. (3.128,130)

When Ruskin firmly denies that beauty and sublimity are separate and distinct aesthetic categories, he departs from Addison, Burke, and Wordsworth, the writers who contributed most to his conception of the

sublime. He is prompted to disagree with his predecessors, because, in keeping with his characteristic desire to derive all aesthetics from the unity of the human spirit, Ruskin wishes to emphasize that the human mind receives undivided pleasures from nature and art. He was not, however, long able to maintain this unified conception of aesthetic effects, and, already, by the next volume of *Modern Painters*, he had reverted, in the manner of earlier theorists, to contrasting beauty and sublimity. The manuscripts of the second and third volumes of *Modern Painters* contain sections on the sublime, which the editors of the *Library Edition* have included in appendices for the appropriate volumes. Although Ruskin did not use these sections in which he partially formulated his own theory of the sublime, his remarks throughout the second and later volumes make it clear that the omitted sections represent Ruskin's true position, and that they reveal the changes which had taken place in his conception of sublimity. In one of the most interesting of the sections originally intended for the second volume, Ruskin contradicted his first view that sublimity can merely be a mode of the beautiful:

> It will readily, I believe, be admitted that many things are sublime in the highest degree, which are not in the highest degree beautiful, and *vice versâ*; *i.e.* that the two ideas are distinct, and one is not merely a particular form or state of the other. (4.369)

This statement shows that Ruskin now accepts that beauty and sublimity are distinct forms of aesthetic pleasure; and, as we shall see, his uses of the terms "sublime" and "sublimity" make it clear that he also tended to oppose the sublime to the beautiful.

Ruskin reversed his initial position, returning to older conceptions of sublimity, because, like the eighteenth-century theorists who first used the sublime as a separate category, he had discovered the need for a means of complementing a classicistic theory of calm, ordered beauty. Ruskin began *Modern Painters* with a partially developed philosophy of beauty which, he thought, would encompass previous notions of both beauty and sublimity; but, in fact, once his ideas of the beautiful had taken form in the second volume of *Modern Painters*, it appeared that they excluded too much; and so, repeating the procedure of the eighteenth-century originators of the sublime, Ruskin used a second aesthetic category to include the pleasures of nature and art which he himself enjoyed so much but which he could not consider beautiful—the pleasures of strong, even violent emotion, of asymmetry, of the awesome, the terrible, and the vast.

That Ruskin tried and failed to create a unified, encompassing system of aesthetics indicates the transitional nature of his position in the history of aesthetics and art theory. It was paradoxical and yet inevitable that after English critics had first opposed beauty to sublimity they would have next attempted to reconcile the two categories once the sublime had become the dominant concern of aesthetic speculation. The sublime allowed the critics to discuss sources of aesthetic pleasure—particularly violent emotional reactions—which they excluded from neoclassical conceptions of beauty. When, however, the sublime dominated mid- and late eighteenth-century English aesthetics, notions associated with the sublime affected the older, neoclassical theories of beauty. Under the influence of the sublime, writers on aesthetics came to believe that beauty was

a matter of emotion and not reason, and that, moreover, it should be described in terms of an emotional
reaction and not in terms of qualities residing in the
perceived object. After changes in conceptions of the
beautiful had removed the basic opposition between
sublime emotions and the qualities of beauty, the way
was open for theorists to bring ideas of beauty and sublimity closer together. If one looks at the history of the
sublime, one can see how it served to introduce new
sources of beauty into modern Western thought. In the
sixteenth century few considered mountains very attractive; in the eighteenth century many were captivated by their sublimity, if not their beauty; and in the
twentieth century most people would regard the usual
sources of eighteenth-century sublimity—mountains,
seas, and skies—as sources of beauty. A parallel change
in theories of sublimity has also taken place in this century, and the usual approach is to merge the sublime
with the beautiful, or to deny that it exists as an aesthetic category.[2] Ruskin, in 1843, wanted to unite these

[2] R. G. Collingwood, son of Ruskin's biographer and himself a prominent interpreter of Ruskin as well as an aesthetician in his own right,
presented, at different stages in his career, two twentieth-century approaches to the problem of beauty and sublimity. In his *Outlines of a
Philosophy of Art* (1925), he attempted to unify sublimity and beauty,
making the sublime an "elementary form of the beautiful." Sublimity
"is beauty which forces itself upon our mind, beauty which strikes us
as it were against our will and in spite of ourselves, beauty which we
accept passively and have not discovered. . . . The sublime is the first
and most elementary form of the beautiful. Sublimity is the mere
revelation of beauty as beauty, the inrush of aesthetic experience."
(*Essays in the Philosophy of Art*, ed. Alan Donagan [Bloomington,
Ind., 1964], pp. 78-79.) In his later *Principles of Art* (1938), however,
Collingwood took a basically Crocean position and stated that the
term "beauty" is merely used to express admiration and consequently
has no aesthetic implication ([Oxford, 1963], pp. 38-39). Both points
of view develop from the idea that beauty is an emotion: Collingwood
thus first believed that since both beauty and sublimity are a matter
of emotional experience, they are forms of the same emotion. He later
assumed, with Croce, that since beauty is merely the successful expres-

two forms of aesthetic experience, but his conservative notions of the beautiful prevented his effecting a satisfactory synthesis.

Since Ruskin's ideas of the sublime draw heavily upon previous writers, it will be useful and appropriate to examine briefly the history of the sublime before considering the details and changes of Ruskin's own theories. He was familiar from childhood with the writings of Addison and Johnson, both of whom discuss important aspects of theories of the sublime; and before beginning *Modern Painters* Ruskin had become well acquainted with Burke, whose treatise was one of the most influential and original aesthetic statements of the eighteenth century. Perhaps of equal importance to Ruskin's notions of sublimity was his early and continued reading of poets, such as Young and Wordsworth, who presented images of the natural sublime about which the theorists and critics had written.

---

sion of emotion, and since all art is expression, to say that something was beautiful only expressed a judgment that this something was a good work of art. Therefore, the term "beauty," and its corollary term, "sublimity," were abandoned, for their use only suggested the presence of what Collingwood felt were nonexistent problems.

Another twentieth-century aesthetician, E. F. Carritt, *The Theory of Beauty* (1914) (6th ed., London, 1962), decided after a detailed discussion that the term "sublime" was too vague to admit of much useful application. In answer to Carritt, a recent writer on this subject, F. R. Sparshott, suggests that "The awe in which we located the distinctive reaction to the sublime is close to the effect ascribed by Rudolf Otto (1917) to 'the holy'; and perhaps advances in the psychology of religion stand the best chance of carrying the study of sublimity beyond the 'indulgence in poetic fiction' which Kant censured." (*The Structure of Aesthetics* [Toronto, 1963], pp. 80-81.) Lastly, the effect of the eighteenth-century sublime on modern aesthetic theory appears with particular clarity in D. W. Prall's statement in *Aesthetic Judgment* (1929) that "One is always struck by great beauty, the feeling is called forth suddenly by a blow upon the senses. Instead of saying that we feel something, we say that something makes us feel, that something strikes us" ([New York, 1967], pp. 5-6).

The discussion of the sublime was perhaps the single most important concern of eighteenth-century British aesthetics; but despite the frequency, or possibly because of the frequency, with which the term appears in eighteenth- and nineteenth-century critical and creative literature, it had no one meaning that would have satisfied its many uses. According to Samuel Holt Monk, whose study of the eighteenth-century sublime is a landmark in modern recognition of the importance of this aesthetic idea, "No single definition of the term would serve in any single decade for all writers . . . ; but the word naturally expressed high admiration, and usually implied a strong emotional effect, which, in the latter years of the century, frequently turned on terror."[3] The origins and functions of the sublime explain why it meant so many things to so many critics. Critics used the sublime as a category in which they could place aesthetic pleasures excluded from neoclassical ideas of beauty. Furthermore, the sublime itself had arisen in sources as different as a new notion of moral psychology, the rediscovery of a Greek rhetorician, and a theological controversy over whether or not the earth was a ruin which recorded man's fall from grace.

In her *Mountain Gloom and Mountain Glory: The Development of the Aesthetics of the Infinite* (1959), Marjorie Hope Nicolson has shown how the theological controversy over the earth's present form, which engaged or influenced most of the important theologians, scientists, and men of letters of the late seventeenth and early eighteenth centuries, created a great interest in the natural sublime. When Thomas Burnet, Master of the Charterhouse and chaplain to King William, published his *Sacred Theory of the Earth* in 1681, he had

[3] Monk, *The Sublime*, p. 233.

hoped to add to science and theology by citing an alternate Biblical tradition which held that the earth, until the Deluge, had been a smooth, featureless, perfectly proportionate sphere, but that afterward it was marred by mountains and scarred by the deep, uneven beds of rivers and seas. According to Miss Nicolson, Burnet

> was convinced that the terrestrial globe of the 1680's was not identical with the original world. Its gross irregularities and lack of symmetry offended his sense of proportion; "there appearing nothing of Order, or any regular Design in its Parts, it seems reasonable to believe that it was not the Work of Nature, according to her first Intention, or according to the first Model that was drawn in Measure and Proportion by the Line and by the Plummet, but a secondary Work, and the best that could be made of broken Materials. . . . [Both earth and moon are] in my Judgment the Image or Picture of a great Ruin, and have the true aspect of a World lying in its Rubbish."[4]

But, as Miss Nicolson has also shown, Burnet was a paradoxical man in a paradoxical age; for although he was prompted to condemn the mountains and seas of the earth on theological grounds, he was simultaneously attracted to them; and in his attraction we have the beginnings of landscape feeling, and of the love of the powerful and asymmetrical, which so moved Ruskin and his predecessors. In a physico-theology that became the expanding, changing work of a lifetime appear the interests that were characteristic of later writers on the sublime:

[4] Nicolson, *Mountain Gloom and Mountain Glory*, pp. 196-197.

Burnet was "rapt" and "ravished" by the vast, the grand, the majestic. Before vastness he experienced the awe and wonder he had associated with God. But he could not understand his own emotions. He knew that his response was not to "Beauty." On every possible occasion, he sharply differentiated between response to Beauty and the new emotions inspired by the grandeur of Nature. Vast and irregular mountains were not beautiful, but, except for the vast and irregular night skies, nothing had ever moved Burnet to such awe or so led his mind to thoughts of God and infinity as did the mountains and the sea.[5]

Burnet's interest in the overpowering aspects of nature, his concern with the effects of this awesomeness on man, his relation of this awe to religion, and his opposition of this new rapturous emotion to beauty prepared for a new aesthetic. Addison, Steele, Joseph Warton, Young, Wordsworth, and Coleridge, among many others, read and were moved by Burnet's *Sacred Theory*. In addition, the controversy that his ideas provoked, when theologians resisted the idea that the earth was a ruin, made his notions a matter of common currency among theologians, scientists, and writers, and turned their attentions to the attractiveness of the external world of mountains and seas.

Although there is no evidence that he read Burnet, we may point out in passing that Ruskin himself was not only concerned with the kind of approach to nature that Burnet had made important but also that in the

---

[5] *Ibid.*, p. 215. "The greatest Objects of Nature are, methinks, the most pleasing to behold; and next to the Great Concave of the Heavens, and those boundless Regions where the Stars inhabit, there is nothing that I look upon with more Pleasure than the wide Sea and the Mountains of the Earth" (p. 214).

fourth volume of *Modern Painters* he frequently dwells on the possibility that the earth is a ruin of a once greater and more perfect beauty. At one point in the fourth volume, which purports to be about mountain beauty but which often verges on a physico-theology, Ruskin asks: "From what first created forms were the mountains brought into their present condition? . . . The present conformation of the earth appears dictated, as has been shown in the preceding chapters, by supreme wisdom and kindness. And yet its former state must have been different from what it is now; as its present one from that which it must assume hereafter. Is this, therefore, the earth's prime into which we are born: or is it, with all its beauty, only the wreck of Paradise?"(6.177). In addition to an interest, similar to Burnet's, in a now vanished state of the earth, Ruskin also parallels his predecessor when he creates "appalling" images of nature in ruins.[6]

6 "There are many spots among the inferior ridges of the Alps, such as the Col de Ferret, the Col d'Anterne, and the associated ranges of the Buet, which, though commanding prospects of great nobleness, are themselves very nearly types of all that is most painful to the human mind. Vast wastes of mountain ground, covered here and there with dull grey grass or moss, but breaking continually into black banks of shattered slate, all glistening and sodden with slow tricklings of clogged, incapable streams; the snow water oozing through them in a cold sweat, and spreading itself in creeping stains among their dust; ever and anon a shaking here and there, and a handful or two of their particles or flakes trembling down, one sees not why, into more total dissolution; leaving a few jagged teeth, like the edges of knives eaten away by vinegar, projecting through the half-dislodged mass from the inner rock, keen enough to cut the hand or foot that rests on them, yet crumbling as they wound, and soon sinking again into the smooth, slippery, glutinous heap, looking like a beach of black scales of dead fish, cast ashore from a poisonous sea; and sloping away into the foul ravines, branched down immeasurable slopes of barrenness, where the winds howl and wander continually, and the snow lies in wasted and sorrowful fields, covered with sooty dust, that collects in streaks and stains at the bottom of all its thawing ripples. I know no other scenes so appalling as these in storm, or so woful in sunshine" (6.158-159).

Burnet's emphasis on external nature and the pleasantly awed reaction it produces in the observer prepared the way for the reception of Longinus's fifth-century fragmentary treatise on the rhetorical sublime. Although there were at least five editions or translations of Longinus during the seventeenth century, critics appear to have paid little attention to the work until Burnet's writings demanded a new vocabulary which Longinus was able to provide. When Boileau translated Longinus's *Peri Hupsous* in 1674, he made available a critical terminology which could be applied to the new interest in external nature which was soon to come into prominence. But although the grand or high style of rhetoric had from its origin the purpose of arousing emotion, critics had to effect a transference of terms from the Longinian rhetorical sublime to the aesthetic natural sublime of the theorists. As Samuel Holt Monk has pointed out: "To write on the sublime style is to write on rhetoric; to write on sublimity is to write on aesthetic. The sublime style is a means to an end; sublimity is an end in itself."[7] Although the terminology of the sublime was rapidly translated from rhetoric to aesthetics, many influential writers on sublimity, including Addison and Shaftesbury, did not employ the word "sublime," and instead used such partial synonyms as "the great," "the unlimited," "the majestic," and "the stupendous."

To John Dennis, Pope's Sir Tremendous Longinus, must go the credit of initiating a sophisticated introduction of Longinian terminology into an aesthetic of the sublime. Dennis's *The Grounds of Criticism in Poetry* (1704) continued trends which Burnet had begun, but also added new important emphases. He con-

[7] Monk, *The Sublime*, p. 12.

tinued the separation of the beautiful and the sublime, and he also maintained the association of the sublime with religious awe. Dennis's most important contribution to the theory of the sublime was that he was the first critic to pay much attention to the effect the sublime object had upon the beholder.[8] According to Miss Nicolson, Dennis's originality lay in the fact that he based his conceptions of sublimity "not upon rhetorical theories but upon his own experience and upon attitudes native to the English, almost unknown to the French."[9] Perhaps most important, Dennis was also the first writer to introduce terror into considerations of the sublime.

Although Dennis was perhaps the most original theorist of the sublime in the first half of the eighteenth century, Joseph Addison had far more influence upon his contemporaries. Since Ruskin knew Addison's writings from childhood, it will be doubly useful to examine the passage in *Spectator* 412 (1712) in which Addison defines his notion of greatness, lists the usual sources of natural sublimity, and explains the psychological mechanism of the aesthetic reaction to sublimity:

> By greatness I do not only mean the bulk of any single object but the largeness of a whole view considered as one entire piece. Such are the prospects of an open champaign country, a vast uncultivated desert, of huge heaps of mountains, high rocks and precipices, or a wide expanse of waters, where we are not struck with the novelty or beauty of the sight but with that rude kind of magnificence which

[8] *Ibid.*, p. 45.
[9] Nicolson, *Mountain Gloom and Mountain Glory*, p. 281.

appears in many of these stupendous works of nature. Our imagination loves to be filled with an object, or to grasp at anything that is too big for its capacity. We are flung into a pleasing astonishment at such unbounded views, and feel a delightful stillness and amazement in the soul at the apprehension of them.[10]

Addison here makes several points that continued to be important in later writings on the sublime. First, he states that in some way the sublime requires a unified magnificence. Second, he cites the usual mountains, deserts, and seas as the most sublime parts of external nature. And, lastly, he analyzes the sublime reaction or effect in terms of a pleasure caused by attempting to fill the mind by "too big" an object. Johnson, Gerard, and Burke, among others, provide similar though often more detailed examinations of the sublime effect. Dr. Johnson, for example, remarked in his "Life of Cowley" that the sublime was not within reach of the metaphysical poets, "for they never attempted that comprehension and expanse of thought which at once fills the whole mind, and of which the first effect is sudden astonishment, and the second rational admiration."[11] Neither Johnson nor Addison (who described feelings of "pleasing astonishment") believed, like Dennis, that sublimity created feelings of terror and horror in the observer. Most writers on the sublime before Burke agreed that the pleasant feelings of awe, delight, and admiration were the result of contemplating mountain

10 *Eighteenth-Century Critical Essays*, ed. Scott Elledge, 2 vols. (Ithaca, N.Y., 1961), I, 45.

11 *Lives of the English Poets*, 2 vols. (London and New York, 1925), I, 12.

ranges, vast seas, and the other usual examples of natural sublimity.

Edmund Burke, whose *Philosophical Enquiry into the Origin of our Ideas of the Sublime and Beautiful* was published in 1757, believed, however, that "terror is in all cases whatsoever . . . the ruling principle of the sublime";[12] and, in keeping with his conception of a violently emotional sublime, his idea of astonishment, the effect which almost all theorists mentioned, was more violent than that of his predecessors: "The passion caused by the great and sublime in *nature* . . . is Astonishment; and astonishment is that state of the soul, in which all its motions are suspended, with some degree of horror. In this case the mind is so entirely filled with its object, that it cannot entertain any other."[13] Since Ruskin, who knew and admired Burke's treatise, made it his point of departure for his own discussion of the sublime in the first volume of *Modern Painters*, it will be useful to look briefly at the most important points in Burke's aesthetic.

In addition to the emphasis which he places on terror, Burke is important because he explained the opposition of beauty and sublimity by a physiological theory. He made the opposition of pleasure and pain the source of the two aesthetic categories, deriving beauty from pleasure and sublimity from pain. According to Burke, the pleasure of beauty has a relaxing effect on the fibers of the body, whereas sublimity, in

---

12 Burke, *On the Sublime*, p. 58.
13 *Ibid.*, p. 57. J. T. Boulton's introduction, which carefully relates Burke's ideas to those of his predecessors, is especially useful, because it enables one to perceive how much of the mainstream of eighteenth-century aesthetics and criticism Ruskin had learned about by reading Burke.

contrast, tightens these fibers. Thus, by using the authority of his ingenious theory, he could oppose the beautiful and sublime: "The ideas of the sublime and the beautiful stand on foundations so different, that it is hard, I had almost said impossible, to think of reconciling them in the same subject, without considerably lessening the effect of the one or the other upon the passions."[14] Burke's use of this physiological theory of beauty and sublimity makes him the first English writer to offer a purely aesthetic explanation of these effects; that is, Burke was the first to explain beauty and sublimity purely in terms of the process of perception and its effect upon the perceiver.

The writings of Addison, Burke, and Johnson, and others with whom Ruskin was familiar, contained two themes particularly important to his own conceptions of the sublime. The first was that the sublime should be discussed in terms of its effects upon the perceiver. This concern with the person who enjoys sublimity marked an important change in the course of English aesthetics, since the reactions of the perceiver became, for the first time, more important than the qualities of the pleasing object; and indeed, this shift of critical interest is the history in outline of English aesthetics during the preromantic period. Classical, Renaissance, and eighteenth-century aestheticians who believed that beauty was derived from order defined the beautiful in terms of the qualities of the beautiful object. Thus, the proportions of the *Venus di Milo* and the proper mixture of unity and variety which it incorporates were, for these critics, the sources of its beauty. On the other hand, those eighteenth-century writers, such as Hume, who derived beauty from utility, and Alison,

14 *Ibid.*, pp. 113-114.

who derived it from association, suggest that aesthetics
should consider the role of the perceiver. But Hume
and Alison, and Reynolds, who derives beauty from
custom, are not concerned with an aesthetic reaction.
Rather they wish to discover what it is that makes certain qualities in a beautiful object pleasing. Thus, according to Hume, men adjudge certain human or
equine proportions to be beautiful because these particular proportions are the most efficient for the well-
being or usefulness of man and horse. On the other
hand, Alison believes that the observer finds certain
proportions beautiful merely because he has become
accustomed to them and because he has associated
pleasant thoughts with them. Although these critics no
longer placed complete emphasis on the formal qualities of the pleasing object, they did not examine very
deeply the process by which these qualities are perceived as beautiful. Dennis, Burke, and other formu-
lators of the theory of the sublime, who were primarily
concerned with the effect of the sublime object upon
the observer, therefore, introduced important new interests into English aesthetics; for theories of sublimity,
not theories of beauty, applied the psychological speculations of Hobbes, Locke, and Hume himself to aesthetics.[15] When the focus of aesthetic considerations

---

[15] Alexander Gerard, in 1759, attempted both to describe sublimity
in terms of qualities, the method usually reserved for discussions of the
beautiful, and to explain the psychological reaction to the sublime
qualities: "Objects are sublime, which possess *quantity*, or amplitude,
and *simplicity*, in conjunction. . . . When a large object is presented,
the mind expands itself to the extent of that object, and is filled with
one grand sensation, which totally possessing it, composes it into a
solemn sedateness and strikes it with deep silent wonder and admiration: it finds such a difficulty in spreading itself to the dimensions of
its object, as enlivens and invigorates its frame: and having overcome
the opposition which this occasions, it sometimes imagines itself present
in every part of the scene which it contemplates; and from the sense

moved from an interest in the qualities of the pleasing object to an interest in the internal emotional reaction caused by the perception of the object, the change was accompanied by an implicit acceptance of subjectivity in aesthetic theory—a subjectivity, which, as we have already seen, Ruskin tried to avoid in his theories of beauty.

Some of the implications which the new emphasis upon internal reactions had for aesthetics appear in Burke's examples of sublimity, among which he included power, obscurity, and privations, such as darkness and silence. Sublime darkness or obscurity are not, like the beautiful curves of a Greek urn or statue, isolable qualities of a particular object. They are rather, qualities which pervade an entire scene, qualities, moreover, which describe the observer's experiential, phenomenological relation to what he observes. Whereas the statue's lines exist independently of the spectator, obscurity, which relates to his manner of perceiving, does not. Many of Burke's examples of sublimity, in fact, cannot be equated with formal qualities of an object, but necessarily characterize that experienced relationship between the observer and the observed.

Turning to the works of Turner and Wordsworth—turning, that is, to the painter and poet whom Ruskin most admired during this early period when he formulated his own ideas about aesthetics—one encounters embodiments of Burke's descriptions of sublimity that make explicit this notion of a subjective, experiential

---

of this immensity, feels a noble pride, and entertains a lofty conception of its own capacity." (*An Essay on Taste* . . . [A Facsimile Reproduction of the third edition (1780) with an introduction by Walter J. Hipple, Jr.] [Gainesville, Fla., 1963], pp. 11-12.)

world. Turner's *Snow Storm: Steamboat off a Harbour's Mouth* (1842) (see Plate 1), one of the paintings in whose defense Ruskin began *Modern Painters*, plunges us into the midst of a storm at sea: the whirling vortex of water, sea-mist, and smoke draws us into the scene, making us look not at the storm but *through* it. The power, magnificence, obscurity, and awe of the Burkean formulation all present themselves as major components of the experience. But, again, the viewer, like the painter before him who immersed himself in the storm on the *Ariel*, does not see these qualities as qualities of an object or scene but as qualities of subjective experience. Furthermore, as Jack Lindsay has shown, Turner's similar early paintings, such as *Snowstorm: Hannibal and his Army Crossing the Alps* (1812) (see Plate 2), demonstrate the painter discarding earlier neoclassical schemes of composition in an attempt to fuse the elements of form, chiaroscuro, and color. "In their place he put a dynamic form of spiral, an explosive vortex, a field of force."[16] In other words, in place of the static composition, rational and controlled, that implies a conception of the scene-as-object, Turner created a dynamic composition that involved the spectator in a subjective relation to the storm. Similarly, certain passages in Wordsworth's *Excursion*, the poem which furnished the epigraph to *Modern Painters*, present us with the phenomenological world of sublime experience. Thus, although the poem frequently employs the term "sublime," mentioning, for instance, a "burst/Sublime of instrumental harmony," "unity sublime," and the "sublime ascent" of man's hopes, sublimity appears not so much in the use of the term as in the

16 *J.M.W. Turner: A Critical Biography* (New York, 1966), p. 120.

199

poet's presentation of sublime experience in the midst
of a majestic dynamic natural scene of which the spectator becomes a part.[17] Wordsworth immerses us in the
natural sublime, taking us out of the role of spectator,
making us sympathetic participants, in the passage
where the Solitary stirs the feelings of the narrator by
recalling the ecstatic joys of wandering amid the
tumult of mountain cataracts:

> How divine,
> The liberty, for frail, for mortal, man
> To roam at large among unpeopled glens
> And mountainous retirements . . .
> . . . regions consecrate
> To oldest time! and, reckless of the storm
> That keeps the raven quiet in her nest,
> Be as a presence or a motion—one
> Among the many there; and while the mists
> Flying, and rainy vapours, call out shapes
> And phantoms from the crags and solid earth
> As fast as a musician scatters sounds
> Out of an instrument; and while the streams
> (As at a first creation and in haste
> To exercise their untried faculties)
> Descending from the region of the clouds,
> And starting from the hollows of the earth
> More multitudinous every moment, rend
> Their way before them—what a joy to roam
> An equal among mightiest energies;
> And haply sometimes with articulate voice,
> Amid the deafening tumult, scarcely heard
> By him that utters it, exclaim aloud,

[17] *Works*, v, 146, 306, and 289.

"Rage on, ye elements! let moon and stars
Their aspects lend, and mingle in their turn
With this commotion (ruinous though it be)
From day to night, from night to day, prolonged!"[18]

The Solitary does not gaze, a spectator, upon nature-as-object; for unlike Gilpin, he is not in search of the picturesque. Instead, he immerses himself in nature-as-process, trying with his roaming descent, with his passionate exclamations, to make himself part of the scene he encounters. Many of Burke's "qualities" present themselves to our notice: "the mists/Flying and rainy vapours" exemplify obscurity, the "deafening tumult" loudness, and the "mightiest energies" magnificence and power. But our point is not that the Solitary notices these qualities in a scene before him, but that he immerses himself in the tumult, joining his energy for a brief moment to mightiest energies, as the power, tumult, and magnificence of nature make their incursions upon his consciousness. So powerfully do they act upon him, so powerfully does he project himself toward and into them, that he enters the scene as participant, as one who experiences the sublime. The Solitary's apostrophe to the raging elements suggests chaotic merging of earth, sky, and water—in short, the Turnerian vortex. But it is not the vortex which here chiefly represents the sublime experience. Using a narrative technique that is analogous to cinematic "panning," Wordsworth first places us high on the crags with the speaker, then brings us downward "from the region of the clouds," and finally plunges us into the tumult below. The visual organization, the Miltonic sonorous

18 *Ibid.*, p. 125.

verse, and the apostrophe in the manner of Lear (who also would participate in the energies of the universe) all involve us in the sublime experience. It was this kind of poetry and this kind of painting, then, which Burke's theoretical formulations imply; and it was these works, favorites of Ruskin himself, for which he would have to find adequate description in his critical theory.

In addition to the fact that the writers with whom Ruskin was familiar discuss sublimity in terms of its effects, they also characteristically make a clear division between the sublime and the beautiful. As a corollary of this opposition of the two aesthetic categories, beauty is often considered less important than sublimity. When Burke contrasts the sublime and the beautiful, for example, he clearly reveals that he believes beauty to be a weaker, feminine form of aesthetic pleasure:

> Sublime objects are vast in their dimensions, beautiful ones comparatively small; beauty should be smooth, and polished; the great, rugged and negligent; beauty should shun the right line, yet deviate from it insensibly; the great in many cases loves the right line, and when it deviates, it often makes a strong deviation; beauty should not be obscure; the great ought to be dark and gloomy; beauty should be light and delicate; the great ought to be solid, and even massive.[19]

In the first volume of *Modern Painters*, Ruskin agrees neither with Burke's separation of beauty and sublimity into two distinct aesthetic categories, nor with his presentation of beauty as less powerful or less important than sublimity. Ruskin wishes, as part of his

[19] Burke, *On the Sublime*, p. 124.

defense of painting, to demonstrate that beauty is important to human life, and, consequently, he could not admit the view that beauty was little more than prettiness. Since Ruskin believed that the perception of beauty was a moral and religious act, he could not permit the implicit depreciation of the beautiful which accompanied Burke's opposition of it to the sublime. The need to emphasize the importance of beauty, as well as his own characteristic preference for a unified aesthetic, prompted Ruskin's denial that the sublime was a separate and distinct aesthetic category.

In his attempt to associate beauty and sublimity more closely, Ruskin naturally transferred some of his views about beauty to his conception of the sublime. He believed, for example, that beauty, like sublimity, was a matter of disinterested emotion; and since he wished to emphasize disinterestedness, one of his major points about aesthetics, he allowed the ingenuity, but not the truth, of Burke's idea that the sublime is derived from pain and from the desire for self-preservation:

> It is not the fear, observe, but the contemplation of death; not the instinctive shudder and struggle of self-preservation, but the deliberate measurement of the doom, which is really great or sublime in feeling. . . . There is no sublimity in the agony of terror. (3.129)

This theoretical position marks a change from the attitudes of his youth, for, as the verse of his childhood and adolescence reveals, he had previously accepted the aesthetic of horror and congenial dread. For example, these lines he wrote in his fourteenth year refer to the pleasures of terror:

> It is a terror, yet 'tis sweet,
> Upon some broken brow
> To look upon the distant sweep
> Of ocean spread below. (2.4)

In contrast to this quatrain's use of natural sublimity, one also encounters Ruskin's interest in the more theatrical sublime—and delicious shudder—of Thomas Warton and the gothic novel. His long poem, "The Broken Chain," written the year before he began *Modern Painters*, contains the following horrific lines:

> The chapel vaults are deadly damp,
> Their air is breathless all;
> The downy bats they clasp and cramp
> Their cold wings to the wall;
> The bright-eyed eft, from cranny and cleft,
> Doth noiselessly pursue
> The twining light of the death-worms white,
> In the pools of the earth-dew. (2.153)

When Ruskin came to write the first volume of *Modern Painters*, however, he found he could accept neither Burke's straightforward emphasis on terror nor his physiological explanations. In addition to the fact that he no longer believed one could enjoy terror, he wished to show that sublimity was an aspect of beauty, and Burke's grounding beauty and sublimity in two opposing physiological reactions effectively contradicted Ruskin's unification of the two. Furthermore, Burke's explanation made both beauty and sublimity dependent upon physical causes, whereas Ruskin believed that aesthetic reactions, which take place in the theoretic, or contemplative, faculty, are primarily mental, not physical, in character.

Despite his reservations, in the first volume of *Modern Painters* Ruskin accepted many points which Burke and others had made about the sublime. First, Ruskin believed that the sublime is concerned with greatness, and, second, that it is a matter of emotion: "Sublimity is . . . only another word for the effect of greatness upon the feelings"(3.128). In addition, when he mentioned greatness of matter, space, power, and virtue (3.128), he chose the usual sources of the sublime. Finally, he maintained the traditional relation of religion, the idea of the holy, to sublimity.

In the second volume of *Modern Painters*, which appeared three years after the first, Ruskin accepted even more traditional conceptions of the sublime. Most important, he opposed beauty to sublimity. This opposition most clearly (and most appropriately) appears in the sections on typical beauty in which Ruskin discusses the beauties of order. In the section on the beauty of symmetry, for example, he contrasts this form of the beautiful to the sublimity produced by irregularity and asymmetry: "Where there is no symmetry, the effects of passion and violence are increased, and many very sublime pictures derive their sublimity from want of it, but they lose proportionally in the diviner quality of beauty"(4.127). From this statement it would appear that Ruskin not only contrasts beauty and sublimity but that he also allows that passion, violence, and asymmetry create pleasing effects. His acceptance of asymmetry apparently widens his initial definition of the sublime. The chapter on the typical beauty of infinity, on the other hand, contains another opposition between beauty and sublimity which is more in line with Ruskin's first idea that sublimity is merely the effect of greatness upon the feelings. Although writers from Burnet to

Burke and after had made the infinite one of the chief sources of sublimity, Ruskin concentrated on rather tame features of the infinite, such as its incorporation in variety and in curved lines. At the close of his chapter, however, he mentions a form of the infinite which creates the sublime: "Farther expressions of infinity there are in the mystery of Nature, and, in some measure, in her vastness; but these are dependent on our own imperfections, and therefore, though they produce sublimity, they are unconnected with beauty"(4.91).

The contrast between beauty and sublimity which appears in these chapters was to have been a major subject of the sections on sublimity which Ruskin stated that he would place in the second volume(4.312-313), but which he left incomplete and did not finally include. But whether or not Ruskin omitted his proposed definitions and discussions of sublimity because they would have overtly conflicted with his theories of the beautiful, his uses of the terms "sublime" and "sublimity" throughout the last four volumes of *Modern Painters* demonstrate that he not only came to accept the opposition of the sublime and the beautiful, but that he also made use of the sublime, as had eighteenth-century theorists, as an aesthetic catchall, as a category into which he could place forms of aesthetic emotion excluded from his theories of beauty.

In the last four volumes of *Modern Painters* and his other writings Ruskin employed the terms "sublime" and "sublimity" in most of their usual eighteenth-century acceptations. The basic notion that sublimity is derived from a large, vast unified object appears frequently, as, for example, when he states that "a mass of one species of tree is sublime"(4.96), and that "the greater the number of objects which . . . become mem-

bers of one another, the more extended and sublime is their unity"(4.96). This basic notion of the sublime as that which is simultaneously unified and vast appears throughout *Modern Painters*. In the fifth volume, for instance, Ruskin mentions a chapter in Michelet's work *L'Insecte*, which, he says, is "so vast in scope, and therefore so sublime"(7.232). The sublimity of magnitude, which he records in many of his Alpine drawings (see Plate 10), is the subject of an unused manuscript passage originally intended for the third volume of *Modern Painters*. There Ruskin describes a form of sublimity entirely dependent upon size for its effect:

> In order to produce these peculiar impressions of sublimity on the human mind, certain degrees of this material largeness are absolutely necessary. No beauty of design in architecture, or of form in mountains, will entirely take the place of what may be called "brute largeness." That is to say, of the actual superiority in feet and inches, over the size of Humanity, our constant standard, the general truth being that . . . the greatest effect of sublimity will be produced by the largest truth which can be clearly manifested to us. (5.434)

Although Ruskin may not have been aware of it, when he derived sublimity from the relation of the vast object and the size of the human observer, he opposed sublimity to beauty almost as strongly as did Burke's physiological theory. Whereas Ruskin tried to derive both typical and vital beauty from divine nature and law, he here based sublimity on the size of man—"our constant standard." It could be further argued that since Ruskin is here concerned with an individual sense of relation to the sublime object, he introduces an ele-

ment of subjectivity. The sublimity of magnitude, then, is not, like beauty, the incarnation of permanent qualities, the shadow of God; it is, if the shadow of anything, the reflected shadow of man, the feeling produced when man compares himself with something greater than himself.

Ruskin did not finally include this section on sublimity of size in *Modern Painters*, Volume III, but he had previously made similar remarks in *The Seven Lamps of Architecture* (1848), and he continued to express these views throughout his career. For example, he frankly made man his standard for sublimity in the first of the Oxford "Lectures on Landscape" (1871), in which he argued that all landscape receives its interest from the presence—actual or imagined—of man. Holding up a small stone before his listeners, he explained that the most magnificently pictured Alpine scene, if unrelated to humanity, would be no more a landscape than his little piece of rock; for, he insisted, there is no such quality as bigness or littleness without reference to man. Similarly, there is "no more sublimity—*per se* —in ground slope at an angle of forty-five, than in ground level; nor in a perpendicular fracture of a rock, than in a horizontal one. The only thing that makes the one more interesting to you in a landscape than the other, is that you could tumble over the perpendicular fracture—and couldn't tumble over the other" (22.14-15). In other words, sublimity derives from an envisaged practical effect upon man: the size of a mountain or the angle of its slope become sublime only in relation to man's size, capacities, and potential movement. It becomes clear, then, that for a scene to be sublime, the spectator must imaginatively place either himself or another human being within it.

This notion that the sublime requires an imagined human presence as an emotional "center" appears implicitly in Ruskin's many remarks on mountain sublimity. First of all, the mountain sublime is only partially produced by size; for, as Ruskin points out, it also comes from association of terror or danger. In the fourth volume, which is largely devoted to a discussion of mountain beauty, Ruskin writes of "sublime and threatening forms"(6.199), and mentions that "some sense of danger might always be connected with the most precipitous forms, and thus increase their sublimity"(6.135). Although Ruskin states that size has a role in the sublimity of mountains, he is more concerned with the emotional effects these mountains create in the observer, and it is, indeed, in terms of emotional effects that Ruskin most interestingly discusses the sublime.

Some of the emotions which Ruskin included under the class name "sublime" have little to do with his initial idea that sublimity is a name for the simple effect of greatness upon the feelings; and, although there is no evidence that he was influenced by Richard Payne Knight, Ruskin adopted a view of the sublime similar to that which Knight had presented in his *Analytical Inquiry into the Principles of Taste* (1790). According to Knight, "All sympathies, excited by just and appropriate expression of energetic passion; whether they be of the tender or violent kind, are alike sublime."[20] Ruskin's statement that "impressions of awe and sorrow" are "at the root of the sensation of sublimity"(7.119) suggests that, like Knight, he believed all emotions, gentle as well as extreme and violent, were sublime. The "sad sublime"(6.296), which he mentions in describing a melancholy scene, is an example of this

[20] 3rd ed. (London, 1806), pp. 371-372.

gentler form of sublimity which was not described in the first volume of *Modern Painters*. Ruskin also appears to have abandoned his original theory that sublimity was the emotional effect caused by greatness when he wrote that "in the shock and shiver of a strong man's features, under sudden and violent grief, there may be something of [the] sublime"(4.203). Grief, although more intense than sadness, is not necessarily the effect of greatness—unless Ruskin later defined greatness of cause merely in terms of a resultant intense emotional reaction.

Although Ruskin does allow that mild or gentle feelings, such as sadness, are sublime, he usually uses the term "sublime" to describe violent emotions, such as awe, terror, and horror. Again intensity of the emotion, rather than a powerful efficient cause of the emotion, is the central factor. For example, Ruskin wrote that when certain effects of a mountain environment are combined, "the result [upon the inhabitants of mountain districts] is even sublime in its painfulness"(6.410). Even painfulness was sublime. Ruskin's editors note that brief manuscript passages exist for a section on the sublimity of fear and horror(4.371); so it is likely that Ruskin intended to change his original position even more and accept the idea that fear and terror have a role in sublimity. His remarks that the suggestion of danger increases the sublimity of a precipice(6.135) would seem to support the conclusion that Ruskin felt that fear and terror have a role in the sublime. He also seems to have associated other emotions, or other qualities which stimulate emotions (he did not always distinguish between them), with the sublime, and he may even have considered them sources of the sublime. In the fourth volume of *Modern Painters* he wrote of

"sublime and threatening forms"(6.199) and also mentioned in the same passage the terrific, the strange, and the majestic. It is likely that these qualities and emotions entered Ruskin's later conceptions of sublimity. Ruskin also mentioned another kind of sublimity in the 1848 "Addenda" to the second volume, in which he wrote of Linnell's painting *Eve of the Deluge* that "its sublimity was that of splendour, not of terror"(4.334). We see here how casual Ruskin was in his use of the terms "sublime" and "sublimity," for whereas terror is an emotion, splendor is not; and, according to his own definition, it would have been proper to call the form of sublimity produced by splendor the sublime of admiration, awe, or wonder, or whatever he considered the effect of splendor upon the feelings. In view of the fact that Ruskin used these two terms in so many ways, it seems necessary to conclude that he not only reversed his earliest position, finally deciding that sublimity was a distinct aesthetic category, but also that, like previous writers, he used the sublime as an embracing aesthetic category in which he placed all forms of pleasing emotion; sorrow, grief, pain, horror, terror, awe, admiration, when contemplated, were all sublime.

Ruskin employs many of these meanings of the term "sublime" in *The Seven Lamps of Architecture*, which contains his most detailed formulation of a theory of sublimity. "The Lamp of Power," the chapter that explicates the "elements of sublime architecture"(8.110), warrants careful attention, since it not only grounds his uses of the term in a precisely formulated theory, but also applies this theory to the details of a sister art.[21]

[21] Such recognition that Ruskin wrote in detail about the sublime style demands particular attention, since architectural historians, who apparently cite him without carefully reading his works, frequently

This chapter on the stylistics of a sublime architecture opens significantly, not with remarks on the art of building, but with a discussion of its effect upon the human mind:

> In recalling the impressions we have received from the works of man . . . it often happens that we find a strange pre-eminence and durability in many upon whose strength we had little calculated, and that points of character which had escaped the detection of the judgment, become developed under the waste of memory. . . . In thus reverting to the memories of those works of architecture by which we have been most pleasurably impressed, it will generally happen that they fall into two broad classes: the one characterised by an exceeding preciousness and delicacy, to which we recur with a sense of affectionate admiration; and the other by a severe, and, in many cases, mysterious, majesty, which we remember with an undiminished awe, like that felt at the presence and operation of some great Spiritual Power. (8.100)

When Ruskin elucidated his theory of typical beauty he concentrated almost entirely upon elements in the beautiful that lay outside the mind of man. "The Lamp

charge he pays no attention to the actual appearance of buildings. For example, Carroll Meeks's, *The Railroad Station* (New Haven, 1956), which makes a fine attempt to define the style of nineteenth-century architecture as "picturesque eclecticism," pretty much dismisses Ruskin with the comment that "the most eloquent and prolific critic of the day . . . dealt less with visual effects than with moral qualities" (p. 7); and while this assertion may often be correct, it does not explain a complete neglect of Ruskin's precise statements about the specifics of architectural style here and in other places. Similarly, Roger B. Stein, *John Ruskin and Aesthetic Thought in America, 1840-1900* (Cambridge, Mass., 1967), spends little time on Ruskin's specific notions of style, makes no mention of his idea of sublime architecture, and characterizes *The Seven Lamps* as only "superficially" (p. 64) a work on architecture.

of Power," in contrast, opens with this discussion of the way we recollect in tranquillity emotions inspired by architecture. As we have already observed, when Ruskin writes about architecture, perhaps the most human of the arts, he always emphasizes its effects on man; and when setting forth an aesthetic theory concerning this sister art, he here dwells at length on association, memory, sympathy, and emotional effects. His emphasis that the most important reactions to the art of building occur deep within the mind and rise slowly into consciousness, bypassing the judgment, characterizes the subjective, human, pole of his aesthetic theories, and it is at this pole that he remains during this entire chapter.

For example, when continuing his essentially Burkean distinction between the two modes of architecture, he explains that their difference "is not merely that which there is in nature between things beautiful and sublime. It is, also, the difference between what is derivative and original in man's work. . . . [The original] depends for its dignity upon arrangement and government received from human mind, becomes the expression of the power of that mind, and receives a sublimity high in proportion to the power expressed"(8.101-102). Thus, whereas beauty in architecture derives from what exists external to man, architectural sublimity derives both from external nature and from the human imagination. Believing that "men cannot be taught to compose or to invent"(8.134), Ruskin only mentions briefly this highest element of imaginatively created power in architecture, and he therefore devotes most of his discussion to explaining how the architect can create sublimity by sympathizing "with the vast controlling powers of Nature herself"(8.102). Even when

213

writing of the way man draws upon natural sublimity, Ruskin does not chiefly emphasize qualities outside man. According to him, the structures which man erects should embody not only "worship and following" of the spirit of beauty but also that which builds earth's

> barren precipices into the coldness of the clouds, and lifts her shadowy cones of mountain purple into the pale arch of the sky; for these, and other glories more than these, refuse not to connect themselves, in his thoughts, with the work of his own hand; the grey cliff loses not its nobleness when it reminds us of some Cyclopean waste of mural stone; the pinnacles of the rocky promontory arrange themselves, undegraded, into fantastic semblances of fortress towers; and even the awful cone of the far-off mountain has a melancholy mixed with that of its own solitude, which is cast from the images of nameless tumuli on white sea-shores, and of the heaps of reedy clay, into which chambered cities melt in their mortality. (8.102-103)

Ruskin begins his comments on the natural sublime which the builder must emulate by writing of it as the incarnation, the bodying forth, of vast powers which lie outside man and which dwarf him. But as soon as he elaborates upon the sublimity of mountains and grey cliffs, he makes it apparent that nature considered purely external to the human consciousness does not much interest him. Instead, sounding much like the Associationist Alison, he holds up before us "this power and majesty, which Nature herself does not disdain to accept from the works of man"(8.103). Although he had been unwilling, two years earlier, to admit that human

associations play a role in the beautiful, here he readily emphasizes the importance to the sublime of what the human imagination confers upon the external world. In "Tintern Abbey," a poem often quoted by Ruskin, Wordsworth had proclaimed his continuing love for nature as he apprehends it with eye and ear—"both what they half create, / And what perceive." Harold Bloom comments of the phrase "half create," that though "the boundaries between man and nature have wavered, Wordsworth wishes to avoid the suggestion of the total absorption of nature into man."[22] Ruskin's theoretical statements about beauty mark his attempt to absorb man into a nature symbolic of God, but in *The Seven Lamps of Architecture* he has reversed himself, now making nature part of man. For when he emphasizes that nature accepts from human works that sublimity "transferred by association to the dateless hills"(8.103), he makes it clear that nature colored by human thought, nature as it exists within the mind of man, most interests him.

Having thus explained the subjective character of the natural sublime, Ruskin proceeds to detail the ways in which the architect can draw upon its power. The central principle of the architectural sublime, insists Ruskin, is "that the relative majesty of buildings depends more on the weight and vigour of their masses, than on any other attribute of their design: mass of everything, of bulk, of light, of darkness, of colour, not mere sum of any of these, but breadth of them"(8.134). He first considers the sublimity of "mere size," explaining that while it might be thought impossible to emulate nature in this respect, such a conclusion does not follow from

22 *The Visionary Company: A Reading of English Romantic Poetry* (Garden City, N.Y., 1963), p. 145.

the laws of human perception. Certainly, the architect must avoid contending with the size of natural objects: he must not build, for example, pyramids in the valley of the Chamouni. But as long as the human builder avoids such obvious comparisons of scale, he can achieve sublimity of magnitude: "The fact is, that the apprehension of the size of natural objects, as well as of architecture, depends more on fortunate excitement of the imagination than on measurements by the eye; and the architect has a peculiar advantage in being able to press close upon the sight such magnitude as he can command. There are few rocks, even among the Alps, that have a clear vertical fall as high as the choir of Beauvais; and if we secure a good precipice of wall, or a sheer and unbroken flank of tower, and place them where there are no enormous natural features to oppose them, we shall feel in them no want of sublimity of size"(8.103-104). Since impressions of size depend largely on the imagination, the artist who can control the imaginations of his audience can thus achieve sublimity of size. All that the architect requires, says Ruskin, are the financial resources and a site sufficient to reach "that degree of magnitude which is the lowest at which sublimity begins, rudely definable as that which will make a living figure look less than life beside it"(8.105).

Once the designer of buildings has determined to create a structure marked by sublimity, he must follow certain stylistic principles. First of all, his building "must have one visible bounding line from top to bottom, and from end to end"(8.106). Ruskin remarks that many writers have held that for a building to show its size, the observer must take it in all at once, but he believes that his principle of the continuous bounding line

is more central to the sublime style. He explains that the architect must take care not to break this bounding line with ledges or cornices that project too far, since they destroy the desired effect: "not because the building cannot be seen all at once,—for in the case of a heavy cornice no part of it is necessarily concealed— but because the continuity of its terminal line is broken, and the *length of that line*, therefore, cannot be estimated"(8.107). By thus emphasizing the effect of the building's profile upon our imagination, Ruskin applies to architecture the commonplace that the sublime object must be vast and uniform. He similarly draws upon conventional ideas of the sublime which emphasize uninterrupted regularity when he writes "that those buildings seem on the whole the vastest which have been gathered up into a mighty square"(8.108). Furthermore, the criterion of unbroken vastness requires that the architect in search of sublimity employ "breadth of surface" in his walls. In this manner, he can achieve the effect of "the flatness and sweep of great plains and broad seas"(8.109). What material the architect uses in a large building matters little, says Ruskin, so long as "the surface be wide, bold, and unbroken" (8.109). To create the effect of sublimity in smaller buildings, such as cottages, the architect must employ a bold masonry like "the rude and irregular piling of the rocky walls of the mountain cottages of Wales, Cumberland, and Scotland"(8.113). Lastly, the architect must deploy large masses of light and shadow, a "Rembrandtism"(8.117) in building, since "after size and weight, the Power of architecture may be said to depend on the quantity (whether measured in space or intenseness) of its shadow"(8.116). His emphasis upon broad masses of shadow leads Ruskin to praise deep-

set windows, the Gothic "method of decoration by shadow"(8.128), and anything which creates a "broad, dark, and simple"(8.135) effect. According to him, "It matters not how clumsy, how common, the means are, that get weight and shadow—sloping roof, jutting porch, projecting balcony, hollow niche, massy gargoyle, frowning parapet; get but gloom and simplicity, and all good things will follow in their place and time" (8.135). Both Ruskin's citation of these architectural details and his major emphasis upon massing of light and shadow reveal that he believed this art must work with height, breadth, *and* depth, shaping space to create a sense of the sublime. "The Lamp of Power," in other words, offered Victorian England a stylistic alternative to what Nikolaus Pevsner has described as the characteristic English emphasis upon linearity and "beautiful surface quality."[23] Although Ruskin has been accused of being both insular and little concerned with the visual appearance of architecture, his remarks in this chapter on power demonstrate that he recognized, as did few architects of his own age, the essential nature of architecture as a three-dimensional art. Twentieth-century architects have agreed with Ruskin, and, although many of his statements about beauty in architecture seem concerned with a kind of building quite foreign to our own century, his characterizations of sublimity, on the other hand, anticipate much of the modern movement. Both the work of Gropius, who considered himself a follower of Ruskin, and of Wright, who early knew all of Ruskin's major works, often seem to embody his conceptions of the architectural sublime: in particular, aspects of Gropius's 1914 model factory

[23] *The Englishness of English Art* (London, 1956), p. 90. See also, pp. 81-106.

in Cologne and Wright's early Larkin building and late Guggenheim Museum embody Ruskinian principles—whether or not they betray a direct influence.[24]

Ruskin's examples of architectural success and failure enable us to envisage even more clearly his conceptions of sublimity in building. According to him, "St. Peter's, among its many other errors, counts for not the least injurious its position on the slope of an inconsiderable hill"(8.103), an error in siting which lessens the sublimity of the church. Moreover, the recessed dome of this building, which from most vantage points does not allow the spectator to perceive the structure as a uniform mass, shows how a broken profile also destroys a potentially sublime effect. From the evidence of St. Peter's and the Duomo in Florence Ruskin concludes that church designers who want to achieve sublimity (as opposed to beauty) cannot employ domes or towers

[24] John Rosenberg's *The Darkening Glass*, pp. 71-76, most valuably explains not only Wright's early knowledge of Ruskin but also the earlier writer's influence upon the architect. Although Peter Blake, *Frank Lloyd Wright: Architecture and Space* (Baltimore, Md., 1960) makes no mention of Ruskin, his analysis of Wright's approach to designing a skyscraper reveals the similarity of the architect's ideas to those of Ruskin: "As a believer in an architecture close to nature, he had a hard time justifying a tall, upright, seemingly anti-nature building. . . . He solved this dilemma in a characteristic fashion, by going to the one source in nature which did suggest a way of building a tall structure: the form of a tree.

"In structural terms a tree is a vertical beam cantilevered out of the ground. Most of its mass is above ground, and most of the stresses applied to a tree—such as wind pressures and snow loads—are applied to it high up, close to its crown. The structural force that keeps a tree from toppling over is, of course, the restraint applied to its roots by the earth. . . .

"This sort of cantilever is, as a matter of fact, one of the simplest and most dramatic expressions of continuity for it represents a delicate balance of forces, each restraining the other through an infinite number of strands and fibers which make the tree a continuous organism. To Wright, the cantilever was also the 'most romantic, most free, of all principles of construction' " (pp. 86-87).

over their central portions, but instead should place high towers either at the west end or "better still, detached as a campanile"(8.107). When he emphasizes the importance of "one bounding line from base to coping" (8.107), he cites the Palazzo Vecchio as an example of a secular building which thus correctly employs a tower. In addition, this building's size, shape, siting, treatment of walls, and massing of shadow would all seem to exemplify the Ruskinian notion of architectural sublimity. Similarly, the Castle San Angelo in Rome and the Venetian Ducal Palace successfully employ a broad expanse of wall surface, correct siting, unbroken bounding lines, and a shape approaching the square.

Ruskin finishes his discussion of architectural sublimity, as he began it, with reference to the nature of mental impressions, emphasizing in both instances the slow yet inevitable workings of memory and emotional reactions. The chapter, which opens with an examination of the audience's reaction to architecture, closes by explaining the architect's reactions to his environment. According to Ruskin, the buildings the young, developing architect sees around him cripple his capacity to create powerful works:

> Of domestic architecture what need is there to speak? How small, how cramped, how poor, how miserable in its petty neatness is our best! . . . I know not how we can blame our architects for their feebleness in more important work; their eyes are inured to narrowness and slightness: can we expect them at a word to conceive and deal with breadth and solidity? They ought not to live in our cities; there is that in their miserable walls which bricks up to death men's imaginations. . . . An architect should live as

little in cities as a painter. Send him to our hills, and
let him study there what nature understands by a
buttress, and what by a dome. (8.136)

Ruskin, who will not accept any specific proportional
canon, holds that the architect must learn to compose
powerfully by sympathizing with the power, the energy, the life of nature. Like Frank Lloyd Wright after
him, he believes that the architect must therefore flee
the city, which stifles our sympathies, and dwell amid
the sublime natural features of earth. Once again in our
examination of Ruskin's aesthetics we return to what
we may call the primal, or archetypal, situation which
lies at the heart of so much of his writings: man, whether artist or spectator, stands alone in the presence of
nature, receiving emotional reactions that strengthen
his capacities for living. His notions of the development
of the architect, like his notions of beauty, sublimity,
and the moral effects of art, demand that man exist, if
only on rare occasion, in a felt relation to the exterior
world. His writings on the sublimity of architecture, the
pre-eminently human art, emphasize that man himself
must be the source of much of these vitalizing emotions
and sympathies. Although mountain peaks, broad
plains, and vast seas must exist outside man to provide
sources of life, man's associations and man's sense of
self must finally create the sublime.

## II. Two modes of the picturesque

CLOSELY related to the gentler forms of the sublime is
Ruskin's conception of the "noble picturesque," which
he presents in the fourth volume of *Modern Painters*.
Several times in the course of his writings he attempts
to explain the nature of what he felt to be a uniquely

modern aesthetic category characteristic of a uniquely modern style and subject matter in painting. In *The Seven Lamps of Architecture* he remarks upon the fact that signs of age appear pleasing to men, and that since the Renaissance, schools of art have arisen which concentrate upon such signs of age, thereby impressing upon "those schools the character usually and loosely expressed by the term 'Picturesque.'" Proposing to examine the nature of this art, he first points out that "probably no word in the language, (exclusive of theological expressions,) has been the subject of so frequent or so prolonged dispute; yet none remain more vague in their acceptance"(8.235). Here he may be referring to the Knight-Price controversy or, more likely, to the various definitions and usages of the term "picturesque" he had encountered in contemporary art periodicals and in the conversation of practitioners of the picturesque, such as his drawing masters J. D. Harding and Copley Fielding. Just how much Ruskin knew about the three main theorists of the picturesque, William Gilpin, Richard Payne Knight, and Uvedale Price, remains unclear.[25] Although his frequent discussions

[25] Among the more important works on the picturesque one may number the following: William Gilpin, *Three Essays: On Picturesque Beauty; On Picturesque Travel; and on Sketching Landscape: to which is Added a Poem, On Landscape Painting* (London, 1792); Richard Payne Knight, *An Analytical Inquiry into the Principles of Taste*, 3rd ed. (London, 1806); Uvedale Price, *An Essay on the Picturesque, as Compared with the Sublime and the Beautiful; and on the Use of Studying Pictures, for the Purpose of Improving Real Landscape*, rev. ed. (London, 1796). Secondary works include W. J. Hipple, Jr., *The Beautiful, the Sublime, and the Picturesque in Eighteenth-Century British Aesthetic Theory* (Carbondale, Ill., 1957); Christopher Hussey, *The Picturesque, Studies in a Point of View* (London and New York, 1927); and John Gage, "Turner and the Picturesque," *Burlington Magazine*, CVII (1965), 16-25, 75-81. Professor Gage's brief article, perhaps the best study of the picturesque, not only corrects some of the outlandish claims made about the effect of this aesthetic upon roman-

of this term never mention any of these writers, type-scripts of his notebooks in the Bodleian mention "Sir Uvedale Price on Picturesque,"[26] but it is unclear whether he had read this or merely planned to. Ruskin, who had read Knight's work on mythology, may also have known his essays on the picturesque, though there is no indication of this, and of Gilpin there exists no evidence that he knew his writings. Far more important to Ruskin were his conversations and lessons with Fielding, Harding, and Prout, three painters, according to him, who were among the ablest and most important practitioners of this mode of art.

In *The Seven Lamps of Architecture* Ruskin described that "peculiar character . . . which separates the picturesque from the characters of subject belonging to the higher walks of art" as *"Parasitical Sublimity"*— "a sublimity dependent on the accidents, or on the least essential characters, of the objects to which it belongs" (8.236). According to him, the characters of line, shade,

---

ticism but also well summarizes the critical theory and shows the role the picturesque played in the work of a major artist. Ruskin, who, as Professor Gage points out, was not interested in Turner's picturesque period, never discusses his favorite artist in terms of the conventional picturesque.

26 This remark is taken from typescripts of Ruskin's notebooks, now in the Bodleian Library, Oxford, which were prepared by Cook and Wedderburn for use in drawing up their edition. The passage is in Eng. misc. c. 214. I have not located the original manuscript. The complete passage reads: "Works to be seen: 'On the Landscape Architecture and the great painters of Italy' by G. L. Masson (Meason?) Esq. Sir Uvedale Price on the Picturesque. 'Walker on the Picturesque' Universal decay is the essence of the picturesque. In landscape therefore the picturesque stands in the same relation to this the beautiful and the sublime that the pathetic does to them in poetry." The last remark about Walker, which suggests that Ruskin had already read this work (and possibly Price as well) is of interest since this Walker was apparently the "recent critic on Art," cited in *The Seven Lamps of Architecture*, who "has gravely advanced the theory that the essence of the picturesque consists in the expression of 'universal decay'" (8.235).

and expression which produce sublimity and hence picturesqueness include "angular and broken lines"(8.237) and bold contrasts of colors and light and shadow. Furthermore, these visual characteristics become even more effective "when, by resemblance or association, they remind us of objects on which a true and essential sublimity exists, as of rocks or mountains, or stormy clouds or waves"(8.237). Ruskin's discussion of the picturesque in the fourth volume of *Modern Painters*, which refers to these earlier remarks, further explains that the "essence of picturesque character" lies in "sublimity not inherent in the nature of the thing, but caused by something external to it; as the ruggedness of a cottage roof possesses something of a mountain aspect, not belonging to the cottage as such"(6.10).[27] His example of the rugged cottage roof reveals that the picturesque is a reduced form of the sublime which possesses its sharp oppositions and asymmetry without the large scale necessary to create impressions of grandeur. Since the irregular variety, which Ruskin takes to be the chief distinguishing mark of the picturesque, lacks any dominant unity, it does not partake of the beautiful; since it lacks vastness, it cannot produce the powerful emotions of the sublime. Depending in part on "resemblance or association"(8.237) of things sublime, the picturesque produces a minor form of delight.

As Ruskin explains in the fourth volume of *Modern*

[27] Ruskin used the same example previously in *The Stones of Venice*: "When a highland cottage roof is covered with fragments of shale instead of slates, it becomes picturesque, because the irregularity and rude fractures of the rocks, and their grey and gloomy colour, give to it something of the savageness, and much of the general aspect, of the slope of a mountain side. But as a mere cottage roof, it cannot be sublime, and whatever sublimity it derives from the wildness or sternness which the mountains have given it in its covering, is, so far forth, parasitical" (11.159).

*Painters*, the "merely outward delightfulness [of picturesque subjects]—that which makes them pleasant in painting, or, in the literal sense, picturesque—is their actual variety of colour and form"(6.15), and this pleasing variety necessitates a particular choice of style and subject:

> A broken stone has necessarily more various forms in it than a whole one; a bent roof has more various curves in it than a straight one; every excrescence or cleft involves some additional complexity of light and shade, and every stain of moss on eaves or wall adds to the delightfulness of colour. Hence in a completely picturesque object, as an old cottage or mill, there are introduced, by various circumstances not essential to it, but, on the whole, generally somewhat detrimental to it as cottage or mill, such elements of sublimity—complex light and shade, varied colour, undulatory form, and so on—as can generally be found only in noble natural objects, woods, rocks, or mountains. This sublimity, belonging in a parasitical manner to the building, renders it, in the usual sense of the word, "picturesque." (6.15)

From this passage and others in which he describes the nature of the picturesque, one can conclude that Ruskin believes it is created by an irregular variety which characterizes a painting's line, lighting, color, and composition. This irregular variety, or "ruggedness" as he most frequently terms it, leads the artist in search of the picturesque to depict objects, such as ruins or rustic cottages, which provide rough, pleasing texture. Having chosen such subjects, the artist will then avoid the open, clear light which Ruskin advocated in his remarks on the beauty of infinity and will, instead, em-

ploy strong shadows in the manner of "Rembrandt, Salvator, or Caravaggio"(8.237). Like these artists, the man in search of the picturesque uses shadow not primarily to depict an object, but as a subject in itself. In other words, the picturesque, a distinctively minor mode of art, uses the creations of man and nature to display technique, rather than employing the artist's skill for further ends. The delight created by a skillful treatment of line and shadow surmounts any potential delight in the objects depicted.

In thus citing ruggedness as the chief distinguishing characteristic of the picturesque, Ruskin agrees with Gilpin, who in the last decade of the eighteenth century had stated: "Roughness forms the most essential point of difference between the beautiful and the picturesque; as it seems to be that particular quality which makes the objects chiefly pleasing in painting."[28] Although Ruskin was probably unaware of Gilpin, he had encountered such a view in many places; for example, J. D. Harding, his drawing master, explained in his *Principles and Practice of Art* (1845) that

> variety is not only an essential property of beauty, but also of the picturesque,—a term which I use as significative of that quality of objects which renders them more peculiarly capable of being effectively and agreeably represented by Art. . . . The refined, chaste, and classical features of Greek architecture are beautiful simply: the wildness of nature is picturesque simply. The Greek ruin is both beautiful and picturesque, because it has mixed up with its refined beauty the irregularity and variety of the picturesque.[29]

[28] *Three Essays*, p. 6.    [29] (London, 1845), p. 79.

Ruskin, who frequently characterizes Harding's work as picturesque, agrees with his emphasis upon irregularity and variety. On the other hand, he does not accept his teacher's notion that "the wildness of nature is picturesque simply," and he several times mildy censures him for sacrificing the beauties of nature to the lesser asymmetries and irregularities of picturesque art. In the first volume of *Modern Painters*, for instance, even as Ruskin presents his friend's work as an example of excellence, he adds that "Harding's choice is always of tree forms comparatively imperfect, leaning this way and that, and unequal in the lateral arrangements of foliage. Such forms are often graceful, always picturesque, but rarely grand; and, when systematically adopted, untrue"(3.601). Whatever his reservations, Ruskin had learned this conception of nature and the stylistic mannerisms necessary to achieve it in art from Harding's drawing lessons and published works, and from the sketching tours they took together.

Ruskin, however, first learned to appreciate the picturesque, not from Harding or Copley Fielding, his other drawing teacher, but from the works of Samuel Prout. In the catalogue he wrote for the exhibition of the artist's works at the Fine Art Society (1879-1880), he described how one of Prout's drawings which "hung in the corner of our little dining parlour at Herne Hill as early as I can remember . . . had a most fateful and continual power over my childish mind. . . . In the first place, it taught me generally to like ruggedness; and in the conditions of joint in moulding, and fitting of stones in walls which were most weather-worn, and like the grey dikes of a Cumberland hillside" (14.385). This love of picturesque ruggedness appears clearly in Ruskin's own drawings, many of which sur-

pass his model. The first volume of *Modern Painters* explains that "the reed pen outline and peculiar touch of Prout, which are frequently considered as mere manner, are in fact the only means of expressing the crumbling character of stone which the artist loves and desires"(3.194; see Plates 17-19), and Ruskin's own pencil drawings of architectural subjects emulate the older artist's style to create similar effects. And like Prout's drawings, many of his own attempt to portray "the knots and rents of the timbers, the irregular lying of the shingles on the roofs, the vigorous light and shadow, [and] the fractures and weather-stains of the old stones"(11.160; see Plate 11). For example, Ruskin's drawings done when he was sixteen years old clearly emulate Prout's studies (illus. facing 1.8), and as he began to lay in washes and depict shadow more completely his works increasingly resemble the older artist's more finished drawings (illus. facing 14.426). Ruskin, on the other hand, never tried to rival Prout's placement of figures, one of the painter's skills he most admired, and, furthermore, since many of his own architectural subjects are delightfully incomplete sketches, they rarely rival the painter's larger works. Although his landscape drawings show the clear influence of his teachers and Turner, the pictures of architecture remain indebted to Prout.

He attributed important advances in the picturesque mode to this artist. In "Samuel Prout"(1849), an anonymous essay in the *Art Journal*, Ruskin pointed out that this artist had extended the picturesque to include urban scenes:

There is not a landscape of recent times in which the treatment of the architectural features has not been af-

fected, however unconsciously, by principles which
were first developed by Prout. Of those principles
the most original were his familiarisation of the sentiment, while he elevated the subject, of the picturesque. That character had been sought, before his
time, either in solitude or in rusticity; it was supposed to belong only to the savageness of the desert
or the simplicity of the hamlet; it lurked beneath the
brows of rocks and the eaves of cottages; to seek it
in a city would have been deemed an extravagance,
to raise it to the height of a cathedral, an heresy.
(12.313)

Part of Prout's accomplishment in creating picturesque
depictions of noble buildings lay in his ability to present the effects of age and human life upon his subjects.
Until Prout, says Ruskin, excessive and clumsy arti-
ficiality characterized the picturesque: what ruins early
artists drew "looked as if broken down on purpose;
what weeds they put on seemed put on for ornament"
(3.216). To Prout, therefore, goes credit for the creation of the essential characteristics lacking in earlier
art, in particular "that feeling which results from the
influence, among the noble lines of architecture, of the
rent and the rust, the fissure, the lichen, and the weed,
and from the writings upon the pages of ancient walls
of the confused hieroglyphics of human history"(3.217).
Prout, in other words, does not unfeelingly depict signs
of age and decay chiefly for the sake of interesting textures, but rather employs these textures and other characteristics of the picturesque to create deeply felt impressions of age nobly endured. In addition, Prout advanced this mode of art beyond concentration on the
"minor elements of the picturesque,—craggy chasms,

broken waterfalls, or rustic cottages"(13.368). Ruskin once wrote that if Turner "had only wanted what vulgar artists think picturesque," any English valley would have provided him with an endless supply "of old tree-trunks, of young tree-branches, of lilied pools in the brook, and of grouped cattle in the meadows"(15.437). Neither Turner nor Prout were vulgar artists, and while Turner concentrated upon the infinite beauties of nature, Prout, more interested by the cityscape, re-deployed aspects of picturesque technique to show the effects of men and time upon noble works of architecture.

In the first volume of *Modern Painters* Ruskin insists that the pleasure we receive from the signs of age that Prout includes in his work distinguishes our delight in his art from "mere love of the picturesque"(3.217), and this distinction between "age mark"(3.207) and the conventional picturesque becomes, in the fourth volume, the Ruskinian opposition of the surface and Turnerian (or noble) picturesque. An examination of the reasons which lay behind Ruskin's continuing suspicion of the conventional picturesque reveals much that characterizes his theories of art. In the first place, he believes that "the modern feeling of the picturesque, which, so far as it consists in a delight in ruin, is perhaps the most suspicious and questionable of all the characters distinctively belonging to our temper, and art"(6.9). This lesser mode of the picturesque not only neglects the higher forms of the beautiful to portray broken rocks and thatched roofs, it also, by its natural concentration on ruin, encourages the artist and spectator to delight in sad, painful things for the sake of interesting lines and colors to the neglect of the human significance of the scene depicted. Thus, "in a certain

sense, the lower picturesque ideal is eminently a *heart-less* one"(6.19), for artists unthinkingly and unfeelingly create images of broken-down windmills and weakened men because they have visual interest. In *The Stones of Venice* Ruskin wrote that the "whole function of the artist in the world is to be a seeing and feeling creature; to be an instrument of such tenderness and sensitiveness, that no shadow, no hue, no line, no instantaneous and evanescent expression of the visible things around him, nor any of the emotions which they are capable of conveying to the spirit which has been given him, shall either be left unrecorded, or fade from the book of record"(11.49). The lesser mode of the picturesque, however, necessarily reduces the artist to a *seeing* creature, forcing him to ignore the emotional—*human*—implications of his subject. This form of art, which requires an unhealthy dissociation of faculties in the artist, can only appeal to the aesthetic sensibilities of fragmented modern man. An example of the immoral abstraction implicit in the lower picturesque appears in Sir Charles Bell's *Anatomy and Philosophy of Expression in the Fine Arts*, which Ruskin several times quotes in his *Modern Painters*: "In Roman Catholic countries the church-door is open, and a heavy curtain excludes the light and heat; and there lie about those figures in rags, singularly picturesque."[30] For Ruskin,

[30] 6th ed. (London, 1872), p. 16. Uvedale Price relates an anecdote which can serve as a parable: One day when Reynolds and Wilson, the two painters, were looking at a scene, Wilson tried to point out a particular detail to his companion. " 'There,' said he 'near those houses—there! where the *figures* are.'—though a painter, said Sir Joshua, I was puzzled. I thought he meant statues, and was looking upon the tops of the houses; for I did not at first conceive that the men and women we plainly saw walking about, were by him only thought of as figures in a landscape" (*An Essay on the Picturesque*, p. 379n).

taking delight in figures in rags corrupted the artist and audience alike.

By the 1850's Ruskin had become increasingly aware of the social and moral implications of the picturesque and several times comments upon them. For example, in his diary entry for 12 May 1854 he wrote of a scene in Amiens:

> All exquisitely picturesque, and as miserable as picturesque. We delight in seeing the figures in the boats pushing them about the bits of blue water in Prout's drawings, but, as I looked to-day at the unhealthy face and melancholy, apathetic mien of the man in the boat, pushing his load of peats along the ditch, and of the people, men and women, who sat spinning gloomily in the picturesque cottages, I could not help feeling how many suffering persons must *pay* for my picturesque subject, and my happy walk.[31]

Ruskin's problem—and his greatness—was that he "could not help feeling." He could not avoid the human implications of the picturesque scene before him: to do so would have required that he become purely a seeing creature, that he use human beings for aesthetic pleasure, that he treat them purely as objects. The attitudes contained in this diary entry appeared in different form six years later in the last volume of *Modern Painters*. Answering a "zealous, useful, and able Scotch clergyman," who had described a "scene in the Highlands to show (he said) the goodness of God," Ruskin proposes to take another look at this picturesque scene:

---

[31] *Diaries*, II, 493. Ruskin quotes this passage with slight changes in phrasing as a note to the chapter on the Turnerian picturesque (6.24n).

It is a little valley of soft turf, enclosed in its narrow oval by jutting rocks and broad flakes of nodding fern. From one side of it to the other winds, serpentine, a clear brown stream, drooping into quicker ripple as it reaches the end of the oval field, and then, first islanding a purple and white rock with an amber pool, it dashes away into a narrow fall of foam under a thicket of mountain-ash and alder. The autumn sun, low but clear, shines on the scarlet ash-berries and on the golden birch-leaves, which, fallen here and there, when the breeze has not caught them, rest quiet in the crannies of the purple rock. Beside the rock, in the hollow under the thicket, the carcase of a ewe, drowned in the last flood, lies nearly bare to the bone, its white ribs protruding through the skin, raven-torn; and the rags of its wool still flickering from the branches that first stayed it as the stream swept it down. A little lower, the current plunges, roaring, into a circular chasm like a well, surrounded on three sides by a chimney-like hollowness of polished rock, down which the foam slips in detached snow-flakes. Round the edges of the pool beneath, the water circles slowly, like black oil; a little butterfly lies on its back, its wings glued to one of the eddies, its limbs feebly quivering; a fish rises, and it is gone. Lower down the stream, I can just see over a knoll, the green and damp turf roofs of four or five hovels, built at the edge of a morass, which is trodden by the cattle into a black Slough of Despond. . . . At the turn of the brook I see a man fishing, with a boy and a dog—a picturesque and pretty group enough certainly, if they had not been there all day starving. I know them, and I know the dog's ribs also, which are nearly as bare as the dead ewe's; and the

child's wasted shoulders, cutting his old tartan jacket through, so sharp are they. (7.268-269)

Ruskin's bitterly ironic presentation of this Highland scene simultaneously exposes the implications of the picturesque and, as a recent writer has pointed out, reveals "the insufficiency of the Wordsworthian view of nature."[32] The passage possesses a unique interest for a student of Ruskin's notions of the sister arts, for it shows him utilizing his own great skills at literary pictorialism rather differently than he had in earlier volumes of *Modern Painters*. Ruskin's usual practice, particularly in his first volume, is to create a word painting which he then frequently uses as a standard for judging a pictorial representation of a scene. In the opening volume of *Modern Painters*, he creates a powerful image of nature's colors near the Italian town of La Riccia to show how far from this splendor the older painters of landscape remain (3.277-279). The final volume of *Modern Painters*, in contrast, uses such literary pictorialism, not to show that nature is more beautiful than art, but to present the ugliness that a sentimentally artistic vision of nature conceals.

Ruskin knew that in order to paint a scene with words he had first to establish a center of perception, a narrative eye, next present recognizable elements of pictorial composition, and then move his narrative eye, camera-like, through the elements of the scene he creates for us. He therefore begins by placing the reader in the midst of the landscape, which exists in the narrative present: "It *is* a little valley." Next, he sketches in the oval shape of the valley, mentioning afterward the rocks and fern to convey its dominant texture and

[32] Rosenberg, *The Darkening Glass*, p. 23.

color. Lastly, he includes the standard pictorial motif of the winding stream, which serves to compose the picture, and then mentions the sunlight, thus focusing the reader's attention on what the light reveals. Thus far we have a verbal presentation, similar to many of those in the first volume, of beautiful landscape, embellished by details of color. But, having established the broad outlines of this Highland valley, the narrative eye moves closer and the increasing clarity of vision destroys the first impression of quiet loveliness. We move from the golden birch leaves to the carcase of a dead ewe, a necessary component, it seems, of life in nature, and we are drawn closer, perceiving the horrible details—the protruding white ribs, the raven-torn skin, and the rags of wool moving in the breeze. After pausing for this scene, the narrative eye moves on once again in a strikingly cinematic technique: we are moved further down the stream until we catch sight of a little butterfly, at which point we are moved closer, perceiving "its wings glued to one of the eddies, its limbs feebly quivering." A fish rises and the butterfly vanishes, an emblem of the way nature's beauties do not always survive natural predators. A third time we move on, catching sight of picturesque cottages and, at the bend of the stream, a "picturesque and pretty group." Lastly, the passage brings us nearer to this picturesque assemblage, forcing us to recognize the poverty and misery implicit in the picturesque. Ruskin's objections to the art in this mode was that it presented an incomplete, fragmentary and fragmenting, vision of nature. Taking neither art nor man seriously enough, it results in an incomplete, immoral delight in things intrinsically painful. His examination of this scene therefore demands that he guide the reader's percep-

tions to an understanding that one cannot divorce the visual from the emotional, the aesthetically pleasurable from the other needs of man.[33]

Although Ruskin always remains highly critical of the lesser picturesque and is quick to point out its implications, he never condemns it entirely, because he believes that it arises in an essentially healthy human need for beauty. Thus, the fourth volume of *Modern Painters* explains that although "the hunter of the picturesque"(6.21) might appear a heartless monster to those of another place and time, in fact he is generally "kind-hearted, innocent of evil, but not broad in thought; somewhat selfish, and incapable of acute sympathy with others; gifted at the same time with strong artistic instincts and capacities for the enjoyment of varied form, and light, and shade, in pursuit of which enjoyment his life is passed, as the lives of other men are for the most part, in the pursuit of what *they* also like,—be it honour, or money, or indolent pleasure" (6.21). Even that "delight which he *seems* to take in misery is not altogether unvirtuous"(6.21), since it contains the seeds of sympathy that could develop into better things. Moreover, this love of the picturesque also indicates a vague desire for the pastoral simplicities, a vague dissatisfaction with present life. As Ruskin previously explained in *The Stones of Venice*, such dis-

[33] *Fors Clavigera* exposes not the moral or artistic implications of the picturesque, but the political and economic ones when Ruskin comments that "to Professors of Art, the Apennine between Lucca and Pistoja is singularly delightful to this day, because of the ruins of these robber-castles on every mound, and of the pretty monasteries and arcades of cloister beside them. But how little we usually estimate the real relation of these picturesque objects! The homes of the Baron and Clerk, side by side, established on the hills. Underneath, in the plain, the peasant driving his oxen. The Baron lives by robbing the peasant, and the Clerk by blessing the Baron" (27.310-311).

satisfaction is the natural condition of modern man in the modern cityscape: surrounded by the grey monotonies of the urban scene, man longs for something, anything, to delight his spirit. Therefore: "All the pleasure which the people of the nineteenth century take in art, is in pictures, sculpture, minor objects of virtù, or in mediaeval architecture, which we enjoy under the term picturesque: no pleasure is taken anywhere in modern buildings, and we find all men of true feeling delighting to escape out of modern cities into natural scenery"(10.207). Shortly after completing *The Stones of Venice,* Ruskin returned in his notebooks to the conditions of modern life which have produced the love of picturesqueness:

> The real reason of it is this—that for more than a couple of centuries we have been studiously surrounding ourselves with every form of vapidness and monotony in architecture. It has been our aim to make all our houses and churches, alike; we have squared our windows—smoothed our walls; straightened our roofs—put away nearly all ornament[,] inequality, evidence of effort, and ambiguity, and all variety of colour. It has been our aim to make every house look as if it had been built yesterday; and to make all the parts of it symmetrical[,] similar and colourless. . . . All this is done directly in opposition to the laws of nature and truth.[34]

The result has been, as he earlier pointed out, that the "picturesque school of art rose up to address those capacities of enjoyment for which . . . there was employment no more. . . . And thus the English school of landscape, culminating in Turner, is in reality nothing

[34] Bodleian Library, Oxford, Eng. misc. c. 218.

else than a healthy effort to fill the void which the destruction of Gothic architecture has left"(11.225-226). Ruskin offers several solutions to the problems created by the modern city. First of all, he wishes to extend the influence, the enriching effects, of the art of Turner and other painters of landscape; secondly, he encourages his audience to revive a healthy mode of architecture, one which would provide the necessary stimulus for the minds and spirits of men; lastly, he tries to change the economic system which has led to such monotonous environments.

One important way to extend the influence of great artists like Turner is to educate the audience to appreciate the higher, or noble, form of the picturesque. In contrast to the "surface-picturesque"(6.16), which dwells on texture at the expense of emotion, the noble picturesque is produced by "an expression of sorrow and old age, attributes which are both sublime"(6.10). In other words, since the "higher condition of art . . . depends upon largeness of sympathy"(6.19), the noble picturesque, the form practiced by Turner, arises, not from neglect of the meaning of the scene depicted, but from concentration upon it. It is produced, then, by expression "of *suffering*, of *poverty*, or *decay*, nobly endured by unpretending strength of heart. Nor only unpretending, but unconscious. If there be a visible pensiveness in the building, as in a ruined abbey, it becomes, or claims to become, beautiful; but the picturesqueness is in the unconscious suffering"(6.14-15). The noble picturesque, a form of the gentler sublime, is an associated, subjective aesthetic pleasure which demands the projection of human characteristics upon old buildings. Indeed, old buildings are to be considered as old, noble men. Much of this sad, pathetic sublimity

is created by age. In the first volume Ruskin had written of the beauties of age itself, and these are apparently part of the sublime emotion which creates the noble picturesque: "There is set in the deeper places of the heart such affection for the signs of age that the eye is delighted even by injuries which are the work of time; not but that there is also real and absolute beauty in the forms and colours so obtained"(3.204). Even at this early period Ruskin distinguishes this pleasure from what he later called the surface-picturesque; for he remarks that although a building may have "age-mark upon it which may best exalt and harmonize the sources of its beauty," our enjoyment of this sign of aging "is no pursuit of mere picturesqueness; it is true following out of the ideal character of the building" (3.207).[35] This distinction between age-mark and mere picturesqueness became, in the fourth volume, the distinction between the noble and lower, or surface-picturesque.

There are good reasons for taking Ruskin's definitions of the noble picturesque as the final and representative statement of his aesthetic position. The picturesque, in some sense, is a combination of the sublime and the beautiful and is midway between them, a reduced, gentler, less exalted form of both. And as an intermediary class it reminds us of Uvedale Price's idea that the picturesque should bridge the sublime and the beautiful.[36] In this last major statement of his aesthetic

[35] It seems extremely difficult to perceive how the ideal character of a Greek temple could be enhanced by rounding its intentionally distinct form, and in this case pursuit of age-mark would have to be pursuit of the signs of age for their own sake.

[36] "Picturesqueness appears to hold a station between beauty and sublimity; and on that account, perhaps, is more frequently, and more happily blended with them both, than they are with each other." Price, *An Essay on the Picturesque*, p. 82. See also above, n. 21.

position, Ruskin tried to formulate a description of that kind of pleasure which he thought most characteristic of the art of his contemporaries, and in so doing he shows his close relation to theorists of the late eighteenth and early nineteenth centuries. Like them, after he had been concerned with the most violent aspects of the sublime, and the most tranquil forms of beauty, he presented what was in effect a third aesthetic category which emphasized calm, more tranquil, yet subjective effects. Ruskin's statements about the picturesque are also characteristic, not only because he related it to an aspect of the contemporary sensibility which troubled him, but because he here most fully accepts an aesthetic which is patently subjectivist and associationist. This change reflects the changes that were going on, or were being prepared for, in Ruskin's thought as he turned increasingly toward the problems of modern man in modern society. The new humanism which fully appears in the last volume of *Modern Painters* is presaged by the picturesque which gains its effect not, as with beauty, from a figuring forth of divine qualities, but from human associations. Ruskin's description of the picturesque, which at so many points contradicts his ideas of beauty, shows how difficult it had been for him to maintain that his beauty of order contained the pleasures most suited to the art of his time. Ruskin had at first denied the sublime the dignity of a separate aesthetic category, but after formulating his theories of beauty, he found it necessary to use sublimity to contain a wide spectrum of aesthetic effects. The picturesque, which is a subcategory of the sublime, is the final expression of this inability to maintain a classicistic theory of beauty.

CHAPTER FOUR

Ruskin's Religious Belief

Who could tell from my books . . . what has been the course of religious effort and speculation in me?

—John Ruskin (35.628)

## I. Ruskin's Evangelical belief

WE HAVE seen that because Ruskin increasingly felt a need to emphasize the role of human, as opposed to divine, elements in his theocentric system of aesthetics, he was unable to maintain his beauty of order. Although he never formulated a second complete theory of beauty, the statements which Ruskin made about the sublime, the picturesque, and the beauty of association in *The Seven Lamps of Architecture* and the last four volumes of *Modern Painters* show that, even as he proposed his theory of beauty, he began to allow room in his aesthetic system for the role of subjective reactions. When he made man, rather than God, the focus of his aesthetics, Ruskin was no longer able to accept his classicistic beauty of order, and he consequently placed more importance on individual, subjective emotional reaction in his writings on aesthetics. As we have seen, the shift of focus in Ruskin's aesthetics was intimately related to the loss of the religion in which he had been raised; and, now, in order to perceive the degree to which the development of Ruskin's aesthetics was representative of the development of his thought and writings about other subjects, we shall examine the nature of his early Evangelical faith, the manner in which he lost his religion, and the effects which this loss had upon the direction of his later work. Before we begin, however, it will be useful to note that the history of Ruskin's religious opinions divides roughly into four periods: in the first years of firm Evangelical belief, which lasted until about 1848, he accepted the religion of his parents; he then experienced ten years of increasingly painful doubts which culminated in his decisive loss of religion

in 1858; seventeen years of confused and often bitter agnosticism followed; and finally in 1875 he came to rest in a personal, rather strange version of Christianity, which he continued to accept until the end of his life.

From her son's earliest years Margaret Ruskin had zealously inculcated the tenets of a strict, often dour, Evangelical Anglicanism. The seventh chapter of *Praeterita* tells us that his mother's "unquestioning evangelical faith in the literal truth of the Bible placed me, as soon as I could conceive or think, in the presence of an unseen world"(35.128). From the time he "could conceive or think" the young boy found himself amid the promise and terror of the Evangelical universe. He found himself in a world where Damnation awaited most and Death waited for all, a world penetrated by the gaze of an immanent, punishing God who, most graciously, permitted a few, a very few, to escape the pain and horror of hell. Before John Ruskin became fully conscious that he was alive, he learned that he was to die; and before he could know much about depravity, he learned that, like all human beings, he was depraved.

Since the doctrines and attitudes of Evangelical Anglicanism so importantly shaped the Ruskinian world, at this point we would do well to examine them in detail. The Evangelical Anglicans, who became the most influential party in the established church during the first three decades of the nineteenth century, are perhaps best remembered today for their fervent and continuing attempts both to cleanse the moral facade of an immoral England and to bring Gospel Christianity to country parishes and new industrial towns neglected by the less zealous Anglican clergy.[1] Combining

[1] I am primarily indebted to the following works: Ford K. Brown,

the beliefs and methods of Wesley, Whitefield, and the seventeenth-century Puritans with those of the Church of England, the Evangelicals made wide use of itinerant preaching and tracts to send forth the Gospel to the many Englishmen they considered dwelling in darkness. Ruskin, like many another earnest Evangelical, both read and, on occasion, recommended such tracts. Thus, in a letter to J. J. Laing, which the editors of the *Library Edition* place in 1854, he advised his correspondent that "the pleasantest and most useful reading I know, on nearly all religious questions whatsoever, are *Ryle's Tracts*"(36.180). John Charles Ryle (1816-1900), perhaps the most important nineteenth-century author of Evangelical tracts—his tracts had a circulation of twelve million[2]—provides us with the example of a prominent Evangelical spokesman who clearly sets forth the points of Ruskin's belief. In attempting to detail the faith to which Ruskin adhered until 1858—the year of his decisive break with Evangelicalism—we shall also draw upon the sermons of his favorite preacher, Henry Melvill. Melvill (1798-1871), the "Evangelical Chrysostom,"[3] whom many, including Gladstone and Ruskin himself, considered the greatest preacher of his age, served as Chaplain to Queen Vic-

*Fathers of the Victorians, The Age of Wilberforce* (Cambridge, Eng., 1961); Horton Davies, *Worship and Theology in England, 1690-1850* (Princeton, 1961); L. E. Elliott-Binns's three works, *The Early Evangelicals: A Religious and Social Study* (Greenwich, Conn., 1959); *English Thought 1860-1900, The Theological Aspect* (London, 1956); *Religion in the Victorian Era*, 2nd ed. (Greenwich, Conn., 1946); John Henry Overton's two works, *The Evangelical Revival in the Eighteenth Century* (London, 1886) and *The English Church in the Nineteenth Century, 1800-1833* (London, 1894); Vernon F. Storr, *The Development of English Theology in the Nineteenth Century, 1800-1860* (London, 1913).

2 Elliott-Binns, *Religion in the Victorian Era*, p. 348.

3 *Ibid.*, p. 460.

toria (1852) and Canon of St. Paul's from 1856 until his death. He was also the minister to whom the Ruskin family sat while they lived at Denmark Hill, and as John Ruskin grew into adulthood he became a friend of this famous preacher to whose sermons he was devoted. Ruskin tells us in *Praeterita* that Melvill "was the only preacher I ever knew whose sermons were at once sincere, orthodox, and oratorical on Ciceronian principles"(35.386), and the serious attention he gave to these graceful sermons appears in his diaries, where he occasionally summarizes them, urges himself to commit one to memory, or praises them as "noble," "admirable," and "forcible and clear in the extreme."[4] In addition to attending Melvill's sermons when in London, Ruskin habitually read published versions of them in *The Pulpit*, a weekly publication entirely devoted to publishing the sermons of eminent Evangelical preachers. In the letters which he wrote to his parents during his 1851-1852 stay in Venice, Ruskin several times mentions Melvill's sermons, thanking his parents for copies they had sent or asking for additional ones. In December 1851, for example, he wrote: "I am very glad to have the sermons of Mr. Melville [*sic*] for today and next Sunday, if the box with the bath is not yet sent off I wish you could put half a dozen or a dozen into it."[5] Such a remark suggests either that sermons sometimes appeared in print before they were delivered, which, however, does not seem very likely, or that Ruskin had access to Melvill's text. In August 1853, when he, his wife, and Millais were at Glenfinlas where the painter was doing

---

[4] *Diaries*, I, 238, 247 (last two phrases).

[5] *Ruskin's Letters from Venice, 1851-1852*, ed. John Lewis Bradley (New Haven, 1955), p. 92. See also pp. 89, 100. Apparently, Ruskin always misspelled Melvill's name.

the famous portrait, he wrote to his father that he was "especially obliged by the Mr Melvill sermon. Would you be so good as to send me some more."[6] In whatever form and from whatever source Ruskin read particular sermons, we can at least be sure that he frequently attended Melvill's preaching, kept accounts of this preaching in his diaries, and, when out of London, read written or published versions whenever able. The student of Ruskin's thought thus finds himself in a particularly fortunate position to determine the nature of his early belief, for however difficult it is to chart the flux of Ruskin's faith after 1858 one can at least be sure that while he adhered to Evangelicalism, Ryle and Melvill, its prominent spokesmen, clearly set forth that set of attitudes and that body of doctrine in which he was raised and to which at first gave loyal allegiance.

One point, surely, on which all Evangelical Anglicans agreed was the need for uncompromising zeal in spreading the word of God. As Melvill emphasized in a sermon which Ruskin took to heart as bearing on his own condition, "Religion . . . is not a thing for half measures."[7] Ryle, who later became Bishop of Liverpool, emphasized the need for an earnest emotional commitment even more strongly: "Zeal, like John Knox pulling down the Scotch monasteries, may hurt the feelings of the narrow-minded and sleepy Christians. It may offend the prejudices of those old-fashioned re-

[6] *Millais and the Ruskins*, ed. Mary Lutyens (London, 1967), p. 85.
[7] "God's People Never Ashamed," *The Pulpit*, LVIII (1850), 45. In his diary entry for 2 July 1850 Ruskin wrote of this Tuesday morning sermon: "Another sermon on 'My people shall never be ashamed.' Dwelling especially on the shame before the world in preaching Christ, caused by consciousness of personal sin. How often and often have I felt this! May I try so to live as to be able to preach unblushingly. But how these impressions wear away" (II, 465).

ligionists who hate everything new, and abhor all change. But Zeal in the end will justify itself."[8] Their zeal, and the fact that they cooperated in missionary ventures with the dissenting sects, led other Anglicans, who stigmatized them as Methodists within the Church, to believe the Evangelicals shared more with the dissenters than with other members of the established Church; and, in truth, they believed that dissenters who shared their main beliefs were closer to God than many nominal Christians in the Anglican communion. Thus, Ryle points out that any Christian who accepted the main tenets of Evangelical faith would be saved whether or not the believer belonged to the Church of England.

According to Ryle, there were "five distinctive doctrinal marks by which the members of the Evangelical body may be discerned":

> The first leading feature in Evangelical Religion is the *absolute supremacy it assigns to Holy Scripture* as the only rule of faith and practice, the only test of truth. . . . The second leading feature in Evangelical Religion is the *depth and prominence it assigns to the doctrine of human sinfulness and corruption.* . . . [Third] is the *paramount importance it attaches to the work and office of our Lord Jesus Christ.* . . . An experimental knowledge of Christ crucified and interceeding, is the very essence of Christianity. . . . [Fourth] is the *high place which it assigns to the inward work of the Holy Spirit in the heart of man.* Its theory is that the root and foundation of all vital Christianity in any one, is a work of grace in the heart. . . . [Fifth] is the *importance it attaches to the*

[8] *Be Zealous* (New York, 1853), p. 28.

*outward and visible work of the Holy Ghost in the life of man.*[9]

As he explained, the primary conviction of Evangelical Anglicanism was "that man is required to believe nothing, as necessary to salvation, which is not read in God's Word written, or can be proved thereby. It totally denies that there is any other guide for man's soul, co-equal or co-ordinate with the Bible."[10] Casting away Church tradition as without authority, the Evangelicals relied solely on scripture which they took to be the literal Word of God. Scorning "the old wives' fables of Rabbinical writers and the rubbish of Patristic traditions,"[11] Ryle emphasized that "A man must make the Bible his rule of conduct. He must make its leading principles the compass by which he steers his course through life. By the letter or the spirit of the Bible he must test every difficult point and question."[12] To make scripture thus the rule of one's conduct required "a patient, daily, systematic reading of the Book."[13]

Margaret Ruskin engaged her son as soon as he "could conceive or think" in such a course of Bible study, making him read the Testaments, memorize

[9] *Knots Untied, Being Plain Statements on Disputed Points in Religion from the Standpoint of the Evangelical Churchman,* 2nd ed. (London, 1898), pp. 4-8. Most of the chapters in this work appeared as separate tracts in England and America during the 1840's and '50's.

[10] *Ibid.,* p. 4.

[11] *Living or Dead? A Series of Home Truths* (New York, 1851), p. 248.

[12] *Startling Questions* (New York, 1853), p. 216.

[13] *Knots Untied,* p. 72. In *Startling Questions* Ryle states: "Neglect of the Bible is like disease of the body. It shows itself in the face of a man's conduct. It tells its own tale. It cannot be hid" (p. 202), and "Show me a person who despises Bible reading, or thinks little of Bible preaching, and I hold it to be a certain fact that he is not yet born again. . . . Tell me what the Bible is to a man, and I will generally tell you what he is" (p. 219).

them, and then repeat to her daily the passages he had
committed to memory. In addition, for many years he
also kept notebooks in which he collated scriptural passages and plumbed the implications of God's word.
This early training not only gave him his close knowledge of the Bible and his habit of citing scripture for
proof or example, a habit which remained after he had
lost the belief in its literal truth, but also did much to
shape his early prose style. Equally important was the
manner in which Evangelical modes of reading the
Bible formed his ways of interpreting secular works of
art and literature. For example, there can be no doubt
that Ruskin's characteristic attention to the minute details of a painting or a poem, a technique which often
produces his most brilliant insights, derives from Evangelical injunctions to read scripture closely, particularly since in *Praeterita* he credits Melvill with "all
sorts of good help in close analysis, but especially, my
habit of always looking, in every quotation from the
Bible, what goes before it and after"(35.388). When
Ruskin discusses and demonstrates that "word-by-word
examination of your author which is rightly called 'reading' "(1875) in *Sesame and Lilies* (1870), he thus clearly echoes the usual directions of the Evangelical pastor
to his flock. Melvill, for example, similarly instructed
his listeners: "Read the Bible yourselves, and teach
your children to read it, as a book that should be pon-
dered, not hurried over; a book, so to speak, that may
be better read by lines than by chapters."[14] Again, Ruskin appears to be following the pattern of the preacher when he instructs his readers that "you must get into
the habit of looking intensely at words, and assuring
yourself of their meaning syllable by syllable—nay, let-

---

[14] "The Bird's Nest," *Sermons* (London, 1845), p. 209.

ter by letter"(18.64). Not only his habit of close reading but also his theories and procedures of symbolical interpretation clearly derive from Evangelical practice; and when we examine his debt to Evangelical exegetical methods in the following chapter, we shall observe the manner in which he transferred ways of reading the Word of God to the words of men.

According to Ryle, the second "leading feature" of Evangelical Anglican belief is the major emphasis it places on man's fallen state: "Next to the Bible, as its foundation, it is based on a clear view of original sin."[15] A clear view of original sin requires each true believer both to admit intellectually and feel in his heart that "in consequence of Adam's fall all men are as far as possible gone from original righteousness, and are of their own natures inclined to evil."[16] Indeed, Ryle pronounces the sad but essential fact of human depravity with such enthusiasm that he strays dangerously close to the dark heresy of the Manichee, telling his readers that "we are all rather children of the devil, than children of God."[17] Although Melvill guards his expression more closely, he likewise points out the essential corruption that lies at the heart of each of the sons of Adam: "Man is the same, radically the same, in one state and another; he is capable of the same, the very same, villanies. . . ; the polish of civilization may conceal, and the rudeness of barbarianism may bring out, evil tendencies, but those tendencies equally exist."[18] Like Melvill, Ryle, and the seventeenth-century Puritans (whom the Evangelicals regarded as their spiritual ancestors), Ruskin as a young man believed that "there

---

[15] *Knots Untied*, p. 6.  [16] *Ibid.*, p. 5.
[17] *Startling Questions*, p. 48.
[18] "The Examination of Cain," *Sermons* (1845), II, 354-387.

is not any part of our nature . . . uninfluenced or unaffected by the fall"(4.186). With the earnest enthusiasm of a tract the second volume of *Modern Painters*
(1846) describes the "terrible stamp of various degradation" in man's heart, mind, and body: "features seamed
by sickness, dimmed by sensuality, convulsed by passion, pinched by poverty, shadowed by sorrow, brand-
ed with remorse: bodies consumed with sloth, broken
down by labour, tortured by disease, dishonoured in
foul uses; intellects without power, hearts without
hope, minds earthly and devilish"(4.176). This description of man, which an 1883 note characterizes as an
"Evangelical burst of flame upon the 'corruption of human nature' "(4.177n), reveals an important reason why
the second volume of *Modern Painters* was the most
Evangelical of Ruskin's works.

Such Evangelical emphasis on innate human depravity, which he accepted in 1846 so completely, colored
his aesthetics and art criticism in important ways. First
of all, as we have already observed, Ruskin's belief that
the "Adamite curse"(4.184) brought with it an "evil diversity"(4.176) encourages him to support the characteristic romantic demand for particularity and detail
in art; for accepting that original sin has destroyed any
central form of human ideal beauty that may once have
existed, he holds that what ideal beauty still remains
is attainable only in portraiture. Secondly, his emphasis upon the corruptions of the human mind and heart
made it impossible for Ruskin, at this stage in the writing of *Modern Painters*, to allow that subjectivity has
a role in beauty. To admit the role of subjectivity when
he believed that the subject existed in corruption and
diversity would have denied all that Ruskin desired of
his aesthetic theories. In one of Melvill's sermons of

which Ruskin heartily approved, the preacher mentioned "that utter perversion and alienation of affections, which we inherit as creatures whose moral constitution has been deeply deranged."[19] Men "whose moral constitution has been deeply deranged," and whose emotions have been perverted and alienated, can neither experience beauty properly nor receive from it that religious and moral value Ruskin believed present in the beautiful—unless the beautiful itself was grounded in divine nature. Ruskin's Evangelical emphasis upon man's fallen nature, therefore, demanded that he create a theory of beauty as divine order; for just as the sinner could be saved from his innate depravity only by continuous acts of divine grace, so too the individual's perception of beauty could be saved from trivializing subjectivity only by the continuous presence of God. In other words, the aesthetic theories of the second volume of *Modern Painters*, like Evangelical conceptions of the role of God in individual salvation, require the presence of an immanent God.

The third effect of this belief in human depravity appears in Ruskin's attitudes toward the nude in art. Whereas Evangelical belief that Adam's fall had much lessened the human mind could support Ruskin's enterprise of demonstrating the moral stature of art and beauty, the belief that the fall rendered the body essentially sinful, on the other hand, creates moral and aesthetic difficulties for Ruskin the critic. Since for him the body has become the very emblem of depravity, he believes that the artist who paints it always risks that "which is luscious and foul"(4.194). Such an attitude did not hinder his appreciation of landscape and, in-

19 "The Duty of Rejoicing," *The Pulpit*, XLIII (1843), 99. Ruskin briefly summarizes this sermon in *Diaries*, I, 240 (22 January 1843).

deed, may even have contributed much to that love of nature which characterizes Ruskin's first volume; but after he decided to expand the scope of the second volume of *Modern Painters* to include all painting, his puritanical dislike of the human body made it impossible for him to appreciate much of the world's great art. Throughout the second volume one encounters his intense dislike of things physical and physically pleasurable, and no more so than when he encounters the problem of the nude. Ruskin's essential difficulty is that, unlike men of classical and Renaissance times, he finds the body *as body* distasteful, discomforting, and even disgusting. In sharp contradistinction to the statements of his friend and drawing master, J. D. Harding,[20] who felt that the human body was the ultimate source of all beautiful line and form, Ruskin feels that the unclothed human form has little beauty not borrowed from color or expression. In addition, he dislikes the presentation of the nude in painting, because he feels that the body and its pleasures are necessarily dangerous because necessarily debasing. Although Ruskin later cast away the theological basis for his dislike of the physical, admitting in later years that he had come to respect the needs of the body, he always maintained his dislike of sexuality. Thus in an 1883 note he restated his early belief that sexuality has no place whatever in art: "The general tendency of modern art, under the guidance of Paris, renders it necessary to explain now to the reader, what I before left him to feel, that the sexual in-

[20] In his *Principles and Practice of Art* (London, 1845), p. 53, Harding states: "By the perpetual contemplation of the human form, and the study of its perfections, the artist, by invisible steps and inappreciable degrees, beautifies his own conceptions of the forms of all things. From this model he derives the power for his imagination imperceptibly to raise and refine whatever else he touches."

stinct is entirely excluded from consideration throughout the argument of this essay; I take no notice of the
feelings of the beautiful, which we share with flies and
spiders"(4.63n). His statements almost four decades
earlier reveal the extent to which he believed that the
artist who painted the body had to deny the physical
nature of his subject. First of all, as we have seen, he
felt that true human beauty resides in the features, in
facial expression, and not in the body itself. Secondly,
he believed that the artist who had to portray the
naked body must emphasize color, the element of emotion and spirituality, at the expense of qualities which
might suggest flesh:

> The purity of flesh painting depends, in very con-
> siderable measure, on the intensity and warmth of
> its *colour*. For if it be opaque, and clay cold, and de-
> void of all the radiance and life of flesh, the lines of
> its true beauty, being severe and firm, will become
> so hard in the loss of the glow and gradation by
> which nature illustrates them, that the painter will
> be compelled to sacrifice them for a luscious fulness
> and roundness, in order to give the conception of
> flesh; which, being done, destroys ideality of form as
> of colour, and gives all over to lasciviousness of
> surface. (4.194-195)

Ruskin's obvious dislike of "luscious fulness and roundness," of flesh that suggests sexuality, further appears
in his remark that "splendour of colour both bears out
a nobler severity of form, and is in itself purifying and
cleansing, like fire"(4.195). According to Ruskin, then,
flesh must be purified, for it cannot be presented as it
is, as soft material of a living body; it must be presented—or as Ruskin says, "redeemed"—"by severity

of form and hardness of line"(4.196). In other words, whereas Ruskin's emphasis on expression turns the living body into spirit, his emphasis on color and severe form turns flesh into an object, into a sexually neutral thing.

The roles of Christ and divine grace in man's salvation, the third and fourth points of Evangelical belief, receive a strongly emotional coloring from Ryle and other Evangelical ministers of the Gospel. After pointing out that "nothing whatever is needed between the soul of man the sinner and Christ the Saviour, but simple, childlike faith," Ryle goes on to emphasize that, not a mere belief in Christ, but "an experimental knowledge of Christ crucified and interceding, is the very essence of Christianity."[21] This "experimental knowledge of Christ"—Christ felt, seen, *experienced*—can come only as the result of grace, and therefore only an emotional experience of Christ can demonstrate true conversion, true openness to God. According to Ryle, the fourth characteristic tenet of Evangelical Anglicanism is the emphasis it places upon "the *inward work of the Holy Spirit in the heart of man*":

> Its theory is that the root and foundation of all vital Christianity in any one, is a work of grace in the heart, and that until there is real experimental business within a man, his religion is a mere husk. . . . We hold that, as an inward work of the Holy Ghost is a necessary thing to a man's salvation, so it is a thing that must be inwardly *felt*. . . . And we insist that where there is nothing *felt* within the heart of a man, there is nothing really possessed.[22]

First of all, the Holy Ghost must enable the recipient

[21] *Knots Untied*, p. 6.    [22] *Ibid.*, p. 7.

of grace to sense the presence of death close at hand. Before one can turn to Christ and appreciate his gift of eternal life, one must first experience the fear of death and damnation, and therefore the preacher, trying to assist the work of grace, emphasizes that all must die. Similarly, in a tract directed at the young, Ryle thus assures his readers: "Young men, it is appointed unto you to die; and however strong and healthy you may be now, the day of your death is perhaps very near. I see young people sick as well as old. I bury youthful corpses as well as aged."[23] According to William Wilberforce's *Practical Christianity,* one of the most influential of all Evangelical works, such felt experience and conviction of one's own death separates the true believer from "the generality of nominal Christians, who are almost entirely taken up with the concerns of the present world. They *know* indeed that they are mortal, but they do not *feel* it."[24] After feeling the closeness of death, one must feel one's guilt, and finally one must experience the presence of Christ in one's life, feeling both what Christ suffered for man and his grace in one's own actions.

This emphasis upon a felt emotional religious experience, so central to Evangelical belief, provided support for the romantic critical theory upon which Ruskin drew in formulating his own views of art and aesthetics. First of all, the Evangelical preacher and the individual worshipper demanded the same qualities of religious experience as did the romantic poet and theorist: both Evangelicalism and romanticism required spontaneous, personal, intense, sincere emotions upon

23 *Twelve Hints to Young Men* (Philadelphia, n.d.), p. 10.
24 The full title of *Practical Christianity* is *A Practical View of the Prevailing Religious System of Professed Christians, in the Higher and Middle Classes in this Country, Contrasted with Real Christianity,* 18th ed. (London, 1830), p. 122.

which to found one's life or one's art. This convergence of religion and poetry is understandable in the light of the fact that both drew upon theories of moral perception and the sympathetic imagination. In fact, Wilberforce gave Adam Smith's *Theory of the Moral Sentiments*, which presented emotionalist theories of moral perception and sympathy, something very like official party sanction when he cited it frequently in his *Practical Christianity*.[25] In addition, Wilberforce devoted large sections of his devotional and proselytizing work to defending the role of the emotions in religion, something about which the High Church party had grave doubts. His chief argument for the role of the emotions sounds much like Ruskin's own statements on human nature, for he argues that religion must appeal to the whole man, to the emotions as well as to the reason.[26] Introducing emotions into religion always risks the dangers of an isolating, dividing subjectivity, but the Evangelical preachers assured the faithful that faith itself would insure that their emotion was the influence of grace and not, as Swift had asserted, the product of a less divine afflatus. Similarly, Ruskin sought to assure his audience not only that their deeply felt experiences of art and beauty were themselves earnest, noble, and essential to the spiritual life of man, but that they directly derived from God. In particular, Ruskin's theory of the beautiful, which posits the symbolic presence of

25 For example, he quotes Smith's assertion that things closest at hand most strike our imaginations, using this as an argument for bringing the passions into religion (p. 68); see also *ibid.*, pp. 68, 165, 182.

26 "It is her [Christianity's] peculiar glory, and her special office, to bring all the faculties of our nature into their just subordination and dependence; that so the whole man, complete in all his functions, may be restored to the true ends of his being, and be devoted, entire and harmonious, to the service and glory of God" (*ibid.*, p. 54).

God, asserts the religious nature of this mode of aesthetic experience. When we examine his theories of allegory and allegorical imagination in the following chapter, we shall observe other ways that Ruskin's theories try to guarantee the value and truth of aesthetic experience by modeling it upon the life of faith.

Finally, the Evangelical Anglicans believed "that the true grace of God is a thing that will always make itself manifest in the conduct, behaviour, tastes, ways, choices and habits of him who has it,"[27] and although they held that good works could in no way earn salvation, which was entirely the gift of God, they placed great value on them as a sign of divine grace in action. Ryle emphasized: "We affirm confidently that 'fruit' is the only certain evidence of a man's spiritual condition."[28] As first evidence of grace the newly converted member of the faith had to exemplify in his own life the beliefs he professed; he had to make his life an emblem of religion in action, a doctrine which Melvill emphasized in a sermon Ruskin liked enough to summarize in his diary: "The believer has to give an exhibition—a representation of religion; it rests with him to furnish practical evidence of what religion is, and of what religion does."[29] Furthermore, Melvill explains elsewhere: "As the people of God, they must carry religion with them into every business of life, and see to it that all scenes are pervaded by its influence"[30]—an enterprise continually apparent in Ruskin's aesthetics, art criticism, and economic theory.

Then, while the true believer attempted to make himself a living emblem of his faith, carrying "religion

27 *Knots Untied*, p. 8.　　28 *Ibid.*
29 "The Duty of Rejoicing," p. 103.
30 "God's People Never Ashamed," p. 49.

into every business of life," he also had to make others receptive to the words of God. The Evangelical belief in an emotional, felt religion plus this commitment to good works produced that characteristic zeal to aid the spiritual well-being of others. In Melvill's "The Greatness of being Instrumental to Another's Conversion," which Ruskin considered a "fine sermon," the preacher characterized the "true Christian" as "one, who burns with zeal for the glory of God, and who loves his fellow-men, as children of the same Father, and redeemed by the same blood. Show him, then, what he can do to promote God's glory, or to benefit his fellow-men, and you show him what he will eagerly seize upon, as meeting his desires and serving his energies."[31] Not all Evangelicals spoke with Melvill's gentleness and generosity, for this zealous desire to do good for others produced a characteristic Evangelical arrogance well exemplified by Ryle's statement that "zeal will make a man hate unscriptural teaching, just as he hates sin. It will make him regard religious error as a pestilence which must be checked, whatever may be the cost."[32] The cost in other people's feelings never, it seems, appeared too high a price for zealous Evangelicals to pay, and they willingly, all too willingly, censured others with that freedom born of the heady conviction that God approved the words and deeds of the converted. Ryle himself frankly admitted that although many people "think it uncharitable to say anything which appears to condemn others," he for one could not understand such charity: "It seems to me the charity which would see a neighbour drinking slow poison, but never

[31] *The Pulpit*, XLV (1843), 9. Ruskin mentions this sermon in *Diaries*, I, 256 (31 December 1843).
[32] *Rich and Poor* (New York, 1855), pp. 16-17.

interfere to stop him."[33] The Evangelicals willingly interfered, knocking from the Englishman's hand such poison cups as the workingman's sabbath amusements. Although they occasionally accomplished some good, particularly in suppressing the slave trade, they too frequently acted with an arrogant and heavy hand, and after Ruskin had parted from the Evangelicals he disliked them heartily for this proud conviction that they, and only they, possessed the truth. In *Fors Clavigera* Ruskin satirically characterized the father of Frederick the Great as "an Evangelical divine of the strictest orthodoxy," because he was "entirely resolved to have his own way, supposing, as pure Evangelical people always do, that his own way was God's also"(28.68). Similarly, in a lecture which he delivered at Oxford in 1870, he described not only the Evangelical party but all "modern Protestantism" as that religion, "which consists in an assured belief in the Divine forgiveness of all your sins, and the Divine correctness of all your opinions"(22.81). Nonetheless, however much he may have later criticized the arrogant crusading zeal of the Evangelicals, it left firm imprints on his own thought, reinforcing his conviction both that he knew the truth and that he had to bear it to others. Similarly, Evangelical societies for the prevention of vice and the distribution of Bibles, for the converting of the heathen and the saving of waifs and strays, grew out of the same attitudes one may perceive in Ruskin's statements about the working class. And part of Ruskin's arrogance toward artists came from the fact that, like the Evangelicals in religion, he believed he was the bearer of truth who must do good for others—with or without their aid or even desire. By the time he was nine years old, Ruskin

[33] *Living or Dead?*, p. 236.

had copied into his notebooks the Evangelical belief that "He that is not for me is against me,"[34] and the signs of this attitude continued to mark his life and writings many years after he had abandoned Evangelicalism.

Furthermore, Ruskin shared the Evangelical attitude toward criticism by others. At the same time that this Church party easily dismissed the feelings of "narrow-minded" Christians, censuring them at will, they reacted to all criticism of their own group as the clear sign of Satan's work; in fact, they all but cherished such criticism as a martyrdom which the children of God had to bear in an evil, unconverted world. During the first years of the Evangelical movement, which began in the second half of the eighteenth century, many in the Church of England did scorn their indecorous enthusiasm and itinerant preaching. But long after they had attained power within the Church and had become an influence in the nation, the Evangelicals continued to regard themselves, rather incongruously, as a persecuted little sect bravely enduring the jibes of those others who would soon enough find themselves consigned to the flames of hell. Ryle exemplifies the usual martyr complex of the Evangelicals when he warns his readers that "God's true people are still a despised little flock. True Evangelical religion still brings with it reproach and scorn. A real servant of God will still be thought by many a weak enthusiast and a fool."[35] Melvill similarly told his congregation that "The converted

[34] This text appears in some of the rough notes which Ruskin took on the sermons of the Reverend E. Andrews, Beresford Chapel, in preparation for the polished sermon records he made for his mother in 1828. These notes are contained in seven volumes of notebooks and juvenilia in the Yale library. For more on these and other sermon notes, see below, pp. 336-39, 402.

[35] *Living or Dead?*, pp. 314-315.

member, being secretly disliked, will, under some shape or other, be persecuted by the unconverted."[36] Ruskin too had this sense that he and those whose causes he advocated were "persecuted by the unconverted," and this attitude toward hostile criticism often colors his statements both in *Modern Painters*, particularly the first volume, and his later works on political economy. Of course, the fact that he so often espoused unpopular causes—Turner, the Pre-Raphaelites, and Christian socialism come immediately to mind —certainly exposed him to much hostile criticism. And while Ruskin sometimes quietly accepted this criticism to a degree that has not often been realized, he more usually reacted with hostility and sarcasm to any adverse comment, as though, like the Evangelicals in religion, his advocacy of truth had subjected him to martyrdom in the public arena.[37] Although such an attitude surely is largely a matter of individual personality, the religion in which his parents had raised him continually served to reinforce it.

We can also perceive in Ruskin that peculiar ruthlessness associated with the Evangelicals. As one might expect, the Evangelicals' confidence that they possessed the only Right often led them to believe that their great purpose of salvation justified whatever means they, the elect, the men of the second birth, found necessary. Ryle was most characteristic when he stated: "I loathe that squeamishness which refuses to help religious works if there is a blemish about the instrument by which the work is to be carried on."[38] Ford K. Brown's

---

[36] "Christianity a Sword," *Sermons* (London, 1838), pp. 131-158.

[37] For several examples of such acceptance of criticism see my "Ruskin's Revisions of the Third Edition of *Modern Painters*, Volume I," *VN*, XXXIII (1968), 12-16.

[38] *Be Zealous*, p. 33.

*Fathers of the Victorians* has shown how remarkably unsqueamish the Evangelicals could, in fact, be. Believing that they had to make vice unpopular and unfashionable before they could drive it from the land, they willingly used many instruments with blemishes about them. For example, Evangelical organizers of societies to save "fallen women" thought nothing amiss in making well-known rakes, if titled, their patrons and honorary presidents, since such action would in the long run, they believed, serve the interests of morality. Thus, we have the grotesque situation in which those who helped women fall, and delighted when they did, presided over movements to stamp out their favorite pleasures.[39] The Evangelicals did not seek to avoid such hypocritical situations, for as Ryle affirmed, "Zeal in the end will be justified by its results."[40]

Similarly, this confidence that he was in possession of the sole Right was surely one reason that Ruskin continued to cite scripture in support of his arguments, knowing well, as he must, that such a style and such a tone suited the tones of the time and the expectations of many in his intended audience. Furthermore, he was well aware of the hostile public reaction that awaited anyone who left the faith. As he wrote in 1859 to

[39] "The genial and debauched Marquis of Hertford and his genial and debauched son and successor, one or the other the original of Thackeray's Lord Steyne, contributed steadily, as a rule to societies not religious or moral, though like the Regent, his brother York and some other noted performers in the amorous history of the age they seemed to feel the claim on them of the institutions caring for prostitutes, women with venereal disease, and seduced, pregnant or otherwise unhappy unmarried young women" (*Fathers of the Victorians*, pp. 345-346). *Fathers of the Victorians*, which contains a list of Evangelical organizations (pp. 329-340), explains at length this Church party's working principles of moral reform and its tacit assumption that only the vices of the lower orders were to be suppressed (pp. 4-5, 84). See in particular Brown's history of the Vice Society (pp. 428-445).
[40] *Be Zealous*, p. 28.

Charles Eliot Norton, a close friend: "I don't believe in Evangelicalism—and my Evangelical (once) friends now look upon me with as much horror as on one of the possessed Gennesaret pigs"(36.313). Another reason for Ruskin's reticence, at least after 1862, was that in that year he promised Mrs. La Touche, a close friend, not to make any public statements on his loss of belief for another ten years.[41]

## II. Loss of belief

WHATEVER Ruskin's complex reasons, we are led to agree with a statement he made in an intended preface to *Prosperina* (1881) that he knew "no other author of candour who has given so partial, so disproportioned, so steadily reserved a view of his personality. Who could tell from my books, for instance . . . what has been the course of religious effort and speculation in me?"(35.628) It is a fact characteristic of Ruskin that it was not until he had a use for his religious history— not until he believed it would have value for others— that he chose to reveal publicly the story of his "religious effort and speculation," and this he did in two places, *Fors Clavigera* (1878) and *Praeterita* (1886). In *Praeterita* Ruskin tells us that he had already, by the age of fourteen, been unable to accept his mother's faith in the literal truth of the Bible: "It had never entered into my head to doubt a word of the Bible, though I saw well enough already that its words were to be understood otherwise than I had been taught; but the more I believed it, the less it did me any good. It was all very well for Abraham to do what angels bid him,—so would I, if any angels bid me; but none had

[41] Ruskin mentioned this promise in a letter he wrote to his father in 1863 (34.662n).

ever appeared to me that I knew of"(35.189). It soon
entered into Ruskin's mind to question the words of the
Bible. As with so many other Victorians, geology did
much to weaken Ruskin's faith. Geological discoveries
were casting doubt on the possibility of a flood, as described in the Old Testament, and Ruskin confided to
Henry Acland in 1851 that his beloved science, geology,
was destroying his faith and his peace of spirit:

> You speak of the Flimsiness of your own faith. Mine,
> which was never strong, is being beaten into mere
> gold leaf, and flutters in weak rags from the letter of
> its old forms; but the only letters it can hold by at all
> are the old Evangelical formulae. If only the Geolo-
> gists would let me alone, I could do very well, but
> those dreadful Hammers! I hear the clink of them at
> the end of every cadence of the Bible verses.
> (36.115)

In 1862, four years after he lost his religion at the
church service in Turin, a book appeared which was
a great help to Ruskin's peace of mind, for it showed
that he was not alone in his questionings, and that a
man learned in the study of scripture had also come to
the conclusion that the Bible was not historically true.
This book was Bishop John William Colenso's *The
Pentateuch and the Book of Joshua Critically Examined,* and of it Ruskin wrote to Sir John Naesmyth:

> One great worry is over and settled, and in a way
> which Lady Naesmyth and you will be mightily sorry
> for. You will soon hear—if you have not heard—of
> the Bishop of Natal's book. Now for the last four
> years I've been working in the same direction alone,
> and was quite unable to tell anyone what I was

about. . . . I could not speak of anything, because all things have their root in that. . . .

But now the Bishop has spoken, there will be fair war directly, and one must take one's side, and I stand with the Bishop and am at ease, and a wonderful series of things is going to happen—more than any of us know—but the *indecision* is over. (36.424-425)

Ruskin was correct, for there was to be a battle over Colenso's book, a battle in the course of which an attempt would be made to depose, defrock, and, finally, excommunicate the Bishop. The government would not allow this; and although the Evangelical Anglicans, who provided much of the financial support for his missionary work, withdrew their aid, Colenso retained his see and continued as Bishop to become engaged in other controversies. In later years Ruskin held it against the English clergy that they had resisted truth in ways dishonest and unfair: "The clergy, as a body, have, with what energy and power was in them, repelled the advance both of science and scholarship, so far as either interfered with what they had been accustomed to teach; and connived at every abuse in public and private conduct, with which they felt it would be considered uncivil, and feared it might ultimately prove unsafe, to interfere"(28.364). Of course, here in *Fors Clavigera* he refers not only to Colenso but also to the matter of *Essays and Reviews*(1860). Ruskin, like many others, realized that Higher Criticism, geology, and biology were fast overrunning the weakened positions of both the Evangelical and High Church parties, and he would have preferred the Church to beat an honest retreat to surer ground rather than attack those

who advocated such a policy. The Evangelicals did not change their positions, because in fact they could not, and as the decades passed the incursions of science and scholarship drove many from their ranks, weakening this once powerful force in the Church. The result was as Matthew Arnold described it in 1870: "The Evangelical clergy no longer recruits itself with success, no longer lays hold on such promising subjects as formerly. It is losing the future and feels that it is losing it. . . . The best of their own younger generation, the soldiers of their own training, are slipping away from them."[42] Thus, five years later Ruskin could charge, not only against his own former coreligionists but against all men of the Church, that "in general, any man's becoming a clergyman in these days implies that, at best, his sentiment has overpowered his intellect"(28.239).

It was precisely this weakening of the Church and the strengthening of these hostile attitudes that Colenso had tried to forestall in 1862 by removing points of doctrine which men of the mid-nineteenth century found impossible to believe. For him the entire problem centered on the right of the minister to free thought, a right which, as he wrote in a later volume, was denied by a law which bound each minister "by law to believe in the historical truth of Noah's Flood, as recorded in the Bible, which the Church believed in some centuries ago, before God had given us the light of modern science."[43] The blows of the geologist's hammer were here decisive. In the preface to the volume which Ruskin had mentioned in his letter to Sir John

[42] *Dissent and Dogma*, ed. R. H. Super (Ann Arbor, Mich., 1968), p. 110.
[43] *The Pentateuch and the Book of Joshua Critically Examined*, Part II (London, 1863), xxi-xxii.

Naesmyth he would have encountered doubts similar to his own:

> My own knowledge of some branches of science, of Geology in particular, had been much increased since I left England; and I now knew for certain, on geological grounds, a fact, of which I had only had misgivings before, viz., that a *Universal* Deluge, such as the Bible manifestly speaks of, could not possibly have taken place in the way described in the Book of Genesis, not to mention other difficulties which the story contains. I refer especially to the circumstance, well known to all geologists, . . . that volcanic hills exist of immense extent in Auvergne and Languedoc, which must have been formed ages before the Noachian Deluge, and which are covered with light and loose substances, pumice-stone &c., that must have been swept away by a Flood, but do not exhibit the slightest sign of having ever been so disturbed.[44]

Once the Bishop's doubts had been aroused by the facts of geology and further stimulated by the questions of native assistants who were aiding his translation of the Bible, he proceeded to examine "the other difficulties the story contains."

After investigating the details, as presented in Exodus, of camp life, of sacrifice, of numbers of men and animals—details all of which, according to contemporary ecclesiastic law, had to be literally true—Bishop Colenso was led to the conviction, painful, he said, both to himself and his reader, that

> the Pentateuch, as a whole, cannot personally have been written by Moses, or by anyone acquainted per-

[44] *Ibid.*, Part I (1862), vii-viii.

sonally with the facts which it professes to describe, and, further, that the (so-called) Mosaic narrative, by whomsoever written, and though imparting to us, as I fully believe it does, revelations of the Divine Will and Character, cannot be regarded as *historically true.*[45]

To feel the force of these words and to understand the anguish they both caused and relieved, it is necessary to realize how widespread was the view, quoted by Colenso, that "The Bible cannot be less than verbally inspired. *Every word, every syllable, every letter, is just what it would be, had God spoken from heaven without any human intervention.*"[46] In the introductory remarks to the first part of his work, Colenso quotes from Burgon's *Inspiration and Interpretation,* a standard work for ministerial students:

The BIBLE is none other than *the Voice of Him that sitteth upon the Throne!* Every book of it—every chapter of it—every verse of it—every word of it— every syllable of it—(where are we to stop?) every *letter* of it—is the direct utterance of the Most High! The Bible is none other than the word of God—not some part of it more, some part of it less, but all alike, the utterance of Him, who sitteth upon the Throne—absolute—faultless—unerring—supreme.[47]

Colenso adds, "Such was the creed of the School in which I was educated," and such was the school in which Ruskin was educated; and both cast off this creed, choosing to regard the Bible as poetry whose

[45] *Ibid.,* p. 8.
[46] *Ibid.,* preface to Part II, xii.
[47] *Ibid.,* I, 6.

value lay in the fact that it recorded the constancy of man's need for virtue and cognizance of sin.[48]

Ruskin's approval of Colenso's book indicates the cause and course of his doubtings. But, since *The Pentateuch and the Book of Joshua Critically Examined* appeared four years after Ruskin's decisive loss of faith, its only influence can have been the reconfirmation of an earlier "unconversion," and this is also true of other Broad Church writings, such as *Essays and Reviews* (1860), with which Ruskin was familiar.[49] One must be careful not to overstress the importance of influences upon Ruskin, for, unless in any particular instance there is evidence to the contrary, I believe we must accept Ruskin's own statement to his father in a letter of 1861: "Mamma has a horror of these people—Carlyle, etc.—because she thinks they 'pervert' me; but I never understand them till I find the thing out for myself"(36.396). Similarly, two years later Ruskin wrote to his father "I wish you could put out of your mind—that either Carlyle, Colenso, or Froude, much less anyone less than they, have had the smallest share in this change. Three years ago, long before Colenso was heard of, I had definitely refused to have anything more to do with the religious teaching in this [Evangelical] school"(36.460). I think we must conclude that however similar Ruskin's later view of biblical his-

---

[48] *Ibid.,* p. 381.

[49] Ruskin almost certainly knew *Essays and Reviews* when it appeared in 1860; in *Sesame and Lilies* (18.77) and *Time and Tide* (17.360) he refers to the controversy and the trials for heresy (1864) which it caused. I have chosen to discuss Colenso rather than *Essays and Reviews*, because Ruskin seems to have approved so highly of his work. At the same time, one must recognize, as Professor Van Akin Burd has kindly pointed out to me, that Ruskin never gave Colenso any public support despite his initial enthusiasm.

toricity was to that of the Broad Churchmen, he arrived at this view independently.[50]

Ruskin's letter to Joan Severn in 1867 tells us of his
attitude toward scripture seven years after he finished
*Modern Painters*:

> I notice in one of your late letters some notion that
> I am coming to think the Bible the 'Word of God' be-
> cause I use it . . . for daily teaching. But I was never
> farther from thinking, and never can be nearer to
> thinking, anything of the sort. Nothing could ever
> persuade me that God writes vulgar Greek. . . . If
> there is any divine truth at all in the mixed collec-
> tion of books which we call a Bible, that truth is, that
> the Word of God comes *directly* to different people
> in different ways. (36.538-539)

Again, nine years later, Ruskin warned the working
men of England against the notions of the Bible propa-
gated by the Evangelicals within and without the
Church: "Don't suppose that the printed thing in your
hand, which you call a Bible, is the Word of God, and
that the said Word may therefore always be bought at
a pious stationer's for eighteen-pence"(28.587). Instead,
as *Fors Clavigera* had stated two years earlier in 1874,
the Bible is rather "an ill written, and worse trans-writ-
ten, human history, and not by any means 'Word of
God'; and . . . whatever issues of life, divine or human,

---

[50] F. D. Maurice, with whom Ruskin taught at the Workingman's
College, provides an example of a churchman whose views Ruskin
may have approached but who does not seem a plausible influence
upon him. In the first place, as Ruskin tells us in *Praeterita* (35.486),
although he "loved Frederick Maurice, as everyone did who came near
him," yet he "was by nature puzzle-headed, and, though in a beautiful
manner, *wrong*-headed . . . and in his Bible-reading, as insolent as any
infidel." Ruskin never seems to have respected Maurice's intellect, particularly as concerned religion.

there may be in it, for you, can only be got by searching it; and not by chopping it up into small bits and
swallowing it like pills"(28.72). In other words, at this
point in his life he believed the Bible should be read
much like any other human work—studied more atten-
tively and more reverently, possibly, but by no means
taken as divine instruction whose every word merits
equal reverence. Ever the polemical writer defining his
position in contrast to those he opposed, Ruskin now
concerns himself with denying Evangelical statements
about scripture, and this in part explains the unpleasant sarcasm of his remarks. Once he walked out of the
chapel in Turin, Ruskin, I believe, would have agreed
with Matthew Arnold's complaint in 1873 that "we have
been trained to regard the Bible, not as a book whose
parts have varying degrees of value, but as the Jews came
to regard their Scriptures, as a sort of talisman given
down to us out of Heaven, with all its parts equipol-
lent."[51] And like Arnold he felt that "to re-inthrone the
Bible as explained by our current theology, whether
learned or popular, is absolutely and for ever impossible!"[52] Since Ruskin's religious views underwent several
modifications, it is particularly valuable to have his statements about the Bible, for they reveal that although he
may have returned to several of his old points of faith in
later years, once he rejected the notion of a divinely
inspired scripture that his mother had taught him, he
never returned to this belief. Indeed, as *Fors Clavigera*
demonstrates, he seems to have become increasingly
scornful of the Testaments, despite the fact that their
words and phrasing continued to permeate his writing,
shape his political economics, and perhaps even haunt
his thoughts.

[51] *Dissent and Dogma*, p. 159.     [52] *Ibid.*, p. 149.

But, as Ruskin had much earlier written to Acland, the letters of his Evangelical belief—an acceptance of the literal accuracy of the Bible—had been the mainstay of his wavering religion. Once he lost his faith in the Bible, another, equally tormenting problem gained importance until it, finally, drove him from the religion of his parents. This other problem was whether or not there was a life after death. Ruskin felt that he could not believe in an afterlife without also believing in damnation, and yet the horror of damnation seemed too cruel, too terrible, to accept. For a long while his intense need to believe in a life after death was enough to maintain an acceptance of damnation. For like the Pastor in Wordsworth's *Excursion*, that poem which he so loved in his early years, he felt the certain need to hold to

> The head and mighty paramount of truths,—
> Immortal life, in never-fading worlds,
> For mortal creatures, conquered and secured.[53]

In April 1852 Ruskin wrote to his father from Venice of his need to believe:

> I cannot understand the make of the minds that can do without a hope of the future: Carlyle for instance is continually enforcing the necessity of being virtuous and enduring all pain and self denial, without any hope of reward. I do not find myself in the least able to do this: I am too mean—or too selfish; and I find that vexations and labours would break me down, unless I could look forward to a "crown of rejoicing." My poor friend Mr George used to talk of death in exactly the same tone that he did of going to bed, as no evil at all, though expressing no hope

[53] *Works*, v, 188.

whatever of rising from that bed. I cannot do this: so far from it that I could no longer look upon the Alps, or the heavens, or the sea, with any pleasure—because I felt that every breath brought the hour nearer when I must leave them all. To believe in a future life is for me, the only way in which I can enjoy this one.[54]

Like Young, a poet whom with Wordsworth, Milton, and Herbert, Ruskin at this time placed among religious writers, he felt completely that

> 'Tis immortality, 'tis that alone,
> Amid life's pains, abasements, emptiness,
> The soul can comfort, elevate, and fill.[55]

In fact, when we try to sense the tone of his doubts and beliefs, we must turn to the religious poets he most admired, as well as to Evangelical writings; for part of his agony came from the fact that his favorite poets continued to reinforce the doctrines about which he increasingly felt doubt. Young, for example, emphasized the point Ruskin had been making to his father, that only immortality can make earthly life bearable and morality possible:

> Virtue, and vice, are at eternal war.
> Virtue's a combat; and who fights for nought?
> Or for precarious, or for small reward?

And

> The man immortal, rationally brave,
> Dares rush on death—because he cannot die.

<hr>

[54] *Ruskin's Letters from Venice, 1851-1852*, p. 247.
[55] *The Complaint: or, Night-Thoughts on Life, Death, and Immortality* (Glasgow, 1775), p. 161.

But if man loses all, when life is lost,
He lives a coward, or a fool expires.[56]

The poems of Young, to take but one example from the poets Ruskin had with him in Venice, thus encouraged him to hold fast to the belief in an afterlife.[57]

But despite the support which Ruskin's faith received from these believing poets, he had already begun to move away from Evangelical Anglicanism. A clear sign of his gradual movement away from childhood belief appears in *The Stones of Venice*, which reveals him casting off narrow sectarian attitudes and trying to grant other religions their just due. In contrast, if we examine *The Seven Lamps of Architecture* (1848), Ruskin's last major work before writing *The Stones of Venice*, we observe him self-consciously marching forth under the Evangelical banner, accompanied by zeal and intolerance, as he tries to save the Gothic for low church Protestantism by driving off the

[56] *Ibid.*, pp. 186, 184.

[57] Professor Bradley's invaluable edition of *Ruskin's Letters from Venice, 1851-1852* includes Ruskin's description of the religious readings he had with him in December 1851: "I have plenty of religious book[s]—Young—George Herbert—Vinet—d'Aubigné—Milton—Wordsworth and Milner—only there is something very refreshing in Mr Melville. I class Wordsworth as a thoroughly religious book—in fact I believe for all practical use—he is much more so than Milton—It is almost impossible that anything can be more noble or *useful* than the entire passage beginning about 60 lines into the 4th book with 'And what are things eternal' and going on to the end of the speech of the Wanderer—some hundred and 70 or 80 lines, but more especially the passage beginning 'Here then we rest not fearing for our creed.' This passage—and the whole of the poem called the 'Happy Warrior,' and Young's very correspondent description—far in the poem but I forget in which book—of 'the man on earth devoted to the skies'—are as far as I know—the best things that profane poetry has yet done for the help and guidance of mankind—Dante being prevented from having his full effect by his imaginative wildness and Romanism, and George Herbert being the expression in *detail* of that which passages sum up in the most comprehensive and philosophical 'manner' " (pp. 92-93).

claims of Pugin, the Roman Catholics, and men of the High Church. These efforts to rescue the Gothic style for English Protestantism lead him to attack other faiths—both because he believed they persisted in error and because he had to adopt such a manner to attract Evangelicals within and without the Church, who might be suspicious of anyone advocating such Romanist styles of building.[58] Although he occasionally lambasts the Catholics in *The Stones of Venice* with his usual zeal, he now, a brief three years later, defends them on occasion and also heavily censures the Protestant sects as well. For example, although he writes scornfully of "the debased manufacture of wooden and waxen images which is the support of Romanist idolatry all over the world"(10.130), he adds a long appendix explaining that he does

not intend, in thus applying the word "Idolatry" to certain ceremonies of Romanist worship, to admit the propriety of the ordinary Protestant manner of regarding those ceremonies as distinctively idolatrous, and as separating the Romanist from the Protestant Church by a gulf across which we must not look to our fellow Christians but with utter reprobation and disdain. . . . Idolatry is, both literally and verily, not the mere bowing down before sculptures, but the serving or becoming the slave of any images or imag-

[58] Although Ruskin firmly denied that he had been influenced by Pugin (5.428-429), writers have generally assumed that he was not telling the truth. However, one must admit that many of Pugin's ideas were current by the time Ruskin wrote, and he may have come upon them in the art periodicals he read without knowing their major source. In addition, it is quite likely, as Ruskin suggests in his essay on Prout (14.385), that his early love for this artist's style and subject encouraged his defense of Gothic. Carlyle, Rio, and Lindsay may also have served as important influences here as well.

inations which stand between us and God. (10.450-451)

After thus defining idolatry he then confronts his Protestant readers with the searching question: "Which of us is not an idolater? Which of us has the right . . . to speak scornfully of any of his brethren, because, in a guiltless ignorance, they have been accustomed to bow their knees before a statue?"(10.451) Obviously rejecting the Evangelical point of view, he excuses the Catholic worshipper, claiming that even when the ignorant in fact worship the saint's statue "we shall oftener find it the consequence of dulness of intellect than of real alienation of heart from God; and I have no manner of doubt that half of the poor and untaught Christians who are this day lying prostrate before crucifixes, Bambinos, and Volto Santos, are finding more acceptance with God than many Protestants who idolise nothing but their own opinions or their own interests" (10.451-452). Two things of importance stand out in this passage: first, Ruskin has rejected the usual Evangelical intolerance toward other faiths, an intolerance which marks the statements of even a learned and humane Evangelical clergyman such as Melvill, who considers the Catholic Church the Whore of Babylon.[59] Sec-

[59] See for example, "Protestantism and Popery," *Sermons* (1854), I, 307-319. Ruskin's bitterly anti-Catholic mother was greatly troubled by his new attitudes toward religion. After their return from Venice, Effie wrote to her mother that "Mrs R goes to such extremes of anti-popery that I am really afraid of her tormenting John into being more with them than he otherwise would. . . . She says we have been living for a year amongst idolators and infidels and that for that time we have not heard a word of truth. She abuses the Austrians and holds up the Hungarians and Italians by the Hour and if we say anything she says we know nothing but lies. John says he never heard anything like her and that you are nothing to her, now she abuses the Jesuits far more than ever you did" (*Millais and the Ruskins*, p. 16). Effie wrote, not from tolerance, but from an equal desire to protect Ruskin from Roman

ondly, at this point in Ruskin's career, faith, any faith, becomes worthy of reverence and unworthy of sectarian scorn. He himself had been trying so strenuously to retain his own religious faith that he admires and praises all those who had succeeded. His newly acquired public tolerance of other religions, particularly of Catholicism, appears when, in relating the history of the Church of San Donato on Murano, he advises his English Protestant readers that "The legends of the Romish Church, though generally more insipid and less varied than those of Paganism, deserve audience from us on this ground, if no other, that they have once been sincerely believed by good men, and have had no ineffective agency in the formation of the existent European mind"(10.42). Although he tells his readers, who might be expected to despise Catholic legend, that such information will aid their understanding of cultural history, he more significantly points out that these legends deserve attention because "they have once been sincerely believed by good men." Any belief should be reverenced. Similarly, when he describes Torcello he remarks that "the weeping Madonna in the act of Intercession, may indeed be a matter of sorrow to the Protestant beholder, but ought not to blind him to the earnestness and singleness of the faith"(10.27) of Torcello's founders. For Ruskin the most important fact at this period was not the believer's doctrine but that "The mind of the worshipper was fixed entirely upon two great facts, to him the most precious of all facts,— the present mercy of Christ to His Church, and His future coming to judge the world"(10.27). He praises the medieval figures of the Palazzo Ducale for a faith even

---

Catholicism, and her letters prompted her mother, Mrs. Gray, to write to her son-in-law to warn him of the dangers of the Papists.

more general in its points, for he now directs the reader to observe "their simple expression of two feelings, the consciousness of human frailty, and the dependence upon Divine guidance and protection"(10.364). The degree to which his own sincere yearning for faith led him to reverence any such worship appears even more strikingly in his statement that "there is a wider division of men than that into Christian and Pagan: before we ask what a man worships, we have to ask whether he worships at all"(10.67). He concludes that a far greater difference exists between those who do not believe and those who do—whether in Mary, Athena, or the "Syrian Queen of Heaven"(10.67). We may surely conclude, then, that Ruskin so valued any faith that he reverenced its appearance in any form. What he most desired appears in his praise of the pure and simple— if for him unattainable—faith of the Middle Ages, which, centering on the love of God, "comprehended everything, entered into everything; it was too vast and too spiritual, to be defined; but there was no need of its definition"(10.366). This was the kind of faith for which Ruskin desperately yearned; but this was the kind of faith which both his doctrine and his doubts made most difficult to have or to hold.[60]

In fact, as early as 1848 when he still wrote as a firm Evangelical, Ruskin had experienced doubts, and he had tried to still them. At this time Ruskin had written to his father, discussing his own thoughts in Pascal's wager,[61] and in 1852 he wrote to his father in a time of

[60] I agree with Professor Rosenberg (*The Darkening Glass*, p. 55) that Ruskin never approached conversion to Catholicism. For an interesting letter which Ruskin wrote to Mrs. Gray on the subject of his attitudes toward Catholicism, see *Millais and the Ruskins*, pp. 19-21.
[61] Quoted in E. T. Cook, *Life of Ruskin*, 2 vols. (London, 1911), I, 227.

severer trial that the desire for a belief in a heavenly reward, and the need to quiet his tormented spirit, had encouraged him to elect his own version of Pascal's choice:

> I considered that I had now neither pleasure in looking to my past life—nor any hope such as would be any comfort to me on a sickbed, of a future one. And I made up my mind that this would never do. So after thinking a little more about it, I resolved that at any rate I would act as if the Bible *were* true; that if it were not, at all events I should be no worse off than I was before.[62]

This commitment was sufficient to calm his inquiring mind for a short while, but his doubts continued to mount; and by 1858 when he finally experienced his "unconversion," Ruskin was no longer able to continue this willing suspension of disbelief.

Since Ruskin relates two slightly different versions of those decisive few hours in Turin, it is unlikely that we shall ever know precisely what occurred at the moment of crisis. Upon comparing the version which appeared in the April 1877 *Fors Clavigera* with the one that Ruskin presented eleven years later in *Praeterita,* one is struck at once by their markedly different tones and sequences of events. *Fors* thus describes the moment at which he abandoned his religion in 1858:

> I was still in the bonds of my old Evangelical faith; and, in 1858, it was with me, Protestantism or nothing: the crisis of the whole turn of my thoughts being one Sunday morning, at Turin, when, from before Paul Veronese's Queen of Sheba, and under quite

62 *Letters from Venice,* p. 244.

overwhelmed sense of his God-given power, I went away to a Waldensian chapel, where a little squeaking idiot was preaching to an audience of seventeen old women and three louts, that they were the only children of God in Turin; and that all the people in Turin outside the chapel, and all the people in the world out of sight of Monte Viso, would be damned. I came out of the chapel, in sum of twenty years of thought, a conclusively *un*-converted man. (29.89)

Whereas *Fors* mentions that "a little squeaking idiot was preaching to an audience of seventeen old women and three louts"(29.89), *Praeterita* forgoes the strident, savagely indignant invective of 1877 and describes the chapel scene with more generosity:

The assembled congregation numbered in all some three or four and twenty, of whom fifteen or sixteen were grey-haired women. Their solitary and clerkless preacher, a somewhat stunted figure in a plain black coat, with a cracked voice, after leading them through the languid forms of prayer which are all that in truth are possible to people whose present life is dull and its terrestrial future unchangeable, put his utmost zeal into a consolatory discourse on the wickedness of the wide world . . . and on the exclusive favour with God, enjoyed by the between nineteen and twenty-four elect members of his congregation. (35.495)

Thus while *Fors* emphasizes the absurd arrogance of the few who insolently assure themselves of salvation while condemning all other men to eternal torment, *Praeterita*, which does not even mention damnation, concentrates instead on the bleakness, the dullness, the

emptiness of lives which require such cruel consolation. What he earlier attacked *Praeterita* tried to explain. These radically different attitudes toward the same subject derive both from the inconsistency of Ruskin's emotions and from his different intentions in the works which contains the story of his loss of belief. The polemic version in *Fors*, which relies on invective, uses his personal experience to provide a cautionary tale that, he hopes, will warn the workingmen of England against the twin dangers of atheism and Evangelical Protestantism. The gentler version in *Praeterita*, which tries to recapture the past, to recollect and present it in tranquility, seeks understanding rather than victory over an opponent.

But although the books' divergent purposes may help us understand why their tones differ, they do not explain why Ruskin reversed the order of his experiences in the chapel and art gallery. *Fors* tells that the "crisis" of his thought came one Sunday morning "when, from before Paul Veronese's Queen of Sheba, and under quite overwhelmed sense of his God-given power," he went to the Protestant chapel only to hear the preacher assure his Waldensian congregation that they, and only they, would escape the damnation which awaited all others in Turin. "I came out of the chapel, in sum of twenty years of thought, a conclusively *un*-converted man—converted by this little Piedmontese gentleman" (29.89). Thus, Ruskin told the workingmen of England that after an admiring contemplation of Veronese's painting had convinced him God had entered the work of this irreligious painter, he heard a sermon on damnation, which both denied the validity of his recent experience and condemned the painter to hell. Holding to his own sense of Veronese's "God-given power," Rus-

kin believed that the painter had more of God than the
man who preached damnation, and he left the service
an "*un*-converted man." According to *Fors*, then, the
pastor's statements about damnation, which so opposed
Ruskin's sense of the ways of God, finally enabled him
to choose between "Protestantism or nothing"(29.89).
In contrast, *Praeterita* states that he first attended the
Waldensian chapel and heard the sermon, after which
he encountered the painting:

> Myself neither cheered nor greatly alarmed by this
> doctrine, I walked back into the condemned city, and
> up into the gallery where Paul Veronese's Solomon
> and the Queen of Sheba glowed in full afternoon
> light. The gallery windows being open, there came
> in with the warm air, floating swells and falls of mili-
> tary music, from the courtyard before the palace,
> which seemed to me more devotional, in their perfect
> art, tune, and discipline, than anything I remem-
> bered of evangelical hymns. And as the perfect
> colour and sound gradually asserted their power on
> me, they seemed finally to fasten me in the old article
> of Jewish faith, that things done delightfully and
> rightly were always done by the help and in the
> Spirit of God. (35.495)

According to this second version of his past, Ruskin did
not experience revulsion and react strongly against the
sermon, breaking sharply with his Evangelical belief
before he left the chapel. Instead, feeling the sermon
irrelevant, he walked out of the chapel unmoved, and
only later did the music and painting convince him
that there were better ways than the Evangelical to
serve God. When Ruskin inverted the order of events,
placing the sermon before his experience in the gallery,

he changed the point of his narrative; for whereas *Fors* explains how a painting convinced him that his Evangelical religion preached a false doctrine of damnation, *Praeterita* tells how the arts of painting and music taught him how to serve God better than had his earlier belief. In fact, although his autobiography ends the story of this experience with the remark that his "evangelical beliefs were put away, to be debated of no more"(35.496), this later version really emphasizes a new conviction, a new faith in work well done, rather than a loss of religion. *Praeterita* not only fails to mention, as had *Fors*, that his decision was between "Protestantism or nothing," thereby lessening the sense of crisis, but it emphasizes affirmation rather than denial. If one tries to decide which version more accurately portrays Ruskin's feelings at this time of crisis, the evidence of his correspondence, at which we shall look, leads one to conclude that the earlier narrative in *Fors*, which emphasizes his rejection of doctrine, far better describes the event.

However differently *Fors Clavigera* and *Praeterita* describe that decisive moment when Ruskin cast away his Evangelical belief, they both record the fact that many years of thought preceded it. During these years many doubts eroded his faith, and although it would be difficult, and perhaps inaccurate, to name a single dominant cause of his final rejection of Evangelicalism, the following nine factors undoubtedly contributed to that decisive act: (1) Ruskin's lack of a personal, felt religious experience; (2) his analytical turn of mind, and particularly his analytical approach to religion; (3) his interest in the discoveries of geology and consequent loss of faith in the truth of scripture; (4) his reaction against Evangelical intolerance of other religions and

Evangelical resistance to scientific knowledge; (5) his experience of Roman Catholic culture and art; (6) his reaction against his parents, particularly against his mother's Evangelical narrow-mindedness; (7) his acquaintance with those, like the Broad Churchman Maurice and the Catholic Manning, who were Christians but not Evangelicals, and those, like Carlyle, who did not believe in any orthodox religion; (8) his acquaintance with art created by men, such as Veronese, whom he considered irreligious; (9) and his own fear of damnation and his generous moral distaste for a doctrine which would have cast men he considered admirable into eternal torment.

He decided there could not be damnation because there could not be a future existence, and this decision left him confused and embittered for many years. During the period of Ruskin's agnosticism, which lasted from 1858 until 1875, his letters express bitter contempt for religion in general and Evangelicalism in particular. He wrote to Norton in 1861 that he felt "intense scorn of all I had hitherto done or thought, still intenser scorn of other people's doings and thinkings, especially in religion"(36.356). Furthermore, after he had rejected his religious belief, he looked upon his former coreligionists with special contempt, and in *Fors Clavigera* (1875) he admitted that "of all sects . . . I most dislike and distrust the so-called Evangelical"(28.366). In particular, Ruskin so disliked the Evangelical emphasis upon damnation that he charged that their unhealthy concentration on the pains of hell—and not, as Protestants liked to believe, the practices of Roman Catholics—were responsible for the contemporary weakness of Christianity: "It is neither Madonna-worship nor saint-worship, but the evangelical self-worship and

hell-worship—gloating, with an imagination as un-
founded as it is foul, over the torments of the damned,
instead of the glories of the blest,—which have in reality degraded the languid powers of Christianity to
their present state of shame and reproach"(28.82). The
fury with which *Fors Clavigera* here savages the Evangelicals sixteen years after Ruskin walked out of the
chapel in Turin, reveals his continuing hatred for their
idea of damnation.

Although one can thus be sure that Ruskin never regained his earlier belief in damnation during these
years of agnosticism, one finds it difficult to describe
the other aspects of his religious opinions at any one
point between 1858 and 1875. Certainly, he had rejected Evangelicalism and never returned to it. Certainly, he no longer believed in divinely inspired
scripture, damnation, or any life after this one. But just
as certainly, he did not break with Evangelical attitudes as easily as either the savage description of the
Turin chapel scene in *Fors* or the far more gentle one
in *Praeterita* would lead his reader to conclude. During
these years his ideas and attitudes remained in continual flux, for he discovered that after casting off the
doubts and fears of the Evangelical believer, he experienced not peace but new anxieties—anxieties due
largely to the fear of death inculcated by his former
religion. For although he no longer feared death and
subsequent damnation, he now feared death and subsequent nothingness. As an Evangelical, he had been
taught to experience the fear of death as a way to
heaven, and now that heaven no longer existed for him,
he still found himself pursued by this fear. He had always believed that life on earth was only a brief part,
the merest instant, of that unending duration whose

greater portion the soul would experience after death —and now he learned that this brief instant of passage was all. Moreover, he had been born into a life which, he had been taught, was merely a period of pilgrimage—and now he discovered that the pilgrimage had become a journey without purpose. These discoveries made him confused because he found it difficult to re-found anew his way of life, his goals, and the message of his works. And he became bitter, particularly at Evangelicalism, because he felt that his former religion not only had previously led him to misspend much of his life but also continued to make a new beginning impossible.

His letters reveal how troubled he was during this time and how continually his attitudes toward his situation changed. He wrote to the Brownings in May 1861, telling of the shock and confusion caused by his loss of belief:

> I am stunned—palsied—utterly helpless—under the weight of the finding out the myriad errors that I have been taught about these things; every reed that I have leant on shattering itself joint from joint—I stand, not so much melancholy as amazed—I am not hopeless, but I don't know what to hope for. (36.364)

Although in May 1861 he thus claimed he was "not so much melancholy as amazed," in February he had written to Norton that he felt "intense scorn of all I had hitherto done or thought, still intenser scorn of other people's doings and thinkings, especially in religion" (36.356). In another letter to Norton written in August 1861, Ruskin reveals how painfully difficult was the adjustment to his new ways of thought: "I looked for an-

other world, and find there is only this, and that is past for me: what message I have given is all wrong: has to be all re-said, in another way, and is, so said, almost too terrible to be serviceable"(36.381). In other words, he had to make himself like Carlyle, like him whom he had been unable to understand, and, as he wrote to Carlyle, also in August 1861, the difficulties were great:

> The heaviest depression is upon me [that] I have ever gone through; the great questions about Nature and God and man have come on me in forms so strange and frightful—and it is so new to me to do everything expecting only Death, though I see it is the right way—even to play—and *men* who are men nearly always do it without talking about it. (36.382)

But now that he had become convinced that one had to "do everything expecting only Death," he, for a time, gained some peace of mind—though he did not stop talking about his religious difficulties. He wrote to his father in October 1861 that he could never return to his former beliefs, and that he might be useful to his fellow men in this state of unbelief:

> I have your kind note of the 2nd, saying you would give half of all you have if I were feeling like the Nun at Le Puy. Would you rather, then, have me kept in the ignorance necessary to produce that state of feeling? It might have been, once. Never can be now—once emerged from it, it is gone for ever, like childhood. I know no example in history of men once breaking away from their early beliefs, and returning to them again. The Unbeliever may be taught to believe—but not Julian the Apostate to return. However, if you look at the world—take America—

Austria—France—and see what their form of Christianity has done for them—possibly the form that is coming may do more, and I may be more useful, as I always have been, as an iconoclast, than as a conservative. (36.384)

Another letter to his father, written a few months later in December 1861, openly declares his agnosticism:

> You know in that matter of universal salvation, there are but three ways of putting it.
>     1. Either "people *do* go to the devil for not believing."
>     2. Or "they—don't."
>     3. Or—"We know nothing about it."
> Which last is the real Fact, and the sooner it is generally acknowledged to be the Fact, the better, and no more said about Gospel, or Salvation, or Damnation. (36.400)

Upon reading these letters to his father, one finds it hard to decide whether he was trying to spare the older Ruskin the painful doubts he had earlier confessed to Norton and the Brownings, or whether, in fact, he had for a time achieved peace of mind and spirit. At any rate, later correspondence reveals that the fear of death and the need to refound his life continued to trouble Ruskin severely for many years. In 1867, for example, Ruskin is again writing to Norton that "the deadly question with me is—What next? or if anything is next? so that I've no help, but rather increase of wonder and horror from that"(36.534). But two years later, in October 1869, he once again writes to Norton as though, having accepted life without future existence, he has determined to do his best and

worry no more: "That I am no more immortal than a gnat, or a bell of heath, all nature, as far as I can read it, teaches me, and on that conviction I have henceforward to lead my gnat's or heath's life"(36.596).

During this same year Ruskin for a while moved from agnosticism to atheism. A few months before writing to Norton about his belief that human existence ends with death, he told William Holman Hunt that he no longer accepted even the existence of God. According to the painter, when they met in Venice during the summer of 1869 Ruskin confessed:

I am led to regard the whole story of divine revelation as a mere wilderness of poetic dreaming, and, since it is proved to be so, it is time that all men of any influence should denounce the superstition which tends to destroy the exercise of reason. Amongst the chaotic mass there are exquisite thoughts, elevating aspirations, and poetic mental nourishment, and it would be a pity that these riches should be lost to the world. I want you, who have done a great deal of harm by your works in sanctifying blind beliefs, to join with me and others to save these beautiful fragments, lest the vulgar, when indignant at the discovery of the superstition, should in their mad fury destroy what is eternally true in the beautiful thoughts with that which is false. The conviction that I have arrived at leads me to conclude that there is no Eternal Father to whom we can look up, that man has no helper but himself. I confess this conclusion brings with it great unhappiness.[63]

Admittedly, this record of Ruskin's words does not

[63] *Pre-Raphaelitism and the Pre-Raphaelite Brotherhood*, 2 vols. (New York, 1905), II, 265.

sound very much like him, but there seems to be little reason to doubt the truth of Hunt's account, particularly since his other remarks on the course of Ruskin's later religious belief are quite accurate. One can conclude, then, that during these years after Ruskin abandoned his earlier faith his desire for certainty, for rest, led him however briefly to accept atheism.

Nonetheless, whatever were his religious opinions during this time the impress of Evangelicalism remained upon him, and the manner in which Ruskin's rejected belief continued to exercise dominion over his life, influencing his thoughts and acts, appears not only in the fact that he found it difficult to accept life without a future existence, but also in his continued reading and citation of scripture, his observance of the sabbath according to Evangelical rule, and his intermittent need to pray and attend church. We have previously observed his continuing use of biblical word and phrase, and as a further instance of the way he continued an Evangelical practice almost against his will, we may note his habitual observance of the sabbath. As he explained in *Praeterita*, despite the fact that he had long realized that "Christ's first article of teaching was to unbind the yoke of the Sabbath"(35.492), he could not free himself from the old idea of "Sabbath keeping"—"the idea that one was not to seek one's own pleasure on Sunday, nor to do anything useful. . . . The great passages in the Old Testament regarding its observance held their power over me, nor have ceased to do so"(35.492-493). Similarly, just as he felt the need to keep the sabbath, so too he sometimes felt the need to pray, and in 1863 he confided in his father that "Though I am so much of a heathen, I still pray a little sometimes in pretty places, though I eschew Camden

Chapel"(36.428-429). In 1867 he wrote to Joan Agnew (later Severn) of a similar need which had led him to attend church: "Well, I've been to church, and have made up my mind that I shall continue to go. First, you see, the psalms for the day seemed to go straight at what was troubling me. . . . I came away on the whole much helped and taught, and satisfied that . . . I was meant to go to church again"(36.539). As we have already observed, Ruskin broke with Evangelicalism neither as sharply nor as easily as his published statements lead one to believe, and his continuing need for support and solace led him during these years of agnosticism to make his own accommodation with religion.

### III. The return to belief

FINALLY, in December 1875 Ruskin's desire for peace of mind, a meaningful universe, and a life after death both for himself and his loved ones returned him to Christianity. Although he never publicly related the date and cause of his return to Christianity, his letters and the always invaluable introductions of the *Library Edition* demonstrate that on December 20, 1875, a spiritualist séance at Broadlands, the home of his friends Mr. and Mrs. Cowper Temple, convinced him that the ghost of Rose La Touche had appeared at his side. The editors point out that although in earlier years he had attended séances with the Temples, he had not been firmly convinced by them, but in December 1875 "Ruskin was now in a mood to lend himself, not unwillingly, to experiments. Broadlands had been the scene of some of his happiest hours, for there he had been wont to meet the girl he loved. His friend [Mrs. Cow-

per Temple] was eagerly persuaded that the partition between the life of this world and the spirit world was impenetrable only to the hard in heart. Gradually the conviction was borne in upon him also"(24.xxii). His diary entry for 20 December only records that "the truth is shown me, which, though blind, I have truly sought,—so long"(24.xxii). A letter to Norton of January 13, 1876, expresses far less assurance about what had occurred:

> At Broadlands, either the most horrible lies were told me, without conceivable motive—or the ghost of R. was seen often beside Mrs.——, or me.—Which is pleasantest of these things I know, but cannot intellectually say which is likeliest—and meantime, take to geology. (37.189)

Ruskin had not himself seen Rose's ghost, but his faith in others was apparently enough to lead him back to some sort of religious belief; and a letter written to Norton on March 1, 1876, some five weeks later, reveals a pragmatic, still tentative, attitude toward his resumption of belief: "I have no *new* faith, but am able to get some good out of my old one, not as being true, but as containing the quantity of truth that is wholesome for me"(37.194).

His published statements about religion and other letters after this time make clear that this final belief shares neither the tone nor the emphases of his earlier Evangelical Anglicanism, a fact which appears with particular distinctness in the way *Praeterita* defined Christianity in 1886:

> The total meaning was, and is, that the God who made earth and its creatures, took at a certain time

upon the earth, the flesh and form of man; in that flesh sustained the pain and died the death of the creature He had made; rose again after death into glorious human life, and when the date of the human race is ended, will return in visible human form, and render to every man according to his work. Christianity is the belief in, and love of, God thus manifested. Anything less than this, the mere acceptance of the sayings of Christ, or assertion of any less than divine power in His Being, may be, for aught I know, enough for virtue, peace, and safety; but they do not make people Christians. (35.351-352)

Although this Christianity accepts as fact the incarnation, resurrection, and judgment of Christ, it refuses to damn those who do not thus believe, and it will not even assert that such belief is necessary for "virtue, peace, and safety." In further contrast to the sharp blade of Evangelical doctrine, which cut off nominal Christians from the true body of the Church Militant, Ruskin's broadly defined faith does not even mention the Trinity, the fall, the Bible, grace, human depravity, or damnation. Although Ruskin states that Christ will return "and judge every man according to his work," he leaves, perhaps deliberately, the nature of that judgment unspecified, and this vagueness may indicate that he did not much concern himself at this time with the problem whether damnation, mere exclusion from heaven, or some other end awaited those who act badly in this life. *Praeterita* therefore suggests that Ruskin may have been able, finally, to believe in an afterlife without subjecting himself to the corollary belief in hell and damnation.

This peaceful vision of a gentle and tolerant Chris-

tianity, so in contrast to Evangelicalism, dissolves when we consider that while he was insane Ruskin believed himself tormented by Satan and figures of monstrous evil. As a young child he had learned that evil was an active force to be combatted actively, and his painful experiences with the insane young girl he had wanted to marry and his own strong feelings of guilt fed his sense of evil until one cold February night in 1878 this childhood lesson evolved to madness. As Ruskin later described those fearful hours to a physician, "my madness took the form of my ever being in conflict, more or less personal, with the Evil One. . . . I became powerfully impressed with the idea that the Devil was about to seize me, and I felt convinced that the only way to meet him was to remain awake waiting for him all through the night, and combat him in a naked condition"(38.172). Throwing off his clothing, he stalked his room in great agitation all through the dark hours of night. When dawn came he walked to his window "wondering at the non-appearance of my expected visitor. As I put forth my hand towards the window a large black cat sprang forth from behind the mirror! Persuaded that the foul fiend was here at last in his own person . . . I darted at it, as the best thing to do under the critical circumstances, and grappled with it. . . . I had triumphed!"(38.172) After his victory, he staggered exhausted to bed where he was found "in a state of wild delirium"(38.172) in which he remained for several weeks. Ruskin reported that during these painful weeks, "Demons appeared to me constantly, coming out of the darkness and forming themselves gradually into corporeal shapes, almost too horrible to think of. But even worse and more torturing than these were the fantastic, malignant, and awful imps and

devils and witches that formed themselves out of the various articles in the room"(38.172). Surrounded by a grotesque universe of jeering evil, he found himself isolated from all other human beings while the most prosaic objects transformed themselves into taunting, tormenting spirits. Time, like space, changed as he perceived himself falling, again and again, into inexpressible sin. At the very beginning of this first attack, Ruskin reported, time was subdivided "infinitesimally," and at each instant, hearing the cry of a pet peacock, "I thought I was in a farmyard and that I was impelled by the tyrant Devil to do some fearful wrong, which I strove with all my might and main to resist. But my passionate efforts were to no avail; and every time I did the wrong I heard the voice of the Demon—that is, the peacock—give forth a loud croak of triumph"(38.172). Again and again he repeated the fall of Adam, the betrayal of Peter, the horrible sin. Ruskin's mad vision, which was merely the intensification of the usual Puritan conversion experience,[64] allowed the unseen world of spirits to stand forth in visible form as the nightmarish and all-embracing embodiment of his guilt. Ruskin's first and succeeding attacks of madness reveal that although he consciously rejected hell and damnation, they rose up fearful specters to haunt him again and again.

Since we know he tried to remain calm during the periods of sanity when he composed his autobiography, we might surmise that he there presents only the least troubling form of his belief in an attempt to remain undisturbed. On the other hand, it is even more likely that his madness had the purgative effect John D. Rosen-

[64] See John N. Morris, *Versions of the Self, Studies in English Autobiography from John Bunyan to John Stuart Mill* (New York, 1966).

berg has described, so that after his attacks he could, for a time, attain the calm faith he had so long desired.[65] One must then decide how to define his religious convictions: is the belief of madness or the belief of sanity the more real? During these last years his sanity and madness became so entwined that one is forced to conclude that Ruskin simultaneously accepted both his long-desired belief in a gentle, forgiving Christianity and his obsessive conviction of the tempting Satan of Puritanism. In moments of balance his milder, comforting faith reasserted itself, but in those moments when he moved closer to madness he was tormented by a belief in a Satan who led men to fall and a God who punished them when they did.

The complex nature of Ruskin's belief appears with particular clarity when one examines the strange statements he made about hell and the devil almost two decades before he defined Christianity in *Praeterita*. In *Time and Tide . . . Twenty-five Letters to a Working Man of Sunderland on the Laws of Work* (1867) he includes a discussion of Satan in the midst of urging England's desperate need for a society based upon cooperation. After attacking the cash nexus, he comments caustically on the way his nation willingly devotes 150 times as much wealth to the military arts of death as to the arts of life and cooperation. Lamenting that the English do not follow the Bible they profess to believe —a Bible which "primarily forbids pride, lasciviousness, and covetousness"(17.351)—he demonstrates that modern man has lost the capacity for pure and noble enjoyment. He next turns to the causes which militate against a society founded upon honesty and cooperation and which have produced this painful state of na-

---

[65] *The Darkening Glass*, p. 219.

tional mind and soul. His tenth letter begins by arguing against both those who deny the existence of hell and Satan and those who think "that there *must* be such a place as hell, because no one would ever behave decently upon earth unless they were kept in wholesome fear of the fires beneath it"(17.360). At a time in his life when he did not believe in Christianity, the essential truth of scripture, or an afterlife, Ruskin insists: "I do not merely *believe* there is such a place as hell. I *know* there is such a place; and I know also that when men have got to the point of believing virtue impossible but through dread of it, they have got *into* it"(17.360-361). Not they "will get" into it, but they "have got" into it. In other words, despite the strangely ambiguous way he makes his point, Ruskin apparently intends "hell" to mean a present state of mind and soul. But our problem is not so much what Ruskin means but why he chose this oddly misleading manner of statement—if misleading it is.

His long discussion of Satan, which occupies the larger part of this tenth letter, clarifies the reason for this method, revealing darker intentions that lurk beneath the surface of Ruskin's words. Assuring his reader that he writes of the devil neither metaphorically nor rhetorically, Ruskin emphasizes that "in fearful truth, the Presence and Power of Him *is* here; in the world, with us, and within us"(17.361). But after thus apparently affirming the existence of an incarnate force of evil, he offers a broader definition, stating that "whatever influence it is, without or within us" which perverts the good impulses and faculties of our being is " 'Satanic' "(17.363). He then explains his point by leading the reader through an infernal modern landscape in which pride, avarice, and selfish divisiveness

have corrupted man's noble instincts and desires: religion, teaching, mutual help, justice, beauty, and industry have all assumed grotesque forms under the influence of this "deceiving spirit within us, or outside of us" (17.363). Ruskin concludes with a long exhortation, whose mode of statement embodies the peculiar dilemmas in his thought:

> Now observe—I leave you to call this deceiving spirit what you like—or to theorise about it as you like. All that I desire you to recognise is the fact of its being here, and the need of its being fought with. If you take the Bible's account of it, or Dante's, or Milton's, you will receive the image of it as a mighty spiritual creature. . . : if you take Aeschylus's or Hesiod's account of it, you will hold it for a partly elementary and unconscious adversity of fate, and partly for a group of monstrous spiritual agencies connected with death, and begotten out of the dust; if you take a modern rationalist's, you will accept it for a mere treachery and want of vitality in our own moral nature exposing it to loathsomeness or moral disease, as the body is capable of mortification or leprosy. I do not care what you call it,—whose history you believe of it,—nor what you yourself can imagine about it; the origin, or nature, or name may be as you will, but the deadly reality of the thing is with us, and warring against us, and on our true war with it depends whatever life we can win. (17.365)

Ruskin warns against these forces of destruction in a manner as eclectic and undecided as the multifarious styles of Victorian architecture, for like those architects who offered alternate Greek, Gothic, and Renaissance plans, he will not choose a point of view, though

he can present several with skill. Attempting to make his statements accessible and acceptable to the widest possible audience, he presents not a single, embracing definition but three different ones, none of which overtly betrays the impress of authorial belief. This deliberate vagueness about his own position, which appears elsewhere in *Time and Tide,* surely arises as much from the nature of his thought as from rhetorical strategy. His private letters indicate that he would have felt the position of the modern rationalist most intellectually congenial. On the other hand, his vocabulary, his echoes of Puritanism, and his tone suggest a fascination with Satan and the Satanic. Just as many years later Ruskin held in precarious balance a conscious belief in a gentle, undogmatic Christianity and an emotional conviction of Satanic presence, so in 1867 while he accepted no religious convictions he yet felt himself drawn to the idea of the devil. Perhaps one should not even limit the components of his belief to rationalism and Puritanism, for in 1867 he seems almost equally drawn to the Greek conception of evil as part spirit and part "elementary and unconscious adversity of fate." Nonetheless, the main tensions in his thought were between his consciously assumed position of unbelief and his fascination with the idea of a devil. According to John D. Rosenberg, whose *Darkening Glass* has done so much to explain the nature of Ruskin's thought,

> Ruskin was convinced of the reality of Satan, "the Lord of *Pain,*" because to no other power could he attribute the reality of his own torment: his terrifying dreams, his agony over Rose, his fear that the Serpent-Tempter would not only corrupt his soul but unhinge his mind. His fears proved prophetic. A dec-

ade after he wrote *Time and Tide*, a grotesque hallucination of "the Evil One" appeared in his bedroom.[66]

Professor Rosenberg is essentially correct, for undoubtedly this evil force, which Ruskin in 1867 stated might be a weakness within man, an agent of fate, or a conscious spiritual presence, became, finally, the Evil One for whom he waited on that long, cold February night. But in 1867 Ruskin seemed unable to state definitely, either to himself or others, that Satan, the Evil One, the Lord of Lies and Pain, exists as an active, conscious spirit. Several places in *Time and Tide* he appears to admit this, and then, as if drawing himself back from the brink of darkness, he qualifies and broadens his description, offering more palatable alternatives; for however insistently the forces of guilt and horror had begun to push their way up from the depths of the surface of his mind, he still remained unwilling to accept the figure of Satan consciously and intellectually. He felt drawn to the idea of Satan, nonetheless, since he desired something, someone, that would bear responsibility for the suffering which he had both experienced himself and seen around him. Ironically, Ruskin's Evangelical religion, which had been unable to bring him an experiential, felt knowledge of Christ, brought him, finally, such a conviction of Satan. But in 1867 the Puritan and the agnostic, the conscious and the unconscious, yet maintained an uneasy balance.

After his first attack of madness, these opposing positions became even more forcefully contrasted. He was once again a believer, and in calm, sane moments

[66] *Ibid.*, pp. 169-170. Professor Rosenberg demonstrates that a major element in Ruskin's belief in Satan derives from sexual guilt (p. 169n).

he held an unquestioning faith, which accepted the reality of spiritualism and miracles. As the dark clouds
of madness gathered, his sense of evil became ascend-
ant, and he wrote, an Old Testament prophet, as
though he could perceive the hand of a jealous, aveng-
ing God in England's then bizarre weather conditions.
But, as John D. Rosenberg has shown, even in *The
Storm-Cloud of the Nineteenth Century* (1884), in which
Ruskin seems most completely unbalanced, he blended
sanity and madness, for as fantastic as the work seems
now it described accurately the frightening and deadly
effects of the industrial age upon the sky.[67]

After 1875 Ruskin held religious convictions that
were essentially undoctrinal, unquestioning, and even
anti-intellectual. As he wrote in 1876 to his friend
Fanny Talbot, he did "not think the question of the
Trinity or Unity is one for Man to discuss," and, indeed, after the experience at Broadlands he felt that
many points of belief were not "for Man to discuss."[68]
When both his need to remain calm and his need to believe became more desperate, he willingly relinquished
his former analytical attitude toward religion, turning
away from questions that might have disturbed his assurance that he would meet his mother and father and
Rose after death. But although he was finally able to
attain that belief he had long sought, it was not to bring
him peace of mind; for madness irrupted into his life,
bringing terror and darkness. In the end, Ruskin was
unable to escape the bonds of Evangelicalism, for just
as it shaped and gave impetus to his earlier thought
and writing, it provided the form and substance of

[67] *Ibid.*, pp. 214-215.
[68] *Dearest Mama Talbot: A Selection of Letters from John Ruskin
to Mrs. Fanny Talbot*, ed. Margaret Spence (London, 1966), p. 51.

those waking nightmares into which he at last withdrew for the last eleven years of his life.

## IV. Religion, man, and work

Now that we have some idea of the tortuous course of
Ruskin's beliefs, we may turn away from the dark lands
of madness into which they at last guided him and observe the way his religious crisis in 1858 affected his
writings. In particular, the effects of Ruskin's loss of belief are to be seen in the markedly different attitudes
toward man in the second and fifth volumes of *Modern
Painters*. Amid the theocentric aesthetic of *Modern
Painters*, Volume II, man is considered primarily as a
being related to his Maker; and therefore his spiritual
aspects, those which ready him for a future existence
with God, are most important. On the other hand, the
final volume centers upon man and his relation, not to
God, but to the needs of life in this world. In 1860 the
knowledge most important to man no longer comes
from the word of God in the Bible, but rather all
knowledge, including that of God, is said to come from
man's knowledge of himself. Once Ruskin placed man
at the center of his views of the universe, his view of
human nature, human needs, and human art underwent great change.

In the second volume where Ruskin is writing about
the usefulness of art, he proposes, first, to determine
what is most useful to man by examining the nature
and needs of mankind. He writes that the role of man
in the world is "to be the witness of the glory of God,
and to advance that glory by his reasonable obedience
and resultant happiness. Whatever enables us to fulfil
this function is, in the pure and first sense of the word,

Useful to us"(4.28-29). In the fifth volume the center of the universe is man, not God: "All the power of nature depends on subjection to the human soul. Man is the sun of the world; more than the real sun. The fire of his wonderful heart is the only light and heat worth gauge or measure. Where he is, are the tropics; where he is not, the ice-world"(7.262). And now that Ruskin has abandoned his earlier belief that scripture is literally true, man becomes the major source of all spiritual truth. All that we know of God, says Ruskin, must come from what we know of man: "for the directest manifestation of Deity to man is in His own image, that is, in man. . . . The soul of man is still a mirror, wherein may be seen, darkly, the image of the mind of God" (7.259-260). Once Ruskin makes man the center of his attentions, the needs of life, physical as well as spiritual, become important, and this is a change from 1846 when Ruskin had felt the first need was to emphasize man's spiritual dimension:

> People speak in this working age, when they speak from their hearts, as if houses and lands, and food and raiment were alone useful, and as if Sight, Thought, and Admiration were all profitless, so that men insolently call themselves Utilitarians, who would turn, if they had their way, themselves and their race into vegetables; men who think . . . that the meat is more than the life, and the raiment than the body, who look to the earth as a stable, and to its fruit as fodder. (4.29)

The polemical tone of this is obvious: obvious and significant, for Ruskin remains a polemicist throughout his career, developing his own ideas to contrast with and defeat points of view, whether of the periodical re-

viewers or the political economists, which he thinks are harmful or dangerous. Thus in pointed contrast to the Utilitarians, whom Ruskin believes have a debased, animalistic conception of human nature, he emphasizes, in 1846, man's need for "Sight, Thought, and Admiration." On the other hand, in 1860, when he is trying to deal with many of the problems with which the Utilitarians are concerned, his charge in *Unto This Last* is not that these political philosophers are animalistic for paying attention to the needs of this life, but rather that they are mechanistic for proposing inhuman and ultimately impracticable solutions.

When Ruskin becomes concerned with the needs of this life, he rejects much of his earlier Puritanism. Gone, for example, is the view that "The common consent of men admits that whatever branch of any pursuit ministers to the bodily comforts, and regards material uses, is ignoble, and whatever part is addressed to the mind only is noble"(4.33). In the second volume of *Modern Painters* Ruskin also writes that pursuits "whose results are desirable or admirable in themselves and for their own sake, and in which no farther end to which their productions or discoveries are referred . . . ought to take rank above all pursuits which have any taint in them of subserviency to life"(4.34-35). He qualifies this in a note added in 1883: " 'Taint' is a false word. The entire system of useful and contemplative knowledge is one; equally pure and holy: its only 'taints' are in pride, and subservience to avarice or destruction"(4.35n). In another 1883 note Ruskin describes the change in his attitude: "As I grew older, I more and more respected vulgar uses"(4.34n), and we see this new attitude in the final volume of *Modern Painters* where Ruskin judges art by the view of man which it presents:

All art which involves no reference to man is inferior or nugatory. And all art which involves misconception of man, or base thought of him, is in that degree false and base.

Now the basest thought possible concerning him is, that he has no spiritual nature; and the foolishest misunderstanding of him possible is, that he has or should have, no animal nature. For his nature is nobly animal, nobly spiritual—coherently and irrevocably so; neither part of it may, but at its peril, expel, despise, or defy the other. All great art confesses and worships both. (7.264)

This picture of man is based on a conception of unity that remains central to Ruskin's thought throughout his entire career. Although his interests and emphases change, Ruskin's demand for a coherent wholeness continues to be a theme in his writing. Although Ruskin always stresses the integrality of the human body and spirit, he broadens his outlook as he comes increasingly to see the importance of those aspects of man which are "subservient to life." In the fifth volume of *Modern Painters* he adds, to his earlier attacks on an animalistic view of man, a criticism of views which are too ascetic, for "every form of asceticism on one side, of sensualism on the other, is an isolation of his soul or of his body" (7.263).

Ruskin's new humanism and its corollary dislike of asceticism is at the heart of his criticism of religious art in the last volume of *Modern Painters*. There he writes: "The art which, since the writings of Rio and Lord Lindsay, is specially known as 'Christian,' erred by pride in its denial of the animal nature of man;—and . . . by looking always to another world instead of this"

(7.264). At this point it would be well to glance at the writings of Lord Lindsay and Alexis François Rio, because Ruskin is here focusing his comments upon their views of art. In Lord Lindsay's *Sketches for a History of Christian Art*(1847) there is a preface on the character and dignity of Christian painting in which the author describes a hierarchy of body, mind, spirit, and then relates each member of this hierarchy to the arts, respectively, of Egypt, Greece, and Christendom:

> For example, the Architecture of Egypt, her pyramids and temples, cumbrous and inelegant but imposing from their vastness and their gloom, express the ideal of Sense or Matter—elevated and purified indeed, and nearly approaching the Intellectual, but Material still. . . .
>
> But the Sculpture of Greece is the voice of Intellect and Thought, communing with itself in solitude, feeding on beauty and yearning after truth:—
>
> While the Painting of Christendom—(and we must remember that the glories of Christianity, in the full extent of the term, are yet to come—is that of an immortal Spirit, conversing with its God.[69]

Christians have an artistic advantage, says Lindsay, because "we are raised by communion with God to a purer atmosphere, in which we see things in the light of Eternity, not simply as they are, but with their ulterior meanings, as shadows of deeper truths—an atmosphere which invests creation with the glow of love."[70] This heavenly perspective explains "the depth, intensity, grandeur and sweetness of the emotions at

[69] 3 vols. (London, 1847), I, xiii-xiv. The problem of Ruskin's debt to Lindsay calls for a careful investigation. At the very least, Ruskin drew upon him for a great deal of information about iconography.
[70] *Ibid.*, xv.

the command of Christian artists, as compared with those elicited by the ancients."

Similarly, Rio's *De la Poésie Chrétienne* (1836), which had an important influence on Ruskin's ideas of art, characterizes Christian art in terms of its concern with immortality. Rio begins his discussion of Christian painting with the art of the catacombs, which is based, he says, on the notions of love, sacrifice, redemption, and eternity. In its earliest days Christian painting readied man for martyrdom by continually asserting the belief in a heavenly reward, and in all truly Christian art there persists a dislike of things transient and of this world: "Il y a quelque chose de sublime et de bien profondément chrétien dans cette répugnance pour ce qui n'est plus et ne doit plus être: l'instinct de la pérpétuité est inséperable de celui de l'immortalité."[71] Rio continually contrasts mystic and naturalistic arts, criticizing naturalistic ones because they are fascinated by the truths of this world and are led astray by a desire to present these truths accurately. It is not, according to Rio, that there is anything basically wrong in striving for artistic skill, but rather that this striving has almost always distracted men's minds from the more important truths of art.

The truths which were important to Lindsay and Rio are no longer important to Ruskin when he writes

[71] (Paris, 1836), p. 320. Among the many convergences between Rio and Ruskin, one may cite the fact that the Frenchman suggests a theory of painting, like Ruskin's, based on emotion, and he also mentions the history of Venice as a Christian epic, an idea which might have partially inspired *The Stones of Venice*. In addition, Rio's sympathetic treatment of Savonarola points out that the priest "avait vu que la décadence des beaux-arts tenait principalment à la décadence du culte parmi les chrétiens, et il avit conclu que la régénération de l'un conduirait nécessairement à celle des autres" (p. 328). This attempt to improve art by improving the society which produces it is also one of Ruskin's principles.

the last volume of *Modern Painters*. Because Giotto, Fra Angelico, and painters like them believed so firmly in the immortality of the soul, they were not concerned enough with the lives of men in this world, says Ruskin, and they consequently ignored the pain and suffering of human life, which they believed could not be of lasting importance; or else they made this pain and suffering a glorious means of rising above man's animal nature. But for Ruskin it seemed wrong, a diminution of man, to honor suffering and pain because of a supposed relevance to a future life in which he no longer believed. The valuation of life in terms of a heavenly existence seemed irrelevant, dangerously so, for men who must eke out an existence in this world. Referring to the childlike faith which engendered medieval Christian art, Ruskin comments that when such firm, trusting faith is encountered, "unfortunately, it appears that the attainment of it is never possible without inducing some form of intellectual weakness"(7.267).

His rejection of medieval attitudes toward pain and death may be seen as early as 1852, when he included a guide to the Tintorettos in the Scuola San Rocco in the appendix to *The Stones of Venice*. His praise of the *St. Sebastian*, one of the minor pictures in the Scuola, would have been out of place in the first two volumes of *Modern Painters*:

> [It is] one of the finest things in the whole room, and assuredly the most majestic St. Sebastian in existence, as far as mere humanity can be majestic, for there is no effort at any expression of angelic or saintly resignation; the effort is simply to realise the fact of the martyrdom, and it seems to me that this is done to an extent not even attempted by any other painter. (11.419)

Although Ruskin admits that this painting only depicts humanity and has nothing of the saintly or angelic expression of faith for which most artists have tried in pictures of martyrdoms, he yet values it more than other versions of St. Sebastian. Similarly, Ruskin's growing doubts of a future life may also be one reason why, in this guide, he always criticizes pictures of the resurrection and of the raising of Lazarus: his own discomfort in this matter seems to have made it difficult for him to accept as satisfactory any presentation of a future life.

Ruskin's loss of belief, particularly in a future life, is related to his humanistic attitudes, which in turn affect his preferences in art. At the same time, Ruskin's new "religion of humanity," as he called it in *Fors*, concentrates on the problems of an earthly existence, seeking to provide the faith and strength, not to conduct pilgrimages toward a heavenly Jerusalem but to endure and make homes in London and Manchester. Since Ruskin no longer believes that man's purpose is to glorify God and thus gain a heavenly reward, he has to discover—or invent—a purpose. And this purpose is work:

> The right faith of man is not intended to give him repose, but to enable him to do his work. It is not intended that he should look away from the place he lives in now, and cheer himself with thoughts of the place he is to live in next, but that he should look stoutly into this world. (7.267)

This statement of a religion of humanity with a gospel of work appears in the last volume of *Modern Painters*; and although Ruskin gained a new belief in 1875, this credo remained at the center of his ideas about art,

society, and life. As he wrote in 1878, "Human work must be done honourably and thoroughly, because we are now Men;—whether we ever expect to be angels, or ever were slugs, being practically no matter. We *are* now Human creatures, and must, at our peril, do Human—that is to say, affectionate, honest, and earnest work. . . . In resolving to do our work well, is the only sound foundation of any religion whatsoever"(29.88).

Carlyle is here the certain influence. Ruskin gave his copy of Carlyle's *Past and Present,* now in the British Museum, to Alfred MacFee in 1887, writing to his friend, "I now send you a book which I read no more, because it has become a part of myself—and my old marks in it are now useless because in my heart I mark it all."[72] Ruskin's "old marks" confirm what one would expect from reading his published works. He has, for instance, double marked in both margins the following passage:

> Work is of a religious nature:—work is of a *brave* nature; which it is the aim of all religion to be. All work of man is as the swimmer's; a waste ocean threatens to devour him; if he front it not bravely, it will keep its word. By incessant, wise defiance of it, lusty rebuke and buffet of it, behold how loyally it supports him, bears him as its conqueror along.[73]

Work for Ruskin as for Carlyle is occupation, ark, and anodyne all in one. The purposeful action of work keeps man busy, enabling him to *use* his time rather than waste it, and in so doing it saves him both from

[72] The letter is bound in the copy Ruskin presented to MacFee. The British Museum number of Ruskin's presentation copy is c61 a14, and although the volume is entirely devoted to *Past and Present,* it is entitled *Carlyle on History and Historians* (London, 1844).
[73] *Ibid.*, p. 269.

the waste ocean of life and from a morbid and paralyz-
ing awareness of his immersion in those perilous waters. The lone swimmer, the castaway who must keep
moving or sink beneath the waves, needs action not
thought. As Conrad wrote in *Nostromo*, "Action is consolatory. It is the enemy of thought and the friend of
flattering illusions. Only in the conduct of our action
can we find the sense of mastery over the Fates."[74] But
since to pause long in the manner of Conrad at the
Everlasting Nay becomes living death, Carlyle and
Ruskin concern themselves less with remarking upon
the illusions created by action than with encouraging
man to use such action to sustain himself.

Whereas Carlyle sees man in a barren sea, struggling
bravely and striving nobly to keep the waters from
closing over his head, St. Augustine, who centuries
earlier had commented upon the perils of the waste
ocean, believed that once man crossed these dangerous
waters he would arrive, finally, at the heavenly city.
Jorge Luis Borges has suggested that "universal history
is the history of the diverse intonation of a few meta-
phors,"[75] and if we compare the intonations which
Carlyle and earlier writers such as Augustine give to
the ancient metaphor of life's journey, we can observe
a history in brief of changing ideas of human existence.
Turning back to our distant past, we perceive Odysseus
traveling to Ithaca to become fully himself, to become
man, husband, father, and king. Aeneas moves across
the world toward the unfolding destiny of Rome. Every
man, according to Augustine, moves toward heaven
and must guard himself against enjoying the distrac-

---

[74] (New York, 1951), p. 72.
[75] "Pascal's Sphere," *Other Inquisitions, 1937-1952*, trans. R.L.C.
Simms (New York, 1966), p. 8.

tions of the voyage lest he become stranded in mid-journey:

> Suppose we were wanderers who could not live in blessedness except at home, miserable in our wandering and desiring to end it and to return to our native country. We would need vehicles for land and sea which could be used to help us to reach our homeland, which is to be enjoyed. But if the amenities of the journey and the motion of the vehicles itself delighted us, and we were led to enjoy those things which we should use, we should not wish to end our journey quickly, and entangled in a perverse sweetness, we should be alienated from our country, whose sweetness would make us blessed.[76]

But do what he will Ruskin finds himself stranded in mid-voyage. Since he no longer believes in Augustine's heavenly home, he finds himself with only "the amenities of the journey and the motion of the vehicles" to console him. In short, he replaces the conception of man as pilgrim with that of man as castaway, choosing that image which so attracted artists and writers in the nineteenth century. One recalls, among many other examples, Géricault's *Raft of the Medusa* and Turner's shipwrecks, the castaways in Melville, Crane, and Conrad.[77] Sounding like a more bitter version of Carlyle, Stein tells Marlow in *Lord Jim*, "A man that is born falls into a dream like a man who falls into the sea. If he tries to climb out into the air as inexperienced people endeavour to do, he drowns. . . . The way is to the

---

[76] *On Christian Doctrine*, trans. D. W. Robertson, Jr. (New York, 1958), pp. 9-10.

[77] See T.S.R. Boase, "Shipwrecks in English Romantic Painting," *JWCI*, XXII (1959), 332-346, and Lindsay, *The Sunset Ship*, pp. 62-63.

destructive element submit yourself, and with the exertions of your hands and feet in the water make the deep, deep sea keep you up."[78] Ruskin described himself in terms not of the castaway but of the shipwrecked sailor who had reached land. As he wrote to Norton in 1875, a short six weeks before the crucial séance at Broadlands: "It is very strange to me . . . to be now merely like a shipwrecked sailor, picking up the pieces of his ship on the beach"(37.183). He sees himself a shipwrecked mariner, a Robinson Crusoe of the spirit, trying to sustain present life with the wreckage of the past. This image is convincing, for his career after his loss of faith and even after he returned to Christianity reveals a continuing attempt to salvage fragments of his old religion for use in a new life. He wrote to Norton in this same letter that whatever his own losses he could "gather bits up . . . for other people"(37.183). He had long been engaged in such gathering of bits, for his attempt to center man's life on humane, enriching labor surely exemplifies such reapplication of Evangelical doctrine to sustain man in a time of unbelief. Both Carlyle and Ruskin placed the Puritan emphasis upon work in a new context, making labor not the result of the Fall, or a means to salvation, but salvation itself.

With Ruskin's concentration on labor in the world comes the need to determine the right nature of work and to attack all those forces which prevent men from engaging in this right form of work. In *The Stones of Venice* Ruskin discusses the need for pleasurable, enriching labor. The problem in his England "is not that men are ill fed, but that they have no pleasure in the work by which they make their bread, and therefore

---

[78] (New York, 1931), p. 214.

look to wealth as the only means of pleasure"(10.194). Men have been made to do the work of machines and have hence been reduced to machines. But by the time that Ruskin wrote *Unto This Last* (1860), which he published in periodical form shortly after completing *Modern Painters*, his conception of the problem had changed: for seeing that, indeed, men are hungry, that they cannot find work, even dehumanizing work, and that men are forced to compete with one another even for a chance to earn enough for food, Ruskin directed his energies toward replacing the economic system which creates such conditions of life and labor. These concerns led him farther and farther from art, and, after 1860, he became primarily interested in the criticism, not of art, but of society. Despite these new interests, Ruskin continued to occupy himself with the problems of painting, architecture, sculpture, and the applied arts; and while he wrote no more major works on these subjects after finishing *Modern Painters* in 1860, he did produce valuable shorter writings on different aspects of the arts. Yet, when Ruskin lost his religion in 1858, his career took a major change of direction. He turned from the problems of painting to the problems of society; and this central shift of emphasis in Ruskin's thought is anticipated by the replacement of God by man as the focus of his aesthetic theories. Ruskin found his theocentric aesthetic of objective, unchanging order unworkable almost as soon as he proposed it in 1846—at least to the extent that he allowed room for the emotional elements of sublimity, which in the first volume of *Modern Painters* he had left out of his theory of beauty. *The Seven Lamps of Architecture* (1848) further qualified these early theories, because it placed great importance on the role, in beauty, of

human associations—which Ruskin had earlier denied. He defined the picturesque, his most subjective, emotional aesthetic theory, in the fourth volume of *Modern Painters*, which appeared in 1856, two years before the crisis of faith in Turin. The shift in Ruskin's aesthetic theories, which begins in the late 1840's and continues to occur until the late 1850's, first antedates and then plays a role in his loss of faith and his gradual turning away from art.

# CHAPTER FIVE

## Ruskin and Allegory

It is not often realized that all commentary is allegorical interpretation, an attaching of ideas to the structure of poetic imagery. The instant that any critic permits himself to make a genuine comment about a poem (e.g., "In *Hamlet* Shakespeare appears to be portraying the tragedy of irresolution") he has begun to allegorize. Commentary thus looks at literature as, in its formal phase, a potential allegory of events and ideas.

—Northrop Frye[1]

The best refutation of allegories I know is Croce's; the best vindication, Chesterton's. Croce says that the allegory is a tiresome pleonasm, a collection of useless repetitions which shows us (for example) Dante led by Virgil and Beatrice and then explains to us, or gives us to understand, that Dante is the soul, Virgil is philosophy or reason or natural intelligence, and Beatrice is theology or grace. According to Croce's argument (the example is not his), Dante's first step was to think: "Reason and faith bring about the salvation of souls" or "Philosophy and theology lead us to heaven" and then, for *reason* and *philosophy* he substituted *Virgil* and for *faith* or *theology* he put *Beatrice*, all of which became a kind of masquerade. By that derogatory definition an allegory would be a puzzle, more extensive, boring, and unpleasant than other puzzles. It would be a barbaric or puerile genre, an aesthetic sport. . . .

Chesterton . . . denies that the genre is censurable. He reasons that reality is interminably rich and that the language of men does not exhaust that vertiginous treasure. . . . Chesterton infers that various languages can somehow correspond to the ungraspable reality, and among them are allegories and fables.

In other words, Beatrice is not an emblem of faith, a belabored and arbitrary synonym of the word *faith*. The truth is that something—a peculiar sentiment, an intimate process, a series of analogous states—exists in the world that can be indicated by two symbols: one, quite insignificant, the sound of the word *faith;* the other, Beatrice, the glorious Beatrice who descended from Heaven and left her footprints in Hell to save Dante.

—Jorge Luis Borges[2]

[1] *Anatomy of Criticism* (Princeton, 1957), p. 89.

[2] "Nathaniel Hawthorne," *Other Inquisitions, 1937-1952*, trans. R.L.C. Simms (New York, 1966), pp. 51-52.

THE ALLEGORICAL tradition in painting, poetry, and
critical theory, so vital in the Middle Ages and Renaissance, had all but died by 1856 when Ruskin published
the third volume of *Modern Painters*, and it is thus
striking to encounter his statement that "allegorical
painting has been the delight of the greatest men and
of the wisest multitudes, from the beginning of art, and
will be till art expires"(5.134). Arguing against those
who assert that "symbolism or personification should
not be introduced in painting at all," Ruskin expresses
the wish "that every great allegory which the poets ever
invented were powerfully put on canvas, and easily accessible by all men, and that our artists were perpet-
ually exciting themselves to invent more"(5.134). Ruskin, who here draws upon the humanistic theory of
painting, makes allegory one of the major parts of his
conception of *ut pictura poesis*; and in this same chapter which defends allegory in painting he cites the allegory of the *Faerie Queene* as a great example of
poetic imagination. Discussing Spenser's figure of
Envy, he comments that the poet concentrates his ideas
in one powerful image, "so that we feel it fully, and see
it, and never forget it"(5.133). Unlike most nineteenth-
century critics, then, Ruskin believes that allegorical
painting and poetry embody the highest workings of
the artistic imagination.

To his praise of Spenserian allegory one may compare Macaulay's harsh criticism of the *Faerie Queene*:

Even Spenser himself, though assuredly one of the

greatest poets that ever lived, could not succeed in the attempt to make allegory interesting. It was in vain that he lavished the riches of his mind on the House of Pride, and the House of Temperance. One unpardonable fault, the fault of tediousness, pervades the whole of the Faerie Queene. We become sick of Cardinal Virtues and Deadly Sins, and long for the society of plain men and women. Of the persons who read the first Canto, not one in ten reaches the end of the First Book, and not one in a hundred perseveres to the end of the poem. Very few and very weary are those who are in at the death of the Blatant Beast.[3]

Macaulay believes that allegory is dull, intrinsically so, and of all the allegories ever written only one, *Pilgrim's Progress*, escaped boring its readers: "Other allegories only amuse the fancy. The allegory of Bunyan has been read by many thousands with tears."[4] Only the seventeenth-century thinker has achieved "the highest miracle of genius—that things which are not should be as they were, that the imaginations of one mind should become the personal recollections of another."[5] Macaulay's condemnation of the *Faerie Queene* and his praise of *Pilgrim's Progress* reveal that, for him, poetry, which he believes to be largely a matter of the emotions, must convey what it felt like to have been at a particular scene, to have had particular thoughts, and to have experienced particular emotions. For him, in other words, literature must portray the facts of experience-being-experienced, not the truths to be abstracted from experience. Assuming that with one exception allegory

---

[3] "Southey's Edition of the Pilgrim's Progress" (1831), *Essays, Critical and Miscellaneous* (Philadelphia, 1853), p. 129.
[4] *Ibid.*                    [5] *Ibid.*

can appeal only to the fancy, Macaulay stands so completely committed to his romantic conception of art that he cannot even envisage the possibility of successful non-romantic modes. Furthermore, as his remark about the tediousness of the cardinal virtues reveals, the kind of art which makes its audience contemplate the long-known, sure truths of morality and religion bores him; and therefore that delight in discovering commonplace beliefs under strange and wondrous guise, which characterizes the expectations of the medieval and Renaissance reader of allegory, is not only missing in Macaulay, but, more important, is beyond his grasp. Thus interested neither in the specific pleasures of the allegorical mode nor the kind of truths it best conveys, he finds such poetry essentially and irremediably boring.

Many of the points at the heart of Macaulay's criticism of the *Faerie Queene* appear more explicitly stated in Coleridge's distinction between allegory and symbol:

An allegory is but a translation of abstract notions into a picture-language, which is itself nothing but an abstraction from objects of the senses; the principal being more worthless even than its phantom proxy, both alike unsubstantial, and the former shapeless to boot. On the other hand a symbol . . . is characterized by a translucence of the special in the individual, or of the general in the special, or of the universal in the general; above all by the translucence of the eternal through and in the temporal. It always partakes of the reality which it renders intelligible; and while it enunciates the whole, abides itself as a living part in that unity of which it is the

representative. The other are but empty echoes which the fancy arbitrarily associates with apparitions of matter.[6]

Whereas the symbol, which develops organically, partakes of that which it represents, allegory, a mere mechanical device, has no such intimate, natural relation to the signified. Therefore, allegory can signify only arbitrarily and artificially. This basic difference in the natures of the two modes arises from the fact that whereas the imagination creates the symbol, fancy, a lesser faculty, produces allegory: the symbol comes into being as a forming, synthesizing mode of vision which may finally reveal the mind in possession of more truth than it had consciously realized, but allegory, which "cannot be other than spoken consciously" never adds new truths. In other words, while the symbol precedes conscious formulation of an idea, thus itself advancing knowledge, allegory must always follow behind, the mere embellisher of thoughts already formulated.

Similar attitudes appear in Matthew Arnold's statements about allegory. He begins his "Dante and Beatrice" with the assertion that "Those critics who allegorize the *Divine Comedy*, who exaggerate, or, rather, who mistake the supersensual element in Dante's work, who reduce to nothing the sensible and human element, are hardly worth refuting. They know nothing of the necessary laws under which poetic genius works, of the inevitable conditions under which the

6 *The Statesman's Manual*, ed. W.G.T. Shedd (New York, 1875), pp. 437-438. Quoted by Angus Fletcher, *Allegory: The Theory of a Symbolic Mode* (Ithaca, N.Y., 1964), p. 16n. For a discussion of Coleridge's attitudes toward allegory, see also pp. 15-18.

creations of poetry are produced."[7] Arnold's remark about the "necessary laws under which poetic genius works" refers, it would seem, to the belief (which he shared with Coleridge) that allegory cannot be imaginative. Since Arnold believes great poetry imaginative and the *Divine Comedy* great poetry, it cannot, he would argue, be an allegory. His other comment that to consider the *Divine Comedy* allegory would "reduce the sensible and human element to nothing" shows that, like Macaulay, he believes allegory has no human element and deals only with rather uninteresting abstractions. His statement in this same essay that "The *Divine Comedy* . . . is no allegory, and Beatrice no mere personification of theology" further demonstrates that for Arnold allegory equates, clearly and unmistakably, with "mere personification."[8] He holds that allegory concerns itself only with personified abstractions, abstractions which have been emptied of all human interest; for example, he holds that to consider Beatrice a figure in an allegory necessarily means, first, that the reader must neglect whatever literal meaning this figure might have in the poem, and, second, that in allegory a simple abstraction, here theology, equates clearly and simply with that which represents it. Arnold, of course, is quite correct: Dante did not write *this kind* of an allegory, but, then, neither did any one else before the eighteenth century.

Carlyle's attitudes toward allegory are more complex, largely because he employs the term ambiguously. In *Heroes and Hero-Worship*, he comments that

[7] *Lectures and Essays in Criticism*, ed. R. H. Super (Ann Arbor, Mich., 1962), p. 3.

[8] *Ibid.*, p. 4.

"Dante's Hell, Purgatory, Paradise, are a symbol withal, an emblematic representation of his Belief about this Universe:—some Critic in a future age . . . , who has ceased altogether to think as Dante did, may find this . . . all an 'Allegory,' perhaps an idle Allegory! It is a sublime embodiment, or sublimest, of the soul of Christianity. It expresses, as in huge world-wide architectural emblems, how the Christian Dante felt Good and Evil to be the two polar elements of this Creation."[9] Like Coleridge before him, he apparently believes that allegory cannot embody thought, and yet, as other passages reveal, he does not distinguish between allegory and symbol. Like Arnold after him, he believes that Dante, as a great and sincere poet, could not have written the *Divine Comedy* consciously as an allegory. The central problem for Carlyle with an allegorical interpretation of the *Divine Comedy* is that "Men do not believe an Allegory," and yet he is positive that "to the earnest Dante it is all one visible Fact; he believes it, sees it; is the Poet of it in virtue of that. Sincerity, I say again, is the saving merit, now as always."[10] Carlyle's prime difficulty arises in his theory of the creative act, a theory which differs at significant points from Ruskin's. According to Carlyle, all great poetry and all great truths must well up from within the deeps of the mind, growing unconsciously and organically. Unlike Coleridge, from whom he apparently derives this emphasis upon unconscious creation, Carlyle holds that the artist must believe literally and completely in the vision he creates. So suspicious is Carlyle of the workings of the conscious mind, that he

[9] *Works, Centenary Edition*, ed. H. D. Traill, 30 vols. (London, 1896-1899), v, 97.
[10] *Ibid.*

holds no organic, sincerely believed, art could arise
even partially in the conscious mind. Therefore although we, who come centuries after Dante in a
changed time, can read Dante's poem as an allegory,
we cannot, says Carlyle, hold that Dante could have
created it as one.

His discussion of the allegorical interpretation of
pagan religious myth in "The Hero as Divinity" confirms this interpretation of his conception of allegory.
He admits the partial truth of those writers who attribute pagan myth to allegory. "It was a play of poetic
minds, say these theorists; a shadowing-forth, in allegorical fable, in personification and visual form, of
what such poetic minds had known and felt of this Universe. Which agrees, add they, with a primary law of
human nature . . . , That what a man feels intensely, he
struggles to speak-out of him, to see represented before
him in visual shape, and as if with a kind of life and historical reality in it." Admitting there is doubtless such
a law, Carlyle yet asks, "Think, would *we* believe, and
take with us as our life-guidance, an allegory, a poetic
sport?" Nonetheless, a few sentences later he states
"Pagan Religion is indeed an Allegory, a Symbol of
what men felt and knew about the Universe; . . . but it
seems to me a radical perversion, and even *in*version,
of the business, to put that forward as the origin and
moving cause, when it was rather the result and termi-
nation. . . . We ought to understand that this seeming
cloudfield was once a reality; that not poetic allegory,
least of all that dupery and deception was the origin of
it."[11] In other words, Carlyle, who feels that allegory
consciously conceived must be insincere, "a poetic
sport," yet holds that those who created pagan myth

[11] *Ibid.,* pp. 5-7.

unconsciously created allegory from stories which they firmly believed. Looking back, Carlyle and men of the nineteenth century may perceive that these beliefs were in fact allegories, but the men who created them could not have been aware of this themselves. As accurate a rendering of primitive mythology as this may be—and it is surely an advance on the usual Renaissance and eighteenth-century conception of the origins of myth[12]—Carlyle's view of allegory, when applied to literature, requires that one believe poets such as Dante did not know what they were doing. Ruskin, who knew the *Epistle to Can Grande* and the *Convito*, could not hold such a conception of allegory.

Carlyle's one concession to an allegorical literature appears in his statement in the same passage that "The *Pilgrim's Progress* is an Allegory, and a beautiful, just and serious one: but consider whether Bunyan's Allegory could have *preceded* the Faith it symbolises! The Faith had to be already there, standing believed by everybody;—of which the Allegory could then become a shadow; and with all its seriousness we may say a *sportful* shadow, a mere play of the Fancy, in comparison with that awful Fact and scientific certainty, which it poetically strives to emblem."[13] Here the ground has shifted, apparently, for Carlyle now argues that, at least as far as Bunyan was concerned, sincere allegory was possible; and yet when a chapter later he discusses Dante, he does not allow that possibility. Carlyle does not tell us much about Bunyan here, so we may reason either that he believes Dante a far greater

[12] See Jean Seznec, *The Survival of the Pagan Gods: The Mythological Tradition and its Place in Renaissance Humanism and Art*, trans. Barbara F. Sessions (New York, 1961) and Frank E. Manuel, *The Eighteenth Century Confronts the Gods* (New York, 1967).

[13] *Works*, v, 6.

writer than Bunyan, one who has to work in a more unconscious way, or that he may even have thought that
Bunyan himself literally believed what he wrote. Or,
finally, that Carlyle's habit of stating everything in the
strongest possible terms leads him to major inconsistencies. Whatever the answer, Carlyle clearly remains
deeply suspicious of allegorical art and will not allow
that great, true, sincere art can be written consciously
as allegory.

## II. Ruskin's "language of types" and
## Evangelical readings of scripture

IN contrast to many other nineteenth-century critics,
Ruskin does not oppose allegory and symbolism to each
other, for he holds that allegory, an imaginative mode,
forms one kind of symbolism and not a lesser replacement for it. Not unexpectedly, his conceptions of allegory and allegorical art enable him to read painting,
poetry, and architecture composed in this mode more
sensitively than most of his contemporaries. In addition, Ruskin allegorizes not only art but natural phenomena as well—not only Dante, Spenser, and Giotto
but also the facts of geology and meteorology. Like his
theories of beauty, his interpretative methods partake
of a larger vision of an orderly universe in which God
has ordained that all phenomena bear moral and religious valences. As Mircea Eliade has pointed out, "the
*completely* profane world, the wholly desacralized cos-
mos, is a recent discovery in the history of the human
spirit."[14] Ruskin, we must observe, had not yet made
that discovery, and although many men of the eight-

---

[14] *The Sacred and the Profane: The Nature of Religion*, trans. Wil-
lard R. Trask (New York and Evanston, 1959), p. 13.

eenth and nineteenth centuries had long accepted what
has come to be the modern view of the universe, the
universe emptied of the spirit of God, he did not. In
fact, for all Ruskin's interest in scientific geology, he
still existed within a conception of the world more congenial in many ways to the Middle Ages than to the age
of Queen Victoria.

Believing that God intended natural phenomena, the
rock, the tree, and the cloud, to bear moral meanings,
Ruskin reads them in a manner that makes parts of
*Modern Painters* much resemble earlier physico-theol-
ogies. In the fourth volume, for example, he remarks
that "there is one lesson evidently intended to be taught
by the different characters"(6.132) of the rocks which
form the earth and its mountains:

> It can hardly be necessary to point out how these
> natural ordinances seem intended to teach us the
> great truths which are the basis of all political sci-
> ence; how the polishing friction which separates, the
> affection that binds, and the affliction that fuses and
> confirms, are accurately symbolized by the processes
> to which the several ranks of hills appear to owe
> their present aspect; and how, even if the knowledge
> of those processes be denied to us, that present as-
> pect may in itself seem no imperfect image of the
> various states of mankind: first, that which is power-
> less through total disorganization; secondly, that
> which, though united, and in some degree powerful,
> is yet incapable of great effort or result, owing to the
> too great similarity and confusion of offices, both in
> ranks and individuals; and finally, the perfect state
> of brotherhood and strength in which each character

330

is clearly distinguished, separately perfected, and employed in its proper place and office. (6.132-133)

Ruskin, like the Physiologus, conceives himself living in an allegorical universe in which natural fact reverberates with further meanings. Unlike the eighteenth-century divines, Ruskin is not primarily interested in argument from analogy. He concerns himself more with allegory, reading "Nature-scripture"(5.191) as he had been taught to read God's written Word—in terms of type and shadow. In his treatise *On Christian Doctrine* St. Augustine writes that the world divides between things and signs, and only in the world of the Bible can one take things as signs, rocks and mountains for bearers of meaning. By turning this earth into scripture, "Nature-scripture," Ruskin finds himself able to interpret "the ordinances of the hills"(6.117). The faith of some would move mountains; Ruskin prefers to read them, and just as he finds the laws of politics and morality embodied in the crystalline rocks, he finds in the sky an "ordinance of the firmament" that states the presence of God to all men: "God means us to acknowledge His own immediate presence as visiting, judging, and blessing us"(6.113). Ruskin does take into account the argument from design and from analogy, but he concerns himself far more with explicating the meaning of the world in which we find ourselves. Thus, Ruskin explains that the "conditions of mountain structure" have been invariably "calculated for the delight, the advantage, or the teaching of men; prepared, it seems, so as to contain . . . some beneficence of gift, or profoundness of counsel"(6.385). In short, God has constructed the mountains and the seas, the forests and the

plains, for man: they offer sustenance for the body, beauty for the soul, and instruction for the mind. Nature-scripture, then, was "written" the way Augustine, Dante, and other men of the Middle Ages believe the Bible to have been: with a literal sense that upon inspection revealed further, deeper, richer significance.

Ruskin also conceives the laws of human life to be similarly founded so that principles can be read for significance. *The Seven Lamps of Architecture* thus explains that "there is no branch of human work whose constant laws have not close analogy with those which govern every other mode of man's exertion. But, more than this, exactly as we reduce to greater simplicity and surety any one group of these practical laws, we shall find them passing the mere condition of connection or analogy, and becoming the actual expression of some ultimate nerve or fibre of the mighty laws which govern the moral world"(8.22). Whenever Ruskin can choose between analogy and allegory, he chooses allegory, as he has done here.

Realizing that "to the minds of many persons nothing bears a greater appearance of presumption than any attempt at reasoning respecting the purposes of Divine Being," Ruskin argued in a footnote against the notion that "the modesty of humanity" should limit its inquiries to "the ascertaining of physical causes": "Wisdom can only be demonstrated in its ends, and goodness only perceived in its motives. He who in a morbid modesty supposes that he is incapable of apprehending any of the purposes of God, renders himself also incapable of witnessing His wisdom" (6.134n). Few ever accused Ruskin of morbid modesty, to be sure, and even when his conventional faith had disappeared the

impulse to interpret the world to others and to convert them to his vision remained.

Long after Ruskin had both lost his Evangelical faith and then returned to his own version of Christianity, he added a note to the fourth volume of *Modern Painters* that significantly altered his conception of these "natural ordinances." "I should have said now," he wrote in 1885, "rather than 'seem intended to teach us,' '*do*, if we will consider them, teach us' "(6.132n). Having lost the faith which allowed him to allegorize the world, he now becomes willing to use natural phenomena for examples and analogies. But it was his early views which formed his readings of art, life, and nature, and to them we must turn to perceive the sources and reasoning of his interpretation.

In 1852 when Ruskin published the last volume of *The Stones of Venice*, he was aware that he stood alone, like a prophet, in a vision of things not shared by many; and yet he expressed hope:

> that someday the language of Types will be more read and understood by us than it has been for centuries; and when this language, a better one than either Greek or Latin, is again recognised amongst us, we shall find, or remember, that as the other visible elements of the universe—its air, its water, and its flame—set forth, in their pure energies, the life-giving, purifying, and sanctifying influences of the Deity upon His creatures, so the earth, in its purity, sets forth His eternity and His TRUTH. I have dwelt above on the historical language of stones; let us not forget this, which is their theological language. (11.41)

333

Ruskin's use of the word "type" here and elsewhere throughout his writings indicates his debt to Evangelical Anglican readings of scripture. Although he has obviously extended the meaning of the term beyond its chief exegetical use as "forerunner of Christ," one must examine Evangelical methods of reading the Bible to understand the habits of mind which shape his criticism, his conception of the world, and his theories of art.

As a young child Ruskin, like all Evangelicals, learned that daily Bible reading, the duty of every worshipper, had to be a search for Christ. The famous tracts of Bishop Ryle, which Ruskin later recommended to others, characteristically advised the reader:

> *Read the Bible with Christ continually in view.* The grand primary object of all Scripture is to testify of Jesus. Old Testament ceremonies are shadows of Christ. Old Testament judges and deliverers are types of Christ. Old Testament history shows the world's need of Christ. Old Testament prophecies are full of Christ's sufferings, and Christ's glory yet to come.[15]

Bible reading had to be a meditation on the types of Christ, but the believer did not read his Bible figurally to authenticate Jesus Christ as the true Savior of man, for the devout reader was already convinced of this truth. Instead, he read the Bible as a means of discovering and meditating upon the universal role of Christ's coming in human history. The Evangelical was supposed to read continually to perceive foreshadowings of Christ, to feel wonder at the universal beauty of

[15] *Startling Questions*, pp. 247-248.

334

God's plan, and to exercise his intellect in the service of his own soul's salvation. Bible reading was to be not only devotional exercise, unraveling of the greatest of all puzzles, but also the aesthetic appreciation of divine order.

These attitudes toward studying scripture, which Ruskin learned as a child, recall similar attitudes underlying medieval and Renaissance allegorical imagery. According to Rosemond Tuve, "Men do not weary of meeting, especially in interesting disguise, ideas and beliefs that they hold with real firmness. We shall have little sympathetic understanding of this mediaeval and Renaissance taste in imagery unless we can conceive of readers who thought deliverance from hell to heaven was extraordinarily interesting good news."[16] Similarly, we can have little feeling for the fusion of aesthetic, intellectual, and spiritual concerns that prompted both Victorian preachers and congregations to look forward with pleasure to two long sermons every Sunday, unless we conceive of the Evangelical love of discovering evidences of Christ. Since Ruskin learned his habits of reading in such a milieu, it is not surprising that when he later transferred religious exegetics to secular works, he maintained a similar fusion of apparently diverse attitudes.

Although the Evangelicals and other groups, such as the Baptists and Presbyterians who shared their methods, made full use of tracts and biblical commentaries, they considered preaching the most effective

---

[16] *Allegorical Imagery: Some Mediaeval Books and Their Posterity* (Princeton, 1966), p. 331. Richard D. Altick's *The English Common Reader* (Chicago, 1963), pp. 121-122, points out that editors and authors of religious tracts and periodicals tried to provide the excitement of prohibited works of fiction. The sermon satisfied another intellectual taste in an acceptable form.

weapon of the elect; and consequently it is in sermons that we find the most important use of biblical types. While still a young child Ruskin had learned from sermons the correct way to search the Bible for types and shadows of Christ, and the degree to which typological exegetics had become a commonplace to him appears in one of the *Letters Addressed to a College Friend,* which Ruskin wrote to the Reverend Edward Clayton in 1843: "To-day being the first Sunday of the month, Mr. Melville [*sic*] preached at the Tower, and his curate gave us a sermon on 'Unto Adam also, and to his wife, did the Lord God make coats of skins,' etc. 'Now,' thought I, when he began, 'I know what you're going to say about that; you'll say that the beasts were sacrificed, and that the skins were typical of the robe of Christ's righteousness' "(1.490). He could thus anticipate the curate in such a superior manner because the sermons of Melvill and other preachers, particularly the Reverend E. Andrews of Beresford Chapel, Walsworth, had long before instructed him in the practice of typological readings of scripture. When Ruskin was only nine years old he made elaborate summaries of sermons, probably those of Andrews, which demonstrate the theological and exegetical sophistication which he had attained by 1828.[17] In Sermon X, "The

---

[17] The following passages are taken from a notebook now in the Coniston Museum which contains Sermons IX, X, XI, and part of XII. The rough notes for these sermons are to be found among Ruskin's juvenilia at Yale. Marjorie G. Wynne, Research Librarian at the Beinecke Rare Book and Manuscript Library at Yale has kindly advised me that Professor Helen Gill Viljoen has expressed the intention to publish Ruskin's childhood sermon notes, but attempts to confirm this or to locate the other four notebooks containing final drafts have not proved successful. A comparison of Ruskin's first and final drafts proves his sophistication at the age of nine. The tenth sermon, "The law of sacrifice," for example, has the following opening in the rough draft: "Today Remarks on the law of Moses. Leviticus 1st. is

law of sacrifice," Ruskin makes use of the characteristic
Evangelical application of figural reading to Leviticus.
This third book of the Pentateuch, which sets forth the
Judaic ceremonies of sacrifice used before the destruction of the Temple, apparently had little to offer the
Christian reader, since it details the outmoded rules of
an abrogated law. Ruskin, explaining that he will "follow up the law of the shadow of sacrifice to its substance Christ," points to the difficulties created by
Levitical ceremonies when he mentions "the beginning
of the 10th chapter, of Hebrews where it is said that
the law, having a shadow of good things to come, and
not the very image of these things, can never make the
comers thereunto perfect, & it goes on to say that the
blood of bulls and goats can never take away sin. Now,
if it is impossible, that blood can take away sin, can we
suppose that these momentous ordinances, were only
for show, for ceremony[?] Can God institute anything
of no moral worth[?]" Such apparent irrelevance
would have created great difficulties for Evangelical
belief, which held not only that God had directly inspired every word of the Bible but also that each of its
parts bore equal value. Since they did not accept an

the first to which we should go for it contains more specifically law
of sacrifice which is foundation of Mosaic economy. Let us consider
the doctrine of atonement and sacrifice here then in Christ. Law
Shadow First A real sacrifice is brought before us." The Coniston Ms.
version reads: "The 1st chapter of Leviticus, from the beginning. I
think that in the remarks on the law of Moses which are to employ
us today it is better to enter upon Leviticus as the book which contains
more specifically the details of the law of sacrifice, which is the very
foundation of the Mosaic economy. We shall first consider the doctrine
of atonement here & then follow it up to its antitype, the death of
Christ. Now this is a real form of sacrifice, and a simple form. It is
not for confirmation of testimony, now announcement, now instruction
to be communicated." I am especially grateful to Mr. W. Rawdon-
Smith, Low How, Coniston, for his generous aid in obtaining copies of
this Ms.

evolutionary theory of scripture, they found themselves
forced to make the best of this unpromising material,
and their universal solution was that God had instituted Levitical sacrifices as types to prefigure Christ's
sacrifice: "As the law threw forward a shadow to another economy these sacrifices must be to intimate[?]
that sacrifice is necessary in the other economy and
sacrifice, which shall be capable of taking away all sin.
Now . . . in the Gospel this sacrifice of animals is done
away with, and yet we know that we must have sacrifices of some sort[;] we are shut up to the death of
Christ as the very essence of atonement. The law[s] of
sacrifices derive their value only because they referred
to the Gospel and if this be correct, the view which
[we] have taken of them, must be referred to Christ.
. . . As the law is a shadow of good things to come and
as sacrifice is the foundation of the law[,] we have a
striking proof of the efficacy of the atonement of
Christ." In the next sermon, "Sacrifices of the old law,"
Ruskin again makes use of the usually circular argument from types. After stating that ceremonial law
"was to shadow forth the future sacrifice of Christ," he
adds "[I]f these were not shadow[s] of this great sacrifice, they were trivial ceremonial forms and unworthy
of the being who appointed them." Such clearly could
not be the case.

Ruskin here follows a very common Evangelical
authentication of types. Ryle, for example, arguing
from the assumption that God had written the Bible
with types and shadows, uses this principle to attack
the Socinians who believed that Christ was mortal.
Their belief, he held, strikes "at the root of the whole
plan of salvation which God has revealed in the Bible,
and . . . [would] nullify the greater part of the Scrip-

tures. It overthrows the priesthood of the Lord Jesus, and strips him of His office. It converts the whole system of the law of Moses touching sacrifices and ordinances, into a meaningless form. . . . It turns man adrift on a sea of uncertainty, by plucking from under him the finished work of a divine mediator."[18] In other words, if Christ were not divine, God could not and would not have instituted types; and if God had not instituted types, the Bible would have become all too frequently the record of "meaningless form." The Evangelicals perceived themselves living in a universe of divinely instituted order of which the Bible was the key; and types, which reveal a consistent principle in the Bible, the principle of Christ, create order and meaning in the Bible.

In addition to the fact that these childhood sermon records demonstrate Ruskin's early acquaintance with the usual Evangelical applications of typology, they gain further interest because the ideas he draws upon when he was nine years old appear again twenty years later in *The Seven Lamps of Architecture*. In his first chapter, "The Lamp of Sacrifice," he asks "the broad question, Can the Deity be indeed honoured by the presentation to Him of any material objects of value. . . ?"(8.31) Summoning the tone, vocabulary, and arguments of an Evangelical preacher, Ruskin examines the nature of sacrifice in the Bible, coming to the conclusion that this second question "admits of entire answer only when we have met another and far different question, whether the Bible be indeed one book or two, and whether the character of God revealed in the Old Testament be other than His character revealed in the New"(8.32). Drawing upon the theory of

[18] *Living or Dead?*, pp. 239-240.

types, Ruskin argues that since the same principle—
salvation by Christ—unites Old and New Testaments,
"God is one and the same, and is pleased or displeased
by the same things for ever, although one part of His
pleasure may be expressed at one time rather than another, and although the mode in which His pleasure is
to be consulted may be by Him graciously modified to
the circumstances of men. Thus, for instance, it was
necessary that, in order to the understanding by man
of the scheme of the Redemption, that scheme should
be foreshown from the beginning by the type of bloody
sacrifice"(8.32). Ruskin so emphasizes the notion of the
figural significance of ceremonial law that he holds
"God had no more pleasure in such sacrifice in the time
of Moses than He has now; He never accepted, as a
propitiation for sin, any sacrifice but the single one in
prospective"(8.32-33). Arguing that it was not "necessary to the completeness, as a type, of the Levitical sacrifice, or to its utility as an explanation of divine purposes, that it should cost anything," since the sacrifice
it prefigured "was to be God's free gift"(8.33), he concludes that "costliness, therefore, must be an acceptable
condition in all human offerings at all times"(8.33-34).
Hence Ruskin, using Evangelical method and manner,
can convince Evangelicals to build costly Gothic houses
of worship. He directed *The Seven Lamps of Architecture* at his English Protestant audience which, he knew,
would not accept Gothic architecture as long as it
seemed a Roman Catholic style. Ever a polemical
writer, he adapts himself to his readers, wielding the
phrases of the preacher and the evidence of scripture,
to convince them that an Evangelical reading of the
Bible demanded sacrifice.

"The Lamp of Sacrifice" shows how thoroughly

typology had permeated Ruskin's habits of thought. But although his Evangelical habits of scriptural interpretation thus enabled him on occasion to conduct arguments that would appeal to an Evangelical reader, the major effects of these modes of reading appear in his art and literary criticism. In order to gain a sense of the exegetical procedures that so impressed themselves upon Ruskin's thought, we would do well to examine the sermons of Henry Melvill, Ruskin's favorite preacher. This preacher's gracefully written sermons, to which Ruskin paid such close attention, frequently take the form of elaborate revelations and explanations of typical resemblances. Like many other Evangelicals, he believed that the presence of types in the Bible is its distinguishing characteristic. Consequently, he warns his listeners: "If we fail to search the scriptural narratives for lessons and types, it is evident that we shall practically take away from a great part of the Bible its distinctive character as a record of spiritual truth."[19] Melvill's sermons are of particular interest to a student of Ruskin's criticism not only because he makes sophisticated use of figuralism, but also because in the course of elaborating Christ's types and shadows he provides rules for the applications of typology.

One of his sermons, "The Death of Moses," which was delivered sometime between 1836 and 1843, provides a good example of his methods. Speaking on Deuteronomy XXII:48-50, in which God orders Moses to leave his people before they entered Canaan, Melvill asks why Moses was not permitted to enter the Promised Land. The preacher carefully sets his listeners within the narrative, reminding them of Moses's past actions, the wanderings in the wilderness, the beauties

[19] "The Well of Bethlehem," *Sermons* (London, 1843), p. 170.

of Canaan, and the prophet's great desire to see the land of milk and honey. One of Melvill's principles, which he elucidated in another sermon, is that "We should never spiritualize any narrative of facts, till the facts have carefully been examined as facts, and the lessons extracted which their record may have been designed to convey."[20] He thus proceeds to examine the details of the narrative, searching for any explanation for God's forbidding Moses to enter the Promised Land. He then reminds the congregation that, on one occasion, Moses had sinned: when the water supply failed just as the Jews were about to enter Canaan, God directed Moses, "speak ye unto the rock before their eyes, and it shall give forth his water." But Moses became angered at his people, because they forgot that God had saved them before in Horeb when a similar thirst prevailed, and they reproached him for leading them into the desert: "And Moses and Aaron gathered the congregation together before the rock, and he said unto them, Hear now, ye rebels, must we fetch you water out of this rock? And Moses lifted up his hand, and with his rod he smote the rock twice." According to Melvill, Moses sinned because he allowed himself to become subject, not to righteous indignation, but to human anger, because he displayed arrogance in speaking as though he and Aaron could fetch water out of the rock alone, and because, falling into unbelief, he disobeyed God's command, not speaking to the rock but striking it twice. From the punishment of Moses's sins of "passion, and arrogance, and unbelief," and from the fact that Moses accepted God's punishment, all men are to learn, says Melvill, that their sins are great and that even the most mighty need obey God. Furthermore,

[20] "The Well of Bethlehem," p. 196.

342

Moses's acceptance of God's sentence that he go up the mount and die teaches all men how to accept death, which comes only by God's will. These moral lessons, or tropological applications of history, are, however, not all that Melvill finds in this incident.

This mild act of disobedience, this brief moment of human weakness, does not seem enough to explain why Moses was prevented from entering Canaan, and therefore Melvill searches for, finds, and elucidates the typological significance of the story. At this point, we come to a major principle of figural interpretation: when a detail appears particularly striking, unnecessary, or puzzling it probably demands the application of types. Melvill states this principle in a sermon devoted to Jacob's ladder, where he remarks that "If nothing had been intended beyond the assuring Jacob of divine favour and protection, the ladder with its attendant circumstances, seems unnecessarily introduced; for the words, spoken by God would have sufficed."[21] Melvill here makes the same demand for meaning that Ruskin did when he held that unless the Levitical sacrifices signified beyond themselves, unless they foreshadowed Christ, they were "trivial" and "unworthy of the being who appointed them." Evangelical devotion to typological interpretation arises in a demand for meaning and a desire to recognize God's orderly purpose in human history; and though they led to an occasional abuse of scripture, they more commonly produced careful and ingenious readings of the Bible. In addition to this demand for proper significance, Melvill requires an appropriateness in the manner in which the truth is conveyed. Thus he comments that if the ladder is to convey the unwearied communication of God with man

21 "Jacob's Vision and Vow," *Sermons* (London, 1838), p. 10.

343

via the angels, "the figure . . . scarcely seems distinguished by the aptness and force which are always characteristic of scriptural imagery."[22] Finally, since every part of God's dealings with man "is generally significative, and none can be shown to have been superfluous," we must search farther. Melvill concludes that the ladder typically signifies Christ, for Christ is both man's way to heaven and man's way of communicating with God, and he substantiates his traditional interpretation by the usual reference, made by Simeon and others, to John I:51 where Christ says to Nathaniel, "Verily, verily, I say unto you, Hereafter ye shall see heaven open, and the angels of God ascending and descending upon the Son of Man." Therefore, another principle of typological exegetics is that Christ's (or in some cases Paul's) confirmation is final proof.

Returning to "the Death of Moses," we can now recognize the gravity of Moses's sin. When he struck the rock in Horeb on divine command, he did so because God wanted to make the rock typify Christ: "The circumstance of the rock yielding no water, until smitten by the rod of Moses, represented the important truth, that the Mediator must receive the blows of the law before he could be the source of salvation to a parched and perishing world."[23] By striking the rock a second time, Moses disrupted God's scheme, or would have done so had not God's later action allowed the preacher to realize the significance of Moses's action:

Having been once smitten, there is nothing needed, in any after dearth, but that this rock should be

22 *Sermons* (1838), p. 11.
23 *Sermons* (London, 1836), pp. 163-164.

spoken to; prayer, if we may use the expression, will open the pierced side of the Lamb of God, and cause fresh flowings of that stream which is for the cleansing of the nations. Hence it would have been to violate the integrity and beauty of the type, that the rock should have been smitten again; it would have been to represent a necessity that Christ should be twice sacrificed, and thus to darken the whole Gospel scheme.[24]

God punished Moses, then, in order to draw attention to his act, and thereby suggest another entry in the book of Christ's revelations.

Melvill next proceeds to examine the story once more, finding another reason, in a figural significance, why Moses could not enter Canaan. "You will all remember that Moses, though he must die before entering Canaan, was to rise, and appear in that land, ages before the general resurrection. When Christ was transfigured on Mount Tabor, who were those shining forms that stood by him, and 'spake of the decease which he should accomplish at Jerusalem?' Who but Elias and Moses. . . ? . . . Moses was the representative of the myriads who shall rise from the grave; Elias, of those, who, found alive upon earth, shall be transformed without seeing death."[25] As part of the transfiguration, Moses then becomes part of a type which has not yet been fulfilled.

Melvill then returns once more to his original question, and for a third time finds an answer. Why has Moses not been allowed to complete his great work of deliverance? "Why, except that Moses was the repre-

[24] *Sermons* (1836), pp. 165-166.    [25] *Sermons* (1836), pp. 184-185.

345

sentative of the law, and that the law of itself, can never lead us into heavenly places? The law is as 'a schoolmaster, to bring us unto Christ [Gal. iii]."[26] Moses, then, as representative of the Jewish law, could not enter the Promised Land, because to have done so would have mistakenly suggested that the old dispensation could earn that salvation made possible only through Christ.

Something very interesting has happened here: by the recognition of this typical significance, Melvill seems to be saying that what the man Moses, as emblem, signifies is more important than what the man as agent does. One feels that no matter what the prophet had done, the burden of figural meaning, of reference beyond himself, would have prevented him from entering the land of milk and honey. According to a figural interpretation of history, such as we encounter here, the personages exist simultaneously on several planes and in separate worlds. First of all, there is Moses the human being, a man who has direct dealings with the Lord; he exists here in this life as we all do. Secondly, every one of his actions, like those of all men, has a moral meaning, for he exists in a moral universe; and because the prophet is more important than most men are or have been, each action is doubly significant, each action is emblematic of the actions of morality in human life. Thirdly, there is the fact that Moses exists as a part of the Gospel scheme which God created before —or perhaps outside—time. Furthermore, Moses exists in several different ways, or dimensions, within this typical structure that underlies or is intertwined with earthly history and time. Moses is, first of all, a figure

[26] *Sermons* (1836), p. 185.

346

of Christ, for like Christ he brings the law and guides his people; secondly, he, as a representative of the law, is the type of those who do not attain heaven, the Promised Land, because they do not have Christ; thirdly, he enforces another type, when, signifying the law, he strikes the rock, now a figure of Christ, thus showing that Christ must die by the law which he has come to replace; fourthly, by striking the rock a second time, he is again a type of those who will not reach heaven because they disobey God, because they hurt Christ by their sinning, and because they do not pray to Christ. What has happened is that while Moses is conceived as dwelling solidly within the world of physical fact, of the visible here and now, he is also seen to exist multivalently in a realm of sacred meaning.

What is most striking about this vision of history is that Melvill, unlike some earlier Evangelical preachers, does not hold that reading figural significances is primarily important as a meditational exercise. Instead, Melvill states that many types are as yet unfulfilled, that they await completion, that man, even man in the time of Queen Victoria, lives within a typologically structured universe. We have already seen that because Moses figures forth those who, at the resurrection, will rise from the grave, he takes part in a yet unfinished typological scheme that embraces the preacher's contemporaries. Melvill also holds that not only individual men, but even entire nations, must be seen as partaking in divine schemes whose fulfillment awaits the fullness of time. For example, the history of the Jews, who are to be regarded as "a typical people," shadows forth both the histories of the human race and the Christian

347

church.[27] So also with those who have oppressed the Jews, for

> from the first the enemies of God and his people which one age has produced, have served as types of those who will arise in the latter days of the world; and . . . the judgments by which they have been overtaken, have been so constructed as to figure the final vengeance on Antichrist and his followers. Hence it is that so many prophecies appear to require as well as to admit a double fulfilment: they could hardly delineate the type and not delineate also the antitype.[28]

Types, as Melvill so well phrases it, are to be seen "spreading . . . over the whole of time, and giving outlines of the history of this world from the beginning to the final consummation."[29] Thus, when he preaches upon the text of Zechariah X:1, which directs that we should ask the Lord for rain in the time of latter rain, Melvill comments "that time must include the whole christian dispensation, and . . . must comprehend such days as our own."[30] The preacher insists that his listeners still exist within biblical history, within prophetic and figural time.

That Ruskin, like his favorite preacher, finds himself living within sacral, figural time perhaps appears in those arguments which draw upon the typical laws in Leviticus to demonstrate the sacredness of color and

27 "Seeking after Finding," *Sermons* (London, 1845), p. 159. This commonplace appears also in "The Resurrection of Dry Bones," *Sermons* (London, 1848), pp. 64-73. See, in addition, "The Dispersion and Restoration of the Jews," *Sermons* (New York, 1854), I, 207-217.
28 "Seeking after Finding," *Sermons* (1845), p. 156.
29 "The First Prophecy," *Sermons* (London, 1833), p. 6.
30 "The Latter Rain," *Sermons* (1843), p. 279.

the need for sacrifice in architecture. Here, however, he chiefly emphasizes, not that types have yet to be ful- filled, but that the truths contained in typical law re- main valid. A far clearer indication that he accepts a figural conception of history occurs when *The Stones of Venice* uses the destinies of Tyre and Venice as types for nineteenth-century England. The opening pages of this work demonstrate forcibly that when he wrote it, he believed God structured time so that the events of the scriptural narrative would prefigure contemporary history.

Although Ruskin evidently shared with Melvill and other Evangelicals this sense of dwelling in figural time, his conception of the world as allegory plays a far more central role in his writings. Similarly, although he frequently makes skillful use of typology, as in his in- terpretations of Giotto, his uses of allegory are more important than his applications of figuralism. Both this allegorical conception of the world and his ideas of al- legory in general derive from Evangelical typology, for despite the fact that members of this Church party, in- cluding Wilberforce and Melvill, mention allegory with distaste and distrust,[31] many preachers unknowingly practiced allegorization under another guise: the Evan- gelical Anglican penchant for elaborate figural inter- pretation frequently prompts nineteenth-century exe- getes to move from typology to allegory, thus repeating a phenomenon familiar in the history of scriptural ex- position. Whereas typology (or figuralism), which traces the connections between two unique events,

---

31 Wilberforce, who quotes Swift's *Tale of a Tub* against forced alle- gorical interpretations of scripture, seems far more conservative than Melvill, though even he is usually quite skeptical of allegorization (as opposed to typological exegetics).

stresses what an historian of exegetics has called a "similar situation,"[32] allegory, which interprets one thing as in reality signifying another, does not attempt to establish this unique situational parallel. Strictly speaking, Moses is not a type of Christ. Rather "Moses leading the children of God from Egyptian slavery into the Promised Land" acts as a type for "Christ leading men from spiritual slavery into the heavenly kingdom." Thus, although writers often sound as though one person or thing may foreshadow another, in fact situation and action are also required to have a true type. Another difference between figural and allegorical interpretation is that, whereas in typology one real, physically existing being or event represents another real, physically existing being or event, in allegory a thing may often represent a doctrine or abstract idea, such as grace, whose duration cannot be confined to one moment or one period in time. Thus, although both typological and allegorical interpretations are meta-historical, typology must work within human time, while allegory may often work outside of it. We can perceive this shift from typological to allegorical reading of the Bible in Melvill's sermons. For example, when he uses the traditional notion, found in Scott, Simeon, and others, that God's creation of the waters typified grace, he has in fact applied allegory and not typical symbol-

[32] R.P.C. Hanson, *Allegory and Event, A Study of the Sources and Significance of Origen's Interpretation of Scripture* (Richmond, Va., 1959), p. 22. Other works to which I am here indebted include Henri de Lubac, *Exégèse médiévale, les quatre sens de l'écriture*, 4 vols. (Paris, 1959-1964); Beryl Smalley, *The Study of the Bible in the Middle Ages* (Notre Dame, 1964); Eric Auerbach, *Mimesis: The Representation of Reality in Western Literature* (Princeton, 1953); D. W. Robertson, Jr., *A Preface to Chaucer: Studies in Medieval Perspectives* (Princeton, 1962); Victor Harris, "Allegory to Analogy," *PQ*, XLV (1966), 1-23; and Miss Tuve's *Allegorical Imagery*.

ism; although one can perhaps argue that the physical creation of water figures forth countless individual acts of grace that have occurred and are yet to occur throughout history, this is not true "prefiguring," since the first event is linked not to one but to an infinite number of following events, and since the weakened connection between events is far less important than the fact that one thing, water, is seen to represent a theological doctrine. In other words, whereas a type focuses attention on both its historical existence and its meaning, an allegory places most importance on its significance. The difference between the two is often not very great, and therefore Evangelical attempts to perform intricate typological readings frequently lead the interpreter to shift unknowingly from type to allegorization.

Working within this Evangelical tradition of scriptural interpretation, Ruskin himself frequently extends the primary sense of type to include allegory and symbol. Nonetheless, however far he extends the original meaning of the term "type," his uses of it almost always bear overtones of that original meaning. For example, because typology assumes that on the narrative level there must be a real, historically existing person or thing, it places much greater emphasis upon the literal level than does allegory. Unlike most nineteenth-century critics, including Arnold, who believe that once the meanings of allegory make themselves clear the narrative tends to disappear like a useless husk, Ruskin places essentially equal emphasis upon both signifier and signified. The influence of typology appears in Ruskin's theory of typical beauty, which emphasizes *both* the formal elements of the beautiful and its deeper theological significance. Similarly, his theories

351

of art formed under the influence of typology encourage him to maintain a balance between the formal elements of a painting, its aesthetic surface, and its complex significances. Thus, as we shall observe in a later section of this chapter, when he interprets the allegory of one of Turner's works, he tends to pay close attention both to form and iconography.

Although such a relation between typology and Ruskin's theories of allegory may explain why he rather unfashionably defended the values and procedures of allegorical art and literature, it presents us with another problem; namely, how in the first place could Ruskin and other Evangelicals have maintained a belief in typology, a belief that was obviously an anachronism by the Victorian age. The answer to the question how the Evangelicals could sustain this belief in a hostile intellectual environment lies in their belief, never officially accepted by the Church of England, that God had literally dictated the words of the Bible. This noncanonical doctrine of Verbal Inspiration created that conception of language fundamental to allegorical and typological readings of scripture. As Thomas P. Roche has pointed out in his study of Spenser, "Allegorical reading (or more simply allegory) is a form of literary criticism with a metaphysical basis. It postulates a verbal universe at every point correspondent with the physical world in which we live, that is a Realistic view of language."[33] Allegory and allegorical interpretation both depend upon and implicitly create a Realistic view of language, a view which since the late seventeenth century has become increasingly difficult to ac-

[33] *The Kindly Flame: A Study in the Third and Fourth Books of Spenser's "Faerie Queene"* (Princeton, 1964), p. 7.

cept. As long as men assumed that language had, corresponded to, or participated in essences, allegorical art and an allegorical reading of scripture were possible and perhaps inevitable. But after Hobbes and Locke referred language not to metaphysics but to psychology, a Realistic conception of language which provides the basis for allegory became largely untenable. Hobbes, who denied that words have essences, believed that language is merely the means "whereby men register their Thoughts."[34] Thus, there is no such thing as "an *Universall*; there being nothing in the world Universall but Names; for the things named, are every one of them Individuall and Singular."[35] Similarly, Locke states that language functions as a sign for ideas within the speaker's mind that communicates these ideas to another person.[36] According to Locke, human convention, not participation in essences or correspondence to them, establishes meaning. Furthermore, because man has no access to any metaphysical existence, he therefore cannot define his words by reference to something that thus lies above or beyond him. Words are defined ultimately by reference to the speaker's mind. Once Hobbes and Locke moved the reality of language from metaphysics to psychology, from the external realm of forms to the internal realm of the mind, they simultaneously dissolved the linguistic foundations of allegory.

The Evangelical Anglicans did not maintain their Realistic conception of biblical language by consciously opposing Locke and his philosophical heirs, the Scot-

[34] *Leviathan* (New York, 1950), p. 22.    [35] *Ibid.*, p. 24.
[36] *An Essay Concerning Human Understanding*, ed. Alexander Campbell Fraser, 2 vols. (New York, 1959), II, 3, 9-11.

tish empiricists such as Thomas Reid, Dugald Stewart, and Adam Smith. Smith's *Theory of the Moral Sentiments*, in fact, received something very like official sanction when William Wilberforce's *Practical Christianity* (1797), cited it approvingly. But although the Evangelicals accepted empiricist philosophy, they were nonetheless able to read scripture figurally and allegorically, because they believed, as Melvill stated, that "The Bible is as actually a divine communication as though its words came to us in the voice of Almighty, mysteriously syllabled, and breathed from the firmament."[37] This Evangelical doctrine that the Bible was literally the Word of God placed the scriptures in a special category unaffected by empiricist theories of language. For since God had dictated the words of scripture, these words, unlike any others, necessarily participated in a greater reality. In other words, the Evangelicals had accepted the Lockean notion that the context created by the mind of the speaker ultimately defines language, and then referred scriptural language to the eternal mind of God.

Only the conservatism of the Evangelical party, which insulated it for a time from the corrosive implications of contemporary historical and scientific speculation, enabled its members to maintain their non-canonical belief in Verbal Inspiration. Ruskin soon lost that belief, but not before his habits of reading had been formed. By the middle of the nineteenth century, when the great Evangelical preachers were perfecting their elaborate methods of figural and allegorical interpretation, the combined forces of natural science,

[37] "The Advantages Resulting from Possession of the Scriptures" (New York, 1854), I, 159.

biblical criticism, and comparative philology were already clearly demonstrating that the Bible could not be literally true.[38] Geology, Ruskin's favorite science, had shown that scriptural accounts of the physical world, particularly the age of the earth, could not be correct,[39] while biblical studies emanating from Germany demonstrated that the Bible was not a homogenous document, but one which had evolved throughout a long history. Both Colenso's work and *Essays and Reviews* were two of many factors that increasingly undermined Evangelical doctrine. Comparative philology, which revealed that Hebrew was not, as most Evangelicals believed, unique and set apart from other languages, further eroded the doctrine that the Bible was the Word of God. Their belief in Verbal Inspiration had enabled the Evangelicals to interpret the Bible figurally and allegorically long after the general linguistic basis of such interpretation disappeared, but once the corrosive forces of historical and scientific scholarship undermined Evangelical belief in Verbal Inspiration, it became apparent even to many of the Evangelical party that typology and allegory could not be used to interpret scripture. Thus, at the very time that Melvill and other Evangelical clergymen most closely paralleled medieval exegesis, the intellectual climate of the nineteenth century was beginning to wear away fundamental doctrines of the Evangelical party. In the second half of the nineteenth century this segment of the Anglican Church lost power, as Englishmen turned increasingly either to less conservative parties in the

[38] Vernon F. Storr, *The Development of English Theology in the Nineteenth Century, 1800-1833* (London, 1894), pp. 175-176.

[39] See Francis C. Haber, *The Age of the World, Moses to Darwin* (Baltimore, Md., 1959).

Church or to unbelief. Having already observed the way Ruskin's own faith gradually changed, vanished, and returned in a new form, it now remains for us to examine other sources of typological interpretation that he had encountered as a boy and young man.

### III. Typological symbolism in the readings of Ruskin's childhood

RUSKIN, who learned to read the language of types chiefly from Evangelical sermons, frequently encountered typological symbolism in the readings of his boyhood as well. *Paradise Lost*, which all devout Evangelicals read as a doctrinal work, exemplifies that literature which exercised methods of interpretation Ruskin learned in Beresford and Camden Chapels. Milton's explicit explanation of types appears in Book XII when Michael comforts Adam with a vision of salvation to come, first instructing him that God will communicate laws to His chosen people through Moses

> part such as appertain
> To civil Justice, part religious Rites
> Of sacrifice, informing them, by types
> And shadows, of that destin'd Seed to bruise
> The Serpent, by what means he shall achieve
> Mankind's deliverance. But the voice of God
> To mortal ear is dreadful; they beseech
> That *Moses* might report to them his will,
> And terror cease; he grants what they besought,
> Instructed that to God is no access
> Without Mediator, whose high Office now
> *Moses* in figure bears, to introduce
> One greater, of whose day he shall fortell,

And all the Prophets in thir Age the times
Of great *Messiah* shall sing.[40]

Michael further explains to Adam that since man in his
fallen state will be unable to keep God's moral law,
only Christ will be able to crush Satan:

> Doubt not but that sin
> Will reign among them, as of thee begot;
> And therefore was Law given them to evince
> Thir natural pravity, by stirring up
> Sin against Law to fight; that when they see
> Law can discover sin, but not remove,
> Save by those shadowy expiations weak,
> The blood of Bulls and Goats, they may conclude
> Some blood more precious must be paid for Man,
> Just for unjust, that in such righteousness
> To them by Faith imputed, they may find
> Justification towards God, and peace
> Of Conscience, which the Law by Ceremonies
> Cannot appease, nor Man the moral part
> Perform, and not performing cannot live.
> So Law appears imperfet, and but giv'n
> With purpose to resign them in full time
> Up to a better Cov'nant, disciplin'd
> From shadowy Types to Truth, from Flesh to Spirit,
> From imposition of strict Laws, to free
> Acceptance of large Grace, from servile fear
> To filial, works of Law to works of Faith.
> And therefore shall not *Moses*, though of God

40 Ed. Merritt Y. Hughes (New York, 1962), p. 297. For Milton's figural symbolism see: William G. Madsen, "Earth and Shadow of Heaven: Typological Symbolism in *Paradise Lost*," and Northrop Frye, "The Typology of *Paradise Regained*," both in *Milton: Modern Essays in Criticism*, ed. Arthur E. Barker (New York, 1965), pp. 246-263 and 429-446.

Highly belov'd, being but the Minister
Of Law, his people into *Canaan* lead;
But *Joshua* whom the Gentiles *Jesus* call,
His Name and Office bearing, who shall quell
The adversary Serpent, and bring back
Through the world's wilderness long wander'd man
Safe to eternal Paradise of rest.[41]

In these lines Milton not only explains the need for types and shadows but also, like the Evangelical preachers two centuries later, explains how Moses himself functions in the scheme of salvation.

Furthermore, as commentators have pointed out, Milton subtly emphasizes his typological vision of sacred history throughout *Paradise Lost,* thus simultaneously revealing the curse of the Fall and the promise of salvation. At the moment in Book x when the voice of God accuses Adam and Eve of their transgression and states the future enmity between their descendents and Satan, the poet mentions "*Jesus* son of *Mary* second *Eve*," who will bring salvation.[42] Similarly in the fifth book Raphael greets Eve, yet unfallen, with "Hail"—"the holy salutation us'd/ Long after to blest *Mary*, second *Eve*."[43] The poem, in fact, begins with Milton's request that he be inspired by the Heavenly Muse which inspired Moses, "That Shepherd, who first taught the chosen Seed."[44] Milton, then, continually emphasizes both the individual historical role of each agent, whether Adam, Eve, or Moses, and the symbolic function that each plays in sacred time. The forces of evil are revealed in their typical roles as well, for when Satan climbs into Eden, Milton points out how his act prefigures future evil:

41 *Paradise Lost,* pp. 298-299.     42 *Ibid.,* p. 240.
43 *Ibid.,* p. 123.     44 *Ibid.,* p. 5.

So clomb this first grand Thief into God's Fold:
So since into his Church lewd Hirelings climb.[45]

Similarly, the continual shifting of verb tenses in "The Morning of Christ's Nativity," which serves to reveal the interpenetration of human time, God's divine scheme of salvation, and Christ's presence, has its counterpart in these consistent reminders to the reader of *Paradise Lost* of the spiritual beauty of God's plan.

Confident both of the reality of types and that his readers will perceive them in the poem, Milton makes many subtle uses of figuralism. Thus, the eleventh book opens with Adam and Eve able to pray since God had enabled Grace to descend to them "from the Mercy-seat above."[46] Milton would have expected his readers to have recognized the mercy-seat as the image of Aaron's tabernacle in Exodus 25:17-20, traditionally the type of intercession of Angels or Christ in heaven. Furthermore, the prophecy that Christ would bruise the head of Satan appears six or seven times throughout the poem, always emphasizing the future appearance of the Savior. In their ability to read figurally the Evangelicals clearly earn themselves a place in Milton's "fit audience though few." It is characteristic of the seriousness with which this party in the Church of England regarded *Paradise Lost* that Wilberforce's *Practical Christianity* should use Milton's words to illustrate man's fallen state.[47] Similarly, when Melvill's ser-

---

[45] *Ibid.*, p. 89.    [46] *Ibid.*, p. 265. See also p. 265n.
[47] Wilberforce (p. 40) quotes Adam's closing speech in Book x:

> What better can we do [ . . . ], than prostrate fall
> Before him reverent; and there confess
> Humbly our faults, and pardon beg; with tears
> Watering the ground, and with our signs the air
> Frequenting, sent from hearts contrite, in sign
> Of sorrow unfeign'd, and humiliation meek?

mon, "Eve Parleying with the Tempter," which Ruskin summarized in his diary, appeared in *The Pulpit*, the Victorian editor followed the sermon by Milton's ll. 735-784 of the ninth book as the natural accompaniment to the preacher's words.[48]

*Pilgrim's Progress*, one of the few books Margaret Ruskin allowed her son to read on Sundays, further exemplifies the way his childhood readings reinforced Evangelical interpretations of scripture. After returning home from Beresford Chapel where he had heard Reverend Andrews preach on the types in Leviticus, Ruskin would have come upon many of these same figures of Christ in Bunyan. For example, the verses prefatory to *Pilgrim's Progress* thus cite God's use of types in Levitical law to defend the author's allegory and metaphor:

> *Was not God's laws,*
> *His Gospel-laws, in olden times held forth*
> *By Types, Shadows and Metaphors? Yet loth*
> *Will any sober Man be to find fault*
> *With them, lest he be found for to assault*
> *The highest Wisdom. No, he rather stoops*
> *And seeks to find out what by Pins and Loops,*
> *By Calves, and Sheep, by Heifers, and by Rams,*
> *By Birds and Herbs, and by the blood of Lambs,*
> *God speaketh to him; and happy is he*
> *That finds the Light & Grace that in them be.*[49]

Believing firmly that in the service of God one can employ those devices of language and art sanctified by "the highest wisdom," Bunyan casts his narrative in the form of an allegory and embellishes his text with fre-

[48] XLIII (1843), 432. Ruskin mentions and summarizes this "noble sermon" in *Diaries*, I, 243 (12 February 1843).

[49] Ed. James B. Wharey (Oxford, 1928), p. 4.

quent echoes of scripture, many of which bear figural significance.

Occasionally he will explicitly mention typology in the narrative, but usually his practice is more indirect. At one point, however, Christian explains to Hopeful that *"Esau's* Birth-right was Typical."[50] More characteristic is that scene in the second half of the *Progress* which indirectly expounds the Levitical types cited in the prefatory verse. After Christiana's son Matthew has fallen ill from a guilty conscience, Mr. Skill "made him a Purge, but it was too weak. 'Twas said it was made of the Blood of a Goat, the Ashes of a Heifer, and with some of the Juice of Hyssop, &c. When Mr. *Skill* had seen that that Purge was too weak he made him one to the purpose. 'Twas made *ex Carne & Sanguine Christi.*"[51] Combining the belief that Christ has come to fulfill sacrificial law with the belief that only Christ can cure the ills of the world, this passage shows that in one's journey to heaven one especially needs the Gospel and the intercession of Christ *after* one has realized his own guilt. For the reader to understand this incident he must be familiar with figural interpretations of Levitical law. For him to enjoy it he must delight in discovering the truths of religion in novel contexts. Bunyan obviously expects these figural embellishments upon the main narrative to attract and exercise the reader's skill at biblical interpretation, and he makes frequent use of them. For instance, when Christiana, Great-Heart, and Gaius sit down to dinner with the others, they find on their table "a *Heave-shoulder* and a *Wave-breast,*" the sacrificial offerings enjoined by Leviticus 7:32-34 and 10:14-15.[52] Here the typo-

50 *Ibid.*, p. 136.　　　　　51 *Ibid.*, p. 242.
52 *Ibid.*, p. 275.

logical symbolism functions more indirectly than did Mr. Skill's purge, for the reader must first recognize that the pilgrims dine on the Levitical offering, then realize that this offering prefigures Christ, and finally perceive that the pilgrims sustain themselves with the body and blood of Christ thus typically prefigured. This love of solving divine riddles appears again in many of the visions and emblems which the pilgrims encounter throughout their journey. For example, when the angels present Christiana with a vision of Jacob's ladder and Abraham's sacrifice of Isaac, the well-prepared reader would have received figural instruction as well as the overt moral instructions that Bunyan included.[53]

In other words, the reader has to interpret *Pilgrim's Progress* in the same way the Evangelicals—and the Puritans before them—interpreted the Bible. Like Milton, Bunyan believed that since his allegory reveals Christ's role in human salvation he could fittingly employ typology. Unlike Milton, whose figuralism generally advances the main narrative, Bunyan uses types to embellish his tale of life's journey. Both works achieved great popularity with the Evangelicals who regarded the seventeenth-century Puritans as honored precursors to their party, and Ryle described the story of Christian's pilgrimage through life as "a religious work . . . unrivalled in its way since the time of the apostles."[54] The fact that Bunyan's absorbing story both

[53] Bunyan's primary use of the visions are tropological. Thus after Prudence has shown Christiana the holy places and things of religion she sings the following song to her (p. 246):

> *An Anchor you received have;*
> *But let not these suffice,*
> *Until with* Abra'm *you have gave*
> *Your best, a Sacrifice.*

[54] *Living or Dead?*, p. 18.

enforced Evangelical doctrine and exercised the reader's skill at understanding the Word of God made it especially appropriate reading for the young. Although many Victorian children must have read the story literally, completely missing Bunyan's use of types and shadows, Ruskin, who at the age of nine could already explicate Levitical law with utmost sophistication, would have understood *Pilgrim's Progress* more fully.

George Herbert, who throughout Ruskin's life remained one of his favorite poets, similarly makes extensive use of figuralism. For example, "The Sacrifice," a soliloquy spoken by Christ, emphasizes both that Jesus came as a second Adam and that he was the antitype, the fulfillment, of Moses:

> My face they cover, though it be divine.
> As *Moses* face was vailed, so is mine,
> Lest on their double-dark souls either shine.[55]

Similarly, Herbert's "Sunday" employs the notion that Sampson was a type of Christ, showing that the tremor which shook the earth at the moment Christ died fulfilled Sampson's destruction of the temple which he pulled down upon himself. In particular, the poem argues that just as the Old Testament hero pulled down the heathen temple, so Christ pulled down the old religious order—worship on Saturday—replacing it with worship on Sunday, the day of His resurrection:

> The rest of our Creation
> Our great Redeemer did remove
> With the same shake, which at his passion
> Did th' earth and all things with it move.

[55] *Works*, ed. F. E. Hutchinson (Oxford, 1941), p. 31.

As Sampson bore the doores away,
Christs hands, though nail'd wrought our salvation,
    And did unhinge that day.[56]

The use of typology for Herbert's wit of paradox, evident in "Sunday," characterizes many of his other poems, and, as a recent critic has demonstrated, not only individual poems but also the entire structure of *The Temple* itself employ typological symbolism.[57] Ruskin, who encountered in Herbert the uses of figuralism that he had learned from the sermons of Andrews and Melvill, would here have found his habits of scriptural reading reinforced and exercised in the most delightful manner.

In addition, Ruskin exercised his knowledge of figural interpretation in reading not only the works of these seventeenth-century writers but also those of his own century. Wordsworth, who perhaps more than any other poet influenced Ruskin's early years, employs typology in ways that would have confirmed Ruskin's own usage of this mode of symbolism. *The Excursion*, upon which he drew for the epigraph to *Modern Painters*, several times uses figuralism in its strict biblical application. For example, when the Solitary is musing upon the rite of baptism, he mentions the commonplace that Noah's ark was a type of the church:

At the baptismal font ... when the pure
And consecrating element hath cleansed
The original stain, the child is there received
Into the second ark, Christ's church, with trust

[56] *Ibid.*, p. 76. See the editor's commentary, p. 503.
[57] John David Walker, "The Architectonics of George Herbert's *The Temple*," ELH, XXIX (1962), 289-305.

That he, from wrath redeemed, therein shall float
Over the billows of this troublesome world
To the fair land of everlasting life.[58]

In other words, just as Noah, following the Word of
God, built an ark that the virtuous few might survive
the divine wrath of the punishing flood, so Christ established the church to enable the virtuous few of a later
day to survive the "billows of this troublesome world."
Such use of a biblical type does not draw much attention to itself, for it arises as a natural means of expression to those accustomed to reading the scriptures for
signs of Christ. And Wordsworth, while not an Evangelical, still read the Bible in this manner and still
found the language of types a natural mode in which
to discuss the truth of scripture. A similar use of figuralism occurs in Book VI, "The Churchyard among
the Mountains," when the betrayed Ellen tells her
mother that the grace of God enabled her to endure the
"pang of despised love":

There was a stony region in my heart;
But He, at whose command the parchèd rock
Was smitten, and poured forth a quenching stream,
Hath softened that obduracy, and made
Unlooked-for gladness in the desert place,
To save the perishing.[59]

Here the use of the scriptural type is more indirect
than in the previous passage. Although the analogy
which Ellen draws between Moses striking the rock in
the wilderness and God relieving her distress functions

---

[58] *Works*, v, 162.
[59] *Ibid.*, 216. Ruskin borrows this image for use in his poem "The
Broken Chain" (2.174).

quite effectively without a recognition that this is a common type, such a recognition adds to the power of the comparison. For if the reader perceives that when Moses struck the rock he prefigured, as Melvill pointed out, Christ's death by the law which brought grace to men, then the further connections between the suffering of Ellen and her Savior make the passage even more moving.

Wordsworth's most interesting types are those symbols drawn from the world of nature which foreshadow things to come. Thus, upon looking at the glory of a mountain sunset, the effusive clergyman of *The Excursion* "in holy transport" thanks God for

> this local transitory type
> Of thy paternal splendours, and the pomp
> Of those who fill thy courts in highest heaven,
> The radiant Cherubim.[60]

The notion of type here is of course somewhat ambiguous, for the speaker might be using it in the extended sense of "symbol"—that the sunset provides an earthly image of eternity—or he might intend it to mean that this terrestrial beauty literally prefigures the beauties of the life which follows. At any rate, since in either case the earthly, temporal beauty signifies that which is outside time and space, and since that which exists in eternity clearly relates to Christ, who brought men the good news of eternal life, the basic notion of the biblical type applies. On the other hand, the magnificent "Simplon Pass," which presents the tumult and peace, the darkness and light of the Alpine pass as a type of the Apocalypse, clearly and unambiguously makes use of figuralism:

[60] *Works*, v, 307.

—————Brook and road
Were fellow-travellers in this gloomy Pass,
And with them did we journey several hours
At a slow step. The immeasurable height
Of woods decaying, never to be decayed,
The stationary blasts of waterfalls,
And in the narrow rent, at every turn,
Winds thwarting winds bewildered and forlorn,
The torrents shooting from the clear blue sky,
The rocks that muttered close upon our ears,
Black drizzling crags that spake by the wayside
As if a voice were in them, the sick sight
And giddy prospect of the raving stream,
The unfettered clouds and region of the heavens,
Tumult and peace, the darkness and the light—
Were all like workings of one mind, the features
Of the same face, blossoms upon one tree,
Characters of the great Apocalypse,
The types and symbols of Eternity,
Of first, and last, and midst, and without end.[61]

Against Wordsworth one might argue that natural phenomena cannot be types, since they only appear in the Bible and only there because God dictated its words. But to Wordsworth, as to Ruskin, such argument would fail to recognize their assumption that the earth, in a most literal sense, is the book of God. Believing as he does in the sacred language of the earth, Wordsworth has no difficulty in discovering types of a changed earth, the future earth of the Apocalypse, in the magnificence of an Alpine pass.

Carlyle, whose influence upon Ruskin increased about the time Wordsworth's began to fade, further

[61] *Ibid.*, II, 212-213.

provided him with an example of symbolism ultimately rooted in biblical typology. Unlike the essentially orthodox use of figuralism which Wordsworth extended to include the natural world, Carlyle's conception of the symbol had been largely emptied of its original Christian meaning. This genetic relation of the Carlylean symbol to type or *figura* appears most distinctly in *Sartor Resartus* where, after emphasizing that men live by symbols, Carlyle's Professor points out how much greater are symbols with intrinsic meaning than banners and emblems: "Let but the Godlike manifest itself to Sense; let but Eternity look, more or less visibly, through the Time-figure (*Zeitbild*)! Then is it fit that men unite there; and worship together before such a Symbol. . . . Of this latter sort are all true Works of Art: in them (if thou know a Work of Art from a Daub of Artifice) wilt thou discern Eternity looking through Time; the Godlike rendered visible."[62] Carlyle's use of the term "Time-figure," which obviously recalls "figure" or *figura*, the usual Latin term for type, would seem to demonstrate his debt to traditional readings of scripture. Similarly, the emphasis upon "Eternity looking through Time" and "the Godlike rendered visible" apparently arise in conventional typology. Throughout Carlyle's writings one can perceive similar hints that his notions of symbolism derive from a typology emptied of christological significance. *Sartor*, for example, emphasizes that "in what we can call a Symbol, there is ever . . . some embodiment and revelation of the Infinite; the Infinite is made to blend itself with the Finite, to stand visible, and as it were, attainable there."[63] Without the emphasis upon Christ, without the emphasis upon an eternal plan unfolding in human

[62] *Works*, I, 178.    [63] *Ibid.*, 175.

368

time, there remains the notion essential to typology that the type both exists in itself and signifies further—that an incursion from eternity stands forth in the world of man, bearing news from the infinite. Similarly, although Carlyle's "Chartism" removes the Carlylean notion of sacred history far from its original source, we can still perceive habits of mind acquired in the Christian tradition: "Events are written lessons, glaring in huge hieroglyphic picture-writing, that all may read and know them: the terror and horror they inspire is but the note of preparation for the truth they are to teach."[64] Here in "Chartism," though we are far from the gospel of salvation that typology reveals, the terminology remains Christian. Like the fundamentalist preacher, whether Presbyterian, Evangelical, or Methodist, Carlyle considers events as "written lessons," and like the preacher he uses the notion of "hieroglyphic," teaching by event, and a meaningfully structured history.

When Carlyle drew upon Christian typology for his ideas of symbolism, he emptied his source both of orthodox Christian significance and its emphasis upon the literal. As we have already seen, typology, unlike Hellenistic allegory, maintains the integrity of both the signifier and the signified: Moses, though far less than Christ, is still real. A conception of symbolism or allegory, such as Ruskin's, which is based on typology therefore emphasizes the reality and the importance of the literal. Carlyle, on the other hand, remains without confidence in the essential reality of this world. His central attitude appears in his statement in *Heroes and Hero-Worship* that "this so solid-looking material world is, at bottom, in very deed, Nothing: is a visual and

tactual Manifestation of God's power and presence—a
shadow hung-out by Him on the bosom of the void Infinite; nothing more."[65] The difference between Carlyle
and Ruskin is a matter of emphasis, surely, but an all-
important one; for although Ruskin, like Wordsworth,
believes this world to be a mere shadow of things to
come, he never loses sight of the essential reality of the
material, the earthly. This divergence between Ruskin
and Carlyle, a divergence which goes far to explain
why Carlyle so distrusted the art which Ruskin loved,
suggests that Carlyle had little effect on Ruskin's notions of symbolism, which, at any rate, had formed
themselves before Carlyle had an important influence
upon his thought.

### IV. The Symbolical Grotesque—theories of allegory, artist, and imagination

RUSKIN'S chapters on the grotesque in *The Stones of
Venice* and *Modern Painters*, Volume III, make it abun-
dantly clear that his theories of allegory derive from
Evangelical versions of traditional Christian beliefs
about revelation, prophecy, and scriptural language.
Many of his statements about the way allegory permits
man to grasp truth otherwise beyond his capacities appear as commonplace in Evangelical sermons. For example, Henry Melvill assured his congregation that although type and allegory are presently necessary for
man to receive divine revelation, "hereafter so
strengthened will be our faculties, so enlarged our
capacities, and so exalted our place among the orders
of creation, that God will be visible to us in such sense
as he is visible to any finite beings; not in dim shadow,

---

[65] *Ibid.*, v, 69.

and mystic type, and material representation, but in the splendour, the spirituality, the immenseness, the eternity of Deity."[66] In man's present state, dim shadow and mystic type remain the only way his shattered, limited capacities can perceive God and His ways. The second volume of *Modern Painters* similarly insists that "what revelations have been made to humanity inspired, or caught up to heaven, of things to the heavenly region belonging, have been either by unspeakable words, or else by their very nature incommunicable, except in types and shadows"(4.208). Ruskin believes that these "types and shadows," which he subsumes under the term "Symbolical Grotesque" (11.182), are always that mode in which the revelations of the prophet and artist appear.

His very choice of that rather strange term for allegory demonstrates his debt to the notion that allegory and type are necessary to accommodate spiritual truths otherwise beyond the capacities of fallen man; for according to him, the highest form of the grotesque is that "arising from the confusion of the imagination by the presence of truths which it cannot wholly grasp" (5.130). The Symbolical Grotesque, then, "arises out of the use or fancy of tangible signs to set forth an otherwise less expressible truth; including nearly the whole range of symbolical and allegorical art and poetry" (5.132). In *The Stones of Venice* Ruskin carefully explains that man's present state necessitates the grotesque: "the fallen human soul, at its best, must be as a diminishing glass, and that a broken one, to the mighty truths of the universe round it; and the wider the scope of its glance, and the vaster the truths into which it obtains an insight, the more fantastic their dis-

66 "Heaven," *Sermons* (New York, 1854), I, 388.

tortion is likely to be, as the winds and the vapours trouble the field of the telescope most when it reaches farthest"(11.181). Yet even were it not for man's fallen state, the very fact that he exists in space and time would require the grotesque as a mode of perception and statement. Even were it not for Adam's fall the problem still remains, as Augustine had recognized centuries earlier, that whereas God's world is "an utterance outside time," man exists in the prison house of time and space. The fact that an infinite, eternal God speaks to man from outside time and space places necessary limitations on the capabilities of human language to portray the essential truths of religion. Ruskin, who described the allegorical works of Carpaccio and Dante as "picture writings for children who live in the nursery of Time and Space"(24.355), made this limitation of man one of the prime defenses of allegory. According to him, when "the truth is seen by the imagination in its wholeness and quietness, the vision is sublime; but so far as it is narrowed and broken by the inconsistencies of the human capacity, it becomes grotesque; and it would seem to be rare that any very exalted truth should be impressed on the imagination without some grotesqueness"(11.181). In other words, although the vision of truth is sublime, men, in their present state, rarely encounter any truth not too great for their capacities, so that almost all truths of the spirit appear to man in the form of grotesques.

So truth appeared to Moses, so it appeared to the prophets, and so it must still appear to great artists and poets. According to Ruskin, "in all ages and among all nations, grotesque idealism has been the element through which the most appalling and eventful truth has been wisely conveyed, from the most sublime

words of true Revelation, to the . . . [words] of the oracles, and the more or less doubtful teaching of dreams; and so down to ordinary poetry. No element of imagination has a wider range, a more magnificent use, or so colossal a grasp of sacred truth"(5.134). He takes quite seriously and quite literally the idea that to imagine deeply is to prophesy, and that to be an artist and poet is to be a prophet; and he can do this because his theory of the allegorical imagination derives from a theological tradition which holds that such a mode is necessary to accommodate divine truths to the human condition.[67] In the second volume of *Modern Painters,* Ruskin, who elsewhere states that "this power of prophecy is the very essence"(4.225) of imagination, writes that this faculty's "first and noblest use is, to enable us to bring sensibly to our sight the things which are recorded as belonging to our future state, or as invisibly surrounding us in this . . . [and] to give to all mental truths some visible type in allegory, simile, or personification, which shall more deeply enforce them" (5.72-73). The imagination, then, "that prophetic action of mind"(4.234), acts as solace and salvation for man, who confined to the prison house of this world, can sustain his faith and correct his life with its aid. Sounding much like Dante, upon whom he frequently draws in discussing the allegorical in art, Ruskin reminds us that "Imagination is a pilgrim on the earth—and her home is in heaven"(4.288). The imagination allows us to escape the bounds of time and space for the sake of our spiritual welfare, for according to Ruskin this faculty is "an eminent beholder of things *when* and *where* they are NOT; a seer, that is, in the prophetic sense, calling

[67] See Joseph Mazzeo, *Structure and Thought in the Paradiso* (Ithaca, N.Y., 1958).

'the things that are not as though they were,' and for
ever delighting to dwell on that which is not tangibly
present . . . its great function being the calling forth, or
back, that which is not visible to bodily sense"(5.181).
The imagination is prophetic in two ways: it can move
through time, reinforcing hope in the central truth of
Christianity, eternal life, while in the form of the Symbolical Grotesque it can also convey to us spiritual
truths, the truths that originate beyond our terrestrial
existence.

Ruskin's theory of the prophetic imagination permits
him to take literally the conception of the artist-poet as
seer or vates. Citing the words of St. Paul and Plato to
the effect that the highest wisdom must come from
heaven,[68] *The Stones of Venice* asserts that the noblest
kinds of imagination necessarily make a prophet of
their possessor: "The noblest forms of imaginative
power . . . are in some sort ungovernable, and have in
them something of the character of dreams; so that the
vision, of whatever kind, comes uncalled, and will not
submit itself to the seer, but conquers him, and forces
him to speak as a prophet, having no power over his
words or thoughts"(11.178). In the third volume of
*Modern Painters*, Ruskin again returns to this descrip-

---

[68] In a note Ruskin explains: "This opposition of art to inspiration
is long and gracefully dwelt upon by Plato in his *Phaedrus*; using, in
the course of his argument, almost the words of St. Paul . . .: 'It is
the testimony of the ancients, that *the madness which is of God is a
nobler thing than the wisdom which is of men;*' and again, 'He who
sets himself to any work with which the Muses have to do' (*i.e.*, to
any of the fine arts) 'without madness, thinking that by art alone he
can do his work sufficiently, will be found vain and incapable, and the
work of temperance and rationalism will be thrust aside and obscured
by that of inspiration.' The passages to the same effect, relating especially to poetry, are innumerable in nearly all ancient writers; but in
this of Plato, the entire compass of the fine arts is intended to be em-
braced" (11.178-179n).

tion of the artist as prophet, emphasizing the creator's essential passivity when he is captured by vision:

> All the great men *see* what they paint before they paint it,—see it in a perfectly passive manner,—cannot help seeing it if they would; whether in their mind's eye, or in bodily fact, does not matter; very often the mental vision is, I believe, in men of imagination, clearer than the bodily one; but vision it is, of one kind or another,—the whole scene, character, or incident passing before them as in second sight, whether they will or no, and requiring them to paint it as they see it; they not daring . . . to alter one jot or tittle of it as they write it down or paint it down; it being to them in its own kind and degree always a true vision or Apocalypse, and invariably accompanied in their hearts by a feeling correspondent to the words,—"Write the things *which thou hast seen*, and the things which *are*."(5.114)

Ruskin's citation of Revelation 1:19 and his use of the stock phrase "jot and tittle," which Evangelical preachers employ in their discussions of typological exegesis (to emphasize that nothing, not "one jot and tittle," will pass away until the types are fulfilled) show him employing scriptural language to create religious authority for the artist.

The attribution of the nature of prophet to poet had, with varying emphases, long been a critical commonplace, and Ruskin would have encountered it in writers other than Plato, Dante, and Carlyle. This description of the poet's nature was a favorite of the English Renaissance, and Sir Philip Sidney, whose *Apologie for Poetrie* (1595) Ruskin probably knew, presents the usual arguments for the prestige of this art. Following

the lead of Horace, Sidney first points out: "Among the Romans a Poet was called *Vates*, which is as much as a Diuiner, a Fore-seer, or Prophet, as by his conioyned wordes *Vaticinium* and *Vaticinari* is manifest: so heauenly a title did that excellent people bestow vpon this hart-rauishing knowledge." Next, he mentions that "both the Oracles of *Delphos* and *Sibillas* prophecies were wholy delivered in verses. For that same exquisite obseruing of number and measure in words, and that high flying liberty of conceit proper to the Poet, did seeme to haue some dyuine force in it." Lastly, he cites the evidence of the Bible "to shew the reasonablenes of this worde *Vates*," since "holy *Dauids* Psalmes are a diuine Poem."[69] In a similar fashion, George Puttenham's *Arte of English Poesie* (1589) both uses the historical argument for the prestige of poetry and points out that "King *Dauid* also & *Salomon* his sonne and many other of the holy Prophets wrate in meeters," while Sir John Harington's preface to the translation of *Orlando Furioso* argues that scripture, which uses fiction and parable, shows the near relation of poetry and prophecy.[70] Although these attempts to bolster the reputation of the poet's art readily refer to the opinions of the respected ancients, none of them asserts, as Ruskin was willing to do, that poetry, poetry written by their contemporaries, was prophecy. For example, Francis Meres's *Wits Treasury* (1598) informs his reader that Cicero believed poetry required "celestiall instruction," and that "our famous English Poet Spenser . . . saith most sweetly to the same," but he himself will not directly make that claim.[71] In fact, while Renaissance critics frequently cite the Roman

---

[69] *Elizabethan Critical Essays*, ed. C. Gregory Smith, 2 vols. (Oxford, 1904), I, 154.
[70] *Ibid.*, II, 10; 205-206.     [71] *Ibid.*, p. 313.

equivalence of poet and vates, employing this as an argument from prestige, they never make such equivalence themselves. Instead, perhaps too aware of the heretical implications of such an assertion, they content themselves with pointing out the indirect relations of poetry and prophecy: the ancients believed poets to be prophets, ancient oracles used verse, and the Bible contains both verse and figurative language.

One of the most important reasons that Ruskin could take literally the notion of the artist-poet as prophet was that his theories of imagination and imaginative conception of truth derived from religious sources. Whereas Carlyle, who here almost certainly confirmed Ruskin's original ideas rather than added to them, frequently speaks of the artist as prophet and seer, he does so in a way characteristically oracular and vague. Ruskin, in contrast, holds a precise theory of imagination which both makes his equation of artist and prophet more understandable and relates it directly to a particular mode of art.[72]

This conception of the great artist as prophet allows Ruskin to avoid problems intrinsic to romantic art and

[72] James A. W. Heffernan, "Wordsworth on Imagination: The Emblemizing Power," *PMLA*, LXXXI (1966), 389-399, would seem to suggest that Wordsworth, rather than Carlyle, was a more likely influence. Professor Heffernan's fine essay explains that Wordsworth's "statements on the imagination—and particularly those of his later years—seem to point substantially in one direction: that the primary effect of imaginative power is the evocation of meaning from the material world, the manifestation of a visible object as the *emblem* of invisible truth. . . . Wordsworth read all of nature as a living testament, a world whose material forms had been consecrated by their appearance in Scripture; and in its achievement of the eternal through the temporal, of the infinite through the finite, and of the invisible through the visible, poetry was for him the brother of religion, bearing witness to the Word made flesh. Its nature and purpose were evangelical" (p. 389). The essay concentrates on examining the poet's idea of imagination in *The White Doe of Rylstone*, a poem which Ruskin praises highly for its truth, grace, and imaginative power (4.392).

its theory. Although he makes use of the romantic description of the poet as a sensitive, emotional man, extending it to include the painter as well, Ruskin paradoxically distrusts the effects of emotion on art. In the second volume of *Modern Painters* he exposes the dilemma at the heart of romantic critical theory when he states that, "though we cannot, while we feel deeply, *reason* shrewdly, yet I doubt if, *except* when we feel deeply, we can ever *comprehend* fully"(4.180-181). When emphasizing that only intense feeling and emotional sympathy can perceive human truths, the truths of morality and art, he uneasily admits that feeling prevents true rational judgment; and yet he can avoid confronting the difficulty because he is then emphasizing that emotional and imaginative perceptions contribute more than reason to human existence. On the other hand, when in the third volume he comes to consider characteristically modern distortions of landscape caused by emotion, he places major emphasis upon the fact that "an excited state of the feelings" makes a man "for the time, more or less irrational"(5.205). From this awareness of the effect of the emotions comes his definition of the pathetic fallacy: "All violent feelings have the same effect. They produce in us a falseness in all our impressions of external things, which I would generally characterize as the 'pathetic fallacy' "(5.205). Ruskin's discussion of the pathetic (or emotional) fallacy, which contains his most direct confrontation of the problems of a theory of art centered on the feelings, makes overt the dilemma which had figured large in his thought from the first volume. He had always tried to demonstrate that an art centered on the feelings was not inevitably solipsistic, and this continuing struggle to protect his notions of painting and poetry from the

dangers of subjectivity is as paradigmatic of the problems of his age as was the course of his religious belief.

Although deeply concerned with the solipsistic tendencies of his aesthetic theory, Ruskin opens his chapter "Of the Pathetic Fallacy" by refusing to employ the terms "objective" and "subjective." Both his reasons for thus proceeding and his manner of argument reveal much characteristic of his thought. He begins with a proclamation that "German dulness, and English affectation, have of late much multiplied among us the use of two of the most objectionable words that were ever coined by the troublesomeness of metaphysicians, —namely, 'Objective,' and 'Subjective' "(5.201). Declaring that these terms are completely useless, Ruskin explains that certain philosophers hold that the word "blue" means the sensation of color which the eye receives in looking at the open sky or at a bell gentian; and, according to these men, since one only receives this "blue" sensation when looking at the object, and since the object produces no sensation when nobody looks at it, therefore when not looked at the object is not blue. These troublesome metaphysicians continue that qualities which thus depend upon human perception should be called "subjective," while those, such as roundness or squareness, which remain independent of human perception, should be called "objective." Ruskin's reason for so scornfully attacking the use of these terms appears in his next statement that it is very easy to move from such a philosophical theory to the opinion that "it does not much matter what things are in themselves, but only what they are to us; and that the only real truth of them is their appearance to, or effect upon, us. From which position, with a hearty desire for mystification, and much egotism, selfishness, shallow-

ness, and impertinence, a philosopher may easily go so far as to believe, and say, that everything in the world depends upon his seeing or thinking of it, and that nothing, therefore, exists, but what he sees or thinks of"(5.202). The very intensity of Ruskin's scorn for these terms betrays how much he felt threatened by them. The same scornful tone, the same use of rhetorical climax, and the same attack on the egotism and immorality of an opposing view marked his tirade a decade earlier against Associationist theories of beauty. The second volume of *Modern Painters* had argued that to call the pleasure of association beauty "is no theory to be confuted, but a misuse of language to be set aside, a misuse involving the positions that in uninhabited countries the vegetation has no grace, the rock no dignity, the cloud no colour, and that the snowy summits of the Alps receive no loveliness from the sunset light, because they have not been polluted by the wrath, ravage, and misery of men"(4.71). In both his attack on Associationist aesthetic theory and the notion of subjective qualities Ruskin's vehemence arises from his fear that the opposing view, if allowed, would reduce the value of art and its role in human life. Although he in fact did come to accept an Associationist theory of beauty, he continued to oppose the philosophic position implicit in the use of the dangerous terms "objective" and "subjective."

In his attempt to rid himself and his reader of these "troublesome words," Ruskin proposes that "blue" means not the sensation produced but "the *power* of producing that sensation: and this power is always there, in the thing, whether we are there to experience it or not, and would remain there though there were not left a man on the face of the earth"(5.202). We have

encountered this view before, since it is simply his theory of beauty generalized to an entire epistemology. Whereas in Typical Beauty the "power" in the beautiful object was the symbolization of God's nature, which necessarily affects man, here the nature of the power remains unspecified.

Putting aside these "tiresome and absurd words," Ruskin proceeds to his main subject—"the difference between the ordinary, proper, and true appearances of things to us; and the extraordinary, or false appearances, when we are under the influence of emotion, or contemplative fancy"(5.204). His phrasing here, specifically his mention of "emotion" and "contemplative fancy" leads one to inquire about the relation of the pathetic fallacy to Ruskin's theory of the creative faculties. Since he mentions the fancy when introducing the problems of false appearances, and since, moreover, he always emphasizes that imagination perceives truthfully, one might be tempted to attribute poetry which employs the pathetic fallacy to the action of the fancy. According to this view, the greatest poems, the *Iliad*, the *Divine Comedy*, and *King Lear*, which do not use the pathetic fallacy, *arise in* the imagination, while the fancy produces the *Immortality Ode* and *Maud*. Ruskin's other comments in this chapter, however, make it clear that he does not align the pathetic fallacy with fancy. In the first place, he obviously considers the fine poets of the second rank—those such as Wordsworth, Keats, and Tennyson—men of high imagination; and, secondly, fancy cannot play any important role in the pathetic fallacy, which is a matter of emotional distortion and projection, since this lower faculty, as he explained in his previous volume, concerns itself chiefly not with feeling—the province of imagination—but

with "mere vivid sight of reality" and "witty suggestion of likeness," passing in its highest mode to a "ghostly sight of what is unreal"(4.293). Thus, although in its highest form fancy comes to resemble imagination, it never partakes of that "deep heart feeling"(4.298) which characterizes imaginative power. He emphasizes that "fancy," since "she stays at the externals, can never feel"(4.257). Ruskin's own elaborate version of the Coleridgean distinction between imagination and fancy, which was derived not from Coleridge but from Wordsworth's prefaces and Leigh Hunt's *Imagination and Fancy*, does not therefore match his division of poetry into that which does and does not use the pathetic fallacy.

His introduction of the problem of false appearances reveals two kinds of poetic falsehood or distortion, only one of which he calls the pathetic fallacy. Before concerning himself with the distortions of deep emotion, he first explains the delightful fallacies of fancy. As an example he quotes these lines from Oliver Wendell Holmes's *Astrea* which describe "The spendthrift crocus, bursting through the mould/Naked and shivering, with his cup of gold"(5.204). Ruskin first comments that, while very beautiful, these lines are nonetheless untrue, for the crocus is not spendthrift but hardy, not gold but saffron. These lines exemplify "the fallacy of wilful fancy, which involves no real expectation that it will be believed"(5.205). In contrast to the fanciful, self-conscious distortions of wit Ruskin opposes "the other error, that which the mind admits when affected strongly by emotion"(5.205), and as instance he presents these lines from Kingsley's *Alton Locke*: "They rowed her in across the rolling foam—/The cruel, crawling foam." According to Ruskin, grief has

so affected this speaker's mind, so distorted his vision of the world, that he attributes to the foam the characteristics of a living being. In so doing he tells us more about his state of mind, his interior world, than he does about the world which exists outside his mind, and it is this psychological truth that moves and delights the reader. The distorted version of reality does not itself please us, but we can ignore it, for "so long as we see that the *feeling* is true, we pardon, or are even pleased by, the confessed fallacy of sight which it induces: we are pleased, for instance, with those lines of Kingsley's above quoted, not because they fallaciously describe foam, but because they faithfully describe sorrow" (5.210).

In other words, considered in relation to the interior state of the speaker the pathetic (or emotional) fallacy tells the truth, for by presenting the world *as experienced* by a man under the influence of powerful emotion, this device can tell us much about the inner life of another. From this point of view, then, the distorting effects of emotion, once understood correctly, are not solipsistic, are not isolating. Rather, by manipulating a portion of reality which both speaker and listener share, the pathetic fallacy allows one to glimpse the passions within the consciousness of another human being. Since we know that foam does not crawl and since we know it cannot be cruel, when someone thus describes the sea we understand that he suffers from grief. The distortions of the pathetic fallacy function like the voice inflections which a speaker gives to a common, shared language: they permit something to be communicated which it would be difficult to state "directly." The pathetic fallacy, then, allows the poet to dramatize grief and joy, communicating them far

more effectively than would the simple statement that the speaker suffers from sorrow or feels joy.

This idea that the pathetic fallacy effectively conveys truths of man's inner world makes it fulfill what Ruskin takes to be the role of art, which is to present things, not as they are in themselves—the role of natural science—but "as they appear to mankind. Science studies the relations of things to each other: but art studies only their relations to man: and it requires of everything . . . only this,—what that thing is to the human eyes and human heart, what it has to say to men, and what it can become to them" (11.48). The truth conveyed by the pathetic fallacy is phenomenological truth, the truth of experience, the truth as it appears to the experiencing subject. In particular, these emotional distortions of exterior reality much resemble the Ruskinian notion of imaginatively depicted landscape. The higher mode of landscape, we remember, presents not the topographical facts of a scene but the impression which its trees and rocks, sky and water made upon the great, imaginative painter. Although the emotional and imaginative interpretation of a landscape might seem a mere distortion of facts to the uneducated or unreflective viewer—as indeed Turner's late works appeared to the critics—such depiction contains truths unattainable by other methods. According to Ruskin, therefore, imaginative painting of landscape has the advantage over our presence at the depicted scene precisely because its "expression of the power and intelligence of a companionable human soul" gives us the "penetrative sight" (5.187) our own more limited faculties cannot provide.

On the other hand, the pathetic fallacy differs from the art of high imagination in that it so distorts exterior reality that it presents truthful depictions of *only* an

interior state. Thus, whereas Turner's *Snow Storm: Steamboat off a Harbour's Mouth* conveys both the truthful appearance of a scene and of the state in which it was experienced, the lines from *Alton Locke* tell us accurately only about the feelings of the speaker. The problem with poetry which employs this emotional distortion is that it is too restricted: it perceives everything from a single point of view, and while the resulting restriction can effectively convey emotional and psychological truth, it also creates inevitable narrowness and lack of balance. When the poetic speaker feels happy, everything appears perfect, all rings with joy; when he experiences grief, everything appears colored by his grief—the waves either reflect it or cruelly mock it. Although such a poetry proves eminently valuable in its ability to educate the reader about the experiences of life, it can never present a balanced, complete view of nature and man's existence. In contrast, the very greatest poetry, as Matthew Arnold would have agreed, presents life whole. For instance, when Homer announces the death of Castor and Pollux he states "them, already, the life-giving earth possessed, there in Lacedaemon, in the dear fatherland." And Ruskin comments that "The poet has to speak of the earth in sadness, but he will not let that sadness affect or change his thoughts of it. No; though Castor and Pollux be dead, yet the earth is our mother still, fruitful, life-giving. These are the facts of the thing"(5.213). Similarly, Dante's broad view of life will not permit his deep sympathies to distort reality; and when he "describes the spirits falling from the bank of Acheron 'as dead leaves flutter from a bough,' he gives the most perfect image possible of their utter lightness, feebleness, passiveness, and scattering agony of despair, without, however, for

an instant losing his own clear perception that *these* are souls, and *those* are leaves"(5.206). Ruskin's remark that the author of the *Divine Comedy* does not lose his embracing, clear vision of things even "for an instant" emphasizes that the greatest poets surmount the flux of consciousness; they do not present all reality, all human life, as it appears to them during the brief instant they experience an intense emotion.

Thus, although Ruskin, like many other romantic theorists, continually emphasizes the need for intensity of emotion, he does not follow Poe and Baudelaire in praising the lyric above other modes; for his desire to avoid the dangers of a limiting subjectivity, his wish to escape the limited moment of an instant, leads him to prefer the epic and the dramatic—the more "objective" forms. However much he delights in Wordsworth, Byron, Keats, and Tennyson, his favorites remain Homer, Dante, and Shakespeare. Furthermore, he prefers the dramatic lyric to the pure lyric, and when discussing the pathetic fallacy he makes it clear that it achieves most when the speaker clearly is a character and not the author. The irony possible in the dramatic lyric elevates it almost to the level of the broader vision of life. In the manuscript for the section which mentions Homer's revelation of the deaths of Castor and Pollux, Ruskin had praised "the insurpassably tender irony of the epithet—'life-giving earth' "(5.213n), and one may emphasize that this delight in the ironic, dispassionate view of life is quite appropriate to Ruskin's aesthetic theories which stress a calm beauty of restraint.

As we have frequently observed, Ruskin continually concerned himself throughout his career to find ways to protect a theory of the arts centered on emotion

from the potentially limiting and distorting effects of that emotion. In particular, his theories of beauty both try to demonstrate the objective existence of an unchanging standard of beauty by deriving it from divine attributes and attempt to guard against the dangers of emotion by elevating calmness, restraint, and balance into an aesthetic ideal. Similarly, he initially attempted to deny the importance of association to protect the objectivity of the beautiful, just as he initially denied the sublime the status of a separate aesthetic category to avoid the dangers of violent emotion. Furthermore, his praise of epic and dramatic work as the highest modes, his concern with allegorical art, and his criticism of the pathetic fallacy all serve the same purpose —to protect art from the dangers of excessive emotion. Characteristically, his most elaborate and extended discussion of the dangers of emotion in this chapter "Of the Pathetic Fallacy" occurs in his portrait of the ideal artist-poet, the point at which he draws most upon the notion of artist as prophet. Ruskin's habitual procedure throughout his writings is to relate various modes of art to the psychological nature of the artists who produce them. Thus, when describing topographical and imaginative landscape, Gothic architecture, and the purist, naturalist, and grotesque modes, he draws psychological portraits of the artist-poet; and when setting forth his views of the pathetic fallacy he proceeds in his usual manner.

According to him, one may divide men into three classes: first, "the man who perceives rightly, because he does not feel"; secondly, "the man who perceives wrongly, because he feels"; and, thirdly, "the man who perceives rightly in spite of his feelings"(5.209). Thus, although he admits that the "temperament which ad-

mits the pathetic fallacy . . . is a more or less noble state, according to the force of the emotion which has induced it," he points out that far more noble is that ideal mind, possessed by the greatest artists and poets, in which "the intellect also rises, till it is strong enough to assert its rule against, or together with, the utmost efforts of the passions; and the whole man stands in an iron glow, white hot, perhaps, but still strong"(5.208). The ideal artists and poets, Homer, Dante, and Shakespeare, Giotto, Tintoretto, and Turner, were such men who could remain cool in the midst of burning emotion; and so the ideal artist-poet must always be. Ruskin thus modifies previous notions of the romantic poet, positing an ideal creator who is paradoxically sensitive and impassive, moved and yet serene:

> He is tender to impression at the surface, like a rock with deep moss upon it; but there is too much mass of him to be moved. The smaller man, with the same degree of sensibility, is at once carried off his feet . . . ; he is gay or enthusiastic, melancholy or passionate, as things come and go to him. Therefore, the high creative poet might even be thought, to a great extent, impassive (as shallow people think Dante stern), receiving indeed all feelings to the full, but having a great centre of reflection and knowledge in which he stands serene, and watches the feeling, as it were, from afar off. (5.210)

The artist, the poet to be truly great must combine "the two faculties, acuteness of feeling, and command of it. A poet is great, first in proportion to the strength of his passion, and then, that strength being granted, in proportion to his government of it"(5.215). Although Ruskin frequently emphasizes that "If you are without

strong passions, you cannot be a painter at all"(22.17), he emphasizes with equal frequency that the artist must control these emotions which give his art meaning and human value. As he commented in "The Relation of Art to Religion" (1870), "Not only the highest, but the most consistent results have been attained in art by men in whom the faculty of vision, however strong, was subordinate to that of deliberative design, and tranquillized by a measured, continual, not feverish, but affectionate, observance of the quite unvisionary facts of the surrounding world"(20.56).

The very nature of the prophetic vision avoids many difficulties and limitations of an emotionally centered art. First of all, "The true Seer always feels as intensely as any one else; but he does not much describe his feelings"(5.334); and therefore the rare artist, whose work has been raised by vision to the heights of prophecy, automatically avoids the dangers of mawkishness to which an emotionally centered art is vulnerable. Equally important, because the artist-poet of the highest order does not concentrate on consciously expressing his own emotional reactions, he avoids the egotism to which romantic art has too often succumbed. According to Ruskin, who uses the author of the *Iliad* and *Odyssey* as his chief example, "The choice, as well as the vision, is *manifested* to Homer. The vision comes to him in its chosen order. Chosen *for* him, not *by* him. . . . And, from a bee to Paul Veronese, all masterworkers work with this awful, this inspired unconsciousness"(5.118,122). Thus clearly echoing Carlyle's emphasis upon unconscious creation, Ruskin believes that the great artist, the creator truly inspired, "can never be egotistic. The whole of his power depends upon his losing sight and feeling of his own existence,

and becoming a mere witness and mirror of truth, and a scribe of visions,—always passive in sight, passive in utterance"(5.125). Lastly, the artist-seer not only escapes the dangers of self-consciousness, egotism, and mawkishness, he also surmounts the problem of the division between objective and subjective, self and other, feeling and fact. The apocalyptic vision of the greatest painters and poets carries them out of themselves, out of the restrictions of place, time, and emotion, granting them truths contained in the symbolical grotesque. Ruskin, who has cited St. Paul and Revelation, and who has followed Dante and Milton as well, believes that for a brief instant the greatest artists and poets find themselves in that region where to see is to see truly. Since the vision is granted by God (as it is to the highest), then the vision must be true. Furthermore, since, as Milton realized, the division between objective and subjective appeared when Adam fell, the prophet's vision briefly allows him to evade man's fallen, limited state. Such a theory of the highest artists does not solve the problems of a romantic art for any but the greatest, but, by allowing Ruskin to show the veracity of these ideal men, his theory that they are prophets provides an ultimate justification for all art and a shelter within which to include its weaker, more ordinarily human forms.

At the same time that Ruskin conceives the greatest artists as prophets captured by vision, he does not hold that anyone can become such a great artist, nor does he believe that the great artist does not have to work at his art. For as he warns in *The Stones of Venice,* "Only, if the whole man be trained perfectly, and his mind calm, consistent, and powerful, the vision which comes to him is seen as in a perfect mirror, serenely, and in consist-

ence with the rational powers; but if the mind be imperfect and ill trained, the vision is seen as in a broken
mirror, with strange distortions and discrepancies, all
the passions of the heart breathing upon it in cross ripples, till hardly a trace of it remains unbroken"
(11.178-179). The great artist must work a lifetime, pre-
paring himself, storing visual truths in his memory,
learning the ways of man and nature, so that, ultimately, he may become a vehicle for truth. If the artist
perceives high truths without proper training, then the
result will be distorted, broken—grotesque in the worst
sense. All the highest truths must be grasped first by
grotesques, but even these allegories must be prepared
for by years of learning, by decades of practice, if they
are to be whole, to be truthful.

Since Ruskin described the way the highest imagination makes a prophet of its possessor between 1851 and
1856 when his religious faith had weakened, one may
ask how he could have thus asserted that artists and
poets attain divine truth when he himself was in doubt
about the validity of religious teachings. The answer,
I believe, lies in the fact that it was not despite this
weakening faith but because of it that Ruskin advanced
such a portrait of the ideal artist; for as he began to believe that God came in diverse ways to men, pagan,
Catholic, and Protestant, he also came to accept that
throughout the ages God had made prophets of great
men, thus ensuring that His wisdom reached man. Of
course, had not Ruskin's habits of thought continued
to be essentially religious despite this loss of belief, he
could never have transferred the idea of prophecy
from scriptural to secular writing.

Now that we have examined Ruskin's theories of
artist and imagination in relation to the Symbolical

Grotesque, we may turn to his description of this allegorical mode of the arts. In the third volume of *Modern Painters,* he defines the allegorical image, which he terms a "grotesque," and exemplifies it with Spenser's image of envy. This example of Ruskin's close reading warrants quoting at length, not only because it exemplifies his practice as literary exegete, but because it once more demonstrates the way his theories derive from his criticism.

> A fine grotesque is the expression, in a moment, by a series of symbols thrown together in bold and fearless connection, of truths which it would have taken a long time to express in any verbal way, and of which the connection is left for the beholder to work out for himself; the gaps, left or overleaped by the haste of the imagination, forming the grotesque character.

> For instance, Spenser desires to tell us, (1) that envy is the most untamable and unappeasable of the passions, not to be soothed by any kindness; (2) that with continual labour it invents evil thoughts out of its own heart; (3) that even in this, its power of doing harm is partly hindered by the decaying and corrupting nature of the evil it lives in; (4) that it looks every way, and that whatever it sees is altered and discoloured by its own nature; (5) which discolouring, however, is to it a veil, or disgraceful dress, in the sight of others; (6) and that it never is free from the most bitter suffering, (7) which cramps all its acts and movements, enfolding and crushing it while it torments. All this it has required a somewhat long and languid sentence for me to say in unsymbolical

terms,—not, by the way, that they *are* unsymbolical altogether, for I have been forced, whether I would or not, to use *some* figurative words; but even with this help the sentence is long and tiresome, and does not with any vigour represent the truth. It would take some prolonged enforcement of each sentence to make it felt, in ordinary ways of talking. But Spenser puts it all into a grotesque, and it is done shortly and at once, so that we feel it fully, and see it, and never forget it. I have numbered above the statements which had to be made. I now number them with the same numbers, as they occur in the several pieces of the grotesque:—

> "And next to him malicious Envy rode
> (1) Upon a ravenous wolfe, and (2,3) still did chaw
> Between his cankred teeth a venemous tode,
> That all the poison ran about his jaw
> (4,5) All in a kirtle of discolourd say
> He clothed was, y-paynted full of eies;
> (6) And in his bosome secretly there lay
> An hateful snake, the which his taile uptyes
> (7) In many folds, and mortall sting implyes."

There is the whole thing in nine lines; or, rather in one image, which will hardly occupy any room at all on the mind's shelves, but can be lifted out, whole, whenever we want it. All noble grotesques are con-centrations of this kind, and the noblest convey truths which nothing else could convey; and not only so, but convey them, in minor cases with a delightful-ness,—in the higher instances with an awfulness,—which no mere utterance of the symbolised truth would have possessed, but which belongs to the ef-

fort of the mind to unweave the riddle, or to the sense it has of there being an infinite power and meaning in the thing seen, beyond all that is apparent therein, giving the highest sublimity even to the most trivial object so presented and so contemplated. (5.132-133)

According to Ruskin, who here draws upon one of the most ancient justifications of allegory, the puzzling, riddling, enigmatic nature of the allegorical imagery stimulates the mind, delighting it with the joys of discovery which commit truth thus discovered to memory. Although one could cite countless works which have similarly explained the advantages of the dark conceit, one need only go to those works Ruskin knew and liked best to see a history in brief of such theoretical justifications. In fact Ruskin first learned about allegory in the books of his childhood, in the *Holy War*, *Pilgrim's Progress*, and Quarles's *Emblems*. From Bunyan, in particular, he would have learned many of the usual points about allegory, the pleasures of enigma, and the dark conceit. For example, "The Author's Apology for his BOOK," which prefaces *Pilgrim's Progress*, explains that "*Dark Clouds bring Waters, when the bright bring none.*"[73] Moreover, Bunyan's prefatory doggerel defends his choice of dark conceits by pointing to the example of scripture:

> *Was not Gods Laws,*
> *His Gospel-Laws, in olden times held forth*
> *By Types, Shadows and Metaphors? Yet loth*
> *Will any sober Man be to find fault*
> *With them, lest he be found to assault*
> *The highest Wisdom....*

[73] *Pilgrim's Progress*, p. 3.

394

*Am I affraid to say that Holy Writ*
*Which for its Style and Phrase puts down all wit,*
*Is every where so full of these things,*
*(Dark Figures, Allegories,) yet there springs*
*From that same Book, that lustre, & those rays*
*Of light, that turns our darkest nights to days.*[74]

Furthermore, making the same point Ruskin made in *Modern Painters*, Bunyan explains that truth set forth in this covered, hidden, dark fashion both pleases the mind and remains there longest:

*And to stir the mind*
*To a search after what it fain would find,*
*Things that seem to be hid in words obscure,*
*Do but the Godly mind but more allure;*
*To study what those Sayings should contain*
*That speak to us in such Cloudy strain.*
*I also know, a dark Similitude*
*Will on the Fancie more it self intrude,*
*And will stick faster in the Heart and Head,*
*Than things from Similies not borrowed.*[75]

In addition, Ruskin, who had of course encountered Spenser's mention of the dark conceit and Dante's description of his poem as "la mia narrazion buia," had long known Dante's injunction that the reader of right understanding should note the doctrine that lay hidden beneath the veil of his strange lines:

O voi ch'avete li 'ntelletti sani,
    mirate la dottrina che s'asconde
    sotto 'l velame de li versi strani.[76]

[74] *Ibid.*, pp. 4, 5.          [75] *Ibid.*, p. 181.
[76] *La Divina Commedia*, ed. Daniele Mattalia, 2 vols. (Milan, 1960), *Inferno*, IX, pp. 191-192; ll. 61-63.

Ruskin also knew Carlyle's description of the way a symbol effectively mixes speech and silence: "In a Symbol there is concealment and yet revelation: here, therefore, by Silence and Speech acting together, comes a double significance. And if both the Speech be itself high, and the Silence fit and noble, how expressive will their union be! Thus, in many a painted Device, or simple Seal-emblem, the commonest truth stands-out to us proclaimed with quite new emphasis."[77] When placed within the context of traditional defenses of allegorical method, Carlyle's explanation of the power of the symbol becomes less oracular, less idiosyncratic, essentially a commonplace assertion about the pleasures of enigma. Indeed, one may speculate that many of his remarks which today seem veiled in clouds of Carlylean prophecy were notions, like this one, long familiar to his contemporaries from religious instruction, preaching, and the works of Bunyan.

The writings of St. Augustine were the ultimate source of these conceptions of enigma. *On Christian Doctrine*, perhaps the work which most shaped the exegetics of medieval Christendom, advances what became the standard justification of the dark conceit. According to Augustine, "things are perceived more readily through similitudes and . . . what is sought with difficulty is discovered with more pleasure."[78] Petrarch and others transferred this idea of happily contrived obscurity to secular poetry and it became a Renaissance commonplace. It is uncertain whether Ruskin knew *On Christian Doctrine*, though it seems likely, yet even if he did not, he had encountered similar arguments in the *Confessions*, which he several times men-

[77] *Sartor Resartus, Works*, I, 175.   [78] *On Christian Doctrine*, p. 38.

tions.[79] For Augustine the ability to conceive properly the nature of scriptural meaning represents both a sign and means of salvation, and the narrative of his pilgrimage to God repeatedly returns to his own difficulties. In his early years, he tells us, he had to learn a double lesson about the nature of the spiritual: first, that God and spirit are not, as the Manicheans claimed, merely invisibly minute particles of matter but something essentially different from it; and, second, that just as God exists in a spiritual realm, set apart from the material, so does His Word. To *begin* to comprehend God man must first realize there is existence beyond the material; to begin to understand His Word one must realize there is meaning, a spiritual sense, beyond the literal narrative. When Augustine himself arrived at truth after a long, hard journey, he wondered at the newly perceived glories of the Bible, "because while all

[79] Ruskin, who had read Origen, Aquinas, and Augustine as well as other figures important in medieval theology, alarmed his wife and his mother by his interest in the writings of the Church Fathers. In July 1852 Effie wrote to her mother: "Manning is out of town and goes shortly to Rome. I do not believe that John will have further personal intercourse with them—but what *I* dislike about him is his wish to understand the Bible throughout—which nobody in this world will ever do—and unless they receive it as a little child it will not be made profitable to them. He wishes to satisfy his intellect and his vanity in reading the Scriptures and does not pray that his mind and heart may be softened and improved by them. He chuses to study Hebrew and read the *Fathers* instead of asking God to give him Light. His whole desire for knowledge appears to me to originate in Pride and as long as this remains and his great feeling of *Security* and doing every thing to please himself he is ready for any temptation and will be permitted to fall into it. I do what I can but I require to be very careful what I say: for he has no respect for what his Mother says and yet it worries him intensely feeling that she thinks so differently" (*Millais and the Ruskins*, p. 17). Professor M. H. Abrams has kindly pointed out to me that Ruskin may also have known Keble's *Tract 89* or his translations of the second-century theologian St. Irenaeus, either of which would have informed him about not only traditional attitudes toward scriptural language but also polysemous interpretations of the Bible.

can read it with ease, it also has a deeper meaning in which its great secrets are locked away. Its plain language and simple style make it accessible to every one, and yet it absorbs the attention of the learned. By this means it gathers all men in the wide sweep of its net."[80] The simplicity of the literal sense attracts all, while the spirit, the allegorical senses, engage those with greater abilities and greater responsibilities. According to Augustine, God, Who pities the weakness of fallen man, compensates "for the ease with which our mortal senses tire by providing that a single truth may be illustrated and represented to our minds in many ways by bodily means."[81] Another point at which the author of the *Confessions* may have influenced Ruskin appears when he marvels, "How wonderful are your scriptures! How profound! We see their surface and it attracts us like children. And yet, O my God, their depth is stupendous. We shudder to peer deep into them, for they inspire in us both the awe of reverence and the thrill of love."[82] This remark sounds much like Ruskin's explanation of the effect when one perceives the difference between the insignificant surface of an allegorical image and its deeper meaning: "Even if the symbolic vision itself be not terrible, the scene of what may be veiled behind it becomes all the more awful in proportion to the insignificance or strangeness of the sign itself; and, I believe, this thrill of mingled doubt, fear, and curiosity lies at the very root of the delight which mankind take in symbolism"(11.182). From Augustine and Carlyle, from Bunyan and Dante, Ruskin formulates his own sophisticated notions of allegory, but his praise of allegorical art and the arguments he summons

---

[80] Trans. R. S. Pine-Coffin (Baltimore, Md., 1961), pp. 117-118.
[81] *Ibid.*, p. 328. See also p. 335.    [82] *Ibid.*, p. 290.

to its defense reveal, not only that Ruskin borrows widely, but that he still finds himself within the medieval Christian universe which founded such conceptions of art. For Ruskin allegorical art and poetry appear as natural modes with which to comment upon a world endowed with sacred meaning.

## V. Myth as allegory

RUSKIN, who reads myth allegorically, considers it a special form of the Symbolical Grotesque which can veil "a theory of the universe under the grotesque of a fairy tale"(19.297).[83] Like other forms of the Symbolical Grotesque, a myth indicates the presence of deeper meanings by an enigmatic literal or narrative level. According to *The Queen of the Air* (1869), "A myth, in its simplest definition, is a story with a meaning attached to it, other than it seems to have at first; and the fact that it has such a meaning is generally marked by some of its circumstances being extraordinary, or, in the common use of the word, unnatural"(19.296). Ruskin further explains that if he informed his reader "Hercules killed a water-serpent in the lake of Lerna, and

---

[83] Although James Kissane's "Victorian Mythology," *Victorian Studies*, vi (1962-1963), 5-28, is quite superficial in its treatment of Ruskin's *Queen of the Air*, the only work by him it discusses, it nonetheless provides a helpful survey of Victorian attitudes toward myth. Charles T. Dougherty, "Of Ruskin's Gardens," *Myth and Symbol*, ed. Bernice Slote (Lincoln, Neb., 1963), pp. 141-151, offers a suggestive, if incomplete, reading of the serpent and woman figures in Ruskin's mythology. One cannot, however, accept Professor Dougherty's assertion that "the allegorical vein in Ruskin's thought remained submerged until the events of 1857-1858 brought it dramatically to the surface" (p. 142) since, as these pages have already demonstrated, this allegorical bent clearly marks Ruskin's writings as early as 1846. Incidentally, Ruskin did not study, as Professor Dougherty states, "the female Melancholia in Dürer's 'Knight and Death'" (p. 145). The *Melancholia* is a separate work, and is illustrated in the *Library Edition of Modern Painters*, Volume v.

if I mean, and you understand, nothing more than that fact, the story, whether true or false, is not a myth" (19.296). If, however, he intends this story of Hercules's victory to indicate that the hero "purified the stagnation of many streams from deadly miasmata, my story, however simple, is a true myth"(19.296). But since no audience would pause to consider with care such a simple tale, it becomes necessary, says Ruskin, "to surprise your attention by adding some singular circumstance. . . . And in proportion to the fulness of intended meaning I shall probably multiply and refine upon these improbabilities"(19.296). In other words, Ruskin has here applied to myth the points he made about the Symbolical Grotesque some thirteen years earlier; for myth, like Spenserian allegory, communicates "truths which nothing else could convey"(5.133) with a combination of delight and awe "which belongs to the effort of the mind to unweave the riddle, or to the sense it has of there being an infinite power and meaning in the thing seen, beyond all that is apparent therein"(5.133).

Ruskin, who was characteristically eclectic in formulating his theories of mythology, had encountered the notion of myth as enigmatic allegory in several authors he knew well. For example, Francis Bacon argued in *The Wisdom of the Ancients,* a work Ruskin cites (17.208,212), that a valuable sign "these fables contain a hidden and involved meaning" is "that some of them are so absurd and stupid on the face of the narrative taken by itself, that they may be said to give notice from afar and cry that there is a parable below. For a fable that is probable may be thought to have been composed merely for pleasure, in imitation of history. But when a story is told which could never have entered any man's head either to conceive or relate on its

own account, we must presume that it had some further reach."[84] Bacon, of course, and Ruskin after him,
here applies to pagan myth the same argument that St.
Augustine and nineteenth-century clergy applied to
difficult passages in the Bible, namely, that where the
passage states something immoral, incongruous, or in
any other way unsuitable, an allegorization becomes
necessary.

Bacon further explains that the enigmas of myth had
been anciently employed "as a method of teaching,
whereby inventions that are new and abstruse and re-
mote from vulgar opinions may find an easier passage
to the understanding. On this account it was that in the
old times, when the inventions and conclusions of human reason . . . were as yet new and strange, the world
was full of all kinds of fables, and enigmas, and parables, and similitudes."[85] Richard Payne Knight, whose
*Symbolical Language of Ancient Art* Ruskin also cites
(19.381n), similarly commented that "it seems to have
been a very generally received opinion, among the
more discreet Heathens, that divine truth was better
adapted to the weakness of human intellect, when
vailed [*sic*] under symbols, and wrapped in fable and
enigma, than when exhibited in the plain and undis-
guised simplicity of genuine wisdom or pure philosophy."[86] This same emphasis upon the value of enigma
to convey ideas effectively occurs in a third likely
source of Ruskin's ideas of mythology—the notes to
Pope's translation of Homer. In a letter to Norton, of
which the editors of the *Library Edition* include a line
or two as a note to *The Queen of the Air*, Ruskin con-

---

[84] *Works*, eds. James Spedding, Robert Leslie Ellis, and Douglas
Denon Heath (Boston, 1860), XIII, 78.
[85] *Ibid.*, 80.                        [86] (New York, 1879), p. 6.

fided to his friend: "Of course these stories are all first fixed in my mind by my boy's reading of Pope" (19.312n), and it is quite likely that he had early encountered those allegorical interpretations which appear frequently in the notes. One of these notes, for example, explains that Homer learned allegory from the Egyptians:

> Our author, like most of the *Greeks*, is thought to have travelled into *Egypt*, and brought from the priests there, not only their learning, but their manner of conveying it in fables and hieroglyphics. . . . For whoever reflects that this was the mode of learning in those times, will make no doubt but there are several mysteries both of natural and moral philosophy involved in the *Iliad*, which otherwise in the literal meaning appear too trivial or irrational; and it is but just, when these are not plain or immediately intelligible, to imagine that something of this kind may be hid under them.[87]

The notes to Homer, which make the usual remarks that one should look further than the literal sense when it appears "too trivial or irrational," stress the notion that myth contains arcane truths, veiling them from the eyes of the vulgar and uninitiated. Ruskin, however, espouses another view, that enigma conveys truths most effectively to the limited understandings of men.

[87] *The Whole Works of Homer*, trans. Alexander Pope, ed. William Melmoth (London, n.d.), p. 102n. The Yale Mss. of Ruskin's juvenilia, interestingly enough, show that Ruskin had encountered this explanation of Greek mythology as derived from Egypt in the sermons of Reverend Andrews. One rather hard to decipher passage reads: "If we notice the character of the Gods of Egypt it [could] assist us. Greece was colonized from Egypt, that is colon[ists] from Egypt settled in Greece and we must regard the mythology of Greece to that of Egypt, and the stream being so foul [full?] what must the fountain have been [?]"

Ruskin had met this notion of myth as hieroglyphic both in Knight and Bacon. The author of *The Wisdom of the Ancients* commented, for example, that "Parables have been used in two ways, and (which is strange) for contrary purposes. For they serve to disguise and veil the meaning, and they serve also to clear and throw light upon it."[88] Knight, who cited Demetrius to the effect that "Mysteries are expressed in allegories, for the purpose of inciting confusion of mind and terror," also believed that "many of the gross fictions which exercised the credulity of the vulgar heathens, sprang from abstruse philosophy conveyed in figurative and mysterious expressions."[89] Although Ruskin, as we shall observe, occasionally used the term "hieroglyph" as a synonymn for "myth," he does not present this theory that the creators of myth employed it to protect truth from the vulgar. Indeed, his entire emphasis falls rather upon the opposite point, that myth reveals the mysteries of nature and of morals.[90]

Ruskin further believes that myth, like other forms of the Symbolical Grotesque, arises in an act of the prophetic imagination. In *The Queen of the Air* Ruskin thus explains that "all the greatest myths have been seen, by the men who tell them, involuntarily and passively—seen by them with as great distinctness (and in some respects, though not in all, under conditions as far

[88] *Works*, XIII, 79.

[89] *Symbolical Language of Ancient Art*, pp. 5, 25.

[90] *Fors*, however, once mentions the way enigma and parable conceal as well as illuminate: "All the teaching of God, and of the nature He formed round Man, is not only mysterious, but, if received with any warp of mind, deceptive, and intentionally deceptive. The distinct and repeated assertions of this in the words of Christ are the most wonderful things, it seems to me, and the most terrible, in all the recorded action of the wisdom of Heaven. 'To *you*' (His disciples) 'it is given to know the mysteries of the Kingdom,—but to others, in parables, that, hearing, they might *not* understand' " (28.319-320).

beyond the control of their will) as a dream sent to any of us by night when we dream clearest"(19.309). Myth, then, resembles not only the vision of Dante and Spenser but also, as he emphasizes in *The Ethics of the Dust*, "the visions spoken of in the Bible"(18.351) as well. In other words, Ruskin's studies of mythology, which increasingly occupy his time after he lost his Evangelical faith, provide another example of the manner in which he transferred ideas originally derived from Evangelicalism to art and to the study of cultural history. As he became convinced that the Evangelicals could not possibly possess the only sources of religious and moral truth, he turned increasingly to other repositories of vital truth, among which mythology was one of the most important. The degree to which Ruskin believes ancient mythology similar to biblical parable and prophecy appears in his statement that myth "is founded on constant laws common to all human nature; that it perceives, however darkly, things which are for all ages true . . . ;—and that its fulness is developed and manifested more and more by the reverberation of it from minds of the same mirror-temper, in succeeding ages"(19.310). Myth, somewhat like the typological evidences of Christ and His Gospel, gradually becomes meaningful as individual after individual contributes to the final vision of truth.

Ruskin's commitment to mythology, one might say, is the extreme form of his protestant temper; for as an individual worshipper he no longer depends solely on his own experience and his own reading of the Bible, but now finds religious truth, which has appeared in many diverse forms, wherever he can. Ruskin's interest in mythology was by no means purely antiquarian: believing myth a repository of divine and human truth,

he turned to it as a partial replacement for his now vanished faith, and, not surprisingly, he found many of the same ideas in the fables of the ancient Greeks as he had in his Bible. His loss of religion accounts therefore both for the seriousness with which he devotes himself to the study of mythology and for the many pleas for tolerance he makes in its behalf. Carlyle had argued that "We shall begin to have a chance of understanding Paganism, when we first admit that to its followers it was, at one time, earnestly true,"[91] but Ruskin, in many ways his disciple, goes even further, holding that indeed myth *remains* true. Both Ruskin and Carlyle, of course, are reacting against the venerable Christian tradition, arising in the earliest days of the Church, which held that myth arose in corrupt pagan religions.[92] He had encountered other oppositions to this view in the work of Knight, who pointed out, for instance, that "complications and a forced literal construction of the mythological fables, were adroitly but most ungenerously seized upon by the adversaries of the popular worship to show the debasing influence of the ancient religions. . . . The interpretation of Euhemerus which transformed the Gods into men, that of Tertullian which gave them substantial existence as evil demons, and the gross sentiment of Epicurus and Lucretius, which made the myths only frivolous fables invented to amuse, having no specific aim or meaning, were so many forms of calumny and misrepresentation."[93] Ruskin, who usually did not have a very high regard for Knight, certainly agreed with him here, for he frequently defends ancient mythology against similar

[91] *Heroes and Hero-Worship, Works*, v, 5.
[92] See Seznec, *Survival of the Pagan Gods*, pp. 11-20.
[93] *Symbolical Language of Ancient Art*, p. xv.

charges. In *The Art of England* (1883), for example, he scorned the "supercilious theory" that "mythology is a temporary form of human folly," going so far as to make the extreme "counter statement, that the thoughts of all the greatest and wisest men hitherto, since the world was made, have been expressed through mythology"(33.294). Similarly, *The Queen of the Air* pleads with its audience to grant the Greek myths of Athena a fair hearing: "We cannot justly interpret the religion of any people, unless we are prepared to admit that we ourselves, as well as they, are liable to error in matters of faith; and that the convictions of others, however singular, may in some points have been well founded, while our own, however reasonable, may in some particulars be mistaken"(19.295). This gentle plea for tolerance reminds one how far Ruskin had traveled from his anti-Catholic rants in *The Seven Lamps of Architecture*. He more explicitly states his belief that God can give truth to all, Christian and pagan alike, in *The Ethics of the Dust*, which, after mentioning visions of death in the Old and New Testaments, inquires: "Is there anything impious in the thought that the same agency might have been expressed to a Greek king, or a Greek seer, by similar visions?"(18.350) A zealous sectarian, and certainly Ruskin himself in earlier years, might well have replied, "Yes, such a thought *is* impious, since God reveals himself only in the Bible and then only to the true believer." But once Ruskin lost his initial belief and accepted the idea that God comes differently to each man and each age, he willingly accepts moral and spiritual truths wherever he finds them.

Moreover, when he lost his Evangelical religion, he not only began to regard mythology, like the Bible, as a source of spiritual and ethical truth, but also inter-

preted it, like the Bible, in terms of multiple meanings. For example, in the last volume of *Modern Painters* when he is discussing Turner's *Garden of the Hesperides* (see Plate 6) Ruskin explains: "The fable of the Hesperides had, it seems to me, in the Greek mind two distinct meanings; the first referring to natural phenomena, and the second to moral"(7.392). Quoting at length from Smith's *Dictionary of Greek and Roman Geography*, he concludes that the "nymphs of the west, or Hesperides, are . . . natural types, the representatives of the soft western winds and sunshine, which were in this district most favourable to vegetation. In this sense they are called daughters of Atlas and Hesperis, the western winds being cooled by the snow of Atlas. The dragon, on the contrary, is the representative the Sahara wind, or Simoom, which blew over the garden from above the hills on the south, and forbade all advance of cultivation beyond their ridge. . . . But, both in the Greek mind and in Turner's, this natural meaning of the legend was a completely subordinate one. The moral significance of it lay far deeper" (7.392-393). Explaining that in this second sense the Hesperides are connected not "with the winds of the west, but with its splendour"(7.393), he draws upon Hesiod to demonstrate that they represent those moral forces and attitudes which produce "household peace and plenty"(7.396).

Ruskin again expounded this notion of myth as polysemous allegory nine years later in *The Queen of the Air*, explaining that "in nearly every myth of importance . . . you have to discern these three structural parts—the root and the two branches:—the root, in physical existence, sun, or sky, or cloud, or sea; then the personal incarnation of that; . . . and, lastly, the

moral significance of the image, which is in all the great myths eternally and beneficently true"(19.300). In addition to these literal, physical, and moral senses of myth, he also believes that many myths have a long lost historical meaning or reference as well; but these last meanings, less important than the moral or physical, he willingly relinquishes to "the masters of history"(19.299). The same theory of mythology, which he also explains in *The Ethics of the Dust*, appears in the 1877 *Fors Clavigera* as well. There he reminds his readers, "I have often told you that everything in Greek myths is primarily a physical,—secondly and chiefly a moral—type"(29.128). Since the idea of interpreting myth this way undoubtedly developed both from his reading of mythographers, such as Bacon and Knight, and from his habits of reading scripture, it is particularly interesting to observe that at the point in his life when he considered myth as a form of scripture, he also considered scripture myth; and he read the Bible, therefore, in terms of physical and moral senses. For example, in the 1876 *Fors Clavigera* he explains that the three sons of Ham, Mizraim the Egyptian, Phut the Ethiopian, and Sidon the Sidonian represent "the three African powers,—A, of the watered plain, B, of the desert, and C, of the sea"(28.561). In their moral sense they signify, respectively, "slavish *strength* of body and intellect," "slavish *affliction* of body and intellect," and "slavish *pleasure* of sensual and idolatrous art"(28.561-562). From this body of interpretations he concludes that "the spiritual meaning of Egyptian slavery is *labour without hope*"(28.562). In other words, although by this time he had returned to some personal form of Christianity, he interprets the Bible primarily as he had in *Unto This Last* (1860)—as ostensible source and authoritative con-

firmation of his theories of social justice. Augustine and the Evangelicals—to name some of those with whom Ruskin was most familiar—always interpret the period of Egyptian bondage as part of their typical readings of scripture, finding that it stands for the soul unredeemed, without grace, and in a state of sin. In contrast, Ruskin, who still centers human life on the idea of occupying, enriching labor, sees slavery within the context of his own gospel.

The notion that scripture may be read in terms of physical and moral allegory appears in Bacon's *Advancement of Learning*, a work Ruskin knew well. Citing Acts 7:22, Bacon explains that of Moses it is said "he was *seen in all the learning of the Egyptians.* . . . Take a view of the ceremonial law of Moses; you shall find, besides the prefiguration of Christ, . . . the most learned Rabbins have travelled profitably and profoundly to observe, some of them a natural, some of them a moral, sense."[94] It is most likely, however, that Ruskin interpreted the meaning of the sons of Ham in a manner resembling Bacon's theories of scriptural exegetics, not because he borrowed them but because he independently arrived at a similar notion from his methods of reading mythology. Although the writers on mythology whom Ruskin knew alternately interpret myth physically and morally, none of them, like Ruskin, believes that myth consistently provides two levels of allegorical meaning. Nonetheless, he may have encountered occasional interpretations of myth which explain several senses of a particular incident. For example, the notes to the *Iliad* offered such multiple explanation of Jove's punishment of his wife in Book xv:

*Homer* mysteriously explains in this place the nature

94 *Works*, VI, 139.

of the *Air*, which is *Juno*; the two anvils which she
had to her feet are the two elements, earth and water; and the chains of gold about her hands are the
*aether*, or fire which fills the superior region; the two
grosser elements are called anvils, to shew us, that
in these two elements only, arts are exercised. We do
not know but that a moral allegory may here be
found, as well as a physical one; the poet, by these
masses tied to the feet of *Juno*, and by the chain of
gold with which her hands were bound, might signify, not only that domestic affairs should be like fet-
ters to detain the wife at home, but that proper and
beautiful works like chains of gold ought to employ
her hands.[95]

To this one can only reply that the moral injunction to
housewives does not seem well served by the image of
Juno tormented by Zeus for her treacherous murder of
Hercules. Indeed any of the interpretations Ruskin
would have found both in Pope's Homer and in the
writings on mythology that he knew tend to be similarly ill-founded, inappropriate, and unconvincing.
Ruskin's own readings of mythology, as we shall see,
tend, in contrast, to be both more tactful and subtle, in
part because unlike many of his sources of information
about myth he interprets figures and incidents not in
terms of simple equations but in terms of complex relations between moral or physical forces. This habit of
reading myth tactfully and with great attention to the
context suggests, once more, that Ruskin's methods of
interpretation owe much less to writings on myth than
to his Evangelical training in scriptural exegesis.

That Ruskin, despite his loss of religion, still empha-

[95] *The Whole Works of Homer*, p. 208n.

sizes the truths and methods of his former belief appears most clearly in the way he derives Christian interpretations from classical myth. Returning to the *Garden of the Hesperides*, we come upon his reminder that "the reader may have heard, perhaps, in other books of Genesis than Hesiod's, of a dragon being busy about a tree which bore apples, and of crushing the head of that dragon"(7.398). His closing words refer, of course, to the prophecy in Genesis which Christian poets and preachers, including Milton and Melvill, always interpreted typologically as Christ's future victory over Satan. After utilizing the evidence of Homer, Hesiod, Euripides, Vergil, Dante, Spenser, Milton, Bacon, and the Bible, Ruskin concludes that the Hesperian dragon "is, in fine, the 'Pluto il gran nemico' of Dante; the demon of all evil passions connected with covetousness; that is to say, essentially of fraud, rage, and gloom. Regarded as the demon of Fraud, he is said to be descended from the viper Echidna, full of deadly cunning, in whirl on whirl; as the demon of consuming Rage from Phorcys; as the demon of Gloom, from Ceto; —in his watching and melancholy, he is sleepless (compare the Micyllus dialogue of Lucian); breathing whirlwind and fire, he is the destroyer, descended from Typhon as well as Phorcys; having, moreover, with all these, the irresistible strength of his ancestral sea" (7.400-401). His interpretation demands several remarks: first of all, Ruskin, unlike the eighteenth-century commentators of Homer, does not conceive allegory as mere equation of one vice or virtue with the stated figure. Instead, he sees the poetic or painterly symbol just as Evangelicals saw the narrative in the Bible—as cause to meditate upon man and his nature, upon sin and salvation. His conception of allegorical

myth, in other words, demands a love of interpretation and a delight in unraveling the fine points of spiritual truth that had largely disappeared from the critical scene several hundred years before. Secondly, we should observe that his interpretations are self-consciously Christian; for here the Hesperian dragon embodies, quite clearly, the spirit of cupidity, covetousness, and Mammon to which Ruskin devotes so much attention in his later writings. One must realize that when Ruskin chose such an interpretation of the Turnerian employment of Greek myth, he did so not in naïve ignorance of other interpretations of myth, but from the declared belief that the same truths he had learned in Beresford Chapel appear in Greek mythology. He knew Knight's discussion of the employment of serpent myths and symbols in phallic ritual, his discussion of Neoplatonic interpretations of mythology, and his citation of evidence from Hindu, Orphic, Egyptian, ancient Scandinavian, Japanese, Tartar, and American Indian sources. Ruskin, whose notion of a bivalent natural-moral meaning in myths corresponds to that of recent anthropologists,[96] was well aware of the ambivalent nature of mythic symbolism. In *The Queen of the Air*, for example, he first points out that "as the worm of corruption, it [the serpent] is the mightiest of all adversaries of the gods—the special adversary of their light and creative power— Python against Apollo"(19.363). At the same time, the serpent, which embodies the earthly, also represents fer-

[96] Victor Turner, *The Forest of Symbols: Aspects of Ndembu Ritual* (Ithaca, N.Y., 1967), p. 28, writes that all "dominant Ndembu symbols possess two clearly distinguishable poles of meaning. At one pole is found a cluster of *significata* that refer to components of the moral and social orders of Ndembu society, to principles of social organization, to kinds of corporate grouping, and to the norms and values inherent in structural relationships. At the other pole, the *significata* are usually natural and physiological phenomena and processes."

tility—"the power of the earth upon the seed"(19.363). Furthermore, "there is a power in the earth to take away corruption, and to purify . . . ; and in this sense, the serpent is a healing spirit,—the representative of Aesculapius, and of Hygieia"(19.364). Despite the presence of these other complicating meanings, Ruskin holds that the serpent signifies, essentially and inevitably, the corrupt, the evil, the forces of death.

Ruskin urges this interpretation upon his readers because he believes that God created the serpent as "a divine hieroglyph of the demoniac power of the earth, —of the entire earthly nature"(19.363). The serpent, in other words, serves as a word in what Ruskin seventeen years earlier had called the "language of types." In *The Queen of the Air*, where his term for the language of types has become "natural myth," he remarks that when studying mythology one should not forget that God as well as man endows myths with significance. Complaining that most students of mythology have "forgotten that there are any such things as natural myths," Ruskin emphasizes that we must look with care into these "dark sayings of nature"(19.361), both because they convey important truths and because they found all human myths; in fact, "all guidance to the right sense of the human and variable myths will probably depend on our first getting at the sense of the natural and invariable ones. The dead hieroglyph may have meant this or that—the living hieroglyph means always the same; but remember, it is just as much a hieroglyph as the other; nay, more,—a 'sacred or reserved sculpture,' a thing with an inner language" (19.361). These remarks on natural myth reveal that Ruskin still accepts what we have earlier observed to be an essentially medieval conception of the universe.

Eleven years after he had walked out of the chapel service in Turin, he still finds himself within a world which bears the impress of God's moral law. He continued to believe, like his medieval forebearers, that God intended man to search nature, "reading" the lamb and the crocodile as the linguistic elements of a verbal universe.

What is most strange about Ruskin's continued allegorizations of the natural world is that he did not turn his back on the developments of contemporary science thus to become a Victorian Physiologus. Indeed, a note to *The Queen of the Air* assures his reader that the "facts" upon which he is about to dwell "are in nowise antagonistic to the theories which Mr. Darwin's unwearied and unerring investigations are every day rendering more probable"(19.358n). The accompanying text explains that evolutionary theory, which shows how species develop, remains irrelevant to the *meanings* which God may have impressed upon the species once formed:

> Whatever the origin of species may be . . . the groups into which birth or accident reduce them have distinct relation to the spirit of man. It is perfectly possible, and ultimately conceivable, that the crocodile and the lamb may have descended from the same ancestral atom of protoplasm; . . . but the practically important fact for us is the existence of a power which creates . . . crocodiles and lambs, . . . the one repellent to the spirit of man, the other attractive to it, in a quite inevitable way, representing to him states of moral evil and good, and becoming myths to him of destruction or redemption, and, in the most literal sense, "Words" of God. (19.358-359)

Ruskin's conception of natural myth resembles his theories of beauty at important points and may, in fact, have been patterned after them. In the first place, he believes that men receive pleasure from beauty "instinctively and necessarily"(3.109), and, similarly, men experience pleasure or displeasure from natural myth "in a quite inevitable way." Men react more or less uniformly to beauty as they react to natural myth, because God created man in harmony with the moral laws of the universe and the nature of His own being. Moreover, both beauty and natural myth first evoke an instinctive emotional response and, when studied with care, reveal a deeper moral meaning. In addition, the emotions produced both by beauty and natural myth are essentially disinterested; for just as beauty is not derived from utility or practical effect upon man, the practical relation of man to the lamb or crocodile, the snake or bird, has less importance than the fact God created these living hieroglyphs with an inner meaning. For example, men do not fear and abhor snakes chiefly because they threaten human life. In fact, "there is more poison in an ill-kept drain,—in a pool of dishwashings at a cottage door,—than in the deadliest asp of Nile." Our "horror" of the snake "is of the myth, not of the creature"(19.362). Lastly, natural myth serves the same polemical purpose as do Ruskin's theories of beauty, for both contribute to a kind of "objectivity" in art and aesthetics. Both insure that human reactions, which are emotional and subjective, occur uniformly.

Although Ruskin thus dwells briefly on the divinely ordained core of certain myths, throughout his writings he concerns himself far more with mythology as creation of man and his society. Unlike all other forms of the Symbolical Grotesque and unlike most of the artis-

tic phenomena he discusses, myth and the mythic element in art are in some sense group enterprises. Mythologies develop slowly, gradually gathering meaning, and they require the contributions of many men over long periods of time. When discussing the symbolic decorative patterns of Greek vases, Ruskin commented in *Fors Clavigera* that "A symbol is scarcely ever invented just when it is needed. Some already recognized and accepted form or thing becomes symbolic at a particular time"(27.405). One might apply this conception of the gradual development of a symbol from something at first without further meanings to Ruskin's conception of mythology, for he believes that myths similarly grow forth from a story often without important meaning. Consequently, since myths thus grow and change, becoming richer and more meaningful, "the question is not at all what a mythological figure meant in its origin; but what it became in each subsequent mental development of the nation inheriting the thought"(18.348). Moreover, "the real meaning of any myth is that which it has at the noblest age of the nation among whom it is current"(19.301). Myths which arise within a nation receive much of their importance because they embody the ideals and aspirations of its members, and therefore, according to Ruskin, it signifies little whether or not the legend which men accept has a basis in fact, for a legend which has no factual basis may be more valuable to a society and tell us more about its beliefs than one easily proved:

> Whenever you begin to seek the real authority for legends, you will generally find that the ugly ones have good foundation, and the beautiful ones none. Be prepared for this; and remember that a lovely

legend is all the more precious when it *has* no foundation. Cincinnatus might actually have been found ploughing beside the Tiber fifty times over; and it might have signified little to any one;—least of all to you or me. But if Cincinnatus never was so found, nor ever existed at all in flesh and blood; but the great Roman nation, in its strength of conviction that manual labour in tilling the ground was good and honourable, invented a quite bodiless Cincinnatus; and set him, according to its fancy, in furrows of the field, and put its own words into his mouth, and gave the honour of its ancient deeds into his ghostly hand; *this* fable, which has no foundation;—this precious coinage of the brain and conscience of a mighty people, you and I—believe me—had better read, and know, and take to heart, diligently. (27.357-358)

Such a myth to which all in a nation pay homage both figures forth and reinforces its central beliefs. A belief in Cincinnatus reveals Roman "conviction that manual labour . . . was good and honourable," a belief in Hercules's conquest of the water serpent reveals Greek conviction of the truth of heroism, and a belief in the battle of Apollo and Marsyas reveals a conviction that in the conflict "between intellectual, and brutal, or meaningless, music"(19.343), the orderly and meaningful must prevail.

Although the ordinary person accepted these myths as historical narratives, says Ruskin, he rarely thought of their deeper meanings. In fact, "literal belief [in a myth] was, in the mind of the general people, as deeply rooted as ours in the legends of our own sacred book; . . . a basis of unmiraculous event was as little suspected, and an explanatory symbolism as rarely traced,

by them, as by us"(19.298). This overt comparison between the Bible and Greek mythology, which demonstrates once again how Ruskin granted all but equal
value to the legends of ancient Greece and Christianity,
also indicates his conviction that only a nation's spiritual leaders really understand its mythology. "But, for
all that, there was a certain undercurrent of consciousness in all minds, that the figures meant more than they
at first showed; and according to each man's own faculties of sentiment, he judged and read them"(19.298-299).
The great men of a nation, its artists and spiritual leaders, see farthest into these myths. They build upon them,
reshape them, add to their meaning.

Because the artists and other spiritual leaders see so
much more in legends than do the common people,
mythology remains essentially the creation of great in-
dividuals. Although the great myth-maker, like the
great artist-poet, draws upon the ideals and beliefs of
his fellow men, he advances beyond their expectations
and can never be fully understood by them. But because the people accept the basic truth of myth, the
ancient creator of myth never found himself alienated
from his society the way Turner did. Thus, even though
Ruskin believes that mythology develops to some extent
as a cooperative enterprise, his essentially Carlylean
conception of the artist-seer leads him to conclude that
the creator of myth belongs to a group composed primarily, not of his contemporaries, but of his great
predecessors.

Turner, as a great artist, takes his place with the
ancient creators of myth, for he, too, accepts the meanings of the past and then recasts them in new ways. For
the great English painter thus to add new meaning to
the old myths, he had both to know them and have in-

418

sight into their significance. In the course of explicating the import of the dragon in the *Garden of the Hesperides*, Ruskin remarks: "How far he had really found out for himself the collateral bearings of the Hesperid tradition I know not; but that he had got the main clue of it, and knew who the Dragon was, there can be no doubt"(7.401-402). As Ruskin explains, the painter's conception of the dragon "fits every one of the circumstances of the Greek traditions"(7.402). This convergence of ancient and modern arises partly in the fact that Turner perceived the "natural myth" at the heart of his subject and partly in his knowledge of the Greek tradition. In reading this painting, Ruskin, as we have already observed, draws upon Homer, Hesiod, Euripides, Vergil, Dante, Spenser, Milton, and the Bible, just as in similarly interpreting the vices and virtues on the columns of the Ducal Palace in Venice he refers to Dante, Spenser, Orcagna, Giotto, and Simon Memmi. These artists and poets, with a few others, represent for Ruskin the Western tradition upon which all the great thinkers, including Turner, have drawn. Several times in *Fors Clavigera* Ruskin paused to set forth lists of essential writings which he believed all should know. For example, when he proposed to set up a library for the St. George's Guild he wrote that "for the standard theological writings which are ultimately to be the foundation of this body of secular literature, I have chosen seven authors . . . the men who have taught the purest theological truth hitherto known to the Jews, Greeks, Latins, Italians, and English, namely, Moses, David, Hesiod, Vergil, Dante, Chaucer, and, for the seventh, summing the whole with a vision of judgment, St. John the Divine"(28.500). Although Ruskin changes and reshuffles his lists to suit his purpose at the moment,

it is clear that he considers the authors upon whom he draws as the sources of the best in the Western tradition, as the key to myth, and that he believes Turner to have known their works.

## *VI. Ruskin's allegorical interpretations of Turner*

RUSKIN most elaborately applies his mythological theories to art criticism when he explains Turner's *Garden of the Hesperides* (1806) and *Apollo and Python* (1811) in the fifth volume of *Modern Painters*. He begins his reading of the earlier canvas by first explaining the significance of the Hesperid nymphs and the dragon, then comments upon the Goddess of Discord and the gloomy atmosphere of the picture, and finally draws his conclusions. First, he explicates the moral ideas embodied in the nymphs. "Their names are, Aeglé,—Brightness; Erytheia,—Blushing; Hestia, —the (spirit of the) Hearth; Arethusa,—the Ministering"(7.395). He then comments that these four were perfectly fitted to guard "the golden fruit which the earth gave to Juno at her marriage":

> Not fruit only: fruit on the tree, given by the earth the great mother, to Juno (female power), at her marriage with Jupiter, or *ruling* manly power (distinguished from the tried and *agonizing* strength of Hercules). I call Juno, briefly, female power. She is, especially, the goddess presiding over marriage, regarding the woman as the mistress of a household. Vesta (the goddess of the hearth), with Ceres, and Venus, are variously dominant over marriage, as the

fulfilment of love; but Juno is pre-eminently the housewives' goddess. She therefore represents, in her character, whatever good or evil may result from female ambition, or desire of power: and, as to a housewife, the earth presents its golden fruit to her, which she gives to two kinds of guardians. The wealth of the earth, as the source of household peace and plenty, is watched by the singing nymphs—the Hesperides. But, as the source of household sorrow and desolation, it is watched by the Dragon. (7.395-396)

The dragon, to whom Ruskin devotes the largest part of this explication, embodies covetousness and the fraud, rage, gloom, melancholy, cunning, and destructiveness associated with it. Thus, whereas "Geryon is the evil spirit of wealth, as arising from commerce . . . the Hesperian dragon is the evil spirit of wealth as possessed in households; and associated, therefore, with the true household guardians, or singing numphs" (7.403).

Turning to the Goddess of Discord, Ruskin finds that in this painting she signifies essentially "the disturber of households"(7.404), though in fact she is the same power as Homer's spirit of the discord of war. "I cannot get at the root of her name, Eris. It seems to me as if it ought to have one in common with Erinnys (Fury); but it means always contention, emulation, or competition, either in mind or in words;—the final work of Eris is essentially 'division,' and she is herself always double-minded; shouts two ways at once (in *Iliad*, xi. 6), and wears a mantle rent in half (*Aeneid*, viii. 702). Homer makes her loud-voiced, and insatiably covetous" (7.404). According to Ruskin, Turner combined this

conception of discord with Spenser's symbolical grotesque Ate in the fourth book of the *Faerie Queene*,
adding a "final touch of his own. The nymph who
brings the apples to the goddess, offers her one in each
hand; and Eris, of the divided mind, cannot choose"
(7.405-406). The presence of the Goddess of Discord,
who darkens the joys of home and family, also accounts
in part for the unusual gloom with which Turner rendered the Hesperid Garden, though the artist's darkened palette "was certainly caused chiefly by Spenser's
describing the Hesperides fruit as growing first in the
garden of Mammon"(7.406-407). Color, like form, according to Ruskin, bears allegorical significance in this
painting, and the critic who would explicate it in full
must pay close attention to this essential aspect of
technique.

After he has thus interpreted the major elements of
the *Garden of the Hesperides*, Ruskin concludes: "Such
then is our English painter's first great religious picture; and exponent of our English faith. A sad-coloured
work, not executed in Angelico's white and gold; nor
in Perugino's crimson and azure; but in a sulphurous
hue, as relating to a paradise of smoke. That power, it
appears, on the hill-top, is our British Madonna: whom,
reverently, the English devotional painter must paint
. . . Our Madonna,—or our Jupiter on Olympus,—or,
perhaps, more accurately still, our unknown God"
(7.407-408). In brief, Turner's darkened, dragon-watched
garden sets forth in visible form the spiritual condition
of England. It testifies that England, having exchanged
faith in God for faith in gold, turns away from the path
of life, embracing that of death, and longs to enter an
earthly paradise that will be, not Eden, the garden of
God, but the garden of Mammon in which the head of

the serpent, unbruised by Christ, gazes about in icy triumph. Ruskin calls this a religious picture because it expounds the faith by which his contemporaries live and work, the faith, that is, to which their deeds, though not their words, testify. In "Traffic," a lecture he delivered in April 1864, he mentions "the real, active, continual, national worship; that by which men act, while they live; not that which they talk of, when they die. Now, we have, indeed, a nominal religion, to which we pay tithes of property and sevenths of time; but we have also a practical and earnest religion, to which we devote nine-tenths of our property, and six-sevenths of our time. And we dispute a great deal about the nominal religion: but we are all unanimous about this practical one; of which I think you will admit that the ruling goddess may be best generally described as the 'Goddess of Getting-on,' or 'Britannia of the Market' "(18.447-448). Like the Evangelicals who continually emphasize the difference between nominal and practical, or true, Christianity, Ruskin frequently informs the unconverted that they profess a nominal worship but live by a far different "practical and earnest religion." England, having traded *caritas* for *cupiditas*, has chosen to live, not by love and cooperation, the laws of life, but by competition, the law of death. In *Sesame and Lilies* (1865), for instance, he warns that England busily engages itself in exchanging greatness for gold and life for death:

A great nation [does not] send its poor little boys to jail for stealing six walnuts; and allow its bankrupts to steal their hundreds of thousands with a bow, and its bankers, rich with poor men's savings, to close their doors "under circumstances over which they have no control," with a "by your leave"; and large

423

landed estates to be bought by men who have made
their money by going with armed steamers up and
down the China Seas, selling opium at the cannon's
mouth, and altering, for the benefit of the foreign
nation, the common highwayman's demand of "your
money *or* your life," into that of "your money *and*
your life." Neither does a great nation allow the lives
of its innocent poor to be parched out of them by
fog fever, and rotted out of them by dunghill plague,
for the sake of sixpence a life extra per week to its land-
lords; and then debate, with drivelling tears, and
diabolical sympathies, whether it ought not piously
to save, and nursingly cherish, the lives of its mur-
derers. . . . And, lastly, a great nation does not mock
Heaven and its Powers, by pretending belief in a
revelation which asserts the love of money to be the
root of *all* evil, and declaring, at the same time, that
it is actuated, and intends to be actuated, in all chief
national deeds and measures, by no other love.
(18.82-83)

Five years before Ruskin thus charged that Victorian
England had sacrificed all to Mammon, he wrote that
Turner's mythological painting proclaimed the same
practical worship: "The greatest man of our England,
in the first half of the nineteenth century, in the
strength and hope of his youth, perceives this to be the
thing he has to tell us of utmost moment, connected
with the spiritual world. . . . Here, in England, is our
great spiritual fact for ever interpreted to us—the Assumption of the Dragon"(7.408). Turner, the greatest
of England's artists, looks about him, observes the
triumph of Mammon, and firmly, if sadly, sets down in
the guise of a symbolical grotesque the truth he has
observed.

He darkens his palette to "a sulphurous hue, as relating to a paradise of smoke"(7.407-408), for, in truth, "the fair blooming of the Hesperid meadows fades into ashes beneath the Nereid's Guard"(7.408). Choosing to live beneath the watchful glance of the Dragon of Mammon which guards the Nereids, England, says Turner, has entered the dark ages. In a previous volume of *Modern Painters* Ruskin had pointed out that "the title 'Dark Ages,' given to the mediaeval centuries, is, respecting art, wholly inapplicable. They were, on the contrary, the bright ages; ours are the dark ones. . . . We build brown brick walls, and wear brown coats. . . . There is, however, also some cause for the change in our own tempers. On the whole, these are much *sadder* ages than the early ones; not sadder in a noble and deep way, but in a dim wearied way,—the way of ennui, and jaded intellect, and uncomfortableness of soul and body"(5.321). When he comes to interpret Turner's *Garden of the Hesperides* Ruskin concludes that the ennui, the sadness, the lack of light and color arise, as he believed Turner to have stated, in the worship of the Goddess of Getting-on.

Before we consider the validity of Ruskin's brilliant, if perhaps surprising, reading of this painting, let us examine his similarly complex interpretation of *Apollo and Python*, the second canvas to which he devotes a chapter in the fifth volume of *Modern Painters*. This chapter, "The Hesperid Aeglé," opens as Ruskin compares this later work to the one he has just discussed at length: "Five years after the Hesperides were painted, another great mythological subject appeared by Turner's hand. Another dragon—this time not triumphant, but in death-pang, the Python slain by Apollo"(7.409). This painting, which he had earlier described in his

notes to the Turner Bequest (1856) as "one of the very noblest of all Turner's works"(13.122), is far simpler than the *Garden of the Hesperides*. The nude Apollo, the sole figure in the picture, kneels, his head radiating light, and watches with arrow in hand the cataclysmic writhings of the dying Python, whose death pangs have splintered trees and sent huge rocks crashing down behind him. As Ruskin's chapter title emphasizes, this is essentially a picture of triumph and light, not gloom; for whereas the keynote of his discussion of the *Garden of the Hesperides* was the dragon, "The Nereid's Guard" of the title, he here emphasizes the Hesperid Aeglé—the nymph who embodies "Brightness."

Although he does not go as deeply into the literary sources of this picture as he did in the *Hesperides*, since he expects the meaning of this battle will appear obvious, he reads it many ways, explicating not only the physical and moral significance of the work but also its meaning as an emblem of Turner himself and of the beauties of art in general. Employing the term "type" in an extension of its figural sense, he comments that "The picture is at once the type, and the first expression of a great change which was passing in Turner's mind. A change, which was not clearly manifested in all its results until much later in his life; but in the colouring of this picture are the first signs of it; and in the subject of this picture, its symbol"(7.409). This victory of god over serpent, which represents in physical allegory the victory of sun and light over mist and darkness, further signifies, in the moral sense, the victory of love, life, and purity over sin and death. Ruskin also takes it as the perfect emblematic representation of Turner's increasing discovery of the joys and beauty of color, and as such it raises the problem of the role of color in art. He

explains that Turner "had begun by faithful declaration of the sorrow there was in the world. It is now permitted him to see also its beauty. He becomes, separately and without rival, the painter of the loveliness and light of the creation. . . . Of its light: light not merely diffused, but interpreted; light seen pre-eminently in colour"(7.410). Thus, although Turner did not fully develop his coloristic gifts until after 1820, this picture exhibited in 1811 already foreshadows the artist's coming victory over the gloom of his predecessors and the brown violin of Sir George Beaumont. Telling the story in brief of Turner's artistic development, Ruskin explains how the artist "went steadily through the subdued golden chord, and painted Cuyp's favourite effect, 'sun rising through vapour,' for many a weary year. But this was not enough for him. He must paint the sun in his strength, the sun rising *not* through vapour. If you glance at that Apollo slaying the Python, you will see there is rose colour and blue on the clouds, as well as gold; and if then you turn to the Apollo in the Ulysses and Polyphemus . . . you see he is not 'rising through vapour,' but above it; —gaining somewhat of a victory over vapour, it appears" (7.411). The painting, then, must be seen as a symbolic representation of Turner's own victory over darkness. But it also represents a second battle, the battle with the audience, for "The public remonstrated loudly in the cause of Python. . . . They would neither look nor hear;—only shouted continuously, 'Perish Apollo. Bring us back Python' "(7.412). Four years earlier, in his notes on the Turner Bequest, Ruskin had explained that *Ulysses Deriding Polyphemus* (1829; see Plate 3) similarly provides an unconsciously created type of the painter's own destiny.

427

He had been himself shut up by one-eyed people, in
a cave "darkened by laurels" (getting no good, but
only evil, from all the fame of the great of long ago)
—he had seen his companions eaten in the cave by
the one-eyed people—(many a painter of good promise had fallen by Turner's side in those early toils of
his); at last, when his own time had like to have
come, he thrust the rugged pine-trunk—all ablaze—
(rough nature, and the light of it)—into the faces of
the one-eyed people, left them tearing their hair in the
cloud-banks . . . and got away to open sea as the
dawn broke over the Enchanted Islands. (13.136-137)

When Ruskin compares this painting to the *Temeraire*
(see Plate 4) of a decade later he points out how the
changed subjects embody the career and life of the
artist, as if his sympathy were best evoked by situations similar to his own:

The one picture, it will be observed, is of sunrise;
the other of sunset.
The one of a ship entering on its voyage; and the
other of a ship closing its course for ever.
The one, in all the circumstances of its subject, unconsciously illustrative of his own life in its triumph.
The other, in all the circumstances of its subject,
unconsciously illustrative of his own life in its
decline. (13.168-169)

Although Ruskin does not hold that Turner intended
such a personal allegory, one might argue, with Jack
Lindsay, that the artist included covert personal reference in many of his works. Arguing from the evidence
of Turner's unpublished poetry, for example, Lindsay
deduces from Turner's poem, "Love is a raging ocean,"

that the painter early "used the shipwreck-image for personal disaster."[97] Ruskin, who had access to Turner's notebooks and who emphasized the significance of his poetry, may well have drawn his conclusions from such evidence. But whether he did or not, Ruskin's elaborate exegesis of Turner's works in this manner testifies to his sense of the painter's career, his feeling for the painter's concerns, and, most important, for his confidence that art bears meaning.

After Ruskin has pointed out the implicit, if possibly unintended, significance of *Apollo and Python* as a symbol of Turner's battle with his public, he examines the meaning of the cry, " 'Perish Apollo. Bring us back Python.' . . . for herein rests not merely the question of the great right or wrong in Turner's life, but the question of the right or wrong of all painting. Nay, on this issue hangs the nobleness of painting as an art altogether, for it is distinctively the art of colouring, not of shaping or relating. Sculptors and poets can do these, the painter's own work is colour"(7.412). Here, then, seventeen years after he had begun his defense of Turner the great colorist, Ruskin once again defends the role of color, *bright color*, in art; and despite the many changes that have taken place in his knowledge of art, religious belief, and theoretical emphases, one is not too surprised to see him explicate the glories of color the way he had much earlier explicated the glories of beauty—with an appeal to types. First, he points out Turner's particular gift to art: "the perfection of the colour chord by means of *scarlet*. Other painters had rendered the golden tones, and the blue tones, of sky; Titian especially the last, in perfectness. But none had dared to paint, none seem to have seen,

97 *The Sunset Ship*, p. 63.

the scarlet and purple. . . . His most distinctive inno-
vation as a colourist was the discovery of the scarlet
*shadow*"(7.413). Continuing the battle of the Rubenistes
against the Poussinistes, of Delacroix against Ingres, of
Turner against the reviewers, Ruskin asks, is color, in
fact, sensual, immoral, the lesser, debasing part of
painting? Are the Hesperides, Aeglé and Erytheia,
"sensual goddesses,—traitresses"(7.413). In a footnote
which occupies almost six pages in the *Library Edition,*
he sets forth his arguments in favor of color, but the
main point, which he emphasizes in the text, is simply
"that colour generally, but chiefly the scarlet, used with
the hyssop, in the Levitical law, is the great sanctifying
element of visible beauty, inseparably connected with
purity and life"(7.414-415). Not wishing, he says, to discuss in detail "the mystical connection between life and
love, set forth in that Hebrew system of sacrificial religion to which we may trace most of the received ideas
respecting sanctity, consecration, and purification"
(7.416), he refers the reader to Leviticus and limits
himself to the assertion that color is "the type of love"
(7.419).

The sky and its clouds, the medium which bears the
golds and scarlets of the sun to man, is, for Ruskin as
he believes for Turner, what he later called a natural
myth. The cloud, or the firmament, Ruskin advises the
reader,

> signifies the ministration of the heavens to man. That
> ministration may be in judgment or mercy—in the
> lightning, or the dew. But the bow, or colour of the
> cloud, signifies always mercy, the sparing of life;
> such ministry of the heaven as shall feed and prolong
> life. And as the sunlight, undivided, is the type of the

wisdom and righteousness of God, so divided, and softened into colour by means of the firmamental ministry . . . is the type of the wisdom of God, becoming sanctification and redemption. (7.418)

Arguing once more from his knowledge of the typical sacrifices enjoined in Leviticus, which prefigured a coming sanctification and redemption, Ruskin can therefore conclude that color is the symbol of love, its embodiment, the word of God's love in visible form. In art it is the Word become Flesh.

To the ancient Greek, the conflict of Apollo with Python therefore represented the battle of light and color with darkness, of life with death, of purity with sin and disease. Whereas the Hesperid dragon guarded treasure, this "worm of eternal decay," ("THE CORRUPTER,") destroys it. "Apollo's contest with him is the strife of purity with pollution; of life with forgetfulness; of love, with the grave . . . of youth and manhood with deadly sin—venomous, infectious, irrecoverable sin"(7.420). Ruskin thus reads this painting as the definitive Turnerian image of all the battles men and nations must fight, and though Apollo, the "conqueror of death"(7.420), the healer of the people, here kneels triumphant, this victory, like all over sin, death, and time, is necessarily a qualified one ever to be repeated: man can meet final defeat but not final victory in these contests. Ruskin, who elsewhere quotes Plato to the effect that "Our battle is immortal"(29.82), believes that Turner's encompassing vision of life necessarily mixes victory and new danger, the end of one battle and the suggestion of another. As evidence he points to a smaller serpent rising out of the blood of defeated Python, and he exclaims: "Alas, for Turner! This

smaller serpent-worm, it seemed, he could not conceive to be slain. In the midst of all the power and beauty of nature, he still saw this death-worm writhing among the weeds"(7.420). Turner, says Ruskin, was without hope: he could not conceive final victory, he could not conceive the rose without the worm, beauty without decay. As the notes to the Turner Bequest point out: "There seemed through all his life to be one main sorrow and fear haunting him—a sense of the passing away, or else the destructive and tempting character of beauty. The choice of subject for a clue to all his compositions, the 'Fallacies of Hope,' marked this strongly"(13.159). *Apollo and Python* thus gives us the image of Turner's mind, an emblem of the emblematic man of the nineteenth century—courageous, loving beauty, visionary but without hope, without belief, without solace.

RUSKIN's interpretations of *Apollo and Python* and the *Garden of the Hesperides,* which skillfully apply his sophisticated theory of artistic meaning to individual paintings, not only demonstrate his ability at close analysis but also show how widely and how well he summons literary tradition to explicate pictorial art. At the heart of these readings of painting, poetry, and myth lies a characteristic Ruskinian assurance that all things bear meaning, that all aspects of a work, if examined, will reveal meanings relevant to man. His remarkable ability first to perceive the significant details of a painting or poem and then to explicate them in the light of literary, artistic, and mythological tradition produces interpretations which anticipate the methods of recent criticism. Certainly, Ruskin's uses of close reading, formal analysis, biographical data, personal

symbolisms, myth, and iconographic traditions mark
him as the honored predecessor of much of this century's best criticism and scholarship.

Although there thus can be little doubt about Ruskin's major importance as a defender, theorist, and
interpreter of the arts, the student of his work must
answer the crucial question how appropriate, how
valid, are his readings of Turner. Joan Evans instructs
us that "Ruskin had no comprehension of Turner's
vision of this world, and 'interpreted' him in the light
of sciences and moralities that must have been wholly
alien to a man who was a poet in paint."[98] This is a
charge that must be investigated. When Miss Evans
scornfully dismisses Ruskin's influential works of social
criticism as "fights against windmills of political economy,"[99] anyone aware of the great influence attributed
to Ruskin's work by those more knowledgeable in politics and economics—including Gandhi, R. H. Tawney,
and numerous Members of Parliament—can discount
her remarks with the realization that she has wandered
into unfamiliar territory and has not done enough to
acquaint herself with the lay of the land.[100] Her charges

[98] *John Ruskin* (London, 1954), p. 93.     [99] *Ibid.*, p. 305.
[100] For R. H. Tawney, see "John Ruskin," in his *Radical Tradition:
Twelve Essays on Politics, Education, and Literature*, ed. Rita Hinden
(Penguin Books: n.p., 1966), pp. 42-46. John Rosenberg writes that
"Clement Atlee, who became a socialist after reading the works of
Ruskin and William Morris, wrote that the modern Labour Party
was born in 1906, when twenty-nine independent Labourites were returned to the House of Commons; according to a questionnaire circu-
lated among them, the book which most profoundly influenced their
thought was *Unto This Last*. By 1910 one hundred thousand copies had
been sold and several unauthorized editions had been printed in
America. Translations appeared in French, German, and Italian; and
a then obscure disciple of Ruskin translated it into Gujarati, an Indic
dialect" (*The Darkening Glass*, p. 131). Gandhi, who was the then obscure disciple, explained in his autobiography that *Unto This Last*
marked the turning point in his life. For Professor Rosenberg's sources,
see pp. 240-241.

about Ruskin's interpretations of Turner, on the other hand, remain more serious, since as an art historian she writes with some authority. Therefore, to determine the validity of Ruskin's approaches to the works of his favorite artist, I propose first to examine the nature of both men's assumptions about art and then look at the extent to which Turner held the political and moral views his critic attributed to him.

Certainly, Turner and Ruskin held nearly identical conceptions of poetry and painting as sister arts, for both not only considered the artist a poet but also emphasized the importance of poetic subject and method to the pictorial arts. Turner placed great value on poetic allusions and on his own "Fallacies of Hope," and Ruskin, like few others, perceived their significance for his art. Both also shared the view of the artist as prophet. Turner, for example, once wrote, "Why say the Poet and Prophet are not often united?—for if they are not they ought to be."[101] Ruskin, who quite literally transfers his notions of Old Testament prophets to men of art, asserted in the first volume of *Modern Painters* that Turner himself united the nature of artist and seer: "Turner—glorious in conception—unfathomable in knowledge—solitary in power—. . .[is] sent as a prophet of God to reveal to men the mysteries of His universe, standing, like the great angel of the Apocalypse, clothed with a cloud, and with a rainbow upon his head, and with the sun and stars given unto his hand"(3.254). The periodical critics attacked this description of Turner as blasphemous, and when Ruskin changed most of the chapter in which it appeared for the third edition he did not employ this passage—

[101] Quoted without source in Lindsay's *The Sunset Ship*, p. 48.

though he still continued to identify Turner as a prophet.[102] Turner's *Angel standing in the Sun* (1852; see Plate 9) may well be, as Jack Lindsay suggests, the artist's vindication of Ruskin's and his own conception of the artist-seer.[103]

In addition to sharing these basic conceptions of art and artist, both men believed Turner's work formed a coherent whole, a unified body of pictorial poetry. *The Harbours of England* (1856) thus notes the artist's "earnest desire to arrange his works in connected groups, and his evident intention, with respect to each drawing, that it should be considered as expressing part of a continuous system of thought"(13.9). As a note to the fifth volume of *Modern Painters* explains, Ruskin recalled Turner's injunction to him concerning his works: " 'Keep them together.' He seemed not to mind how much they were injured, if only the record of the thought were left in them, and they were kept in the series which would give the key to their meaning" (7.434n).[104]

102 On the attacks by *Blackwood* and *The Athenaeum* see *Library Edition* of *Works*, 3.254n and my "Ruskin's Revisions of the Third Edition of *Modern Painters*, Volume I," *VN*, XXXIII (1968), 13.

103 *Turner*, p. 213.

104 Characteristically, Miss Evans makes no mention of this recognition. She does, however, point out that when Ruskin chose one hundred water colors from the Turner Bequest for exhibition he "published a Catalogue of them, arranged rather childishly to illustrate a supposed tour up the Rhine, through Switzerland to Venice and back" (p. 235). Miss Evans unfortunately does not mention that Ruskin made a practice of following Turner's sketching tours in an attempt to locate the artist's originals, a practice which provided Ruskin with much solid evidence about the way Turner imaginatively rearranged particular scenes. Martin Hardie's authoritative *Water-Colour Painting in Britain*, eds. Dudley Snelgrove, Jonathan Mayne, and Basil Taylor, 3 vols. (London, 1967), II, 44, takes such procedure as representative of Ruskin's thoroughness as a critic of Turner. Ruskin's arrangement of the water colors, I believe, derives importantly from his desire to create a unified group of work such as Turner always desired.

Equally important, Ruskin both perceived and shared the artist's allegorical intentions. Turner's characteristic habits of mind appear in an anecdote related by Thornbury:

> When the plate of Wickcliffe's birthplace was being engraved for Whitaker's "Yorkshire," in touching the proof he (Turner) introduced a burst of light which was not in the drawing. To the engraver's enquiry as to why he had done so he replied, "That is the place where Wickcliffe was born and there is the light of the glorious Reformation." "But what do you mean by those large fluttering geese in the foreground?" "Oh! those—those are the old superstitions which the genius of the Reformation is driving away."[105]

This anecdote clearly demonstrates that the complex and unexpected symbolical intentions Ruskin attributed to Turner are in no way, as Miss Evans believes, alien to the artist. Another example of Turner's complex symbolical and allegorical methods appears in the paintings of Carthage and Rome. Here the artist makes use of the histories of ancient times to set forth both the fallacies of human hope and the way greed and corruption destroy nations. In addition, as Jack Lindsay has shown, Turner's shipwrecks, biblical scenes, and other works often contain elaborate political and moral allegories.[106]

Closely related to this employment of ancient history was Turner's knowledge and use of mythology. Although the painter may not have known or drawn upon the precise texts Ruskin cited in his explications, there

[105] Lindsay, *The Sunset Ship*, pp. 62-63, quotes this passage, which, in turn, appears in one of Ann Livermore's essays.
[106] See, for example, *The Sunset Ship*, pp. 46-49, and n.117 below.

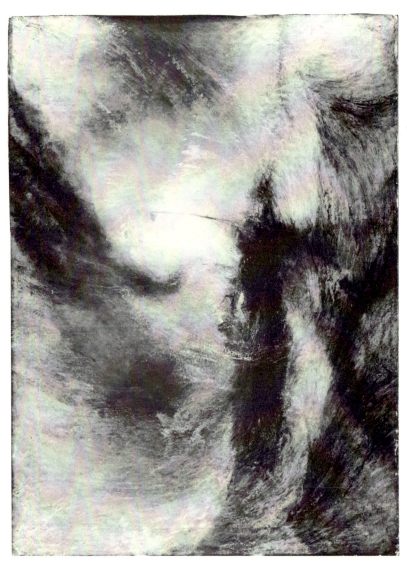

1. J.M.W. Turner. *Snowstorm: Steamboat off a Harbour's Mouth making Signals in Shallow Water, and going by the Lead. The Author was in this Storm on the Night the Ariel left Harwich.* Oil on canvas, 36 x 40 in. Exhibited at the Royal Academy, 1842. Courtesy of the National Gallery, London (no. 530; Turner Bequest)

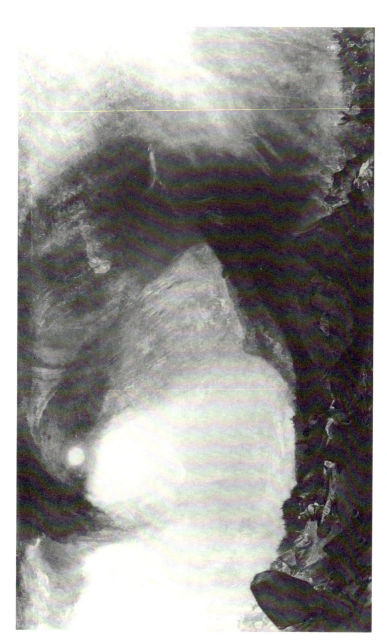

2. J.M.W. Turner. *Snowstorm: Hannibal and his Army Crossing the Alps.* Oil on canvas, 57 x 9¾ in. Exhibited at the Royal Academy, 1812. Courtesy of the Tate Gallery, London (no. 490; Turner Bequest)

3. J.M.W. Turner. *Ulysses Deriding Polyphemus—Homer's Odyssey.* Oil on canvas, 50¼ x 80½ in. Exhibited at the Royal Academy, 1829. Courtesy of the National Gallery, London (no. 508; Turner Bequest)

4. J.M.W. Turner. *The Fighting Temeraire Tugged to her last Berth to be broken Up, 1838*. Oil on canvas, 35¾ x 48 in. Exhibited at the Royal Academy, 1839. Courtesy of the National Gallery, London (no. 524; Turner Bequest)

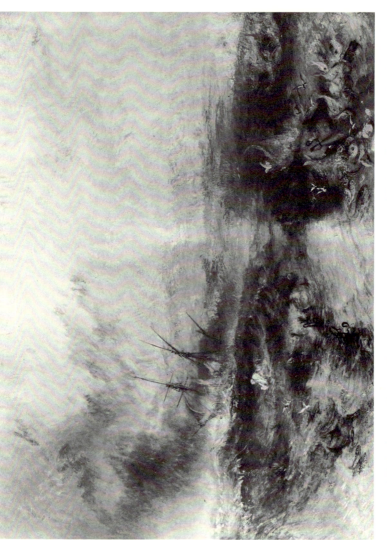

5. J.M.W. Turner. *Slavers Throwing Overboard the Dead and Dying—Typhon Coming On* [*The Slave Ship*]. Oil on canvas, 35¾ x 48 in. Exhibited at the Royal Academy, 1840. Courtesy of the Museum of Fine Arts, Boston (H. L. Pierce Fund)

6. J.M.W. Turner. *The Goddess of Discord choosing the Apple of Contention in the Garden of the Hesperides.* Oil on canvas, 59½ x 84 in. Exhibited at the British Institution, 1806. Courtesy of the Tate Gallery, London (no. 477; Turner Bequest)

7. J.M.W. Turner. *Apollo and Python* (or *Apollo killing the Python*). Oil on canvas, 57¼ x 93½ in. Exhibited at the Royal Academy, 1811. Courtesy of the Tate Gallery, London (no. 488; Turner Bequest)

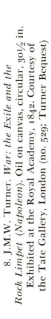

9. J.M.W. Turner. *The Angel standing in the Sun.* Oil on canvas, 30½ x 30½ in. Exhibited at the Royal Academy, 1846. Courtesy of the Tate Gallery, London (no. 550; Turner Bequest)

8. J.M.W. Turner. *War: the Exile and the Rock Limpet (Napoleon).* Oil on canvas, circular, 30½ in. Exhibited at the Royal Academy, 1842. Courtesy of the Tate Gallery, London (no. 529; Turner Bequest)

10. John Ruskin, *The Matterhorn*, 1849. Drawing, 10½ x 14½ in.
Courtesy of the Fogg Art Museum, Harvard University (Prichard Fund)

11. John Ruskin. *Tom Tower, Christ Church College, Oxford.*
Drawing, 12¼ x 10¼ in. Courtesy of the Fogg Art Museum,
Harvard University (Gift of Dr. Denman W. Ross)

12. John Ruskin. *Sculptural Details of the Cathedral, St. Lo.*
Drawing, 19 x 14¼ in. Courtesy of the Fogg Art Museum, Harvard University
(Gift of Samuel Sachs)

13. Henry Wallis. *The Death of Chatterton*. Oil on canvas, 23¾ x 35¾ in. Exhibited at the Royal Academy, 1856. Courtesy of the Tate Gallery, London (no. 1685)

14. Sir John Everett Millais. *Ophelia*. Oil on canvas, 30 x 44 in. Exhibited at the Royal Academy, 1852. Courtesy of the Tate Gallery, London (no. 1506)

15. William Lindsay Windus. *Too Late*. Oil on canvas, 38 x 30 in. Exhibited at the Royal Academy, 1859. Courtesy of the Tate Gallery, London (no. 3597).

16. Arthur Hughes. *April Love*. Oil on canvas. Exhibited at the Royal Academy, 1856. Courtesy of the Tate Gallery, London (no. 2476)

17. Samuel Prout. *Ratisbonne*. Pencil drawing, 10⁹⁄₁₆ x 8⅛ in. Courtesy of the Fogg Art Museum, Harvard University (Gift of Dr. Denman W. Ross)

18. Samuel Prout. *St. Andrew, Brunswick*. Pencil drawing, 15¹⁵⁄₁₆ x 10⁷⁄₁₆ in. Courtesy of the Fogg Art Museum, Harvard University (Grenville L. Winthrop Bequest)

19. Samuel Prout. *Ypres, Cloth Hall and Square*. Drawing, 16½ x 11⅛ in. Courtesy of the Fogg Art Museum, Harvard University

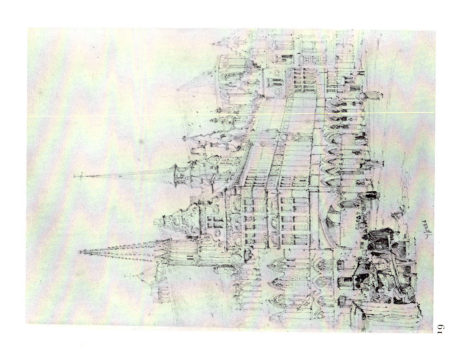

69

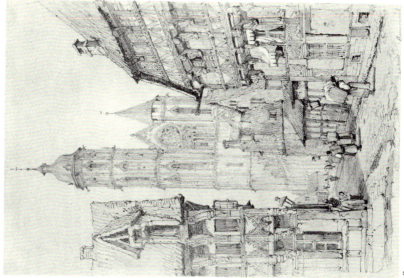

81

is little doubt that Turner knew a great deal of mythology and that he understood it essentially the way his interpreter claimed. According to the editors of the *Library Edition*, much of Turner's knowledge of myth came from Lemprière's *Classical Dictionary*. They comment: "It is often objected that Turner had no deep mythological meanings in his classical compositions, for that Lemprière was his only source of inspiration. Such criticism shows a want of acquaintance with that book, for the author nearly always adds to his bald versions of the myths an interpretation, according to his lights, of their physical and moral meanings"(13.108-109n). One need not, however, rest one's defense of Ruskin on the argument that Turner's major source, Lemprière, advanced such intricate allegorical readings of mythology; for, indeed, as Jerrold Ziff and Jack Lindsay have shown, the artist's debt to Akenside accounts for much of his intimate knowledge of classical culture. For example, the argument to Akenside's *Hymn to the Naiads* explains:

> The Nymphs, who preside over springs and rivulets, are addressed at day-break in honour of their several functions, and of the relations which they bear to the natural and to the moral world. Their origin is deduced from the first allegorical deities, or powers of nature; according to the doctrine of the old mythological poets, concerning the generation of the gods and the rise of things. They are then successively considered, as giving motion to the air and exciting summer breezes; as nourishing and beautifying the vegetable creation; as contributing to the fulness of navigable rivers, and consequently to the maintenance of commerce; and by that means, to the mari-

time part of military power. Next is represented
their favourable influence upon health, when assisted
by rural exercise: which introduces their connection
with the art of physic, and the happy effects of min-
eral medicinal springs. Lastly, they are celebrated
for the friendship which the true Muses bear them.[107]

Akenside's use of mythology reads much like Ruskin's
and provides another source of the ideas the critic attributed to the *Garden of the Hesperides*. A self-
educated man, Turner did not possess Ruskin's knowledge of original classical sources, but he had encountered considerable uses of myth, not only in classical
dictionaries, and the work of other artists, but also in
the poems of Thomson, Akenside, Pope, and other
eighteenth-century poets; then, too, he knew Ovid,
Homer, and other sources of mythology in translation.
Therefore, neither the knowledge nor the employments
of myth Ruskin attributed to Turner was in any way
foreign to the artist.

Furthermore, Turner, whose deathbed utterance is
reputed to have been "The Sun is God," clearly held
the views about light and color which his chief advocate attributed to him.[108] In particular, the painter employed color with precise allegorical or symbolical
intentions. The first volume of *Modern Painters* describes the "crimson and scarlet" of *The Slave Ship*
(see Plate 5) as a judgment upon the guilty vessel: "It
labours amidst the lightning of the sea, its thin masts
written upon the sky in lines of blood, girded with condemnation in that fearful hue which signs the sky with
horror, and mixes its flaming flood with the sunlight,

107 Quoted by Lindsay, *Turner*, p. 145.
108 Quoted by Lindsay in *ibid.*, p. 213.

and, cast far along the desolate heave of the sepulchral waves, incarnadines the multitudinous sea"(3.572). In the notes to the Turner Bequest he points out that the lines the artist appended to *War* (see Plate 8), another crimson work, "are very important, being the only verbal expression of that association in his mind of sunset colour with blood . . . :—

> 'Ah, thy tent-formed shell is like
> A soldier's nightly bivouac, alone
> Amidst a sea of blood.—' (13.160)

By the last volume of *Modern Painters* he had found other corroboration and explained that "the very sign in heaven itself which, truly understood, is the type of love, was to Turner the type of death. The scarlet of the clouds was his symbol of destruction. In his mind it was the colour of blood. So he used it in the Fall of Carthage. Note his own written words—

> While o'er the western wave the ensanguined sun,
> In gathering huge a stormy signal spread,
> And set portentous

So he used it in the Slaver, in the Ulysses, in the Napoleon [War], in the Goldau"(7.437-438n). As Ruskin probably knew from arranging the Turner Bequest, the artist had made this association between sunset crimson and blood as early as his 1806-1808 sketchbook in which he wrote the words "Fire and blood"[109] over a setting sun.

Perhaps most important to our investigation is the fact that both men shared the belief that the worship of Mammon destroyed nations and was threatening England. "O Gold," one of the artist's manuscript

[109] Quoted by Lindsay, *The Sunset Ship*, p. 25.

poems, relates "Chaotic strife, elemental uproar wide"[110] to the love of money, while his painting of William III's arrival in England bore the following note: "The yacht in which His Majesty sailed was, after many changes and services, finally wrecked on Hamburg Sands, while employed in the Hull Trade." Jack Lindsay points out that "even when expressing what he considers a high moment of Liberty, Turner reminds us of the twist that distorts men's aims and hopes; the triumphant ship of Liberty is wrecked in the end as the mere instrument of trade."[111] One may add that Turner's mention in another poem of "Shipowners frown/ Gingling their money"[112] would support Lindsay's interpretation. The clearest indication that Turner espoused Ruskin's attitudes toward the effects of greed and gold appear in the last lines of the poem he appended to *The Slave Ship*: "Hope, Hope, fallacious Hope!/ Where is thy market now?" One must agree with Lindsay that this painting attacks not only the already dying slave trade but also English society, a society joined by the cash-nexus, as well.[113] Whether or not one wishes to accept the interpretation of this particular painting, one must admit that Turner's continual connection in his Carthage series of greed, luxury, and corruption as the cause of national decay demonstrates that painter and critic hold the same moral attitudes, condemnation of Mammon, and estimate of its effect on past and present times. *Hannibal and his Army Crossing the Alps* and *The Decline of Carthage*, for example, reveal that Turner's conceptions of history and the use of an earlier nation as a model

110 *Ibid.*, p. 101.
112 *Ibid.*, p. 112.

111 *Ibid.*, p. 62n.
113 *Ibid.*, p. 51.

for England precisely match Ruskin's beliefs and methods both in *The Stones of Venice* and his reading of the *Garden of the Hesperides*.

Lastly, Ruskin correctly observed Turner's sense of isolation, lack of belief, pessimism, and sorrow at the passing of beauty. The sense of being alone, which Ruskin so emphasized in the last volume of *Modern Painters*, appears, for instance, in these lines the artist addressed to a hostile world:

> Let my works
> Outlive the maker who bequeaths them to thee
> For well I know where our possessions end
> Thy praise begins & few there be who weave
> Wreaths for the Poet ('s) brow, till he is laid
> Low in his narrow dwelling with the worm.[114]

Although, as Turner stated in another poem, art "Re-claims . . . fleeting footsteps from the waste/ Of Dark Oblivion,"[115] he realized that the world too often pays little enough attention to art, which grants such gifts, and he mourns the passing of the noble and beautiful: his painting of the *Temeraire*, for example, conveys this sense of loss, this sense of the death of nobility, while his verses "On the Demolition of Pope's House at Twickenham" complains that his nation too quickly forgets to honor the "British Maro."[116]

Perhaps the only important point on which one can fault Ruskin's interpretations of Turner is that they do not adequately emphasize the artist's covert political allegories. According to the recent work of Jack Lindsay and John McCoubrey, Turner concerned himself with contemporary political events, including the Na-

[114] *Ibid.*, p. 127.    [115] *Ibid.*, p. 128.    [116] *Ibid.*, p. 117.

441

poleonic wars and the bills to reform Parliament. Far more a republican than his critic, Turner comments on the continuing battle of liberty and tyranny.[117] Despite the more specific commentary on contemporary issues than Ruskin perceived, Turner, who often relates his political allegories to his attacks on Mammon, frequently arrives at positions similar to Ruskin. Another point of divergence, perhaps, is that Turner may not have developed his elaborate social and political commentaries until 1812, whereas Ruskin interprets paintings exhibited in 1806 and 1811.[118] The last volume of *Modern Painters*, of course, discusses *Apollo and Python* and the *Garden of the Hesperides* as paintings which signal the approaching change in Turner's art, and it is therefore quite possible, though not certain, that Ruskin may have anticipated Turner's allegorical works, reading into earlier ones themes and methods of those painted later. Although Ruskin may possibly have read too deeply in these particular paintings, there can be no doubt that he well understood Turner's aims and methods, and that Turner found in Ruskin a better interpreter and defender than any other artist has had the good fortune to encounter.

[117] Lindsay writes that the closeness of Turner's "reaction to contemporary events may be gauged from his pictures of 1832, the year of radical agitation, insurrection (at Bristol), and successful parliamentary reform. He showed *Childe Harold* with its moral that decadence follows imperial corruption and the failure to uphold Liberty, *Nebuchadnezzar at the mouth of the burning fiery furnace* (in which the three faithful endure the worst that tyranny can do), *Staffa* with a small steamtug defying the stormclouds, and *The Prince of Orange, William III, embarked from Holland.* . . . In the context of the struggle for the Reform Bill, Turner's picture of William landing against elemental opposition to bring about 'the glorious Revolution' can only have one meaning" (pp. 61-62). In a lecture delivered at the Frick Museum (1966) Professor McCoubrey demonstrated Turner's allusions to contemporary affairs in *The Slave Ship* and *Tapping the Furnace*.
[118] See *The Sunset Ship*, p. 60.

## VII. "Constant art" and the
### allegorical ideal

HAVING observed (perhaps unexpectedly) that Ruskin's allegorical interpretations of Turner prove valid, we shall find it no surprise that his similar readings of medieval and Renaissance painting, poetry, and architecture prove appropriate. His long acquaintance with the artist and his works, both public and private, surely account for much of his understanding of Turner, but the fact that they shared the same views both of allegorical art and the themes such art should portray contributes equally to his excellence as a critic of Turner. And, since his methods of interpretation and the habits of mind which produce them derive from older views of allegorical reading, both religious and secular, one should expect that the same sensitivity to detail, the same knowledge of poetic, mythological, and iconographical traditions, which aided in the understanding of a nineteenth-century painter, should become even more obviously useful in his critiques of earlier allegorical arts.

When examining Ruskin's conceptions of the Symbolical Grotesque, we have already seen how sympathetically, how astutely, he interprets Spenser. Raised on typological exegetics, *Pilgrim's Progress*, and Quarles's *Emblems*, Ruskin, one may expect, read Milton and Herbert with equal skill, and when one turns to his writings on medieval works the suitability of his critical methods appears even more evident. For after one has observed that Ruskin, who possesses an essentially medieval conception of the world, reads both scripture and nature-scripture allegorically, one correctly expects him to approach the painting and architecture of

443

the Middle Ages with a sympathy and an attuned sensibility rare in a Victorian critic. His *Bible of Amiens* and the sections on Torcello, St. Mark's, and the Ducal Palace in *The Stones of Venice* provide examples of his fine readings of medieval iconography, while his interpretations of Tintoretto, Veronese, Dürer, and others throughout his works similarly exemplify his skillful exegesis of later art.

Since his allegorical and symbolical interpretations arise in typological readings of scripture, it is particularly interesting to observe the way he applies figuralism to medieval and Renaissance painting. In *Giotto and His Works in Padua*, for example, he employs his knowledge of scriptural types to suggest interpretations of the work of one of his favorite artists. Commenting on Giotto's depiction of Christ's expulsion of the money lenders from the Temple, he explains that Christ's "raising of the right hand . . . resembles the action afterwards adopted by Orcagna, and finally by Michael Angelo in his Last Judgment: and my belief is, that Giotto considered this act of Christ's as partly typical of the final judgment, the Pharisees being placed on the left hand, and the disciples on the right"(24.91). Briefly relating the pose to later works, Ruskin suggests, but does not insist upon, his own typological interpretations. This approach to Giotto's art also appears throughout *Modern Painters*. For instance, in the final volume he again explicates typological symbolism in art when discussing Veronese's *Presentation of the Queen of Sheba*. He mentions that one of the figures on the left side of the painting holds a white falcon "its wings spread, and brilliantly relieved against the purple robe of one of the elders. It touches with its wings one of the golden lions of the throne, on which the light also

444

flashes strongly; thus forming, together with it, the lion and eagle symbol, which is the type [symbol, not *figura*] of Christ throughout mediaeval work. In order to show the meaning of this symbol, and that Solomon is typically [figurally] invested with the Christian royalty, one of the elders, by a bold anachronism, holds a jewel in his hand in the shape of a cross, with which he (by accident of gesture) points to Solomon"(7.293). Such evident delight in explicating symbolism (even after he had lost the faith which provided its basis) provides the necessary complement to his often remarkable ability to perceive the details, formal and iconographical, of a work of art. These same procedures, which make Ruskin such an able critic of medieval and Renaissance symbolism, appear again in his figural reading of Tintoretto's Scuola San Rocco *Annunciation*. He first remarks that the painter has placed the Virgin "houseless, under the shelter of a palace vestibule ruined and abandoned"(4.264), and then calls attention to the carpenter's tools which lie amid the mass of scattered brickwork. Tintoretto, he points out, has composed his picture so that a narrow line of light, the edge of a carpenter's square, "connects these unused tools with an object at the top of the brickwork, a white stone, four square, the corner-stone of the old edifice, the base of its supporting column. This, I think, sufficiently explains the typical character of the whole. The ruined house is the Jewish dispensation; that obscurely arising in the dawning of the sky is the Christian; but the corner-stone of the old building remains, though the builders' tools lie idle beside it, and the stone which the builders refused is become the Headstone of the Corner [Psalms 118.22]"(4.265). These figural interpretations of Renaissance painting,

which again show the effects of Ruskin's Evangelical upbringing upon his practice as art critic, display the same exegetical skill, the same attention to detail, and the same delight in elaborate pictorial symbolism apparent in his writings on Turner.

In addition, Evangelical typology not only contributed heavily to Ruskin's practice as interpretive critic—by providing him both with a thorough knowledge of conventional types and with the attitudes requisite for complex symbolic readings—but also influenced his art theory. Most importantly, the attitudes which Ruskin derived from Evangelical readings of scripture led him to formulate an artistic program for Victorian painting, one, he believed, more suited to the needs of the age than the genre scenes and domestic narratives so popular at the Academy. His pleasure in allegory, which characterizes much of his response to art after the first volume of *Modern Painters*, marks a change from his earlier views, for he had not always voiced such sympathy toward allegory in painting. In an essay which he contributed to Loudon's *Architectural Magazine* in 1838, five years before the beginning of *Modern Painters*, Ruskin voices attitudes much different from those apparent in his frequent later praise of this symbolic mode. Holding that allegory cannot be combined with a realistic style, he obviously believes that a work in this mode must set itself apart, clearly and definitely, from the world of fact: "All allegory must be perfect in itself, or it is absurd; therefore, allegory cannot be combined with nature"(1.256). His other remarks about the "mechanical"(1.256) nature of allegory, which suggest that he believes it requires rigid symmetry, reveal that at this point he had a far more restricted view of pictorial symbolism than he

446

later evolved. In fact, when thus commenting upon allegorical art in 1838, he seems to limit it to emblems of fame which float over the heads of victorious generals. Nonetheless, despite these views, he tentatively allowed in a note that "if the surrounding features could be made a part of the allegory, their combination might be proper." Therefore: "where the allegorical images are representations of truth, bearing a hidden signification, it is sometimes possible to make nature a part of the allegory"(1.256n). This realization that the artist might endow a realistically painted scene with allegorical meanings became the basis for his conceptions of the allegorical grotesque, and his hesitant acceptance of this notion of symbolism in 1838 evolved more than a decade later into the assertion that he awaits "the dawn of a new era of art, in a true unison of the grotesque with the realistic power"(5.137).

The evolution of his habits of scriptural exegesis into a program for contemporary painting was characteristically complex. First of all, his Italian journeys in preparation for the second volume of *Modern Painters,* and his reading of Lindsay and Rio, had convinced him of the major value of medieval and Renaissance art, and, realizing that this art, rather than that of landscape, formed the central tradition of Western art, he increasingly granted it reverence and praise. Captivated by the work of Florence, Rome, and Venice, he turned to it, rather than to the creations of Turner, for his examples of beauty and imagination in the second volume, and then, having apparently led himself and his reader far from their proposed critical itinerary, he saw the need in the third volume to set the art of Turner within a larger context. Thus, he had now first to explain the rise of interest in landscape, something

447

of an anomaly in the history of art, and second he had to explain how he could praise medieval works which did not seem to fit the criteria of his opening volume. In the course of detailing the history of landscape and the art devoted to it, Ruskin pointed out that the painting of Christian times falls "into two great masses—Symbolic and Imitative"(5.262), and that the criteria for one do not fit the other. Afterwards he consistently maintained this distinction, explaining in his commentaries on Giotto, for instance, that the "abstract and symbolical suggestion will always appeal to one order of minds, the dramatic completeness to another. Unquestionably, the last is the greater achievement of intellect, but the manner and habit of thought are perhaps loftier in Giotto [than in later painters]. Veronese leads us to perceive the reality of the act, and Giotto to understand its intention"(24.101).

Such admission of a second major category of imaginative work in no way violates Ruskin's theories of art, for as he previously explained both in *The Stones of Venice* and *Modern Painters*, Volume III, the imagination produces both the Symbolical Grotesque and the higher, Turnerian mode of landscape. In other words, whereas Turner's natural scenes embody the reaction of imagination in the presence of the visible truths of landscape, allegorical painting embodies the reaction of the imagination in the presence of abstract truths: great landscape painting is the art of the visual faculty, great allegory the art of the visionary one. The greatest imaginative art, however, must combine both, using realistic technique to portray the Symbolical Grotesque; and according to Ruskin, this wedding of modern realism with visionary subject should be the aim and continual enterprise of the contemporary artist.

The "modern painter of mythology," for example, must "place, at the service of former imagination, the art which it had not—and to realize for us, with a truth then impossible, the visions described by the wisest of men . . . bringing the resources of accomplished art to unveil the hidden splendour of old imagination" (33.296). This goal, which Ruskin believes aptly describes the arts of men as different in thought and style as Turner, Hunt, Rossetti, and Burne-Jones, appears to him the only way Victorian painting could rise above the trivial and the merely entertaining.

In the last of his commentaries on Giotto, written the same year as his allegorical readings of Turner, Ruskin contrasts the effects of much contemporary art with that of the earlier painter: "The worst characters of modern work result from its constant appeal to our desire of change, and pathetic excitement; while the best features of the elder art appealed to love of contemplation. It would appear to be the object of the truest artists to give permanence to images such as we should always desire to behold, and might behold without agitation; while the inferior branches of design are concerned with the acuter passions which depend on the turn of a narrative, or the course of an emotion" (24.109). This comparison of the repose of Giotto with the emphasis upon story and emotionalism he finds in Victorian painting emphasizes what he finds wrong with Academy painting. Seven years later he analyzed its flaws in more detail and offered a corrective in his brilliant lecture "Modern Art," which a century after its composition remains one of the finest, most perceptive descriptions of the character of Victorian art. He first points out how even its good qualities, in particular its compassionateness, produce narrowness, trivial-

449

ity, and false emotionalism. The compassionateness of contemporary art, he explains, leads artists to portray by choice the poor instead of the noble, the peasant instead of the king, and as a result painters inevitably reduce the scope and value of their art. Furthermore, the work of his contemporaries, even the better work by men such as Wilkie and Leslie, allows "human sympathy" to warp it "away from its own proper sources of power . . . turning the muse of painting into a sister of Charity"(19.198). The resultant sentimentality destroys the value of a painting as art, however much it may make it an effective tract for the times. Deriving his theories of didacticism and beauty from older notions of moral sympathy, Ruskin yet insists that, though the theoretic faculty may rely on sympathetic perception of emotion, the successful in art must avoid playing directly with feelings of artist and audience alike. According to Ruskin, only beauty and symbolism properly exercise the feelings of the spectator, and the art which tries to take short cuts to pleasure or moral value must inevitably go astray.

Secondly, nineteenth-century painting is marked and marred by a characteristic "Domesticity" and concomitant narrowness, superficiality, and complacency. "All previous art," Ruskin asserts, "contemplated men in their public aspect, and expressed only their public Thought. But our art paints their home aspect, and reveals their home thoughts. Old art waited reverently in the Forum. Ours plays happily in the Nursery" (19.200). Thus, whereas the art of past times served the cause of state and religion, Victorian painting greatly limits its subject and potential for good by concentrating on the interests, events, and emotions of home. From this domesticity derive in turn the third and

fourth qualities of contemporary work—its "shallow-ness" and "sanctified littleness"(19.201). As Ruskin explains, a "great part of the virtue of Home is actually dependent on Narrowness of thought. To be quite comfortable in your nest, you must not care too much about what is going on outside"(19.201). The nation which takes its chief artistic delight in domestic scenes could only do so by turning its back on the unpleasantness, troubles, and turmoil of public life. Furthermore, neglecting the broad areas of social, political, and religious concern which had nourished previous great painting, this "Art of the Nest"(19.200) inevitably separates itself from the intellectual and spiritual needs of the age. "And thus while the pictures of the Middle Ages are full of intellectual matter and meaning— schools of philosophy and theology, and solemn exponents of the faiths and fears of earnest religion—we may pass furlongs of exhibition wall without receiving any idea or sentiment, other than that home-made ginger is hot in the mouth, and that it is pleasant to be out on the lawn in fine weather"(19.201). Such art is safe, but it is trivial: it may not disturb the minds of its audience, but the very avoidance of important subject matter which makes it acceptable prevents it from either edifying or providing major pleasure. Although Ruskin clearly dislikes much about contemporary taste, he does not attack the audience for its preferences, he does not attack the age for its art. When he made these criticisms he had lost faith in the truths of religion and himself doubted the public "truths" of contemporary politics and economics; and well aware that the art of his contemporaries portrayed private affairs because public ones were in such doubt, he gently, if accurately, points to the emptiness in English art.

451

With similar perception of underlying causes, Ruskin describes that "eccentricity"(19.202) which characterizes contemporary painting. The quest for novelty which produces eccentricity derives from the need of artist and audience alike to find solace and diversion in private matters. In other words, the eccentricity, like the domesticity, of Victorian painting signifies that the center of nineteenth-century life has not held, that common concerns, traditions, and beliefs have been so weakened by doubt and disagreement that the sources of strength in earlier art have vanished:

> The difficulty of consistent teaching multiplies with our multitudes, and the sense of every word we utter is lost in the hubbub of voices. Hence we have of late learned the little we could, each of us by our own weary gleaning or collision with contingent teachers, none of whom we recognize as wise, or listen to with any honest reverence. If we like what they say, we adopt it and over-act it; if we dislike, we refuse and contradict it. And therefore our art is a chaos of small personal powers and preferences, of originality corrupted by isolation or of borrowed merit appropriated by autograph of private folly. It is full of impertinent insistence upon contrary aims and competitive display of diverse dexterities, most of them ignorant, all of them partial, pitifully excellent, and deplorably admirable. (19.202)

Modern art arises, then, the result of modern individualism—not the individualism of the hero working for his fellows but that of each man who exists, lost and alone, a discrete unit in a formless, competitive society. This "fury" for originality, for novelty, for eccen-

tricity, "though partly the result of everything being made a matter of trade, is yet more the consequence of our thirst for dramatic instead of classic work"(19.209). This "fatal . . . desire of dramatic excitement"(19.203), the sixth and last attribute of contemporary painting, embodies its other unfortunate characteristics. First of all, its emphasis upon action, frequently trivial action, signifies that art has lost its traditional subjects. Since men no longer share major belief, since the artist no longer knows what to say to his audience, he says little; and since, like his audience, he cannot receive pleasure from depictions of religious truths, he paints insignificant, uncontroversial scenes from parlor and nursery. The emphasis upon "dramatic excitement," which reveals how earlier painting's central themes have become inaccessible, also betrays a loss of belief in essential truths, in that which remains constant and unchanging. To this dramatic, changeful painting Ruskin compares the constant art of the great ages: "Constant art represents beautiful things, or creatures, for the sake of their own worthiness only; they are in perfect repose, and are there only to be looked at. They are doing nothing. It is what they are, not what they are doing, which is to interest you"(19.203). Perugino's St. Michael, the Parthenon Theseus, the Venus of Melos stand forth, embodying something as essence—a belief or a beauty—which we regard with pleasure. "Dramatic art, on the other hand, represents an action in some way; the personages of it may be as noble or beautiful as those of the classic school, but they must be doing or suffering something. . . . Leonardo's Cena, Michael Angelo's Last Judgment, and Raphael's Cartoons are received examples of dramatic art"(19.203).

One may of course combine the two modes to produce such great works as Tintoretto's Scuola San Rocco *Christ Before Pilate* or Titian's *Assumption*.

According to Ruskin, the finest painters usually employ the dramatic element in painting with great reserve. "In vulgar art, on the contrary, the drama or story become principal; the spectator does not care whether the figures are beautiful or rightly executed, he only cares about what is going on"(19.204). One reason, says Ruskin, that this dramatic art frequently becomes vulgarized is that "vulgar people can enjoy a story though they cannot judge of perfect form or character. . . . The lower people of course like it, and inferior painters can produce it. For one man who can paint a beautiful form ten can tell a pleasant story, and ten times ten can tell an unpleasant story"(19.204). Ruskin sorrowfully perceived that in his own time the danger always potential in narrative painting had become actual: painting had been sacrificed to narrative, and telling a story in paint, which always risks neglecting the most essential aspects of pictorial art, had in fact produced an art catering to those who could not appreciate the beauties of form and color. Narrative, dramatic, and genre painting had all too frequently resulted in vulgarized art for those unable to appreciate a higher one. Such a condition in painting had perverted the notion that it was a sister to literature, for pictorial art had become, not an analogue or honored rival to poetry, but a mere appendage. Ruskin offers several reasons for the conditions he found in contemporary art: the undeveloped taste of the new middle-class audience, the role of the art market, the loss of important themes and common belief.

To improve the art of England Ruskin proposes that

painters should strive to emulate the older constant art. Citing Turner's *Apollo and Python* as an example of modern art which properly combines the constant and dramatic, the iconic and the narrative, Ruskin holds that such a revival of great art had already been attempted by Rossetti and the Pre-Raphaelites(19.206). Allegory, it is clear, must provide a major source of strength for this artistic program, for it not only enables the painter to present truths otherwise beyond the grasp of his medium, but also permits him to avoid the dangers of overconcentration upon narrative. Returning to the *Apollo and Python,* one observes that, according to Ruskin, this painting embodies the great conflicts of men's lives—the battles of memory with forgetfulness, life with death, and purity with sin—but it does so in a curiously distant way. Almost the entire painting is static, iconic, a permanent image of a permanent truth. In fact, the only action that occurs in the picture is the fall of a huge rock, which, says Ruskin elsewhere, has been loosened by Python's death pangs. The only action, in other words, is movement of natural objects, and one may say that Ruskin, who has high praise for such Turnerian renderings of nature's power and motion as the *Snow Storms,* believed that the motion of nature, though not of man, could be the subject of high art. Just as Ruskin believed the painter should depict trees and rocks in more detail than the form of the human body, he also thought the actions of nature more suitable than man's to the greatest art. For Ruskin, violent human action, such as Apollo's battle, must occur offstage, deducible from the picture but not present in it. Thus, the emphasis upon a calm, classicistic beauty so evident in his aesthetic theories appears again in his conceptions of ideal art, and in each

allegory plays a significant role: the fact that changeful aesthetic emotions figure forth unchanging divine
qualities both makes beauty morally and spiritually valuable and enables it to partake of the eternal; the fact
that the highest art usually employs allegory, God's
way of communicating wisdom to the limited capacities
of men, similarly both makes it a vehicle for essential,
unchanging truths and enables it to incorporate iconic,
emblematic imagery, thus avoiding the dangers of too
much concentration upon the changeful in pictorial
narrative. The delight in repose, balance, and moderation which marks Ruskin's theories of beauty also ex-
pectedly colors his conceptions of ideal art, and his
notions of allegory and symbolism permit him to argue
for these desired qualities; in theories of both art and
aesthetics the characteristic ability of allegory to partake of essences lying outside human space and time
enable it to create a calm, classicistic beauty and a style
of painting appropriate to such an aesthetic.

Before Ruskin completed *Modern Painters* he lost
the original faith which had engendered his conceptions of both beauty and interpretation. This loss of religion severely weakened the value of his aesthetic
theory as a defense of the arts, for as long as he firmly
believed that the beautiful signified God, he could rest
assured that "these visionary pleasures" are "cause for
thankfulness, ground for hope, anchor for faith, more
than . . . all the other manifold gifts and guidances,
wherewith God crowns the years, and hedges the paths
of Men"(4.145). The art which conveys theological
beauty thus is a spiritual force, the perception of
beauty a spiritual act. Once, however, the foundations
of this aesthetic weakened, Ruskin had to find another
major explanation of man's need for art. Even though

this loss of belief did not affect his theory of Vital Beauty, which emphasized moral sympathy and the exercise of the moral faculties, as seriously as it did his more elaborate theological aesthetic, he still needed another chief defense of the moral and spiritual worth of painting and her sisters. Hence it seems quite possible that his increasing emphasis upon allegory, which occupies the center of *Modern Painters*, Volume v, provided Ruskin with such an argument: as he lost faith in the capacity of the visionary pleasures of beauty to provide spiritual value for the arts, he turned to the visionary pleasures of the Symbolical Grotesque. Since, however, the opening volume of *Modern Painters* had announced that a later section of the work would discuss meaning in the arts, such a change of emphasis, though actual, well fit into his original plan and did not distort the overall organization of his study. Nonetheless, his major concern with the Symbolical Grotesque in *The Stones of Venice* and succeeding volumes, and his later emphasis upon allegorically conceived myth clearly show his growing reliance on allegory as a source of value for the arts. Therefore, whether or not one accepts that the fifth volume of *Modern Painters* consciously replaced his earlier defense of painting, it remains clear that such argument from allegory both increasingly occupied his attention and shaped his program for an ideal Victorian art.

# INDEX

Abrams, M. H. 69, 397n
Acland, Henry 266, 274
Addison, Joseph 75, 78, 127, 183, 187, 190, 192-94, 196
Aeschylus 300
age-mark 230. *See also* picturesque
Akenside, Mark 47-48, 437-38
Alberti, Leone Battista 127-29, 132-33
alienation 73
Alison, Archibald 17, 100-4, 109, 129-30, 197-98, 214
allegory: contrasted to typology, 350-51; as corrective to sentimentalism, 452-54; and enigma, 394-98; and ideal artist-poet, 388-90; language of types, 333-34; myth as, 397, 407-8; nature as, 330-31; necessary to receive divine revelation, 370-71; nineteenth-century criticism of, 324-29; polysemous, 332, 407-9; and problems of romantic art and literature, 377-97, 452; and prophetic imagination, 373-76; relation to sublimity, 372-73; role in Ruskin's aesthetics, 455-57; Ruskin's notions of influenced by typology, 349, 351; Ruskin's first opposition to, 446-47; in Spenser, 392-94; symbolical grotesque as, 392-94; in Turner, 420ff. *See also* imagination, mythology, typology
Altick, Richard D. 335n
Andrews, Rev. E. 262n, 336, 360, 402n
Angelico, Fra 29, 31, 37-38, 310
Aquinas, St. Thomas 397n
architecture: 80-85; relation to sculpture, 83; sublime in, 211-221
Aristotle 14, 45, 134-36, 145, 159, 163-66
Arnold, Matthew 9, 15, 268, 273, 324-25, 350, 385
artist: and pathetic fallacy, 378-87; as prophet, 374-77, 387-89, 434-35; same nature as poet, 48, 51, 434. *See also* imagination
association: personal, 104-5; rational, 105-6. *See also* beauty
Auerbach, Erich 350n
Augustine, St. 313-14, 331-32, 372, 396, 397+n, 398

Bacon, Francis 14, 400-1, 403, 409, 411
Baillie, John 76
Barry, James 17, 45
Bate, Walter Jackson 160n
Baudelaire, Charles 386
Baumgarten, Alexander Gottlieb 158
Beattie, James 158
Beaumont, Sir George 427
beauty, Ruskin's theories of:
    *general characteristics*: allegory and, 16, 455-57; as attempt to create meaningful world, 16; characterize his work, 14-15, 89; classical, 92; conservative, 92, 94; eclectic, 14-15; as emotion, 93, 113-14; emphasis upon order, 15, 115; failure to exclude subjective factors, 94, 109-10; formulated originally to defend Turner, 15, 89; instinctive, 93; polemically presented, 13, 15, 89; purifying, 114; as quality, 92, 113; role of expression in, 178; relation to religious belief, 90-91, 148-49, 167-68, 178-79; and sister arts, 86, 149-50; theocentric, 28
    *Typical Beauty*: Apollonian, 146; influence of eighteenth-century theories upon, 92-93, 113, 115-18; origin in personal experience, 111-12; six aspects or modes, 114; (1) of infinity,

459

# INDEX

Cicero 376
Clark, Sir Kenneth 3-4, 13n
Classicism 36
Claude Lorraine 120
Clayton, Rev. Edward 336
Cohen, Ralph 77
Colenso, Bishop William 266-71, 355
Collingwood, R. G. 186n
Coleridge, Samuel Taylor, 182, 190, 323-26, 382
Color 143-44, 348, 429-30
Composition 35, 123-24
Congreve, William 133
Conrad, Joseph 313-14
Cook, E. T. 3, 142n, 280n
Cooper, Anthony, Lord Shaftesbury 92n, 152-54, 156-57, 159, 192
Cormon, Fernand 20
Cowley, Abraham 76
Cowper, William, Mr. and Mrs. (later Cowper Temple, then Lord and Lady Mount-Temple) 140n, 293-95
Cox, David 8
Crane, Stephen 314
Croce, Benedetto 186n, 320
Cuyp, Albert 37

Dante 32-33, 84, 140, 276n, 300, 320, 325-29, 372, 375, 381, 386, 388-90, 395, 398, 404, 411, 419
Darwin, Charles 414
d'Aubigné, Jean Henri Merle 276n
Davies, Horton 245
Delacroix, Eugène 21, 430
Della Quercia, Jacopo 138, 139n
Dennis, John 116, 192-94
de Piles, Roger 48, 116
De Wint, Peter 8
Dickens, Charles 156
didacticism in art 67-68
disinterestedness, aesthetic 98-99, 162
Dougherty, Charles 399n
Doughty, Oswald 13n
Dryden, John 50
Ducal Palace, Venice 59, 84, 220

Du Fresnoy, Charles A. 46, 116
Dulwich Gallery 19
Duomo, Florence 219
Dürer, Albrecht 68, 399n, 444
Dutch painting 55

Elgin Marbles 141
Eliade, Mircea 329
Elliott-Binns, L. E. 245n
emotion: distorting effects of 386-87, 389; Ruskin's opposition to violent in art, 170-72
enigma 392-98, 402. See also allegory, mythology, typology
Epicurus 405
*Essays and Reviews* 267, 271+n
Euhemerus 405
Euripides 411, 419
Evangelical Anglicanism: anticatholicism, 278+n; Bible literally true, 244, 270, 354-55; Bible reading, 334-45; Bible supreme source of doctrine, 248-51; central doctrines, 248-49; damnation, 244, 282, 286-87, 290; experimental knowledge of Christ, 248, 256-59; grace, 259; heir of seventeenth-century Puritans, 244; human depravity, 248, 251-56; intolerance, 276, 385-86; preaching major weapon of the elect, 335-36; Puritan emphasis upon work, 315; ruthlessness, 263-64; Verbal Inspiration, 270, 354-55; zeal, 247-48, 259-64, 276. See also H. Melvill, J. Ruskin (religious beliefs), J. C. Ryle, typology
Evans, Joan 4-5, 17-18, 433, 435n, 436
expressionism 8, 16
expressive theories of art 43, 49, 68-69, 82, 178, 309n

Ficino, Marsilio 128
Fielding, Copley 8, 18, 222-23, 226-27
figuralism: see typology
Finberg, A. J. 12, 45n, 46

461

INDEX

mythology *(cont.)*
techniques of scriptural exegesis upon, 406-7; as symbolical grotesque, 397; and Turner, 420-31, 437-38. *See also* allegory, enigma

Naesmyth, Sir John 266, 268-69
natural myth 413
Newton, Eric 7n
Newton, Sir Isaac 116-17
Nicolson, Marjorie Hope 70n, 188-90, 193
Norton, Charles Eliot 265, 286, 288, 290-91, 294, 315, 401-2
nude in art 169, 171, 254

Opie, John 48
Orcagna 419, 444
Origen 397n
originality 72-73, 83-84. *See also* expressive theories of art
Ossian 46-47
Otto, Rudolph 187n
Overton, Henry 245n
Ovid 46-47, 438

Palazzo Vecchio, Florence 220
Pascal, Blaise 280-81
Pathetic Fallacy 32-33, 378-84. *See also* emotion, ideal artist-poet
Paul, St. 374+n
Perugino, Pietro 38, 422, 453
Petrarch, Francesco 396
Pevsner, Nikolaus 5, 218
Phidias 83
Physiologus 331, 414
picturesque: absent in Homer, 33; age-mark, 230; exemplified by Harding, 227; exemplified by Prout, 227-30; implications of, 236-38; light and shadow in, 225-26; as modern aesthetic, 240; noble picturesque, 238; parasitical sublimity, 223-24; relation to sublime and beautiful, 239-40; role of variety in, 226-27; ruggedness, 225-26; Ruskin's knowledge of writers on,

222-23; as Ruskin's final aesthetic position, 239; as Ruskin's most subjective aesthetic, 239-40; surface picturesque, 238-40; in urban setting, 228-29
Pissarro, Camille 20
Plato 14, 126-28, 374+n, 375, 431
Poe, Edgar Allan 386
poetry, truth of 63
Pope, Alexander 14, 46, 115, 118, 192, 401-2, 438
Poussin, Claude 55
Poussin, Nicolas 171
Poussinistes 430
Prall, D. W. 187n
Pre-Raphaelites, The 12, 144, 174, 263, 455
Price, Uvedale 222+n, 223+n, 231n, 239+n
proportion 123-134. *See also* beauty
Proust, Marcel 6-8, 13, 18
Prout, Samuel 223, 226-29, 279n
Pugin, Augustus Welby 277+n
*Pulpit, The* 246-47, 261n, 360
Purist Art 31
Puritans, seventeenth-century 16, 244
Puttenham, George 376
Pythagoras 126, 128

Quarles, Francis 394, 443

Raphael 141, 171, 453
Rawdon-Smith, William 337n
Read, Sir Herbert 8, 12, 16
realism 24, 31
Reformation 36
Reid, Thomas 154, 354
Rembrandt 12, 143, 217, 226
Renaissance 6, 21, 60
Renoir, Auguste 20
Reynolds, Graham 142n
Reynolds, Sir Joshua 15, 17, 30, 45, 48, 50-63, 99-100, 197, 231n
Richardson, Jonathan 8, 48
Richmond, George 18
Rio, Alexis François 17, 28, 307-8, 309+n, 447